D0914105

LIVY

IV

BOOKS VIII—X

LIVY

WITH AN ENGLISH TRANSLATION

IN FOURTEEN VOLUMES

IV

BOOKS VIII—X

TRANSLATED BY

B. O. FOSTER, Ph.D.

OF STANFORD UNIVERSITY

CAMBRIDGE, MASSACHUSETTS
HARVARD UNIVERSITY PRESS
LONDON
WILLIAM HEINEMANN LTD
MCMLXIII

First printed 1926
Reprinted 1948, 1957, 1963

Printed *in Great Britain*

CONTENTS

TRANSLATOR'S PREFACE

THE Latin text of Vol. IV. (comprising Books VIII.–X.) has been set up from the fifth edition [1] of the Weissenborn-Müller text with German notes, except that the *Periochae* have been reprinted from the text of Rossbach (1910). But the spelling is that adopted by Professors Conway and Walters in their critical edition of Books VI.–X. (Oxford, 1919), which is also the source of most of the rather numerous readings which differ from those of the Weissenborn-Müller text, and has furnished besides the materials from which the textual notes have been drawn up. I have aimed to record every instance where the reading printed does not rest on the authority of one or more of the good MSS., and to indicate the source of the emendation.

In addition to the symbols used by the Oxford editors, I have employed Ω to designate such of the good MSS. as are not cited specifically for some

---

[1] The sixth edition of Books VI.–VIII. did not reach me until my own text was in type.

other reading, and ς to designate one or more of the late MSS. or early printed texts.

Besides the translations mentioned in the preface to Vol. I. (those of Philemon Holland, George Baker, and Canon Roberts), I have had by me the anonymous version printed in London in 1686, in folio, "for Aunsham Churchill at the Black Swan in Ave-Mary Lane, near Paternoster Row."

I am also indebted to the editions of Book IX. by W. B. Anderson, Cambridge, 1909, and by T. Nicklin, Oxford, 1910. The commentaries of Weissenborn-Müller and Luterbacher have, of course, been constantly consulted, and the latter has been especially serviceable in helping to identify the various members of the same family in the preparation of the index.

The text and translation of the *Periochae* of the lost second decade have been included in this volume.

The map illustrating the campaign of the Caudine Forks has been adapted from Kromayer and Veith, *Schlachten-Atlas zur antiken Kriegsgeschichte*, published by Wagner and Debes, Leipzig.

B. O. F.

THE MANUSCRIPTS

V = Veronensis, 4th century.

F = Floriacensis, 9th century.

P = Parisiensis, 10th century.

H = Harleianus prior, 10th century.

T = Thuaneus, 10th century.

t = the first and second leaves of T, by another scribe.

B = Bambergensis, 10th or 11th century.

M = Mediceus, 10th or 11th century.

$Vorm.$ = Vormatiensis (as reported by Rhenanus).

R = Romanus, 11th century.

U = Upsaliensis, 11th century.

u = later part of U, 14th century.

D = Dominicanus, 11th or 12th century.

L = Leidensis, 12th century.

A = Aginnensis, 13th century.

a = later part of A, 14th century.

$Frag.\ Haverk.$ = Fragmentum Haverkampianum (cf. Conway and Walters, vol. i., Praef. p. ix [1]).

M^1, M^2, etc., denote corrections made by the original scribe or a later corrector. When it is impossible to identify the corrector, M^x, etc., are employed.

Ω = such of the above MSS. as contain the passage in question and are not otherwise reported.

ς = one or more of the late MSS. or early printed texts.

_____

$C.I.L.$ = *Corpus Inscriptionum Latinarum.*

P = Mergusianus (11th century).

E = Florentinus Laurentianus.

P = Parisinus, 10th century.

H = Harleianus 5694, 10th century.

J = Vaticanus, 10th century.

i = the first and second hands of i, respectively.

B = Bamberg class (11th or 12th century).

M = Monacensis (both 13th century).

m = Marcianus (as above or 14th century).

R = Romanus, 11th century.

C = Laurentianus, 14th century.

a = Parisinus, 15th century.

b = Laurentianus, 15th or 16th century.

L = Leidensis, 14th century.

T = Laurentianus, 15th century.

q = latter half of T, 15th century.

Vat. Med., as explained in Introduction (in
Schwartz and Müller, vol. i., Praef. p. xxi.)

Vb, Vc, etc., denote corrections made by the original
scribe or an after-scribe. When the
hypothetical scribe of the corrector, etc.,
etc., are implied.

Ω = apex of the above MSS. as containing the
passage in question and $=$ i, unless otherwise
noted.

Σ = the sum of those of the July MSS. or only
principal texts.

LIVY

FROM THE FOUNDING OF THE CITY

BOOK VIII

T. LIVI

AB URBE CONDITA

LIBER VIII

A.U.O.
413

I. Iam consules erant C. Plautius iterum L.[1] Aemilius Mamercus, cum Setini Norbanique Romam nuntii defectionis Privernatium cum querimoniis 2 acceptae cladis venerunt. Volscorum item exercitum duce Antiati populo consedisse ad Satricum allatum 3 est. Utrumque bellum Plautio sorte evenit. Prius ad Privernum profectus extemplo acie conflixit Haud magno certamine devicti hostes; oppidum captum redditumque Privernatibus praesidio valido 4 imposito; agri partes duae ademptae. Inde victor exercitus Satricum contra Antiates ductus. Ibi magna utrimque caede atrox proelium fuit; et cum tempestas eos neutro inclinata spe dimicantes diremisset, Romani nihil eo certamine tam ambiguo fessi 5 in posterum diem proelium parant. Volscis recensentibus quos viros in acie amisissent haudquaquam idem animus ad iterandum periculum fuit; nocte

---

[1] L. (lucius) D^x: licius D? L: titus (*or* t.) Ω.

LIVY

FROM THE FOUNDING OF THE CITY

BOOK VIII

I. THE consuls were now Gaius Plautius (for the B.C. 341
second time) and Lucius Aemilius Mamercus, when
the men of Setia and Norba brought tidings to
Rome that the Privernates were in revolt, with
complaints of a defeat suffered at their hands. It
was also reported that a Volscian army, conducted
by the Antiates, had encamped at Satricum. Both
wars were by lot assigned to Plautius. He marched
first on Privernum and at once gave battle. Without much ado he overcame the enemy, captured
Privernum, and putting in it a strong garrison,
restored it to the inhabitants, but deprived them of
two-thirds of their territory. Thence he led his
victorious army towards Satricum, to oppose the
Antiates. The battle there, which was desperately
fought, with heavy losses on both sides, was interrupted by a storm before victory had inclined to
either army. The Romans, not a whit discouraged
by so indecisive a struggle, prepared to do battle on
the morrow; but the Volsci, when they reckoned
up the men they had lost in the fighting, were by
no means so eager to incur the danger a second
time, and in the night marched off like beaten men

3

LIVY

pro victis Antium agmine trepido sauciis ac parte
6 impedimentorum relicta abierunt. Armorum magna
vis cum inter caesa hostium corpora tum in castris
inventa est. Ea Luae Matri dare se consul dixit
finesque hostium usque ad oram maritimam est
depopulatus.

7 Alteri consuli Aemilio ingresso Sabellum agrum
non castra Samnitium, non legiones usquam op-
positae. Ferro ignique vastantem agros legati
8 Samnitium pacem orantes adeunt; a quo reiecti ad
senatum, potestate facta dicendi, positis ferocibus
animis pacem sibi ab Romanis bellique ius adversus
9 Sidicinos petierunt, quae se eo iustius petere, quod
et in amicitiam populi Romani secundis suis rebus,
non adversis ut Campani, venissent, et adversus
Sidicinos sumerent arma, suos semper hostes, populi
10 Romani nunquam amicos, qui nec ut Samnites in
pace amicitiam nec ut Campani auxilium in bello
petissent, nec in fide populi Romani nec in dicione
essent.

II. Cum de postulatis Samnitium T. Aemilius
praetor senatum consuluisset reddendumque iis
2 foedus patres censuissent, praetor Samnitibus respondit nec quo minus perpetua cum eis amicitia
esset per populum Romanum stetisse, nec contradici
quin, quoniam ipsos belli culpa sua contracti taedium

---

[1] *i. e.* as he burnt them; captured arms were sometimes
burnt as an offering to Vulcan (I. xxxvii. 5), or to Jupiter
Victor (X. xxix. 18). Lua Mater, wife of Saturn, was a
goddess of atonement; at XLV. xxxiii. 1 she is associated
in this rite with Mars and Minerva.

[2] *Sabellus ager* usually includes the territories in Central
Italy inhabited by the Samnites, Sabines, Picentines, Vestini,
Marsi, Paeligni, and Marrucini. Livy uses it here in a re-
stricted sense of the country of the Samnites.

for Antium, with fear and trembling, abandoning B.C. 341
their wounded and a part of their baggage. A
great quantity of arms was found, not only amongst
the slain but also in the enemy's camp. Declaring [1]
that he gave these arms to Lua Mater, the consul
proceeded to lay waste the enemy's country as far
as the coast.

The other consul, Aemilius, having entered the
Sabellian [2] territory, nowhere encountered a Samnite
camp or levies. As he was ravaging their fields
with fire and sword, he was approached by Samnite
envoys, who begged for peace. Being referred by
Aemilius to the senate, they obtained an audience,
and giving over their air of arrogance, besought the
Romans to grant them peace and the right to war
against the Sidicini. These requests, they said,
were the more justifiable, inasmuch as they had
become friends of the Roman People when their
state was flourishing and not, like the Campanians,
in their adversity; moreover, it was against the
Sidicini that they were drawing the sword, a people
always their enemies and never friendly to the
Romans, of whom they had never, like the Samnites, sought friendship in time of peace, nor
assistance, like the Campanians, in time of war;
neither were they under the protection of the Roman
People, nor yet their subjects.

II. Titus Aemilius the praetor laid the petition of
the Samnites before the senate, and the Fathers
voted to renew the treaty with them. The praetor
then replied to the ambassadors that the Roman
People had not been to blame for the interruption
of the friendship, and that, since the Samnites were
themselves grown weary of a war contracted through

5

3 ceperit, amicitia de integro reconcilietur; quod ad
Sidicinos attineat, nihil intercedi quo minus Samniti
4 populo pacis bellique liberum arbitrium sit. Foedere
icto cum domum revertissent, extemplo inde exercitus Romanus deductus, annuo stipendio et trium
mensum frumento accepto, quod pepigerat consul
ut tempus indutiis daret quoad legati redissent.

5 Samnites copiis iisdem quibus usi adversus Romanum bellum fuerant contra Sidicinos profecti, haud
in dubia spe erant mature urbis hostium potiundae,
6 cum[1] ab Sidicinis deditio prius ad Romanos coepta
fieri est; dein, postquam patres ut seram eam
ultimaque tandem necessitate expressam aspernabantur, ad Latinos iam sua sponte in arma motos
7 facta est. Ne Campani quidem—adeo iniuriae
Samnitium quam beneficii Romanorum memoria
8 praesentior erat—his se armis abstinuere. Ex his
tot populis unus ingens exercitus duce Latino fines
Samnitium ingressus plus populationibus quam proeliis cladium fecit; et quamquam superiores certaminibus Latini erant, haud inviti, ne saepius dimicandum
9 foret, agro hostium excessere. Id spatium Samnitibus
datum est Romam legatos mittendi; qui cum adissent senatum, conquesti eadem se foederatos pati
10 quae hostes essent passi, precibus infimis petiere ut

[1] cum A^1 or A^x: tum (before which P^2F^3O have a stop) Ω.

their own fault, they had no objection to renewing
the covenant; as for the Sidicini, the Romans would
not interfere with the free judgment of the Samnite
People regarding peace and war. On the ratifi-
cation of the treaty, the ambassadors went home,
and the Roman army was at once recalled, after
receiving a year's pay and rations for three months,
which the consul had stipulated should be the price
of a truce, to last until the envoys should return.

The Samnites marched against the Sidicini with
the same forces which they had employed in the
war with Rome, and were confidently hoping to
capture the city of their enemies in a little while,
when the Sidicini attempted to anticipate them by
surrendering to the Romans. Then, after the Fathers
had rejected their offer, on the ground that it came
too late and had been wrung from them only by the
direst necessity, they carried it to the Latins, who had
already risen in arms on their own account. Even
the Campanians—so much more vivid was their recollection of the injury done them by the Samnites
than of the kindness of the Romans—could not
refrain from joining in this expedition. One great
army, gathered out of all these nations, invaded the
borders of the Samnites, under a Latin general, but
wrought more havoc by pillage than in battle; and
although the Latins came off best in all encounters,
they were not unwilling to retire from the enemy's
country, that they might not have to fight so often.
The Samnites thus had time to send ambassadors to
Rome. Appearing before the senate, they complained that they were suffering the same treatment
as allies that they had experienced while enemies,
and besought the Romans, with the utmost humility,

A.U.C.
413
satis ducerent Romani victoriam quam Samnitibus
ex Campano Sidicinoque hoste eripuissent, ne vinci
11 etiam se ab ignavissimis populis sinerent; Latinos
Campanosque, si sub dicione populi Romani essent,
pro imperio arcerent Samniti agro, sin imperium
12 abnuerent, armis coercerent. Adversus haec responsum anceps datum, quia fateri pigebat in
potestate sua Latinos iam non esse, timebantque,
13 ne arguendo abalienarent: Campanorum aliam condicionem esse, qui non foedere sed per deditionem
in fidem venissent; itaque Campanos, seu velint seu
nolint, quieturos; in foedere Latinos nihil esse quod
bellare cum quibus ipsi velint prohibeant.

A.U.C.
414
III. Quod responsum sicut dubios Samnites quidnam facturum Romanum censerent dimisit, ita Campanos metu abalienavit, Latinos velut nihil iam non
2 concedentibus Romanis ferociores fecit. Itaque per
speciem adversus Samnites belli parandi crebra
concilia indicentes omnibus consultationibus inter se
principes occulte Romanum coquebant bellum. Huic
quoque adversus servatores suos bello Campanus
3 aderat. Sed quamquam omnia de industria cela-
bantur—priusquam moverentur Romani, tolli ab tergo
Samnitem hostem volebant—tamen per quosdam
privatis hospitiis necessitudinibusque coniunctos in-

8

that they would be satisfied to have snatched from B.C. 341
the grasp of the Samnites a victory over their
Campanian and Sidicinian foes, and not suffer them
actually to be conquered by the most cowardly of
nations. If the Latins and Campanians were subject
to the Roman People, let the Romans use their
authority and keep them from invading Samnium;
but if they rejected that authority, let them hold
them in check by force of arms. To this plea the
Romans returned an ambiguous reply, since they
were loath to confess that the Latins were no longer
under their control, and feared to estrange them if
they censured them. The Campanians, they said,
were upon a different footing, having come under
their protection not by treaty but by surrender;
accordingly the Campanians, whether willing or not,
should keep the peace; but there was nothing in
their treaty with the Latins which entitled them to
prevent their going to war with whom they chose.

III. This answer, as it left the Samnites quite at B.C. 340
a loss to forecast the Roman policy, so it alienated
the Campanians with fear, while it persuaded the
Latins that there was no longer any concession the
Romans would not make them, and rendered them
yet more audacious. Accordingly their leaders,
under colour of forwarding the war against the
Samnites, appointed numerous councils, and in all
their deliberations secretly concocted war with Rome.
In this war, too, the Campanians took part, against
their preservers. But though all their measures
were sedulously concealed—for they wished to shake
off the Samnite foe behind them before the Romans
should take the alarm—yet through certain persons
connected by private ties of hospitality and kinship,

4 dicia coniurationis eius Romam emanarunt; iussisque
ante tempus consulibus abdicare se magistratu, quo
maturius novi consules adversus tantam molem belli
crearentur, religio incessit, ab eis quorum imminutum
imperium esset comitia haberi.   Itaque interregnum
5 initum.   Duo interreges fuere, M. Valerius ac M.
Fabius; is creavit[1] consules T. Manlium Torquatum
tertium, P. Decium Murem.

6   Eo anno Alexandrum Epiri regem in Italiam
classem appulisse constat; quod bellum, si prima
satis prospera fuissent, haud dubie ad Romanos
7 pervenisset.   Eadem aetas rerum magni Alexandri
est, quem sorore huius ortum in alio tractu orbis,
invictum bellis, iuvenem fortuna morbo exstinxit.

8   Ceterum Romani, etsi defectio sociorum nominisque
Latini haud dubia erat, tamen tamquam de Samnitibus non de se curam agerent, decem principes
Latinorum Romam evocaverunt, quibus imperarent
9 quae vellent.   Praetores tum duos Latium habebat,
L. Annium Setinum et L. Numisium Circeiensem,
ambo ex coloniis Romanis, per quos praeter Signiam[2]
Velitrasque et ipsas colonias Romanas Volsci etiam
exciti ad arma erant; eos nominatim evocari placuit.
10 Haud cuiquam dubium erat super qua re accirentur;

---

[1] is creavit *cod. Sigon.* (v. xxxi. 9): Fabius creavit *Hertz*:
creauit Ω: creant *U*: creati *A*: creaueꞃt *F*[3]: creauere
D[3]*A*[3]ₓ.

[2] Signiam *UA*[1]?: signia *MOHTDL*: signa *PT*[2]*A*: signium
F[3].

---

[1] Alexander the Epirot's expedition is here placed too
early by some ten years. The story of his death is told in
chap. xxiv.

[2] Olympias, daughter of Neoptolemus.

information of the conspiracy leaked out and was B.C. 340
brought to Rome. The consuls were commanded,
before their time was up, to resign their office, in
order that new consuls might the sooner be chosen
to confront so momentous an invasion; but a scruple
arose at allowing the election to be held by those
whose authority had been abridged, and so they
had an interregnum. There were two interreges,
Marcus Valerius and Marcus Fabius: the latter
announced the election to the consulship of Titus
Manlius Torquatus (for the third time) and Publius
Decius Mus.

It is believed to have been in this year that
Alexander, king of Epirus, sailed with a fleet to
Italy—a war which, had it prospered in its beginning, would doubtless have extended to the Romans.[1]
This was also the era of the exploits of Alexander the
Great, who was the son of this man's sister,[2] and was
doomed to be cut off by sickness while a young man,
in another quarter of the world, after proving himself
to be invincible in war.

But the Romans, though quite certain that the
allies and all the Latins were going to revolt,
nevertheless, as if concerned not for themselves
but for the Samnites, summoned to Rome the ten
chief men of the Latins, that they might give
them such commands as they might wish. Latium
at that time had two praetors, Lucius Annius Setinus
and Lucius Numisius Circeiensis, both from Roman
colonies, through whose contrivance, besides Signia
and Velitrae—likewise Roman colonies—even the
Volsci had been induced to draw the sword. It was
determined to summon these men by name. Nobody
could be in doubt why they were sent for; accord-

itaque concilio prius habito praetores quam Romam
proficiscerentur evocatos se ab senatu docent Romano
et quae actum iri secum credant, quidnam ad ea
responderi placeat referunt.

IV. Cum aliud alii censerent, tum Annius: "Quamquam ipse ego rettuli quid responderi placeret, tamen
magis ad summam rerum nostrarum pertinere arbitror
quid agendum nobis quam quid loquendum sit.
Facile erit explicatis consiliis accommodare rebus
2 verba.   Nam si etiam nunc sub umbra foederis
aequi servitutem pati possumus, quid abest quin
proditis Sidicinis non Romanorum solum sed Samnitium quoque dicto pareamus respondeamusque
3 Romanis nos, ubi innuerint, posituros arma? Sin
autem tandem libertatis desiderium remordet animos,
si foedus,[1] si societas aequatio iuris est, si consangui-
neos nos Romanorum esse, quod olim pudebat, nunc
gloriari licet, si socialis illis exercitus is est quo
adiuncto duplicent vires suas, quem secernere ab
se consilia[2] bellis propriis ponendis sumendisque
4 nolint, cur non omnia aequantur?   Cur non alter
ab Latinis consul datur?   Ubi pars virium, ibi et
5 imperii pars esto.[3]   Est quidem nobis hoc per se
haud nimis amplum, quippe concedentibus Romam
caput Latio esse; sed ut amplum videri posset,

---

[1] si foedus *Madvig*: si foedus est Ω.
[2] consilia *Madvig*: consules Ω: consul *TDLA*.
[3] esto *Mehler*: est Ω: ēē (= esse) M: est? *F³H* (*Drakenborch*): *omitted by* O.

ingly, before setting out for Rome the praetors held a council, and explaining how they had been summoned by the Roman senate, asked instructions touching the answers they should give to the questions which they supposed would be put to them.

IV. While one was suggesting this thing and another that, Annius arose. " Notwithstanding I have myself referred to you," said he, " the question as to what our reply should be, nevertheless I consider that what we are to do is of more importance to the welfare of our nation than what we are to say. It will be easy, when we have straightened out our plans, to frame words suitable to our conduct. For if we are able even now to endure slavery under a shadowy pretence of equal treaty-rights, what is left for us but to give up the Sidicini, and obeying the behest not of the Romans only but also of the Samnites, make answer to the Romans that we are ready to lay down our arms at their beck and call? But if our hearts are pricked at last with a longing for liberty; if treaties, if alliances, mean equality of rights; if we may now glory in the kinship of the Romans, of which we were formerly ashamed; if they mean by "allied army" one which added to their own doubles its numbers, one which they would not wish to make its own war and peace, apart from them;—if these things are so, I say, why are not *all* things equalized? Why is not one consul furnished by the Latins? Where a portion of the strength is, there, too, should be a portion of the authority. For us, indeed, this is not in itself any too great an honour, since we suffer Rome to be the capital of Latium; but we have made it seem an

6 diuturna patientia fecimus. Atqui si quando unquam
consociandi imperii, usurpandae libertatis tempus
optastis, en hoc tempus adest, et virtute vestra et
7 deum benignitate vobis datum. Temptastis pati-
entiam negando militem; quis dubitat exarsisse
eos, cum plus ducentorum annorum morem solve-
8 remus? Pertulerunt tamen hunc dolorem. Bellum
nostro nomine cum Paelignis gessimus; qui ne
nostrorum quidem finium nobis per nos tuendorum
9 ius antea dabant nihil intercesserunt. Sidicinos in
fidem receptos, Campanos ab se ad nos descisse,
exercitus nos parare adversus Samnites, foederatos
10 suos, audierunt nec moverunt se ab urbe. Unde
haec illis tanta modestia, nisi a conscientia virium
et nostrarum et suarum? Idoneos auctores habeo
querentibus de nobis Samnitibus ita responsum ab
senatu Romano esse ut facile appareret ne ipsos
quidem iam postulare ut Latium sub Romano
imperio sit. Usurpate modo postulando[1] quod illi
11 vobis taciti concedunt. Si quem hoc metus dicere
prohibet, en ego[2] ipse audiente non populo Romano
modo senatuque sed Iove ipso, qui Capitolium incolit,
profiteor me dicturum, ut si nos in foedere ac
societate esse velint, consulem alterum ab nobis
12 senatusque partem accipiant." Haec ferociter non
suadenti solum sed pollicenti clamore et adsensu

---

[1] postulando M^2 or M^1ς: postulando. Eo TD: postulando
eo Ω: postulando id ς.
[2] en ego A^3 *Gelenius*: eñgo M: en $PFUO$: ego $HTDLA$:
hem ego ς.

honour by our prolonged submissiveness. And yet,
if ever at any time you have desired to share in the
government and to use your freedom, behold, now is
your opportunity, bestowed on you by your valour
and by Heaven's favour! You have tried their
patience by denying them troops; who can doubt
that they were enraged when we broke the tradition of
two hundred years? Yet they swallowed their resentment. We waged war on our own account with the
Paeligni; those who aforetime withheld from us even
the right to defend our own borders by ourselves,
never interposed. They have heard how we received
the Sidicini into our protection, how the Campanians
have left them and joined us, how we are raising
armies against the Samnites, their confederates,—and
have not stirred from the City. Whence comes this
great restraint on their part, if it come not from the
consciousness of our strength—and their own? I
have good authority for saying that when the Samnites
were complaining of us, the Roman senate answered
in such wise that it might readily appear that even
the Romans themselves no longer demanded that
Latium should be under their authority. Do but
take up in your demands what they tacitly concede
to you. If there is any man whom fear prevents
from saying this, lo, I declare that I myself will say
it, in the hearing not of the Roman People only and
their senate, but of Jupiter himself, who dwells in
the Capitol; that if they wish us to observe the
treaty of alliance, they must receive from us one
consul and a moiety of the senate." These bold
encouragements, and even promises, were received
with a general shout of approval, and Annius was
empowered to act and speak as might seem con-

A.U.C.
414
omnes permiserunt ut ageret diceretque quae e
re publica nominis Latini fideque sua viderentur.

V. Ubi est Romam ventum, in Capitolio eis
senatus datus est. Ibi cum T. Manlius consul egisset
cum eis ex auctoritate patrum, ne Samnitibus
2 foederatis bellum inferrent, Annius, tamquam victor
armis Capitolium cepisset, non legatus iure gentium
3 tutus loqueretur, "Tempus erat," inquit, "T. Manli
vosque, patres conscripti, tandem iam vos nobiscum
nihil pro imperio agere, cum florentissimum deum
benignitate Latium [1] armis virisque, Samnitibus bello
victis, Sidicinis Campanisque sociis, nunc etiam Volscis
adiunctis, videretis ; colonias quoque vestras Latinum
4 Romano praetulisse imperium. Sed quoniam vos
regno impotenti finem ut imponatis non inducitis in
animum, nos, quamquam armis possumus adserere
Latium in libertatem, consanguinitati tamen hoc
dabimus ut condiciones pacis feramus aequas utrisque,
quoniam vires quoque aequari dis immortalibus
5 placuit. Consulem alterum Roma, alterum ex Latio
creari oportet, senatus partem aequam ex utraque
gente esse, unum populum, unam rem publicam
6 fieri ; et ut imperii eadem sedes sit idemque
omnibus nomen, quoniam ab altera utra parte concedi
necesse est, quod utrisque bene vertat, sit haec sane
patria potior, et Romani omnes vocemur."

---

[1] Latium *Madvig* : nunc (tunc *M*) Latium Ω.

16

ducive to the welfare of the Latin state and befitting B.C. 340
his own honour.

V. On the arrival of the Latins in Rome, they
were given audience of the senate in the Capitol.
There, after Titus Manlius the consul had pleaded
with them, as directed by the senate, to make no war
upon the Samnites, united as they were by treaty
with the Romans, Annius held forth like some conqueror who had taken the Capitol by storm, not like
an envoy protected by the law of nations. "It was
high time, Titus Manlius," he said, "and you,
Conscript Fathers, that you should cease at length to
deal with us as in any sort our rulers, perceiving, as
you have, that Latium, by Heaven's blessing, is
flourishing exceedingly in arms and men, after van-
quishing the Samnites in war and receiving as allies
the Sidicini and Campanians, and now even the Volsci
besides, and that your own colonies as well have
preferred the Latin to the Roman sway. But, since
you cannot make up your minds to bring your
impotent sovereignty to a close, we—though able by
force of arms to give Latium her freedom—will
nevertheless concede so much to kinship as to offer
terms of peace fair and equal to both sides, since the
immortal gods have willed that we should be of equal
strength. One consul should be chosen from Rome,
the other from Latium, the senate should be drawn
in equal proportions from both nations, there should
be one people and one state; and that we may have
the same seat of empire and the same name for all,
by all means let this rather be our city, since one
side must make concessions,—and may good come of
it to both peoples!—and let us all be known as
Romans."

7 Forte ita accidit ut parem ferociae huius et Romani consulem T. Manlium haberent, qui adeo non tenuit iram ut, si tanta dementia patres conscriptos cepisset ut ab Setino homine leges acciperent, gladio cinctum in senatum venturum se esse palam diceret, et quemcumque in curia Latinum vidisset, sua manu 8 interempturum. Et conversus ad simulacrum Iovis, "Audi, Iuppiter, haec scelera" inquit; "audite, Ius Fasque. Peregrinos consules et peregrinum senatum in tuo, Iuppiter, augurato templo captus atque ipse [1] 9 oppressus visurus es! Haecine foedera Tullus, Romanus rex, cum Albanis, patribus vestris, Latini, 10 haec L. Tarquinius vobiscum postea fecit? Non venit in mentem pugna [2] apud Regillum lacum? Adeo et cladium veterum vestrarum et beneficiorum nostrorum erga vos obliti estis?"

VI. Cum consulis vocem subsecuta patrum indignatio esset, proditur memoriae adversus crebram implorationem deum, quos testes foederum saepius invocabant consules, vocem Anni spernentis numina 2 Iovis Romani auditam. Certe, cum commotus ira se a vestibulo templi citato gradu proriperet, lapsus per gradus capite graviter offenso impactus imo ita 3 est saxo ut sopiretur. Exanimatum auctores quoniam non omnes sunt, mihi quoque in incerto relictum sit, sicut inter foederum ruptorum testationem ingenti fragore caeli procellam effusam; nam et vera esse et apte ad repraesentandam iram deum ficta possunt.

---

[1] atque ipse Ω: ipse atque *Alschefski.*
[2] pugna Ω: pugnam *M*: pugnae *Gronovius.*

---

[1] See Book I., chap. xxiv and chap. lii.

It so happened that the Romans had, in their consul Titus Manlius, a man who was a match for Annius
in boldness. So far was he from controlling his
indignation, that he openly declared that if the
Fathers were so demented as to receive terms from
a Setine, he would gird on his sword, and entering
the senate would slay with his own hand any Latin
he might see within the Curia. And turning to the
statue of the god, "Hear, Jupiter," he cried, "these
wicked words! Hear ye, Law and Right! Shalt
thou behold, O Jupiter, alien consuls and an alien
senate in thy consecrated temple, thyself overpowered and taken captive? Are these the covenants,
Latins, that Tullus, the Roman king, made with your
Alban forefathers, that Lucius Tarquinius afterwards
made with you?[1] Remember you not the battle at
Lake Regillus? Have you so forgot your old disasters
and our goodness to you?"

VI. The consul's speech having been warmly
seconded by the indignant senators, it is recorded
that in answer to the numerous supplications of the
gods, whom the consuls repeatedly invoked as the
witnesses of treaties, the voice of Annius was heard
spurning the power of the Roman Jupiter. At all
events, as he hurried, beside himself with rage, from
the entrance of the temple, he slipped on the stairs,
and struck his head so hard on the lowest stone that
he lost consciousness. That he was killed is not
asserted by all writers, wherefore I, too, may leave the
question undecided, as also the tradition that while
men were calling on the gods to witness the breaking
of the treaty, there was a loud crash in the heavens,
and a hurricane burst forth; for these things may be
true, or they may be apt inventions to express in a

4 Torquatus missus ab senatu ad dimittendos legatos
5 cum iacentem Annium vidisset, exclamat, ita ut
populo patribusque audita vox pariter sit : " Bene
habet ; di pium movere bellum. Est caeleste numen ;
es, magne Iuppiter ; haud frustra te patrem deum
6 hominumque hac sede sacravimus. Quid cessatis,
Quirites, vosque patres conscripti, arma capere deis
ducibus ? Sic stratas legiones Latinorum dabo,
7 quemadmodum legatum iacentem videtis." Adsensu
populi excepta vox consulis tantum ardoris animis
fecit, ut legatos proficiscentes cura magistratuum
magis, qui iussu consulis prosequebantur, quam ius
gentium ab ira impetuque hominum tegeret.

8   Consensit et senatus bellum ; consulesque duobus
scriptis exercitibus per Marsos Paelignosque profecti
adiuncto Samnitium exercitu ad Capuam, quo iam
9 Latini sociique convenerant, castra locant. Ibi in
quiete utrique consuli eadem dicitur visa species
viri maioris quam pro humano habitu augustiorisque,
10 dicentis ex una acie imperatorem, ex altera exercitum
Deis Manibus Matrique Terrae deberi ; utrius exercitus imperator legiones hostium superque eas se
11 devovisset, eius populi partisque victoriam fore. Hos
ubi nocturnos visus inter se consules contulerunt,
placuit averruncandae deum irae victimas caedi ;

20

lively manner the wrath of Heaven. Torquatus, who had been sent by the senate to dismiss the envoys, saw Annius lying there, and exclaimed in a voice that was heard alike by the people and the senators: "It is well; the gods have begun a righteous war. There *is* a heavenly power; thou *dost* exist, great Jupiter; not in vain have we established thee in this holy seat, the Father of gods and men. Why do you hesitate to arm, Quirites, and you Conscript Fathers, with the gods to lead you? As you behold their ambassador brought low, even so will I cast down the Latin legions." The consul's words were received with approval by the people, and so enraged them, that the envoys, at their setting out, owed their protection from men's wrath and fury more to the care of the magistrates—who attended them at the consul's bidding—than to the law of nations.

The senate also agreed on war; and the consuls, enrolling two armies, marched out through the country of the Marsi and Paeligni, and having added to their forces the army of the Samnites, went into camp near Capua, where the Latins and their allies had already assembled. There in the stillness of the night both consuls are said to have been visited by the same apparition, a man of greater than human stature and more majestic, who declared that the commander of one side, and the army of the other, must be offered up to the Manes and to Mother Earth; and that in whichever host the general should devote to death the enemy's legions, and himself with them, that nation and that side would have the victory. When the consuls had compared these visions of the night, they resolved that victims should be slain to turn away the wrath of Heaven;

LIVY

simul ut, si extis eadem quae in somnio [1] visa fuerant
portenderentur, alter uter consulum fata impleret.

12 Ubi responsa haruspicum insidenti iam animo tacitae
religioni congruerunt, tum adhibitis legatis tribunisque et imperiis deum propalam expositis, ne
mors voluntaria consulis exercitum in acie terreret,

13 comparant inter se ut ab utra parte cedere Romanus
exercitus coepisset, inde se consul devoveret pro

14 populo Romano Quiritibusque. Agitatum etiam in
consilio est ut, si quando unquam severo ullum
imperio bellum administratum esset, tunc utique [2]
disciplina militaris ad priscos redigeretur mores.

15 Curam acuebat quod adversus Latinos bellandum
erat, lingua, moribus, armorum genere, institutis ante
omnia militaribus, congruentes; milites militibus,
centurionibus centuriones, tribuni tribunis compares
collegaeque iisdem in [3] praesidiis, saepe iisdem mani-

16 pulis permixti fuerant. Per haec ne quo errore
milites caperentur, edicunt consules, ne quis extra
ordinem in hostem pugnaret.

VII. Forte inter ceteros turmarum praefectos,
qui exploratum in omnes partes dimissi erant, T.
Manlius consulis filius super castra hostium cum
suis turmalibus evasit, ita ut vix teli iactu ab statione

2 proxima abesset. Ibi Tusculani erant equites;
praeerat Geminus Maecius, vir cum genere inter

---

[1] in somnio *Wesenberg*: somnio Ω: somnia (*with* visu) *F*.
[2] utique *Sigonius*: uti Ω.
[3] iisdem in *Conway*: in iisdem *Wesenberg*: iisdem (*or* isdem
or hisdem) Ω.

and, at the same time, that if the warning of the B.C. 340
entrails should coincide with what thay had seen in
their dream, one or other of the consuls should fulfil
the decrees of fate. The report of the soothsayers
agreed with the secret conviction which had already
found lodgment in their breasts; whereupon they
sent for their lieutenants and the tribunes, and
having openly declared the pleasure of the gods, that
so the consul's voluntary death might not terrify the
soldiers in the fray, they agreed with one another
that on whichever flank the Roman army should
begin to yield, there the consul should devote himself
in behalf of the Roman People and Quirites. It was
also urged in the council that if ever any war had
been conducted with stern authority, now was the
occasion of all others for recalling military discipline
to its ancient courses. Their anxiety was sharpened
by the fact that they must fight against the Latins,
who were like themselves in language, customs,
fashion of arms, and above all in military institutions;
soldiers had mingled with soldiers, centurions with
centurions, tribunes with tribunes, as equals and colleagues in the same garrisons and often in the same
maniples. Lest this might betray the soldiers into
some blunder, the consuls proclaimed that no man
should quit his place to attack the foe.

VII. It chanced that amongst the other squadron-
leaders who had been sent off in all directions to
reconnoitre, Titus Manlius the consul's son had
ridden out with his troopers beyond the enemy's
camp, till he was hardly the cast of a spear from
their nearest outpost. There the Tusculan horse
were stationed, under the command of Geminus
Maecius, who enjoyed a reputation amongst his

3 suos tum factis clarus. Is ubi Romanos equites insignemque inter eos praecedentem consulis filium —nam omnes inter se, utique illustres viri, noti 4 erant—cognovit, "Unane," ait, "turma, Romani, cum Latinis sociisque bellum gesturi estis? Quid interea consules, quid duo exercitus consulares 5 agent?" "Aderunt in tempore," Manlius inquit, "et cum illis aderit Iuppiter ipse, foederum a vobis 6 violatorum testis, qui plus potest polletque. Si ad Regillum lacum ad satietatem vestram pugnavimus, hic quoque efficiemus profecto ne nimis acies vobis 7 et conlata signa nobiscum cordi sint." Ad ea Geminus paulum ab suis equo provectus: "Visne igitur, dum dies ista venit, qua magno conatu exercitus moveatis, interea tu ipse congredi mecum, ut nostro duorum iam hinc eventu cernatur, quantum 8 eques Latinus Romano praestet?" Movet ferocem animum iuvenis seu ira seu detractandi certaminis pudor seu inexsuperabilis vis fati. Oblitus itaque imperii patrii consulumque edicti, praeceps ad id certamen agitur, quo vinceret an vinceretur haud 9 multum interesset. Equitibus ceteris velut ad spectaculum submotis, spatio quod vacui interiacebat campi adversos concitant equos; et cum infestis cuspidibus concurrissent, Manli cuspis super galeam

fellows for his achievements no less than for his noble birth. This man recognized the Roman cavalry, and, conspicuous in their van, the consul's son—for they were all known to one another, particularly the men of mark. "Come now," he cried, "will you Romans wage war on the Latins and their allies with a single squadron? What will the consuls, what will two consular armies be doing in the meantime?" "They will be here soon enough," said Manlius, "and with them will be Jupiter himself, the witness of those covenants which you have violated, who is mightier and more powerful than they. If at Lake Regillus we gave you your fill of fighting, here likewise we shall certainly see to it that you have no great joy of meeting us in the serried ranks of battle." At this, Geminus rode out a little in front of his men, and asked, "Would you like then, while waiting for that great day to come, when with a mighty effort you are to set your hosts in motion—would you like meanwhile, I say, to do battle with me, yourself, that from the outcome of our duel men may see at once how far the Latin horse surpass the Roman?" The youth's bold heart was stirred, whether by anger, or by shame at the thought of refusing the combat, or by the irresistible force of destiny. And so, forgetting the commands of his father and the edict of the consuls, he allowed himself to be swept headlong into an encounter where it would make little difference to him whether he won or lost. They caused the rest of the horsemen to stand back, as though it had been a spectacle, and spurred their steeds against one another across the vacant space between. With lances levelled they rushed together; but the lance of Manlius glanced off

10 hostis, Maeci trans cervicem equi elapsa est. Circumactis deinde equis cum prior ad iterandum ictum
Manlius consurrexisset, spiculum inter aures equi
fixit. Ad cuius volneris sensum cum equus prioribus
pedibus erectis magna vi caput quateret, excussit
11 equitem, quem cuspide parmaque innixum attollentem
se ab gravi casu Manlius ab iugulo, ita ut per costas
12 ferrum emineret, terrae adfixit; spoliisque lectis ad
suos revectus, cum ovante gaudio turma in castra
atque inde ad praetorium ad patrem tendit, ignarus
fati[1] futurique, laus an poena merita esset.

13 "Ut me omnes," inquit, "pater, tuo sanguine
ortum vere ferrent, provocatus equestria haec spolia
14 capta ex hoste caeso porto." Quod ubi audivit
consul, extemplo filium aversatus contionem classico
15 advocari iussit. Quae ubi frequens convenit, "Quandoque," inquit, "tu, T. Manli, neque imperium
consulare neque maiestatem patriam veritus adversus
edictum nostrum extra ordinem in hostem pugnasti,
16 et quantum in te fuit, disciplinam militarem, qua
stetit ad hanc diem Romana res, solvisti, meque in
eam necessitatem adduxisti, ut aut rei publicae mihi
17 aut mei[2] obliviscendum sit, nos potius nostro delicto
plectemur quam res publica tanto suo damno nostra
peccata luat.   Triste exemplum sed in posterum

---

[1] fati *T*[2] *Frag. Haverk.* ς: facti Ω.
[2] mei *Conway*: mei meorum Ω: mei meorumue *H*: mei
meorumque *F*[4]*UD*[3]*A*[2]ς.

the helmet of his enemy, and that of Maecius passed over the neck of the other's horse. Then, as they pulled their horses round, Manlius, who was the first to gather himself up for a second thrust, pricked his enemy's charger between the ears. The smart of this wound made the horse rear and toss his head so violently that he threw off his rider, who, raising himself with spear and shield, was struggling to his feet after the heavy fall, when Manlius plunged his lance into his throat so that it came out between the ribs and pinned him to the ground. He then gathered up the spoils and rode back to his troopers, who attended him with shouts of triumph to the camp, where he sought at once the headquarters of his father, knowing not what doom the future held for him, or whether praise or punishment were his appointed guerdon.

"Father," he said, "that all men might truly report me to be your son, I bring these equestrian spoils, stripped from the body of an enemy who challenged me." On hearing this, the consul straightway turned from his son and commanded a trumpet to sound the assembly. When the men had gathered in full numbers, the consul said, "Inasmuch, Titus Manlius, as you have held in reverence neither consular authority nor a father's dignity, and despite our edict have quitted your place to fight the enemy, and so far as in you lay, have broken military discipline, whereby the Roman state has stood until this day unshaken, thus compelling me to forget either the republic or myself, we will sooner endure the punishment of our wrong-doing than suffer the republic to expiate our sins at a cost so heavy to herself; we will set a stern example, but a salutary

27

LIVY

18 salubre iuventuti erimus. Me quidem cum ingenita
caritas liberum tum specimen istud virtutis deceptum

19 vana imagine decoris in te movet; sed cum aut
morte tua sancienda sint consulum imperia aut
impunitate in perpetuum abroganda, nec[1] te quidem,
si quid in te nostri sanguinis est, recusare censeam
quin disciplinam militarem culpa tua prolapsam poena
restituas—i, lictor, deliga ad palum.''

20 Exanimati omnes tam atroci imperio nec aliter
quam in se quisque destrictam cernentes securem,

21 metu magis quam modestia quievere. Itaque velut
demerso[2] ab admiratione animo cum silentio defixi
stetissent, repente, postquam cervice caesa fusus est
cruor, tam[3] libero conquestu coortae voces sunt ut
neque lamentis neque exsecrationibus parceretur,

22 spoliisque contectum iuvenis corpus, quantum militaribus studiis funus ullum concelebrari potest, structo
extra vallum rogo cremaretur, Manlianaque imperia
non in praesentia modo horrenda sed exempli etiam
tristis in posterum essent.

VIII. Fecit tamen atrocitas poenae oboedientiorem
duci militem, et praeterquam quod custodiae vigili-
aeque et ordo stationum intentioris ubique curae
erant, in ultimo etiam certamine, cum descensum

2 in aciem est, ea severitas profuit. Fuit autem
civili maxime bello pugna similis; adeo nihil apud

---

[1] nec Ω *Walters* (*who punctuates as in the text* restituas—) :
ne *Iac. Gronovius* (*with full stop after* restituas).
[2] demerso *M. Mueller* (*D has* uelud *for* uelut) : emerso Ω :
merso *Madvig* : veluti merso *Zingerle.*
[3] tam *Crévier* : tum Ω.

B.C. 340

one, for the young men of the future. For my own part, I am moved, not only by a man's instinctive love of his children, but by this instance you have given of your bravery, perverted though it was by an idle show of honour. But since the authority of the consuls must either be established by your death, or by your impunity be forever abrogated, and since I think that you yourself, if you have a drop of my blood in you, would not refuse to raise up by your punishment the military discipline which through your misdemeanour has slipped and fallen,—go, lictor, bind him to the stake."

All were astounded at so shocking a command; every man looked upon the axe as lifted against himself, and they were hushed with fear more than with reverence. And so, after standing, as if lost in wonder, rooted to the spot, suddenly, when the blood gushed forth from the severed neck, their voices burst out in such unrestrained upbraiding that they spared neither laments nor curses; and covering the young man's body with his spoils, they built a pyre outside the rampart, where they burned it with all the honours that can possibly attend a soldier's funeral; and the "orders of Manlius" not only caused men to shudder at the time, but became a type of severity with succeeding ages.

VIII. Nevertheless the brutality of the punishment made the soldiers more obedient to their general; and not only were guard-duties, watches, and the ordering of outposts, everywhere more carefully observed, but in the final struggle, as well, when the troops had gone down into battle, that stern act did much good. Now the battle was exceedingly like the battles in a civil war, so little

LIVY

Latinos dissonum ab Romana re praeter animos
erat.

3 Clipeis antea Romani[1] usi sunt; dein, postquam
stipendiarii facti sunt, scuta pro clipeis fecere; et
quod antea phalanx similis[2] Macedonicis, hoc postea
4 manipulatim structa acies coepit esse: postremi[3] in
5 plures ordines instruebantur. Prima acies hastati
erant, manipuli quindecim, distantes inter se modi-
cum spatium; manipulus leves[4] vicenos milites,
aliam turbam scutatorum habebat; leves autem
qui hastam tantum gaesaque gererent vocabantur.
6 Haec prima frons in acie[5] florem iuvenum pube-
scentium ad militiam habebat. Robustior inde aetas
totidem manipulorum, quibus principibus est nomen,
hos sequebantur, scutati omnes, insignibus maxime
7 armis. Hoc triginta manipulorum agmen antepi-
lanos appellabant, quia sub signis iam alii quindecim
ordines locabantur, ex quibus ordo unusquisque tres
partes habebat — earum unam quamque primam[6]
8 pilum vocabant; tribus ex vexillis constabat ordo;
sexagenos milites, duos centuriones, vexillarium
unum habebat[7] vexillum; centum octoginta sex
homines erant; primum vexillum triarios ducebat,
veteranum militem spectatae virtutis, secundum
rorarios, minus roboris aetate factisque, tertium

---

[1] Romani M^1(or M^2) H^1(or H^2) *Frag. Haverk.* ς: romanis Ω.
[2] phalanx similis *Luterbacher*: phalanges similes Ω:
phalange similes A^4.
[3] postremi *Ortmann (and M?)*: postremo M or M^1 Ω.
[4] leves *Gruter*: leuis Ω.
[5] frons in acie $F^3D^3A^4$: frons in aciem U: foris in aciem
(ace H) Ω: in aciem foris L: sors in acie *Conway*.
[6] primam *Lipsius*: primum Ω.
[7] *The words* ordo . . . habebat *are placed here by Conway*
(*Class Quart.* 12 (1918) *pp.* 9–14), *who punctuates as in the*

30

did the Latins differ from the Romans in anything
but courage.

The Romans had formerly used small round
shields; then, after they began to serve for pay,
they made oblong shields instead of round ones; and
what had before been a phalanx, like the Macedonian
phalanxes, came afterwards to be a line of battle
formed by maniples, with the rearmost troops drawn
up in a number of companies. The first line, or
hastati, comprised fifteen maniples, stationed a short
distance apart; the maniple had twenty light-armed
soldiers, the rest of their number carried oblong
shields; moreover those were called "light-armed"
who carried only a spear and javelins. This front
line in the battle contained the flower of the young
men who were growing ripe for service. Behind
these came a line of the same number of maniples,
made up of men of a more stalwart age; these were
called the *principes*; they carried oblong shields and
were the most showily armed of all. This body of
thirty maniples they called *antepilani*, because
behind the standards there were again stationed
other fifteen companies, each of which had three
sections, the first section in every company being
known as *pilus*. The company consisted of three
vexilla or "banners"; a single *vexillum* had sixty
soldiers, two centurions, one *vexillarius*, or colour-
bearer; the company numbered a hundred and
eighty-six men. The first banner led the *triarii*,
veteran soldiers of proven valour; the second banner
the *rorarii*, younger and less distinguished men; the

---

text, making vexillum *subj. of* habebat: *the MSS. give them
after* instruebantur (§ 4).

LIVY

accensos, minimae fiduciae manum ; eo et in postremam aciem reiciebantur.

9 Ubi his ordinibus exercitus instructus esset, hastati omnium primi pugnam inibant. Si hastati profligare hostem non possent, pede presso eos retro cedentes in intervalla ordinum principes recipiebant. Tum

10 principum pugna erat; hastati sequebantur. Triarii sub vexillis considebant sinistro crure porrecto, scuta innixa umeris, hastas suberecta cuspide in terra fixas, haud secus quam vallo saepta inhorreret acies,

11 tenentes. Si apud principes quoque haud satis prospere esset pugnatum, a prima acie ad triarios se sensim referebant.[1] (Inde rem ad triarios redisse, cum

12 laboratur, proverbio increbruit.) Triarii consurgentes, ubi in intervalla ordinum suorum principes et hastatos recepissent, extemplo compressis ordinibus velut claudebant vias, unoque continenti agmine

13 iam nulla spe post relicta in hostem incidebant; id erat formidolosissimum hosti, cum velut victos insecuti novam repente aciem exsurgentem, auctam

14 numero, cernebant. Scribebantur autem quattuor fere legiones quinis milibus peditum, equitibus in singulas legiones trecenis.

Alterum tantum ex Latino dilectu adiciebatur,

---

[1] se sensim referebant *Madvig* : sensim referebantur Ω : redisse referebantur *DA* : redisse referebant *L* : retro se referebant *D²* or *D¹* (*margin*).

---

[1] Of this account of the reorganization of the army see the discussion by Professor Conway (*Class. Quart.* 12 (1918) 9–14). The writer concludes that "in the army which Livy was describing there were only 10 maniples of Hastati, 10 of Principes, and 10 *ordines* of the third division (Triarii+ Rorarii + Accensi). Then the numeration becomes clear ; the third division has 3 times 600, *i.e.* 1800 ; each of the

third banner the *accensi*, who were the least depend- B.C. 340
able, and were, for that reason, assigned to the rearmost line.

When an army had been marshalled in this
fashion, the *hastati* were the first of all to engage.
If the *hastati* were unable to defeat the enemy, they
retreated slowly and were received into the intervals between the companies of the *principes*. The
principes then took up the fighting and the *hastati*
followed them. The *triarii* knelt beneath their
banners, with the left leg advanced, having their
shields leaning against their shoulders and their
spears thrust into the ground and pointing obliquely
upwards, as if their battle-line were fortified with
a bristling palisade. If the *principes*, too, were
unsuccessful in their fight, they fell back slowly
from the battle-line on the *triarii*. (From this
arose the adage, "to have come to the *triarii*,"
when things are going badly.) The *triarii*, rising up
after they had received the *principes* and *hastati* into
the intervals between their companies, would at
once draw their companies together and close the
lanes, as it were; then, with no more reserves
behind to count on, they would charge the enemy
in one compact array. This was a thing exeedingly
disheartening to the enemy, who, pursuing those
whom they supposed they had conquered, all at
once beheld a new line rising up, with augmented
numbers. There were customarily four legions
raised of five thousand foot each, with three
hundred horse to every legion.[1]

An equivalent contingent used to be added from

first two has 1600, each maniple running to 160. This gives
1800+2(1600)=5000, Livy's total."

LIVY

qui ea tempestate hostes erant Romanis eodemque
15 ordine instruxerant aciem; nec vexilla cum vexillis
tantum, universi hastati cum hastatis, principes cum
principibus, sed centurio quoque cum centurione, si
ordines turbati non essent, concurrendum sibi esse
16 sciebat. Duo primi pili ex utraque acie inter triarios
erant, Romanus corpore haudquaquam satis validus,
17 ceterum strenuus vir peritusque militiae, Latinus
viribus ingens bellatorque primus, notissimi inter
18 se, quia pares semper ordines duxerant.[1] Romano
haud satis fidenti viribus iam Romae permissum
erat ab consulibus, ut subcenturionem sibi quem
vellet legeret qui tutaretur eum ab uno destinato
hoste; isque iuvenis in acie oblatus ex centurione
Latino victoriam tulit.
19   Pugnatum est haud procul radicibus Vesuvii
montis, qua via ad Veserim ferebat. IX. Romani
consules, priusquam educerent in aciem, immola-
verunt. Decio caput iocineris a familiari parte
caesum haruspex dicitur ostendisse: alioqui acceptam
dis hostiam esse; Manlium egregie litasse. "Atqui
bene habet" inquit Decius, "si ab collega litatum
2 est." Instructis, sicut ante dictum est, ordinibus
processere in aciem. Manlius dextro, Decius laevo
3 cornu praeerat. Primo utrimque aequis viribus,
eodem ardore animorum gerebatur res; deinde ab

----

[1] duxerant *ς*: duxerunt Ω.

----

[1] A river (Aurelius Victor, 26.4), or possibly a town.
[2] The "head of the liver" was a protuberance on the
upper part of the *right* (*i.e.* Roman) lobe. In the present
instance this protuberance had the appearance of being
mutilated, and so constituted a presage of evil to Decius.

the levy of the Latins, who were now the enemies
of the Romans and had drawn up their battle-line in
the same formation; and they knew that not only
must section meet in battle with section, *hastati*
with *hastati*, *principes* with *principes*, but even—if the
companies were not disordered—centurion with
centurion. In either army the *primus pilus*, or chief
centurion, was with the *triarii*. The Roman was far
from strong in body, but was an energetic man
and an experienced soldier; the Latin was a man of
might and a first-rate warrior; they were well
acquainted with each other, because they had always
commanded companies of equal rank. The Roman,
putting no confidence in his strength, had obtained
permission from the consuls before leaving Rome to
choose whom he liked for his deputy-centurion, to
defend him from the one man marked out for his
opponent. This youth, encountering the Latin
centurion in the battle, won the victory over him.

The engagement came off not far from the foot of
Mount Vesuvius, where the road led to Veseris.[1]
IX. The Roman consuls before leading their troops
into battle offered sacrifices. It is said that the
soothsayer pointed out to Decius that the head of the
liver was wounded on the friendly side; but that
the victim was in all other respects acceptable to
the gods,[2] and that the sacrifice of Manlius had
been greatly successful. "It is well enough," said
Decius, "if my colleague has received favourable
tokens." In the formation already described they
advanced into the field. Manlius commanded the
right wing, Decius the left. In the beginning the
strength of the combatants and their ardour were
equal on both sides; but after a time the Roman

LIVY

laevo cornu hastati Romani, non ferentes impres-
4 sionem Latinorum, se ad principes recepere. In
hac trepidatione Decius consul M. Valerium magna
voce inclamat: " Deorum" inquit "ope, M.[1] Valeri,
opus est; agedum, pontifex publicus populi Romani,
praei verba quibus me pro legionibus devoveam."
5 Pontifex eum togam praetextam sumere iussit et
velato capite, manu subter togam ad mentum ex-
serta, super telum subiectum pedibus stantem sic
6 dicere: " Iane Iuppiter Mars pater Quirine Bellona
Lares Divi Novensiles Di Indigetes Divi quorum
est potestas nostrorum hostiumque Dique Manes,
7 vos precor veneror veniam peto oroque[2] uti populo
Romano Quiritium vim victoriam prosperetis, hostesque populi Romani Quiritium terrore formidine
8 morteque adficiatis. Sicut verbis nuncupavi, ita
pro re publica populi Romani[3] Quiritium, exercitu
legionibus auxiliis populi Romani Quiritium, legiones
auxiliaque hostium mecum Deis Manibus Tellurique
devoveo."
9 Haec ita precatus lictores ire ad T. Manlium
iubet matureque collegae se devotum pro exercitu
nuntiare. Ipse incinctus cinctu Gabino, armatus

---

[1] ope, M. *Alschefski*: opem *M.*: ope Ω: *omitted by L.*
[2] oroque *Forchhammer*: feroque Ω.
[3] pro re publica populi Romani Quiritium *Gronovius*: pro
F̄ p̄ quiritium Ω: pro p̄ r̄ quiritium *U.*

---

[1] See chap. iii. § 5. Apparently it was the custom for a
member of the pontifical college to accompany the army in
order to preside over important rites.
[2] *Indiges* probably means "belonging to a certain place,"
and *di Indigites* would be native, as contrasted with the *di
Novensiles* (or *Novensides*), who were immigrants or new
settlers in the Roman Pantheon.

hastati on the left, unable to withstand the pressure B.C. 340
of the Latins, fell back upon the *principes*. In the
confusion of this movement Decius the consul called
out to Marcus Valerius in a loud voice: "We have
need of Heaven's help, Marcus Valerius.[1] Come
therefore, state pontiff of the Roman People, dictate
the words, that I may devote myself to save the
legions." The pontiff bade him don the purple-
bordered toga, and with veiled head and one hand
thrust out from the toga and touching his chin,
stand upon a spear that was laid under his feet, and
say as follows: "Janus, Jupiter, Father Mars,
Quirinus, Bellona, Lares, divine Novensiles, divine
Indigites,[2] ye gods in whose power are both we and
our enemies, and you, divine Manes,—I invoke and
worship you, I beseech and crave your favour, that
you prosper the might and the victory of the Roman
People of the Quirites, and visit the foes of the
Roman People of the Quirites with fear, shuddering,
and death. As I have pronounced the words, even
so in behalf of the republic of the Roman People of
the Quirites, and of the army, the legions, the
auxiliaries of the Roman People of the Quirites, do
I devote the legions and auxiliaries of the enemy,
together with myself, to the divine Manes and to
Earth."

Having uttered this prayer he bade the lictors go
to Titus Manlius and lose no time in announcing to
his colleague that he had devoted himself for the
good of the army. He then girded himself with
the Gabinian cincture,[3] and vaulting, armed, upon

[3] A peculiar mode of wearing the toga usual in certain
rites and possessing the advantage of rendering the robe less
cumbersome.

in equum insiluit ac se in medios hostes immisit,
10 conspectus ab utraque acie, aliquanto augustior
humano visu, sicut caelo missus piaculum omnis
deorum irae, qui pestem ab suis aversam in hostes
11 ferret. Ita omnis terror pavorque cum illo latus
signa prima Latinorum turbavit, deinde in totam
12 penitus aciem pervasit. Evidentissimum id fuit,
quod, quacumque equo invectus est, ibi haud secus
quam pestifero sidere icti pavebant; ubi vero corruit
obrutus telis, inde iam haud dubie consternatae
cohortes Latinorum fugam ac vastitatem late fece-
13 runt. Simul et Romani exsolutis religione animis
velut tum primum signo dato coorti pugnam integram
14 ediderunt; nam et rorarii procurrebant inter ante-
pilanos addebantque[1] vires hastatis ac principibus,
et triarii genu dextro innixi nutum consulis ad con-
surgendum exspectabant.

X. Procedente deinde certamine cum aliis partibus multitudo superaret Latinorum, Manlius consul
audito eventu collegae cum, ut ius fasque erat,
lacrimis non minus quam laudibus debitis prosecutus
2 tam memorabilem mortem esset, paulisper addu-
bitavit an consurgendi iam triariis tempus esset;
deinde melius ratus integros eos ad ultimum discrimen servari, accensos ab novissima acie ante signa
3 procedere iubet. Qui ubi subiere, extemplo Latini,

---

[1] addebantque *Alschefski* : adderantque *M* : addid(adid-
F)erantque Ω.

his horse, plunged into the thick of the enemy, a B.C. 340
conspicuous object from either army and of an
aspect more august than a man's, as though sent
from heaven to expiate all anger of the gods, and to
turn aside destruction from his people and bring it
on their adversaries. Thus every terror and dread
attended him, and throwing the Latin front into
disarray, spread afterwards throughout their entire
host. This was most clearly seen in that, wherever
he rode, men cowered as though blasted by some
baleful star; but when he fell beneath a rain of
missiles, from that instant there was no more doubt
of the consternation of the Latin cohorts, which
everywhere abandoned the field in flight. At the
same time the Romans—their spirits relieved of
religious fears—pressed on as though the signal had
just then for the first time been given, and delivered
a fresh attack; for the *rorarii* were running out
between the *antepilani* and were joining their
strength to that of the *hastati* and the *principes*, and
the *triarii*, kneeling on the right knee, were waiting
till the consul signed to them to rise.

X. While the struggle continued, and in some
parts of the field the Latins were prevailing by reason
of their numbers, the consul Manlius learned of his
colleague's end, and having paid to so memorable
a death—as justice and piety demanded—its well-
merited meed of tears as well as praise, he was for a
little while in doubt whether the moment were yet
come for the *triarii* to rise; but afterwards deeming
it better to keep them fresh for the final push, he
commanded the *accensi* to advance from the rear
before the standards. No sooner had they gone up,
than the Latins, supposing their enemies had done

LIVY

tamquam idem adversarii fecissent, triarios suos
excitaverunt; qui aliquamdiu pugna atroci cum et
semet ipsi fatigassent et hastas aut praefregissent
aut hebetassent, pellerent tamen [1] hostem, debellatum iam rati perventumque ad extremam aciem,
4 tum consul triariis "Consurgite nunc" inquit, "integri adversus fessos, memores patriae parentumque
et coniugum ac liberorum, memores consulis pro
5 vestra victoria morte occubantis." Ubi triarii con-
surrexerunt integri refulgentibus armis, nova ex
improviso exorta acies, receptis in intervalla ordinum
6 antepilanis, clamore sublato principia Latinorum
perturbant hastisque ora fodientes primo robore
virorum caeso per alios manipulos velut inermes
prope intacti evasere tantaque caede perrupere
cuneos ut vix quartam partem relinquerent hostium.
7 Samnites quoque sub radicibus montis procul instructi praebuere terrorem Latinis.

Ceterum inter omnes cives sociosque praecipua
laus eius belli penes consules fuit, quorum alter
omnes minas periculaque ab deis superis inferisque
8 in se unum vertit, alter ea virtute eoque consilio
in proelio fuit ut facile convenerit inter Romanos
Latinosque qui eius pugnae memoriam posteris
tradiderunt, utrius partis T. Manlius dux fuisset,
9 eius futuram haud dubie fuisse victoriam. Latini ex
fuga se Minturnas contulerunt. Castra secundum
proelium capta, multique mortales ibi vivi oppressi,

---

[1] tamen *Walters*: ui tamen (ui *between points in H and
following a point in* P^2T) Ω: ue tamen UA^4: ut tamen *M*:
-que tandem *Madvig.*

[1] Whether Livy made use of Latin as well as Roman
annalists is unknown; they no doubt existed, as he here gives
us to understand.

B.C. 340

the same, sent in their own *triarii*. These having fought fiercely for some time, and worn themselves out and broken or blunted their spears, yet were driving back the foe, and supposed that they had already won the field and penetrated the last line, when the consul cried out to the Roman *triarii*: "Rise up now, and with fresh strength confront the weary enemy, remembering your country and your parents, your wives and your children, remembering the consul who lies dead that you may conquer." When the *triarii* had got to their feet, fresh and sound in their glittering armour, a new and unforeseen array, they received the *antepilani* into the gaps between their files, and, raising a shout, threw the enemy's front ranks into disorder, and thrusting their spears into their faces, disposed of the fine flower of their manhood and went through the other maniples almost scatheless, as though their opponents had been unarmed, penetrating their masses with such slaughter as scarce to leave a fourth part of their enemies alive. The Samnites, too, drawn up a little way off at the base of the mountain, were a source of terror to the Latins.

For the rest, of all the citizens and allies, the chief glory of that war went to the consuls; of whom the one had drawn all the threats and menaces of the supernal and infernal gods upon himself alone, and the other had shown such valour and ability in the battle that it is readily agreed by both Romans and Latins who have handed down an account of this engagement that whichever side had been led by Titus Manlius would undoubtedly have been victorious.[1] The Latins fled to Minturnae. Their camp was captured after the battle and many men—

A.U.C.
414
10 maxime Campani. Deci corpus ne eo die inveni-
retur, nox quaerentes oppressit; postero die inventum inter maximam hostium stragem coopertum
telis; funusque ei par morti celebrante collega
factum est.

11   Illud adiciendum videtur, licere consuli dictatorique
et praetori, cum legiones hostium devoveat, non
utique se, sed quem velit ex legione Romana scripta
12 civem devovere; si is homo qui devotus est moritur,
probe factum videri; ni moritur, tum signum septem
pedes altum aut maius in terram defodi et piaculum [1] caedi; ubi illud signum defossum erit, eo
13 magistratum Romanum escendere fas non esse. Sin
autem sese devovere volet, sicuti Decius devovit,
ni moritur, neque suum neque publicum divinum
pure faciet, sive hostia sive quo alio volet.[2]   Qui
sese devoverit, Volcano arma sive cui alii divo vovere
14 volet ius est; telo super quod stans consul precatus
est hostem potiri fas non est; si potiatur, Marti
suovetaurilibus piaculum fieri. XI. Haec, etsi omnis
divini humanique moris memoria abolevit nova pere-
grinaque omnia priscis ac patriis praeferendo, haud
ab re duxi verbis quoque ipsis, ut tradita nuncu-
pataque sunt, referre.

2   Romanis post proelium demum factum Samnites

---

[1] piaculum *Walters and Conway* (*in their note*): piaculum
hostia (-am *U*) Ω.
[2] sive . . . volet *placed here by Madvig: after* diuo uouere
uolet Ω: *omitted by HTDLA.*

chiefly Campanians—were caught and slain there. B.C. 340
The body of Decius could not be found that day,
for night overtook the searchers; on the following
day it was found, covered with missiles, in a great heap
of enemies, and was given burial by his colleague in a
manner befitting his death.

It seems proper to add here that the consul, dictator,
or praetor who devotes the legions of the enemy
need not devote himself, but may designate any
citizen he likes from a regularly enlisted Roman
legion; if the man who has been devoted dies, it is
deemed that all is well; if he does not die, then an
image of him is buried seven feet or more under
ground and a sin-offering is slain; where the image
has been buried, thither a Roman magistrate may
not go up. But if he shall choose to devote himself,
as Decius did, if he does not die, he cannot sacrifice
either for himself or for the people without sin,
whether with a victim or with any other offering he
shall choose. He who devotes himself has the right
to dedicate his arms to Vulcan, or to any other god
he likes. The spear on which the consul has stood
and prayed must not fall into the hands of an
enemy; should this happen, expiation must be made
to Mars with the sacrifice of a swine, a sheep, and an
ox. XI. These particulars, even though the memory
of every religious and secular usage has been wiped
out by men's preference of the new and outlandish
to the ancient and homebred, I have thought it not
foreign to my purpose to repeat, and in the very
words in which they were formulated and handed
down.

I find in certain writers that it was not until the
battle was over that the Samnites, who had been

A.U.C.
414

venisse subsidio, exspectato eventu pugnae, apud
3 quosdam auctores invenio. Latinis quoque ab La-
vinio auxilium, dum deliberando terunt tempus,
4 victis demum ferri coeptum; et, cum iam portis
prima signa et pars agminis esset egressa, nuntio
allato de clade Latinorum cum conversis signis retro
in urbem rediretur, praetorem eorum nomine Mili-
onium dixisse ferunt pro paulula via magnam
mercedem esse Romanis solvendam.

5 Qui Latinorum pugnae superfuerant multis itineribus dissipati cum se in unum conglobassent,
Vescia urbs eis receptaculum fuit. Ibi in conciliis
6 Numisius imperator eorum adfirmabat[1] communem
vere Martem belli utramque aciem pari caede pro-
stravisse victoriaeque nomen tantum penes Romanos
esse, ceteram pro victis fortunam et illos gerere;
7 funesta duo consulum praetoria, alterum parricidio
filii, alterum consulis devoti caede; trucidatum
exercitum omnem, caesos hastatos principesque,
stragem et ante signa et post signa factam, triarios
8 postremo rem restituisse; Latinorum etsi pariter
accisae copiae sint, tamen supplemento vel Latium
9 propius esse vel Volscos quam Romam; itaque, si
videatur eis, se ex Latinis et ex Volscis populis
iuventute propere excita, rediturum infesto exercitu
Capuam esse Romanosque nihil tum minus quam

---

[1] adfirmabat *Luterbacher*: adfirmando Ω.

---

[1] *Communis Mars belli*, like *c'est la guerre*, was a phrase that
was often on the lips of the unsuccessful, *cf.* v. xii. l.

waiting for the outcome of the engagement, came up to support the Romans. The Latins, too, were already defeated when the Lavinians, who were consuming time in deliberation, began to march to their assistance ; and receiving word of the disaster to the Latins just as their foremost ensigns and a portion of their column had passed out through the gates, they faced about and returned into the city, their praetor, Milionius, remarking, so it is said, that they would have to pay a large price to the Romans for that little march.

Such of the Latins as survived the battle, after being dispersed over many roads, were reunited, and took refuge in the town of Vescia. In the councils which they held there, Numisius, their commander-in-chief, asserted that the fortune of war had in truth been common,[1] overwhelming both armies with equal carnage. The Romans, he said, were victorious only in name, in all else they too were as though they had been defeated ; both consular headquarters were polluted, the one by the blood of a son, the other by the death of the devoted consul ; their whole army had been cut to pieces, their first and second lines had been massacred, and the slaughter had extended from the troops before the standards to those behind them ; finally the veterans had restored the day ; but though the Latin forces had been equally cut up, yet, for recruiting, either Latium or the Volscian country was nearer than Rome ; if therefore it seemed good to them, he would speedily summon the fighting men from the Latin and Volscian tribes, and would return with an embattled host to Capua, where the unexpectedness of his arrival would strike dismay into the Romans,

45

proelium exspectantes necopinato adventu percul-

10 surum. Fallacibus litteris circa Latium nomenque
Volscum missis, quia qui non interfuerant pugnae
ad credendum temere faciliores erant, tumultuarius
undique exercitus raptim conscriptus convenit.

11 Huic agmini Torquatus consul ad Trifanum—
inter Sinuessam Minturnasque is locus est—occurrit.
Priusquam castris locus caperetur, sarcinis utrimque
in acervum coniectis pugnatum debellatumque est;

12 adeo enim accisae res sunt ut consuli victorem
exercitum ad depopulandos agros eorum ducenti
dederent se omnes Latini deditionemque eam Cam-

13 pani sequerentur. Latium Capuaque agro multati.
Latinus ager Privernati addito agro et Falernus,
qui populi Campani fuerat, usque ad Volturnum

14 flumen plebi Romanae dividitur. Bina in Latino
iugera, ita ut dodrante[1] ex Privernati complerent,
data, terna in Falerno quadrantibus etiam pro lon-

15 ginquitate adiectis. Extra poenam fuere Latinorum
Laurentes Campanorumque equites, quia non desci-
verant. Cum Laurentibus renovari foedus iussum,
renovaturque ex eo quotannis post diem decimum

16 Latinarum. Equitibus Campanis civitas Romana
data,[2] monumentoque ut esset, aeneam tabulam in

[1] dodrante *Linsmayer* : dodrantem (drod- *DLA³*) Ω:
quadrantem *D⁴*A.

[2] Romana data *Drakenborch* : rō data *H* : rodata *TDLR* :
redata *M* : reddata *A* : reddita *D³A²* : data *PFUOT²*.

---

[1] The *iugerum* contained 28,800 square feet; the English
acre contains 43,500.

who just then were looking for anything rather than B.C. 340 a battle. Misleading letters were sent out to all parts of Latium and the country of the Volsci, and since those who received them had not been present at the battle, gained ready credence; and an army of militia was levied in hot haste and brought together from every quarter.

This force Torquatus the consul met near Trifanum, a place situated between Sinuessa and Minturnae. Both armies, without waiting to choose sites for their camps, piled their baggage and fell to fighting, and the war was ended then and there; for the enemy's strength was brought so low that, when the consul led his victorious army to pillage their fields, the Latins all surrendered, and the Campanians followed their example. Latium and Capua were deprived of territory. The Latin territory, with the addition of that belonging to Privernum, together with the Falernian—which had belonged to the Campanian people—as far as the river Volturnus, was parcelled out amongst the Roman plebs. The assignment was two *iugera* in Latium supplemented with three-fourths of a *iugerum* from the land of Privernum, or three *iugera* in the Falernian district,—a fourth of a *iugerum* being added to compensate for its remoteness.[1] The Laurentes and the Campanian knights were exempted from the punishment inflicted on the Latins, because they had not revolted; it was ordered that the treaty with the Laurentes should be renewed, and it has been renewed every year from that time, on the tenth day after the Latin Festival. The Campanian knights received Roman citizenship, and to commemorate the occasion a bronze tablet was fastened up in

47

LIVY

aede Castoris Romae fixerunt. Vectigal quoque
eis Campanus populus iussus pendere in singulos
quotannis—fuere autem mille et sexcenti—denarios
nummos quadringenos quinquagenos. XII. Ita
bello gesto, praemiis poenaque pro cuiusque
merito persolutis, T. Manlius Romam rediit. Cui
venienti seniores tantum obviam exisse constat,
iuventutem et tunc et omni vita deinde aversatam
eum exsecratamque.

2 Antiates in agrum Ostiensem Ardeatem Solonium
incursiones fecerunt. Manlius consul, quia ipse per
valetudinem id bellum exsequi nequierat, dictatorem
L. Papirium Crassum, qui tum forte erat praetor,
dixit; ab eo magister equitum L. Papirius Cursor

3 dictus. Nihil memorabile adversus Antiates ab
dictatore gestum est, cum aliquot menses stativa in
agro Antiati habuisset.

4 Anno insigni victoria de tot ac tam potentibus
populis, ad hoc consulum alterius nobili morte,
alterius sicut truci ita claro ad memoriam imperio,
successere consules Ti.[1] Aemilius Mamercinus Q.[2]

5 Publilius Philo, neque in similem materiam rerum,
et ipsi aut suarum rerum aut partium in re publica
magis quam patriae memores. Latinos ob iram agri
amissi rebellantes in campis Fenectanis fuderunt

6 castrisque exuerunt. Ibi Publilio, cuius ductu

---

[1] Ti. ⟨ Sigonius (Diod. XVI. xci. 1); titius (or ticius) Ω:
t U Cassiod. (C.I.L. i², p. 44, A.U.C. 425).

[2] Q. ⟨ (Diod., l.c.) omitted by Ω.

---

[1] Castor and Pollux were protectors of the Roman knights
and hence appropriately chosen as patrons of the friendly
relations established with the aristocracy of Capua.

[2] The *denarius* was a silver coin weighing 70 grains Troy
and reckoned as equivalent to 16 asses. But silver was not
coined in Rome until 268 B.C.

the temple of Castor at Rome.[1] Moreover, the B.C. 340
Campanian people were commanded to pay them
each a yearly stipend—there were sixteen hundred
of them—amounting to four hundred and fifty
denarii.[2] XII. The war being thus dispatched, and B.C. 339
rewards and penalities distributed in accordance with
everyone's deserts, Titus Manlius returned to Rome;
it is said that on his approach only the seniors went
out to meet him, and that the young men, then and
for all the remainder of his days, abhorred and
execrated him.

The Antiates committed depredations upon the
lands of Ostia, Ardea, and Solonium. Manlius, the
consul, having been unable himself to conduct this
war because of ill-health, appointed as dictator
Lucius Papirius Crassus, who at that time happened
to be praetor, and he in turn named Lucius Papirius
Cursor master of the horse. The dictator accomplished
nothing noteworthy against the Antiates, though he
lay some months encamped in their territory.

To a year that was famous for its victory over so
many and so powerful nations, and also for the
glorious death of one of the consuls and the other's
severity of discipline, which though cruel was nevertheless renowned through the ages, succeeded the
consulship of Tiberius Aemilius Mamercinus and
Quintus Publilius Philo. These men had no such
opportunities, and were, besides, more concerned for
their own or their party's interests than for the
country. The Latins took up arms again, being incensed at the confiscation of their land, and suffered a
defeat and the loss of their camp, in the Fenectane
Plains.[3] While Publilius, under whose command and

---

[3] Named presumably from some unknown town in Latium.

LIVY

auspicioque res gestae erant, in deditionem acci-
piente Latinos populos, quorum ibi iuventus caesa
7 erat, Aemilius ad Pedum exercitus duxit. Pedanos
tuebatur Tiburs Praenestinus Veliternusque populus;
8 venerant et ab Lanuvio Antioque auxilia. Ubi cum
proeliis quidem superior Romanus esset, ad urbem
ipsam Pedum castraque sociorum populorum, quae
urbi adiuncta erant, integer labor restaret, bello
9 infecto repente omisso consul, quia collegae decretum triumphum audivit, ipse quoque triumphi ante
10 victoriam flagitator Romam rediit. Qua cupiditate
offensis patribus negantibusque nisi Pedo capto aut
dedito triumphum, hinc alienatus ab senatu Aemilius
seditiosis tribunatibus similem deinde consulatum
11 gessit. Nam neque, quoad fuit consul, criminari
apud populum patres destitit collega haudquaquam
12 adversante, quia et ipse de plebe erat—materiam
autem praebebat criminibus ager in Latino Falernoque [1] maligne plebei divisus—et postquam senatus
finire imperium consulibus cupiens dictatorem ad-
13 versus rebellantes Latinos dici iussit, Aemilius, cuius
tum [2] fasces erant, collegam dictatorem dixit; ab eo
14 magister equitum Iunius Brutus dictus. Dictatura
popularis et orationibus in patres criminosis fuit, et
quod tres leges secundissimas plebei, adversas
15 nobilitati tulit: unam, ut plebiscita omnes Quirites

---

[1] Falernoque *Tan. Faber*: Falernoque agro Ω.
[2] cuius tum A²ς: tum cuius Ω: tunc cuius *F*: cuius
Walters and Conway.

---

[1] In the city the consuls took turns in exercising supreme
administrative authority, and the twelve lictors, with the rods
(*fasces*), attended the consul who, for the time being, enjoyed
this authority.

B.C. 339

auspices the campaign had been conducted, was receiving the surrender of the Latin peoples whose soldiers had fallen there, Aemilius led his army against Pedum. The Pedani were supported by the people of Tibur, Praeneste, and Velitrae, and auxiliaries had also come from Lanuvium and Antium. Though the Romans proved superior in certain engagements, yet the town of Pedum and the camp of the allied nations, which adjoined it, still remained intact to be dealt with, when suddenly the consul, hearing that his colleague had been decreed a triumph, left the war unfinished and returned to Rome to demand a triumph for himself as well, without staying to obtain a victory. This self-seeking disgusted the Fathers, who denied him a triumph, unless he should capture Pedum or receive its surrender. Estranged from the senate by this rebuff, Aemilius thereafter administered his consulship in the spirit of a seditious tribune. For, all the time that he was consul, he ceased not to accuse the senators to the people, while his colleague, since he too was of the plebs, offered not the smallest opposition. The ground of his accusations was the niggardly apportionment of land to the plebeians in the Latin and Falernian districts. And when the senate, desiring to put an end to the authority of the consuls, ordered that a dictator should be appointed to oppose the rebellious Latins, Aemilius, who then had the rods,[1] named his colleague dictator, by whom Junius Brutus was designated master of the horse. Publilius was a popular dictator, both because of his denunciation of the senate and because he carried through three laws very advantageous to the plebs and prejudicial to the nobles: one, that the decisions of the plebs

51

A.U.C.
415

tenerent; alteram, ut legum, quae comitiis centu-
riatis ferrentur, ante initum suffragium patres
16 auctores fierent; tertiam, ut alter utique ex plebe
—cum eo ventum sit ut utrumque plebeium fieri
17 liceret—censor crearetur. Plus eo anno domi acceptum cladis ab consulibus ac dictatore quam ex victoria
eorum bellicisque rebus foris auctum imperium patres
credebant.

A.U.C.
416

XIII. Anno insequenti, L. Furio Camillo C.
Maenio consulibus, quo insignitius omissa res
Aemilio, superioris anni consuli, exprobraretur,
Pedum armis virisque et omni vi expugnandum ac
delendum senatus fremit; coactique novi consules
2 omnibus eam rem praeverti proficiscuntur. Iam
Latio [1] is status erat rerum ut neque bellum neque
pacem pati possent. Ad bellum opes deerant; pacem
3 ob agri adempti dolorem aspernabantur. Mediis
consiliis standum videbatur—ut oppidis se tenerent,
ne lacessitus Romanus causam belli haberet—et
si cuius oppidi obsidio nuntiata esset, undique ex
4 omnibus populis auxilium obsessis ferretur. Neque
tamen nisi admodum a paucis populis Pedani adiuti
sunt. Tiburtes Praenestinique, quorum ager pro-
5 pior erat, Pedum pervenere; Aricinos Lanuvinosque
et Veliternos Antiatibus Volscis se coniungentes ad
Asturae [2] flumen Maenius improviso adortus fudit.

---

[1] Latio Ω: in Latio *Madvig* (*but cf. Walters and Conway
ad loc.*).
[2] Asturae *Sabellicus* (*Plin. N.H.* III. v. 9, § 57) ς: Saturae
(*or* -e) Ω: saturem *DLA*.

---

[1] See chap. xi. § 13.
[2] A little river emptying into the Mediterranean south of
Antium.

should be binding on all the Quirites; another, that
the Fathers should ratify the measures proposed at
the centuriate comitia before they were voted on;
and a third, that at least one censor should be chosen
from the plebs—since they had gone so far as to
make it lawful for both to be plebeians. The harm
that was wrought at home in that year by the
consuls and the dictator outweighed—in the belief
of the patricians—the increase in empire that resulted
from their victory and their management of the war.

XIII. In the following year, when Lucius Furius
Camillus and Gaius Maenius were consuls, the
senators, in order to render more conspicuous the
negligence of Aemilius in the year before, insisted
angrily that men and arms and every kind of force
must be employed to capture Pedum and destroy
it; and the new consuls were forced to put aside all
other matters and set out for that place. The
Latins were now come to such a pass that they
could endure neither war nor peace; for war they
lacked the means, and they scorned peace, for
they still smarted under the confiscation of their
land.[1] It seemed necessary to adopt a compromise,
and keep to their towns—lest they might provoke
the Romans and afford them a pretext for hostilities—and if tidings were brought that any town
was beleaguered, to send in help to the besieged
from all the surrounding peoples. For all that, the
cities that aided Pedum were very few. The
Tiburtes and Praenestini, whose territories lay near
by, reached Pedum; the Aricini, Lanuvini, and
Veliterni, as they were effecting a juncture with the
Antiate Volsci at the river Astura,[2] were suddenly
attacked by Maenius and routed. Camillus dealt

LIVY

6 Camillus ad Pedum cum Tiburtibus, maxime valido
exercitu, maiore mole quamquam aeque prospero
7 eventu pugnat. Tumultum maxime repentina inter
proelium eruptio oppidanorum fecit ; in quos parte
exercitus conversa Camillus non compulit solum eos
intra moenia, sed eodem etiam die, cum ipsos auxilia-
8 que eorum perculisset, oppidum scalis cepit. Placuit
inde iam maiore conatu animoque ab unius expug-
natione urbis ad perdomandum Latium victorem
circumducere exercitum. Nec quievere antequam
expugnando aut in deditionem accipiendo singulas
9 urbes Latium omne subegere. Praesidiis inde dis-
positis per recepta oppida Romam ad destinatum
omnium consensu triumphum decessere. Additus
triumpho honos, ut statuae equestres eis—rara illa
aetate res—in foro ponerentur.

10   Priusquam comitiis in insequentem annum consules rogarent, Camillus de Latinis populis ad sena-
11 tum rettulit atque ita disseruit : " Patres conscripti,
quod bello armisque in Latio agendum fuit, id iam
deum benignitate ac virtute militum ad finem venit.
12 Caesi ad Pedum Asturamque sunt exercitus hostium ;
oppida Latina omnia et Antium ex Volscis aut vi
capta aut recepta in deditionem praesidiis tenentur
13 vestris. Reliqua consultatio est, quoniam rebellando
saepius nos sollicitant, quonam modo perpetua pace

---

[1] Livy means to include with them the Praenestini.

with the very powerful army of the Tiburtes [1] in the
vicinity of Pedum; the struggle was harder, but
the issue was equally successful. The greatest
confusion was occasioned by a sudden sally of the
townsfolk during the battle; but Camillus, sending
a part of his army against them, not only drove them
back into their city, but having discomfited both
them and their allies, even took the place by
escalade that very day. The consuls then resolved,
with the added energy and courage that came with
the capture of one city, to proceed with their
victorious army to the thorough conquest of the
Latins; nor did they rest until, by storming every
city or receiving its surrender, they had brought all
Latium under their dominion. Then, distributing
garrisons amongst the recovered towns, they departed for Rome, to enjoy the triumph by general
consent awarded them. In addition to the triumph,
they were granted the honour—a rare one in those
days—of equestrian statues put up in the Forum.

Before the consular elections for the following
year were held, Camillus referred to the senate the
disposition of the Latin peoples, and spoke as
follows: "Conscript Fathers, what was needful to
be done in Latium in the way of war and arms has
now by Heaven's favour and the valour of our
troops been brought to a conclusion. The armies
of our enemies have been cut to pieces at Pedum
and on the Astura; all the Latin towns, and
Antium in the land of the Volsci, have either been
carried by storm or have made submission, and are
in the keeping of your garrisons. It remains to
consider, since they so often occasion us anxiety by
a renewal of hostilities, how we may hold them

55

LIVY

14 quietos obtineamus. Di immortales ita vos potentes
huius consilii fecerunt ut, sit Latium deinde an non
sit, in vestra manu posuerint; itaque pacem vobis,
quod ad Latinos attinet, parare in perpetuum vel
15 saeviendo vel ignoscendo potestis. Voltis crudeliter
consulere in deditos victosque? Licet delere omne
Latium, vastas inde solitudines facere, unde sociali
egregio exercitu per multa bella magnaque saepe usi
16 estis. Voltis exemplo maiorum augere rem Romanam
victos in civitatem accipiendo? Materia crescendi
per summam gloriam suppeditat. Certe id firmissi-
mum longe imperium est quo oboedientes gaudent.
17 Sed maturato opus est quidquid statuere placet; tot
populos inter spem metumque suspensos animi
habetis; et vestram itaque de eis curam quam
primum absolvi, et illorum animos, dum exspecta-
tione stupent, seu poena seu beneficio praeoccupari
18 oportet. Nostrum fuit efficere ut omnium rerum
vobis ad consulendum potestas esset; vestrum est
decernere quod optimum vobis reique publicae sit."

XIV. Principes senatus relationem consulis de
summa rerum laudare, sed, cum aliorum causa alia
esset, ita expediri posse consilium dicere, si,[1] ut pro
merito cuiusque statueretur, de singulis nominatim

---

[1] si *placed here by Walters and Conway:* in Ω *it stands
before* de singulis, *but is omitted by* PFUT²(*or* T³).

56

quietly to a lasting peace. The immortal gods have B.C. 338
given you such absolute control of the situation as
to leave the decision in your hands whether Latium
is henceforward to exist or not. You are therefore
able to assure yourselves of a permanent peace, in
so far as the Latins are concerned, by the exercise
of either cruelty or forgiveness, at your discretion.
Would you adopt stern measures against those who
have surrendered or been vanquished? You may
blot out all Latium, and make vast solitudes of
those places where you have often raised a splendid
army of allies and used it through many a
momentous war. Would you follow the example of
your fathers, and augment the Roman state by
receiving your conquered enemies as citizens? You
have at hand the means of waxing great and
supremely glorious. That government is certainly
by far the strongest to which its subjects yield
obedience gladly. But whatever it pleases you to do,
you must determine promptly; you are holding so
many peoples in suspense betwixt hope and fear,
that it behoves you both to resolve your own
anxiety regarding them as soon as may be, and to
be beforehand with them, whether in the way of
punishment or kindness, while they are waiting in a
dull amazement. Our task has been to give you
the power to decide regarding everything; it is
yours to determine what is best for yourselves and
for the state."

XIV. The leading senators praised the motion of
Camillus on the national policy, but said that, since
the Latins were not all in like case, his advice could
best be carried out if the consuls would introduce
proposals concerning the several peoples by name,

LIVY

2 referrent populis. Relatum igitur de singulis decre-
tumque. Lanuvinis civitas data sacraque sua reddita, cum eo ut aedes lucusque Sospitae Iunonis
communis Lanuvinis municipibus cum populo
3 Romano esset. Aricini Nomentanique et Pedani
eodem iure quo Lanuvini in civitatem accepti.
4 Tusculanis servata civitas quam habebant, crimenque
rebellionis a publica fraude in paucos auctores ver-
5 sum. In Veliternos, veteres cives Romanos, quod
totiens rebellassent, graviter saevitum : et muri
deiecti et senatus inde abductus iussique trans Tibe-
6 rim habitare, ut eius qui cis Tiberim deprehensus
esset usque ad mille pondo assium [1] clarigatio esset
nec priusquam aere persoluto is qui cepisset extra
7 vincula captum haberet. In agrum senatorum
coloni missi, quibus adscriptis speciem antiquae
8 frequentiae Velitrae receperunt. Et Antium nova
colonia missa, cum eo ut Antiatibus permitteretur,
si et ipsi adscribi coloni vellent; naves inde longae
abactae interdictumque mari Antiati populo est et
9 civitas data. Tiburtes Praenestinique agro multati,
neque ob recens tantum rebellionis commune cum
aliis Latinis crimen, sed quod taedio imperii Romani
cum Gallis, gente efferata, arma quondam con-

---

[1] pondo assium *Lachmann* (*who wrote* assum): pondo ς:
passum Ω : passuum *UO*ς : passus *F*⁴(*or F*³)*HA*³: assium
Madvig (*with hesitation*).

---

[1] Presumably *cum suffragio*—with full political rights.
[2] Where they would be interned amongst an alien
population.

as each should seem to merit. They were therefore
taken up and disposed of separately. The Lanuvini
were given citizenship,[1] and their worship was
restored to them, with the stipulation that the
temple and grove of Juno Sospita should be held in
common by the burghers of Lanuvium and the
Roman People. The Aricini, Nomentani, and
Pedani were received into citizenship on the same
terms as the Lanuvini. The Tusculans were
allowed to retain the civic rights which they
enjoyed, and the charge of renewing the war was
laid to a few ringleaders, without endamaging the
community. The Veliterni, Roman citizens of old,
were severely punished, because they had so often
revolted : not only were their walls thrown down,
but their senate was carried off and commanded to
dwell across the Tiber,[2] with this understanding :
that if any should be caught on the hither side, his
redemption should be set at a thousand pounds of
bronze, and that he who had captured him might
not release his prisoner from bondage until the fine
was paid. Colonists were settled on the senators'
lands, and on their enrolment Velitrae regained its
former appearance of populousness. To Antium
likewise a colony was dispatched, with an understanding that the Antiates might be permitted, if
they liked, themselves to enroll as colonists ; their
war-ships were taken from them and their people
were forbidden the sea ; they were granted citizenship. The Tiburtes and Praenestini were deprived
of territory, not only because of the fresh charge of
rebellion brought against them in common with the
other Latins, but because they had once, in disgust
at the power of Rome, united in arms with the

LIVY

10 sociassent. Ceteris Latinis populis conubia commerciaque et concilia inter se ademerunt. Campanis equitum honoris causa, quia cum Latinis rebellare noluissent, Fundanisque et Formianis, quod per fines eorum tuta pacataque semper fuisset via, civitas
11 sine suffragio data. Cumanos Suessulanosque eiusdem iuris condicionisque cuius Capuam esse placuit.
12 Naves Antiatium partim in navalia Romae subductae, partim incensae, rostrisque earum suggestum in foro exstructum adornari placuit, Rostraque id templum appellatum.

XV. C. Sulpicio Longo P. Aelio Paeto consulibus cum omnia non opes magis Romanae quam beneficiis parta gratia bona pace obtineret, inter Sidicinos
2 Auruncosque bellum ortum. Aurunci, T. Manlio consule in deditionem accepti, nihil deinde moverant; eo petendi auxilii ab Romanis causa iustior
3 fuit. Sed priusquam consules ab urbe—iusserat enim senatus defendi Auruncos—exercitum educe-
4 rent, fama adfertur Auruncos metu oppidum deseruisse profugosque cum coniugibus ac liberis Suessam communisse,[1] quae nunc Aurunca appellatur,[2] moenia antiqua eorum urbemque ab Sidicinis

---

[1] communisse Ω: commeasse Uς.
[2] appellatur ς (*Madvig*): appellata Ω.

---

[1] The Tiburtes had fought on the Gallic side in 361 and 360 B.C. (VII. xi. 1), the Praenestini possibly in 358 (VII. xii. 8).
[2] The speaker's platform on the line between the Comitium and the Forum is referred to earlier (IV. xvii. 6), but possibly only the *place* is there meant. Certainly Livy seems to imply here that the *platform* was now erected for the first time.
[3] 340 B.C.
[4] Suessa Aurunca was so called in order to distinguish it from the Volscian town Suessa Pometia.

B.C. 338

Gauls, a race of savages.[1] The rest of the Latin peoples were deprived of the rights of mutual trade and intermarriage and of holding common councils. The Campanians, out of compliment to their knights, because they had not consented to revolt along with the Latins, were granted citizenship without the suffrage; so too were the Fundani and Formiani, because they had always afforded a safe and peaceful passage through their territories. It was voted to give the people of Cumae and Suessula the same rights and the same terms as the Capuans. The ships of the Antiates were some of them laid up in the Roman dockyards, and some were burnt and a motion passed to employ their beaks for the adornment of a platform erected in the Forum. This place was dedicated with augural ceremonies and given the name of Rostra or The Beaks.[2]

B.C. 337

XV. In the consulship of Gaius Sulpicius Longus and Publius Aelius Paetus the good-will which their generous conduct had procured for the Romans had been no less efficacious than their power in maintaining a general peace, when a war broke out between the Sidicini and the Aurunci. The Aurunci had surrendered in the consulship of Titus Manlius[3] and had given no trouble since that time, for which reason they had the better right to expect assistance from the Romans. But before the consuls marched from Rome—for the Senate had directed them to defend the Aurunci—tidings were brought that the Aurunci had abandoned their town, in their alarm, and had taken refuge, with their wives and children, in Suessa—now called Aurunca[4]—which they had fortified: and that their ancient walls and their city had been destroyed by the Sidicini. This news

A.U.C.
417

5 deletam. Ob ea infensus consulibus senatus, quorum
cunctatione proditi socii essent, dictatorem dici iussit. Dictus C. Claudius Inregillensis magistrum
6 equitum C. Claudium Hortatorem dixit. Religio
inde iniecta de dictatore, et cum augures vitio
creatum videri dixissent, dictator magisterque equitum se magistratu abdicarunt.

7   Eo anno Minucia Vestalis suspecta primo propter
mundiorem iusto cultum, insimulata deinde apud
8 pontifices ab indice servo, cum decreto eorum iussa
esset sacris abstinere familiamque in potestate
habere, facto iudicio viva sub terram ad portam
Collinam dextra viam [1] stratam defossa Scelerato
campo ; credo ab incesto id ei loco nomen factum.

9   Eodem anno Q. Publilius [2] Philo praetor primum
de plebe adversante Sulpicio consule, qui negabat
rationem eius se habiturum, est factus, senatu, cum
in summis imperiis id non obtinuisset, minus in
praetura tendente.

A.U.C.
418-420

XVI. Insequens annus, L. Papirio Crasso K.
Duillio consulibus, Ausonum magis novo quam
2 magno bello fuit insignis. Ea gens Cales urbem
incolebat ; Sidicinis finitimis arma coniunxerat, unoque proelio haud sane memorabili duorum populorum

---

[1] dextra viam Ω: dextra uiae M^4: dextra uia A^x (*over
erasure*): extra uiam *U* (*Madvig*): iuxta viam *Weissenborn*.
[2] Publilius *Glareanus* (*and Sigonius at chap.* xii. § 5):
publius Ω.

---

[1] Had she manumitted them it would have been illegal to
examine them under torture.
[2] The consul did not act upon his threat, so Livy implies,
upon finding the senators lukewarm in their support.

B.C. 337

made the senate angry with the consuls, by whose tardiness the allies had been betrayed, and they ordered a dictator to be appointed. The nomination fell to Gaius Claudius Inregillensis, who named as his master of horse Gaius Claudius Hortator. A religious difficulty was then raised about the dictator, and on the augurs' reporting that there seemed to have been a flaw in his appointment, the dictator and his master of the horse resigned.

In that year the Vestal Minucia, suspected in the first instance because of her dress, which was more ornate than became her station, was subsequently accused before the pontiffs on the testimony of a slave, and having been by their decree commanded to keep aloof from the sacred rites and to retain her slaves in her own power,[1] was convicted and buried alive near the Colline Gate, to the right of the paved road in the Polluted Field—so called, I believe, on account of her unchastity.

In the same year Quintus Publilius Philo was made praetor,—the first to be chosen from the plebs. Sulpicius the Consul opposed his election and declared that he would receive no votes for him; but the senate, having failed in its opposition to plebeian candidates for the highest magistracies, was less obstinate in the matter of the praetorship.[2]

XVI. The following year, being the consulship of Lucius Papirius Crassus and Caeso Duillius, was remarkable for a war more novel than important, to wit with the Ausonians, who inhabited the city of Cales. They had joined forces with their neighbours, the Sidicini, and the army of the two peoples having suffered a defeat in one—by no means memorable—

B.C. 336–334

LIVY

exercitus fusus propinquitate urbium et ad fugam
3 pronior et in fuga ipsa tutior fuit. Nec tamen
omissa eius belli cura patribus, quia totiens iam
Sidicini aut ipsi moverant bellum aut moventibus
4 auxilium tulerant aut causa armorum fuerant. Itaque omni ope adnisi sunt, ut maximum ea tempestate imperatorem M. Valerium Corvum [1] consulem
5 quartum facerent ; collega additus Corvo M. Atilius
Regulus ; et ne forte casu erraretur, petitum ab
consulibus ut extra sortem Corvi ea provincia esset.
6 Exercitu victore a superioribus consulibus accepto,
ad Cales, unde bellum ortum erat, profectus, cum
hostes ab superioris etiam certaminis memoria pavidos clamore atque impetu primo fudisset, moenia
7 ipsa oppugnare est adgressus. Et militum quidem
is erat ardor ut iam inde cum scalis succedere ad
8 muros vellent evasurosque contenderent ; Corvus,
quia id arduum factu erat, labore militum potius
quam periculo peragere inceptum voluit. Itaque
aggerem et vineas egit turresque muro admovit,
quarum usum forte oblata opportunitas praevertit.
9 Namque M. Fabius, captivus Romanus, cum per
neglegentiam custodum festo die vinculis ruptis per
murum inter opera Romanorum, religata ad pinnam
10 muri reste suspensus, manibus se demisisset, perpulit
imperatorem ut vino epulisque sopitos hostes adgre-

---

[1] Corvum Ω: coruinum (*and* coruino *in* § 5, *where, however,*
O has corino) *UO*.

64

B.C.
336-334

battle, was by the nearness of their cities not only
the more disposed to flight, but found in that same
flight the readier safety. The senators, however,
did not cease to be concerned over this war, so
many times before had the Sidicini either drawn the
sword themselves, or lent aid to those who were
drawing it, or been the occasion of hostilities. They
accordingly bent every effort to elect to his fourth
consulship the greatest soldier of that age, Marcus
Valerius Corvus. To be his colleague, they gave
him Marcus Atilius Regulus ; and lest there should
by chance be some miscarriage, they requested of
the consuls that Corvus be given the command,
without the drawing of lots. Taking over the
victorious army from the previous consuls, he marched
on Cales, where the war had originated, and routing
the enemy—who had as yet not even recovered
from the panic of the earlier encounter—at the first
cheer and onset, he attacked the town itself. The
soldiers, for their part, were so eager that they
wished to attempt the walls at once with scaling-
ladders, and insisted that they could carry the place ;
but Corvus, since this would have been an arduous
achievement, preferred to accomplish his purpose at
the cost of labour rather than of danger to his men.
He therefore constructed a terrace and brought up
mantlets, and moved his towers close to the walls,
but a fortunate circumstance made it unnecessary to
employ them. For Marcus Fabius, a Roman prisoner,
being neglected by his guards on a day of merry-
making, broke his bonds, let himself down by the
wall, hand over hand, into the Roman works, by
a rope which he had made fast to a battlement, and
induced the general to attack the enemy while they

A.U.C.
418-420

deretur; nec maiore certamine capti cum urbe
Ausones sunt quam acie fusi erant. Praeda capta
ingens est, praesidioque imposito Calibus reductae
11 Romam legiones. Consul ex senatus consulto
triumphavit, et, ne Atilius expers gloriae esset,
iussi ambo consules adversus Sidicinos ducere exer-
12 citum. Dictatorem ante ex senatus consulto comitiorum habendorum causa dixerunt L. Aemilium
Mamercinum; is magistrum equitum Q. Publilium
Philonem dixit. Dictatore comitia habente consules
13 creati sunt T. Veturius Sp. Postumius. Ei, etsi[1]
belli pars cum Sidicinis restabat, tamen, ut beneficio
praevenirent desiderium plebis, de colonia dedu-
14 cenda Cales rettulerunt; factoque senatus consulto
ut duo milia quingenti homines eo scriberentur,
tres viros coloniae deducendae agroque dividundo
creaverunt K. Duillium T. Quinctium M. Fabium.

A.U.C.
422

XVII. Novi deinde consules a veteribus exercitu
accepto ingressi hostium fines populando usque ad
2 moenia atque urbem pervenerunt. Ibi quia ingenti
exercitu comparato Sidicini et ipsi pro extrema spe
dimicaturi enixe videbantur et Samnium fama erat
3 conciri ad bellum, dictator ab consulibus ex auctoritate senatus dictus P. Cornelius Rufinus, magister

---

[1] Ei, etsi *Madvig* : etsi Ω.

---

[1] This was the third triumph of Corvus. See VII. xxvii.
8, and xxxviii. 3.   [2] Cf. note on p. 156.

B.C.
336–334

wereovercome with feasting and drinking. The result
was that the Ausonians and their city were captured
with no greater effort than they had been defeated
in the field. Huge spoils were taken, a garrison was
established in the town, and the legions were led
back to Rome. The consul triumphed,[1] in pursuance
of a senatorial decree, and lest Atilius should go
without his meed of glory, both consuls were directed
to march against the Sidicini. But first—being
so instructed by the senate—they named a dictator
to preside at the elections, their choice falling on
Lucius Aemilius Mamercinus, who selected Quintus
Publilius Philo to be master of the horse. Under
the presidency of the dictator, Titus Veturius and
Spurius Postumius were chosen consuls. These
men, although a half of the war—with the Sidicini
—yet remained, nevertheless, in order to anticipate
the desires of the plebs by doing them a service,
brought in a proposal for sending out a colony to
Cales. The senate resolved that twenty-five hundred
men should be enrolled for it, and appointed Caeso
Duillius, Titus Quinctius, and Marcus Fabius a
commission of three to conduct the settlers to the
land and apportion it amongst them.

XVII. The new consuls then took over the army
from their predecessors, and entering the enemy's
territory laid it waste as far as their city walls. At
this juncture, since the Sidicini had themselves
raised an enormous army and seemed likely to make
a desperate struggle in behalf of their last hope, and
since the rumour went that Samnium was arming,
the senate authorized the consuls to nominate a
dictator.[2] They appointed Publius Cornelius Rufinus,
and Marcus Antonius was made master of the horse.

B.C.
334–332

A.U.C.
422

4 equitum M. Antonius. Religio deinde incessit vitio
eos creatos, magistratuque se abdicaverunt; et quia
pestilentia insecuta est, velut omnibus eo vitio con-
tactis auspiciis, res ad interregnum rediit.

5 Ab interregno inito per quintum demum interregem, M. Valerium Corvum,[1] creati consules A.
6 Cornelius iterum et Cn. Domitius. Tranquillis rebus
fama Gallici belli pro tumultu valuit ut dictatorem
dici placeret. Dictus M. Papirius Crassus et magis-
7 ter equitum P. Valerius Publicola. A quibus cum
dilectus intentius quam adversus finitima bella
haberetur, exploratores missi attulerunt quieta
8 omnia apud Gallos esse. Samnium quoque iam
alterum annum turbari novis consiliis suspectum
erat; eo ex agro Sidicino exercitus Romanus non
9 deductus. Ceterum Samnites bellum Alexandri
Epirensis in Lucanos traxit; qui duo populi adversus
regem escensionem [2] a Paesto facientem signis con-
10 latis pugnaverunt. Eo certamine superior Alexander,
incertum qua fide culturus, si perinde cetera pro-
cessissent, pacem cum Romanis fecit.

11 Eodem anno census actus novique cives censi.
Tribus propter eos additae Maecia et Scaptia; censores
12 addiderunt Q. Publilius Philo Sp. Postumius. Romani

---

[1] Corvum Ω: coruinum *UO*.
[2] escensionem*ς*: escensione Ω: excensionem *Aς*: excur-
sionem *D³A³*: ascensionem *U*.

---

[1] The Maecian tribe was presumably named from Castrum
Maecium (near Lanuvium) mentioned at vi. ii. 8, and the
Scaptian from the town of Scaptia which lay between Tibur
and Tusculum. The number of tribes was thus raised to
twenty-nine.

A scruple was subsequently raised about the regularity of their appointment, and they resigned their office; and when a pestilence ensued, it was supposed that all the auspices were affected by that irregularity, and the state reverted to an interregnum.

Finally Marcus Valerius Corvus, the fifth interrex from the beginning of the interregnum, achieved the election to the consulship of Aulus Cornelius (for the second time) and Gnaeus Domitius. Coming, as it did, when all was tranquil, the rumour of a Gallic war worked like an actual rising, and caused the senate to have recourse to a dictator. Marcus Papirius Crassus was the man, and he named Publius Valerius Publicola master of the horse. While they were conducting their levy, more strenuously than they would have done for a war against a neighbouring state, scouts were sent out, and returned with the report that all was quiet amongst the Gauls. Samnium likewise had now for two years been suspected of hatching revolutionary schemes, for which reason the Roman army was not withdrawn from the Sidicine country. But an invasion by Alexander of Epirus drew the Samnites off into Lucania, and these two peoples engaged in a pitched battle with the King, as he was marching up from Paestum. The victory remained with Alexander, who then made a treaty of peace with the Romans; with what faith he intended to keep it, had the rest of his campaign been equally successful, is a question.

In this same year the census was taken and new citizens were assessed. On their account the Maecian and Scaptian tribes were added.[1] The censors who added them were Quintus Publilius Philo and

69

A.U.C.
422
facti Acerrani lege ab L. Papirio praetore lata, qua
civitas sine suffragio data. Haec eo anno domi
militiaeque gesta.

A.U.C.
123
XVIII. Foedus insequens annus seu intemperie
caeli seu humana fraude fuit, M. Claudio Marcello
2 C.[1] Valerio consulibus. Flaccum Potitumque varie
in annalibus cognomen consulis invenio; ceterum in
eo parvi refert quid veri sit; illud pervelim—nec
omnes auctores sunt—proditum falso esse, venenis
absumptos quorum mors infamem annum pestilentia
3 fecerit; sicut proditur tamen res, ne cui auctorum
4 fidem abrogaverim, exponenda est. Cum primores
civitatis similibus morbis eodemque ferme omnes
eventu morerentur, ancilla quaedam ad Q. Fabium
Maximum aedilem curulem indicaturam se causam
publicae pestis professa est, si ab eo fides sibi data
5 esset haud futurum noxae indicium. Fabius confestim
rem ad consules, consules ad senatum referunt,
6 consensuque ordinis fides indici data. Tum pate-
factum muliebri fraude civitatem premi matronasque
ea venena coquere, et si sequi extemplo velint,
7 manifesto deprehendi posse. Secuti indicem et
coquentes quasdam medicamenta et recondita alia

---

[1] C. *Sigonius* (*Diod.* XVII. lxxiv. 1): t Ω.

Spurius Postumius. The people of Acerra became B.C. 332
Romans under a statute, proposed by the praetor
Lucius Papirius, which granted them citizenship
without the suffrage. Such were the events of this
year at home and in the field.

XVIII. A terrible year succeeded, whether owing B.C. 331
to the unseasonable weather or to man's depravity.
The consuls were Marcus Claudius Marcellus and
Gaius Valerius. I find Flaccus and Potitus severally
given in the annals, as the surname of Valerius; but
it does not greatly signify where the truth lies in
regard to this. One thing, however, I should be
glad to believe had been falsely handed down—and
indeed not all the authorities avouch it—namely,
that those whose deaths made the year notorious
for pestilence were in reality destroyed by poison;
still, I must set forth the story as it comes to us,
that I may not deprive any writer of his credit.
When the leading citizens were falling ill with the
same kind of malady, which had, in almost every
case the same fatal termination, a certain serving-
woman came to Quintus Fabius Maximus, the curule
aedile, and declared that she would reveal the cause
of the general calamity, if he would give her a
pledge that she should not suffer for her testimony.
Fabius at once referred the matter to the consuls,
and the consuls to the senate, and a pledge was
given to the witness with the unanimous approval of
that body. She then disclosed the fact that the
City was afflicted by the criminal practices of the
women; that they who prepared these poisons were
matrons, whom, if they would instantly attend her,
they might take in the very act. They followed the
informer and found certain women brewing poisons,

LIVY

8 invenerunt. Quibus in forum delatis et ad viginti
matronis, apud quas deprehensa erant, per viatorem
accitis, duae ex eis, Cornelia ac Sergia, patriciae
utraque gentis, cum ea medicamenta salubria esse
contenderent, ab confutante indice bibere iussae, ut
se falsum commentam in conspectu omnium [1] argue-
9 rent, spatio ad conloquendum sumpto, cum submoto
populo rem ad ceteras rettulissent, haud abnuentibus
et illis bibere, epoto medicamento suamet ipsae
10 fraude omnes interierunt.   Comprehensae extemplo
earum comites magnum numerum matronarum
indicaverunt ; ex quibus ad centum septuaginta
11 damnatae.   Neque de veneficiis ante eam diem
Romae quaesitum est.   Prodigii ea res loco habita
captisque magis mentibus quam consceleratis similis
12 visa ; itaque memoria ex annalibus repetita in seces-
sionibus quondam plebis clavum ab dictatore fixum
alienatasque discordia mentes hominum eo piaculo
compotes sui fuisse,[2] dictatorem clavi figendi causa
13 creari placuit.   Creatus Cn. Quinctilius magistrum
equitum L. Valerium dixit, qui fixo clavo magistratu
se abdicaverunt.

XIX. Creati consules L. Papirius Crassus iterum L.
Plautius Venox ; cuius principio anni legati ex Volscis
Fabraterni et Lucani Romam venerunt, orantes ut in

---

[1] *The words* in conspectu omnium *are found in the MSS.
after* populo.   *Walters and Conway suggest placing them here,
or preferably, after* epoto ; *but in the latter position they would
be inconsistent with* submoto populo, *for the women would not
recall the crowd to witness their own discomfiture.*

[2] fuisse *Crévier* : factas esse *Alschefski* : fecisse Ω.

---

[1] Livy says nothing of the nail in his accounts of the
several secessions at II. xxxii, III. l, and VII. xlii, but in
VII. iii describes the practice as having originated in an
attempt to relieve a pestilence.

and other poisons stored away. These concoctions were brought into the Forum, and some twenty matrons, in whose houses they had been discovered, were summoned thither by an apparitor. Two of their number, Cornelia and Sergia, of patrician houses both, asserted that these drugs were salutary. On the informer giving them the lie, and bidding them drink and prove her charges false in the sight of all, they took time to confer, and after the crowd had been dismissed they referred the question to the rest, and finding that they, like themselves, would not refuse the draught, they all drank off the poison and perished by their own wicked practices. Their attendants being instantly arrested informed against a large number of matrons, of whom one hundred and seventy were found guilty; yet until that day there had never been a trial for poisoning in Rome. Their act was regarded as a prodigy, and suggested madness rather than felonious intent. Accordingly when a tradition was revived from the annals how formerly in secessions of the plebs [1] a nail had been driven by the dictator, and how men's minds, which had been distracted by dissension, had by virtue of that expiation regained their self-control, they resolved on the appointment of a dictator to drive the nail. The appointment went to Gnaeus Quinctilius, who named Lucius Valerius master of the horse. The nail was driven and they resigned their posts.

XIX. The consular election resulted in the choice of Lucius Papirius Crassus (for the second time) and Lucius Plautius Venox. At the outset of this year Volscian ambassadors from Fabrateria and Luca came to Rome asking protection, and promising that, if

2 fidem reciperentur : **si a** Samnitium armis defensi essent, se sub imperio populi Romani fideliter atque 3 oboedienter futuros. Missi tum ab senatu legati denuntiatumque Samnitibus ut eorum populorum finibus vim abstinerent; valuitque ea legatio, non tam quia pacem volebant Samnites quam quia nondum parati erant ad bellum.

4 Eodem anno Privernas bellum initum, cuius socii Fundani, dux etiam fuit Fundanus, Vitruvius [1] Vaccus,[2] vir non domi solum sed etiam Romae clarus; aedes fuere in Palatio eius, quae Vacci prata diruto 5 aedificio publicatoque solo appellata. Adversus hunc vastantem effuse Setinum Norbanumque et Coranum agrum L. Papirius profectus haud procul castris eius 6 consedit. Vitruvio nec ut vallo se teneret adversus validiorem hostem sana constare mens, nec ut longius 7 a castris dimicaret animus suppetere; vix tota extra portam castrorum explicata acie, fugam magis retro quam proelium aut hostem spectante milite, sine 8 consilio, sine audacia depugnat. Ut et levi momento nec ambigue est victus, ita brevitate ipsa loci facilique receptu in tam propinqua castra haud aegre 9 militem a multa caede est tutatus; nec fere quisquam in ipso certamine, pauci in turba fugae extremae, cum in castra ruerent, caesi; primisque tenebris Priver-

---

[1] Vitruvius F^2 (*or* F^3) *Sigonius* : uitrubius Ω : uitrubrius *LA* (*in* §§ 6 *and* 10 *the MSS. give* uitrub-).
[2] Vaccus ς : baccus Ω (*but* uacci *below*).

defended from Samnite aggressions, they would be loyal and obedient subjects of the Roman People. The senate thereupon sent envoys to the Samnites and warned them to do no violence to the territories of those cities. The embassy was effective, not so much because the Samnites desired peace, as because they were unprepared, as yet, for war.

The same year saw the beginning of the war with Privernum. The enemy had the Fundanians for allies, and even a Fundanian general, by the name of Vitruvius Vaccus. He was a man of distinction, not only in his own city, but in Rome as well, where he had a house on the Palatine, at the place which, after the building had been demolished and the area confiscated, was known as the Meadows of Vaccus. He was spoiling, far and wide, the territories of Setia, Norba, and Cora, when Lucius Papirius marched out to confront him, and took up a position not far from the other's camp. Vitruvius had neither the strength of mind to remain behind his rampart in the face of a more powerful opponent, nor the courage to fight at a distance from his works. The last of his troops were scarcely clear of the camp gates and his line deployed, and the soldiers were thinking more of flight than of battle or the enemy, when he began, without showing either prudence or audacity, a critical engagement. He was easily and decisively defeated ; yet, because his camp was so near and so readily accessible, he was able without great difficulty to save his men from heavy losses; indeed, there were hardly any slain in the battle itself, and in the flight only a few amongst the stragglers, as they rushed into the camp. Under cover of the earliest dusk they sought Privernum in a panic-stricken

num inde petitum agmine trepido, ut muris potius quam vallo sese tutarentur.

A Priverno Plautius alter consul pervastatis passim agris praedaque abacta in agrum Fundanum exer-
10 citum inducit. Ingredienti fines senatus Fundanorum occurrit ; negant se pro Vitruvio sectamque eius secutis precatum venisse, sed pro Fundano populo, quem extra culpam belli esse ipsum Vitruvium iudicasse, cum receptaculum fugae Privernum habu-
11 erit, non patriam.[1] Priverni igitur hostes populi Romani quaerendos persequendosque esse, qui simul a Fundanis ac Romanis utriusque patriae immemores defecerint : Fundanis pacem esse et animos Romanos
12 et gratam memoriam acceptae civitatis. Orare se con- sulem ut bellum ab innoxio populo abstineat ; agros urbem corpora ipsorum coniugumque ac liberorum suorum in potestate populi Romani esse futuraque.
13 Conlaudatis Fundanis consul litterisque Romam missis in officio Fundanos esse ad Privernum flexit iter. Prius animadversum in eos qui capita coniurationis
14 fuerant a consule scribit Claudius ; ad trecentos quinquaginta ex coniuratis vinctos Romam missos, eamque deditionem ab senatu non acceptam, quod egentium atque humilium poena defungi velle

Fundanum populum censuerint. XX. Privernum duobus consularibus exercitibus cum obsideretur,

---

[1] patriam A^1 (or A^2) ς : patriam fundanos Ω : patriam fundos ς.

throng, to obtain for themselves the protection of walls in place of a rampart.

From Privernum the other consul Plautius, after everywhere pillaging the fields and driving off the cattle, led his army into the domain of Fundi. As he crossed the border he was met by the Fundanian senate, who said that they had come to plead, not for Vitruvius and his followers, but for the people of Fundi, whom even Vitruvius himself had cleared of responsibility for the war, when he sought refuge in Privernum and not in his native city. It was therefore in Privernum that the Roman People should seek out and punish its enemies, who had fallen away at the same time from Fundi and from Rome, unmindful of either allegiance: the Fundani were peaceful, their sympathies were Roman, and they held in grateful recollection the gift of citizenship. They begged the consul to make no war upon an innocent people, and declared that their lands, their city, their persons, and those of their wives and children were subject to the dominion of the Roman People and would so remain. The consul heartily commended them, and announcing in a dispatch to Rome that the Fundanians were loyal, turned aside and marched against Privernum. Claudius [1] writes that before he set out, the consul executed the leaders of the plot, and sent some three hundred and fifty of the conspirators in chains to Rome; but that the senate would not accept of their surrender, being persuaded that the people of Fundi sought to escape with the punishment of their poor and lowly.

XX. While the two consular armies were laying siege to Privernum, the other consul was recalled to

B.C. 330

B.C. 329

[1] Q. Claudius Quadrigarius, the annalist. See Introd. p. xxx.

A.U.C.
425

alter consul comitiorum causa Romam revocatus.
2 Carceres eo anno in circo primum statuti.

Nondum perfunctos cura Privernatis belli tumultus
Gallici fama atrox invasit, haud ferme unquam
3 neglecta patribus. Extemplo igitur consules novi L.
Aemilius Mamercinus et C. Plautius,[1] eo ipso die,
Kalendis Quinctilibus, quo magistratum inierunt,
comparare inter se provincias iussi, et Mamercinus,
cui Gallicum bellum evenerat, scribere exercitum
4 sine ulla vacationis venia; quin opificum quoque
volgus et sellularii, minime militiae idoneum genus,
exciti dicuntur; Veiosque ingens exercitus contrac-
5 tus, ut inde obviam Gallis iretur; longius discedi,
ne alio itinere hostis falleret ad urbem incedens, non
placuit. Paucos deinde post dies satis explorata
temporis eius quiete a Gallis Privernum omnis
conversa vis.

6 Duplex inde fama est: alii vi captam urbem
Vitruviumque vivum in potestatem venisse, alii
priusquam ultima adhiberetur vis, ipsos[2] se in deditionem consuli[3] caduceum praeferentes[4] permisisse
7 auctores sunt Vitruviumque ab suis traditum. Senatus
de Vitruvio Privernatibusque consultus consulem

---

[1] C. Plautius *T*[2] *Sigon.* (*C.I.L.* i.[2] *p.* 45): G. Plautius (*or*
-ci-) *PFUO*: plautius *MDLA*: placius *H*: plutius T.
[2] ipsos ς: ipsum Ω.
[3] consuli *Doujat* (*Walters*): cōs (*or* cos *or* coñs *or* coƧs) Ω:
consulis ς.
[4] praeferentes ς: praeferentis Ω.

---

[1] The cells were stalls, having a bar across the front which
was thrown down to release the chariots at the start of the
race.
[2] July 1st was the normal day for beginning the official
year from 391 B.C. to 153 B.C., when it was changed to
January 1st.

Rome to hold the elections. Chariot cells were B.C. 329
built this year for the first time in the Circus.[1]

The war with Privernum was not yet out of the
way, when there came an alarming report of a Gallic
rising, a warning which the senate almost never
disregarded. Accordingly, without a moment's
hesitation, the new consuls, Lucius Aemilius
Mamercinus and Gaius Plautius, were directed, on
the very day on which they entered office—the
Kalends of July [2]—to divide the commands between
them, and Mamercinus, to whom the Gallic war had
fallen, was bidden to enlist an army without granting
a single exemption; indeed it is said that a rabble
of craftsmen even, and sedentary mechanics, was
called out—a type the least qualified of all for
military service. An enormous army was brought
together at Veii, which was to be the base for the
campaign against the Gauls; further afield they
would not go, lest the enemy, advancing upon the
City, might slip by them on another road. After
a few days it became quite evident that no disturbance on the part of the Gauls was to be appre-
hended at that time, whereupon the whole array
was directed against Privernum.

From this point there is a twofold tradition:
some say that the city was carried by storm, and
that Vitruvius was taken alive; others, that before
the final assault was made, the people came out
with a flag of truce [3] to the consul and surrendered,
and that Vitruvius was betrayed by his own
followers. The senate, being consulted regarding
Vitruvius and the Privernates, commanded the

---

[3] The *caduceus* (κηρύκειον) was actually a herald's staff.

Plautium dirutis Priverni muris praesidioque valido
imposito ad triumphum accersit: Vitruvium in
carcere[1] adservari iussit, quoad consul redisset, tum
8 verberatum necari. Aedes eius, quae essent in
Palatio, diruendas, bona Semoni Sango censuerunt
consecranda; quodque aeris ex eis redactum est, ex
eo aenei orbes facti positi in sacello Sangus adversus
9 aedem Quirini. De senatu Privernate ita decretum,
ut qui senator Priverni post defectionem ab Romanis
mansisset trans Tiberim lege eadem qua Veliterni
10 habitaret. His ita decretis usque ad triumphum
Plauti silentium de Privernatibus fuit; post triumphum consul necato Vitruvio sociisque eius noxae
apud satiatos iam suppliciis nocentium tutam
11 mentionem de Privernatibus ratus, "Quoniam auctores defectionis" inquit, "meritas poenas et ab dis
immortalibus et a vobis habent, patres conscripti,
12 quid placet de innoxia multitudine fieri? Equidem,
etsi meae partes exquirendae magis sententiae quam
dandae sunt, tamen, cum videam Privernates vicinos
Samnitibus esse, unde nunc nobis incertissima pax
est, quam minimum irarum inter nos illosque relinqui
velim."

XXI. Cum ipsa per se res anceps esset, prout
cuiusque ingenium erat atrocius mitiusve suadentibus,

---

[1] in carcere F^x (*over erasure*) *Madvig*: in carcerem Ω.

---

[1] Semo Sangus—or Sancus—was another name for Dius
Fidius, the god of oaths, and was identified with Hercules,
who was himself closely associated with Jupiter. See Warde
Fowler, *Roman Festivals of the Republic*, pp. 135–145.

[2] See chap. xiv. § 6.

consul Plautius to raze the walls of Privernum, and B.C. 329
placing a strong garrison in the town, to come to
Rome and triumph. Vitruvius was to be held a
prisoner till the consul should return, and then
scourged and put to death; his house on the
Palatine was to be pulled down, and his goods
dedicated to Semo Sangus.[1] Out of the bronze
which his chattels realized were fashioned bronze
disks, which were placed in the shrine of Sangus,
over against the temple of Quirinus. Concerning
the senate of Privernum, it was decreed that any
senator who had remained in Privernum after its
defection from the Romans should dwell across the
Tiber on the same terms as the Veliterni.[2] These
decrees having been promulgated, no more was said
about the Privernates, until Plautius had triumphed.
After his triumph the consul caused Vitruvius and
his associates in wrongdoing to be executed, and
deeming it now safe to take up the question of the
Privernates with men who were already sated with
the punishment of the guilty, spoke as follows:
"Since the authors of rebellion have now received
the reward they merited, at the hands of the
immortal gods, and at your own hands, Conscript
Fathers, what is your pleasure regarding the innocent multitude? For my own part, though it
becomes me rather to ask opinions than to offer
one, yet when I see that the Privernates are neighbours to the Samnites, whose peaceful relations
with ourselves are at this time most precarious, I
could wish that as little bad feeling as possible
might be left between them and us."

XXI. The question was of itself a hard one to
decide, and every senator argued, as his own nature

tum incertiora omnia unus **ex** Privernatibus legatis
fecit, magis condicionis in qua natus esset quam
2 praesentis necessitatis memor; qui interrogatus a
quodam tristioris sententiae auctore quam poenam
meritos Privernates censeret, "Eam" inquit "quam
3 merentur qui se libertate dignos censent." Cuius cum
feroci responso infestiores factos videret consul eos
qui ante Privernatium causam impugnabant, ut ipse
benigna interrogatione mitius responsum eliceret,
4 "Quid si poenam" inquit "remittimus vobis?
Qualem nos pacem vobiscum habituros speremus?"
"Si bonam dederitis" inquit, "et fidam et per-
5 petuam; si malam, haud diuturnam." Tum vero
minari, nec id ambigue, Privernatem quidam, et illis
vocibus ad rebellandum incitari pacatos populos;
6 pars mitior [1] senatus ad meliora [2] responsum trahere et dicere viri et liberi vocem auditam: an
credi posse ullum populum aut hominem denique
in ea condicione cuius eum paeniteat diutius quam
7 necesse sit mansurum? Ibi pacem esse fidam ubi
voluntarii pacati sint, neque eo loco ubi servitutem
esse velint, fidem sperandam esse.

---

[1] mitior *Duker*: melior Ω.
[2] meliora Ω: molliora (*with* melior *instead of* mitior)
Gronovius, Walters and Conway.

B.C. 329

prompted him, for severity or mercy; but the whole
situation was rendered even more uncertain by one
of the deputation from Privernum, who possessed
a livelier sense of the condition in which he had
been born than of the exigencies of the actual
crisis. This man, on being asked by a certain
advocate of harsher measures what punishment he
thought the Privernates merited, replied, "That
punishment which is merited by those who deem
themselves worthy to be free." The consul perceived that this proud answer had increased the
hostility of those who were before assailing the
cause of the Privernates. In the hope that he might
himself, by putting a more kindly question, elicit
a friendlier response, "What," said he, "if we
remit your punishment? What sort of peace may
we hope to have with you?" "If you grant us
a good one," was the answer, "you may look to find
it faithfully and permanently kept; if a bad one,
you must not expect that it will long endure."
Whereat some cried out that the Privernate was
threatening them, and in no ambiguous terms, and
asserted that by such words as those pacified peoples
were roused up to rebellion. But the more merciful party in the senate put a better construction on
his answer, and pronounced it the utterance of a
man, and a man free-born. Was it credible, they
asked, that any nation, or for that matter any
man, should abide longer than he must in a
condition that was painful? That peace, they
asserted, was faithfully observed where the terms
were willingly accepted; they must not hope for
loyalty in a quarter where they sought to impose
servitude.

A.U.C.
425

8   In hanc sententiam maxime consul ipse inclinavit
animos, identidem ad principes sententiarum con-
9 sulares, uti exaudiri posset a pluribus, dicendo eos
demum qui nihil praeterquam de libertate cogitent
10 dignos esse qui Romani fiant. Itaque et in senatu
causam obtinuere, et ex auctoritate patrum latum ad
populum est ut Privernatibus civitas daretur.

11   Eodem anno Anxur trecenti in coloniam missi
sunt; bina iugera agri acceperunt.

A.U.C.
426–427

XXII. Secutus est annus nulla re belli domive insignis, P. Plautio Proculo P. Cornelio Scapula consuli-
2 bus, praeterquam quod Fregellas—Signinorum is
ager, deinde Volscorum fuerat—colonia deducta et
populo visceratio data a M. Flavio in funere matris.
3 Erant qui per speciem honorandae parentis meritam
mercedem populo solutam interpretarentur, quod
eum die dicta ab aedilibus crimine stupratae matris
4 familiae absolvisset. Data visceratio in praeteritam
iudicii gratiam honoris etiam ei causa fuit. Tribunusque[1] plebei proximis comitiis absens petentibus
praefertur.

5   Palaepolis fuit haud procul inde ubi nunc Neapoli
sita est; duabus urbibus populus idem habitabat.[2]
6 Cumis erant oriundi; Cumani Chalcide Euboica

---

[1] tribunusque *Zingerle*: tribunatuque (*wanting in* O) Ω
tribunatumque ⊊ *Gronovius*.
[2] habitabat F³ ⊊: habita at MPF?: habitat OHTDLA
habitat ut UT².

84

The consul himself did the most to bring about B.C. 329
the adoption of these views, by remarking repeatedly
to the consulars, who led in the expression of
opinion, in a voice loud enough for many to over-
hear, that only those who took no thought for anything save liberty were worthy of becoming Romans.
Accordingly they gained their cause in the senate,
and on the authorization of the Fathers a measure
was brought before the people conferring citizenship
on the Privernates.

In that same year three hundred colonists were
sent to Anxur, where they received each two *iugera*
of land.

XXII. The following year, when Publius Plautius B.C.
Proculus and Publius Cornelius Scapula were consuls, 328–327
was not signalised by any military or domestic event,
except that a colony was sent out to Fregellae—the
territory had belonged to the people of Signia, and
afterwards to the Volsci—and a dole of meat was
given to the people by Marcus Flavius, at the funeral
of his mother. Some thought that under colour
of honouring his mother he had paid a price that
he owed the people, because they had acquitted
him, when brought to trial by the aediles, of the
charge of corrupting a married woman. Though
the dole was made for the past favour shown him
in the trial, it was also the cause of his receiving an
office; and at the next election he was chosen
tribune of the plebs in his absence, in preference
to some who canvassed.

There was a city called Palaepolis, not far from
the spot where Neapolis is now, and the two cities
were inhabited by one people. Cumae was their
mother city, and the Cumani derive their origin

LIVY

originem trahunt. Classe, qua advecti ab domo
fuerant, multum in ora maris eius quod accolunt po-
tuere, primo in insulas[1] Aenariam et Pithecusas[2]
egressi, deinde in continentem ausi sedes transferre.

7 Haec civitas cum suis viribus tum Samnitium infidae
adversus Romanos societati freta, sive pestilentiae
quae Romanam urbem adorta nuntiabatur fidens,
multa hostilia adversus Romanos agrum Campanum

8 Falernumque incolentes fecit. Igitur L. Cornelio
Lentulo Q. Publilio Philone iterum consulibus,
fetialibus Palaepolim ad res repetendas missis, cum
relatum esset a Graecis, gente lingua magis strenua
quam factis, ferox responsum, ex auctoritate patrum

9 populus Palaepolitanis bellum fieri iussit. Inter consules provinciis comparatis bello Graeci persequendi
Publilio evenerunt; Cornelius altero exercitu Sam-

10 nitibus, si qua se moverent, oppositus—fama autem
erat defectioni Campanorum imminentes admoturos
castra—ibi optimum visum Cornelio stativa habere.

XXIII. Ab utroque consule exiguam spem pacis
cum Samnitibus esse certior fit senatus: Publilius[3]
duo milia Nolanorum militum et quattuor Samnitium
magis Nolanis cogentibus quam voluntate Graecorum

2 recepta Palaepoli;[4] Cornelius dilectum indictum a

---

[1] in insulas ς: insulas Ω: insulam A.
[2] Pithecusas ς: phitecusas MPFO: fitecusas U: pitecusas
HTDLA.
[3] Publilius edd.: publius Ω (omitted by U).
[4] Palaepoli Walters and Conway: Palaepoli miserat
Sigonius: palaepoli romam miserat (or -nt) Ω.

---

[1] Islands in the northern part of the Bay of Naples. By
Pithecusae Livy seems to mean the islands of this group
other than Aenaria, i.e. Pithecusa itself, Leucothea, and
Sidonia; or perhaps he calls the whole group Pithecusae and
means "Aenaria and the rest of the Pithecusae."

from Chalcis in Euboea. Thanks to the fleet in
which they had sailed from their home, they enjoyed much power on the coast of that sea by which they dwell; having landed first on the island of Aenaria and the Pithecusae,[1] they afterwards ventured to transfer their seat to the mainland. This nation, relying in part on its own strength, in part on the faithlessness shown by the Samnites in their alliance with the Romans, or perhaps on the plague which was reported as having assailed the City of Rome, committed many hostile acts against the Romans dwelling in the districts of Campania and Falerii. When therefore Lucius Cornelius Lentulus and Quintus Publilius Philo (for the second time) were consuls, fetials were dispatched to Palaepolis to demand redress; and on their bringing back a spirited answer from the Greeks— a race more valiant in words than in deeds—the people acted upon a resolution of the senate and commanded that war be made upon Palaepolis. By the division of the commands between the consuls, the war with the Greeks fell to Publilius; Cornelius, with another army, was ordered to be ready for the Samnites, in case they should take the field; and since it was rumoured that they were only waiting to bring up their army the moment the Campanians began a revolt, that seemed to be the best place for the permanent encampment of Cornelius.

XXIII. Both consuls informed the senate that
there was very little hope of peace with the Samnites: Publilius reported that two thousand soldiers from Nola and four thousand Samnites had been received into Palaepolis,—rather under compulsion from the Nolani than by the good-will of

A.U.C.
427–428

magistratibus universumque Samnium erectum ac
vicinos populos, Privernatem Fundanumque et For-
3 mianum, haud ambigue sollicitari. Ob haec cum
legatos mitti placuisset prius ad Samnites quam
bellum fieret, responsum redditur ab Samnitibus
4 ferox. Ultro incusabant iniurias Romanorum, neque
eo neglegentius ea quae ipsis obicerentur purgabant :
5 haud ullo publico consilio auxiliove iuvari Graecos
nec Fundanum Formianumve a se sollicitatos ; quippe
minime paenitere se virium suarum, si bellum placeat.
6 Ceterum non posse dissimulare aegre pati civitatem
Samnitium quod Fregellas ex Volscis captas dirutas-
que ab se restituerit Romanus populus, coloniamque
in Samnitium agro imposuerint, quam coloni eorum
7 Fregellas appellent ; eam se contumeliam iniuri-
amque, ni sibi ab iis qui fecerint dematur, ipsos
8 omni vi depulsuros esse. Cum Romanus legatus
ad disceptandum eos ad communes socios atque
amicos vocaret, "Quid perplexe agimus ? " inquit ;
"Nostra certamina, Romani, non verba legatorum
nec hominum quisquam disceptator, sed campus
Campanus, in quo concurrendum est, et arma et
9 communis Mars belli decernet. Proinde inter
Capuam Suessulamque castra castris conferamus, et
Samnis Romanusne imperio Italiam regat decer-

B.C.
327-326

the Greeks; Cornelius, that the Samnite magistrates
had proclaimed a levy, and that all Samnium was up,
while the neighbouring cities of Privernum, Fundi,
and Formiae were being openly solicited to join.
The senate having, in view of these facts, voted to
send ambassadors to the Samnites before declaring
war, received a defiant answer from them.   Indeed
they actually accused the Romans of improper conduct, yet without neglecting to clear their own
skirts—if they could—of the charges brought
against them : the Greeks, they said, were receiving
no public counsel or support from them, nor had
they asked the Fundani or Formiani to revolt ;
indeed they were quite strong enough to look out
for themselves, if they chose to fight ; on the other
hand, they could not dissemble the chagrin of the
Samnite nation that Fregellae, which they had
captured from the Volsci and destroyed, should
have been restored by the Roman People, and a
colony planted in the territory of the Samnites
which the Roman settlers called by that name; this
was an insult and an injury, which, if its authors did
not themselves recall it, they proposed to resist with
might and main.   When the Roman legate invited
them to discuss the question with the common
allies and friends of both, the Samnite spokesman
said, " Why do we beat about the bush ?   Our
differences, Romans, will be decided, not by the
words of envoys nor by any man's arbitration, but
by the Campanian plain—where we must meet in
battle,—by the sword, and by the common chance
of war.   Let us encamp then face to face betwixt
Suessula and Capua, and settle the question whether
Samnite or Roman is to govern Italy."   The Roman

LIVY

10 namus." Legati Romanorum cum se non quo hostis
wocasset[1] sed quo imperatores sui duxissent ituros
esse respondissent . . .[2]

Iam Publilius inter Palaepolim Neapolimque loco
opportune capto diremerat hostibus societatem auxilii
mutui qua, ut quisque locus premeretur, inter se usi

11 fuerant. Itaque cum et comitiorum dies instaret et
Publilium imminentem hostium muris avocari ab spe
capiendae in dies urbis haud e re publica esset,

12 actum cum tribunis est, ad populum ferrent ut, cum
Q. Publilius Philo consulatu abisset, pro consule rem
gereret quoad debellatum cum Graecis esset.

13 L. Cornelio, quia ne eum quidem in Samnium iam
ingressum revocari ab impetu belli placebat, litterae
missae ut dictatorem comitiorum causa diceret.

14 Dixit M. Claudium Marcellum; ab eo magister
equitum dictus Sp. Postumius. Nec tamen ab
dictatore comitia sunt habita, quia vitione creatus
esset in disquisitionem venit. Consulti augures

15 vitiosum videri dictatorem pronuntiaverunt. Eam
rem tribuni suspectam infamemque criminando
fecerunt: nam neque facile fuisse id vitium nosci,
cum consul oriens de nocte[3] silentio diceret
dictatorem, neque ab consule cuiquam publice

---

[1] vocasset T²₅: uocaset O¹: uocaret O: uocassent Ω₅.

[2] *Madvig thinks that a passage of some length, narrating the
outcome of the embassy, the declaration of war, and the
beginning of the siege of Naples, has been lost.*

[3] oriens de nocte *Drakenborch* (oriens nocte *Rubenius*):
oriende nocte F: oriente nocte Ω: oriente noctis D³A:
oriente sub nocte O.

---

[1] This is the first recorded instance of the continuation of
a consul's powers beyond his year of office, although in 464
a former consul, T. Quinctius, had been invested with
consular authority for a campaign (III. iv. 10).

legates having replied that they should go, not where the enemy summoned them, but where their generals led them . . .

By taking up a favourable position between Palaepolis and Neapolis, Publilius had already deprived the enemy of that mutual exchange of assistance which they had made use of, as one place after another was hard pressed. Accordingly, since the time drew near for the elections, and it was not for the advantage of the state that Publilius, who was threatening the enemy's walls, should be called away from the prospective capture of their city, which might happen any day, the senate got the tribunes to propose a popular enactment, providing that Quintus Publilius Philo should, on the expiration of his consulship, conduct the campaign as proconsul until the Greeks should have been conquered.[1]

To Lucius Cornelius, who had already entered Samnium, and whom they were equally unwilling to withdraw from the vigorous prosecution of the war, they sent a letter directing him to name a dictator for conducting the elections. He named Marcus Claudius Marcellus, who named Spurius Postumius master of the horse. But the comitia were not held by the dictator, inasmuch as the regularity of his appointment was called in question. The augurs were consulted, and announced that the procedure appeared faulty. This sentence the tribunes by their accusations made suspect and infamous; for the flaw, as they pointed out, could not easily have been discovered, since the consul rose in the night and appointed the dictator in silence, neither had the consul written to anyone

LIVY

16 privatimve de ea re scriptum esse nec quemquam
mortalium exstare qui se vidisse aut audisse quid
dicat quod auspicium dirimeret, neque augures
divinare Romae sedentes potuisse quid in castris
consuli vitii obvenisset; cui non apparere, quod
plebeius dictator sit, id vitium auguribus visum?
17 Haec aliaque ab tribunis nequiquam iactata; tandem [1]
ad interregnum res redit, dilatisque alia atque alia
de causa comitiis quartus decimus demum interrex
L. Aemilius consules creat C. Poetelium [2] L. Papirium Mugillanum; Cursorem in aliis annalibus
invenio.

XXIV. Eodem anno Alexandream in Aegypto
proditum conditam, Alexandrumque Epiri regem
ab exsule Lucano interfectum sortes Dodonaei Iovis
2 eventu adfirmasse. Accito ab Tarentinis in Italiam
data dictio erat, caveret Acherusiam aquam Pando-
3 siamque urbem: ibi fatis eius terminum dari. Eoque
ocius transmisit in Italiam ut quam maxime procul
abesset urbe Pandosia in Epiro et Acheronte amni,
quem ex Molosside fluentem in Stagna Inferna [3]
4 accipit Thesprotius sinus. Ceterum ut [4] ferme fugi-
endo in media fata ruitur, cum saepe Bruttias

---

[1] tandem ⟂ *Madvig*: tamen Ω (*wanting in O*).
[2] Poetelium *Madvig* (III. xxxv. 11): petilium (*or* pe-
tillium) Ω.
[3] Stagna Inferna *Walters and Conway* (*Plin., N.H.* IV. i.
4, *Strabo* VII. vii. 5): stagna inferna Ω *edd.*
[4] ceterum ut ⟂ : ut ceterum Ω.

---

[1] The founding of Alexandria and the death of Alexander
of Epirus are placed five years too late. They occurred in
332 or 331 B.C.
[2] The name was doubtless due to the association of the
Acheron in Epirus with the Acheron of the lower world.

regarding the transaction, whether officially or privately, nor was there a single mortal living who could say that he had seen or heard a thing that would bring to naught the auspices; nor yet could the augurs have divined, as they sat in Rome, what obstacle the consul had met with in the camp. Was there anyone, they would like to know, who could not see that the plebeian standing of the dictator was the thing which had seemed irregular to the augurs? These and other objections were made by the tribunes to no purpose; the state at length reverted to an interregnum, and after the comitia had been again and again postponed, on one pretext or another, at last the fourteenth interrex, Lucius Aemilius, procured the election of consuls, viz. Gaius Poetelius and Lucius Papirius Mugillanus—in other annals I find the name of Cursor.

XXIV. It is recorded that in that same year Alexandria in Egypt was founded, and that Alexander, king of Epirus, being murdered by a Lucanian exile, fulfilled by his death the oracle of Jupiter at Dodona.[1] On his being summoned to Italy by the Tarentines, the oracle had warned him to beware of the Acherusian water and the city Pandosia, for there he was destined to end his days. On this account he had passed over with the more speed into Italy, that he might be as far removed as possible from the city of Pandosia in Epirus and from the river Acheron, which, debouching from Molossis into the Infernal Marshes,[2] discharges its waters into the Thesprotian Gulf. But, as generally happens, in seeking to escape his doom he ran full upon it. Having repeatedly defeated the Bruttian

LIVY

Lucanasque legiones fudisset, Heracleam Tarentinorum coloniam ex Lucanis, Sipontum Apulorum,
Consentiamque[1] Bruttiorum ac Terinam,[2] alias inde
Messapiorum[3] ac Lucanorum cepisset urbes et
trecentas familias illustres in Epirum, quas obsidum

5 numero haberet, misisset, haud procul Pandosia urbe,
imminente Lucanis ac Bruttiis finibus, tres tumulos
aliquantum inter se distantes insedit, ex quibus
incursiones in omnem partem agri hostilis faceret;

6 et ducentos ferme Lucanorum exsules circa se
pro fidis habebat, ut pleraque eius generis ingenia
sunt, cum fortuna mutabilem gerentes fidem.

7 Imbres continui campis omnibus inundatis[4]
cum interclusissent trifariam exercitum a mutuo
inter se auxilio, duo praesidia, quae sine rege
erant, improviso hostium adventu opprimuntur;
deletisque eis ad ipsius obsidionem omnes con-

8 versi. Inde ab Lucanis exsulibus ad suos nuntii
missi sunt, pactoque reditu promissum est regem
aut vivum aut mortuum in potestatem daturos.

9 Ceterum cum delectis ipse egregium facinus
ausus per medios erumpit hostes, et ducem
Lucanorum comminus congressum obtruncat;

10 contrahensque suos ex fuga palatos pervenit ad
amnem, ruinis recentibus pontis, quem vis aquae

11 abstulerat, indicantem iter. Quem cum incerto

---

[1] coloniam ex Lucanis, Sipontum Apulorum, Consentiamque Bruttiorum *Weissenborn* : coloniam Consentiam (*M omits*
Consentiam) ex Lucanis Sipontumque Bruttiorum (Bruttiorum coloniam *O*) Ω.
[2] ac Terinam *Sigonius*: acerinam (*or* -um) Ω: acrenti-
nam *M*.
[3] Messapiorum A^3ς: massepiorum(-porum = priorum *L*) Ω
[4] inundatis *Madvig*: inundates *MPT*: inundantes Ω.

and Lucanian levies; having taken Heraclea, a Tarentine colony, from the Lucanians, and Sipontum belonging to the Apulians, and the Bruttian towns Consentia and Terina, and after that other towns of the Messapians and Lucanians; and having sent to Epirus three hundred illustrious families, to be held as hostages, he took up his station not far from the city Pandosia, which looks down upon the borders of Lucania and Bruttium, on three hills that stand some little distance apart from one another, that he might thence make incursions into every quarter of the enemy's country. He had about him some two hundred Lucanian exiles, whom he trusted; but their loyalty, like that of most men of that nation, was prone to change with the change of fortune.

Continuous rains, which flooded all the fields, having isolated the three divisions of the army and cut them off from mutual assistance, the two bodies other than the king's were surprised and overpowered by the enemy, who, after putting them all to the sword, proceeded with their entire strength to blockade Alexander himself. Whereupon the Lucanian exiles sent messengers to their countrymen, and promised that, if assured of restoration, they would give up the king, alive or dead, into their hands. But Alexander, with a chosen band, made a daring attempt, and broke out through the midst of his foes, cutting down the Lucanian general in a hand-to-hand encounter. Then, rallying his followers, who had become scattered in the flight, he came to a river, where the fresh ruins of a bridge, which the violence of the current had swept away, pointed out the road. As his company were making

LIVY

vado transiret agmen, fessus metu ac labore miles,
increpans nomen abominandum fluminis, "Iure
Acheros vocaris" inquit.   Quod ubi ad aures accidit
regis, adiecit extemplo animum fatis suis sub-
12 stititque, dubius an transiret.   Tum Sotimus,
minister ex regiis pueris, quid in tanto discrimine periculi cunctaretur interrogans, indicat
13 Lucanos insidiis quaerere locum.   Quos[1] ubi
respexit rex procul grege facto venientes, stringit
gladium, et per medium amnem transmittit
equum ;   iamque in vadum egressum eminus
14 veruto Lucanus exsul transfigit.   Lapsum inde
cum inhaerente telo corpus exanime detulit
amnis in hostium praesidia.   Ibi foeda laceratio
corporis facta.   Namque praeciso medio partem Consentiam misere, pars ipsis retenta ad ludibrium.
15 Quae cum iaculis saxisque procul incesseretur,
mulier una ultra humanarum irarum fidem saevienti
turbae immixta, ut parumper sustinerent precata,
flens ait virum sibi liberosque captos apud hostes
esse ;   sperare corpore regio utcumque mulcato se
16 suos redempturam.   Is finis lacerationi fuit, sepul-
tumque Consentiae quod membrorum reliquum fuit
cura mulieris unius, ossaque Metapontum ad hostes
17 remissa, inde Epirum devecta ad Cleopatram uxorem

---

[1] quos A^2 (*or* A^3)ς : quod Ω.

---

[1] Acheros is apparently a by-form of Acheron.   The
soldier associated the word with ἄχος, "pain."   The stream
is thought to have been a small tributary of the Neaethus.

[2] Apparently Alexander had a garrison there.

their way across the stream by a treacherous ford, a discouraged and exhausted soldier cried out, cursing the river's ill-omened name, " You are rightly called the Acheros !" [1] When the king heard this, he at once bethought him of the oracle, and stopped, undecided whether he should cross or not. Whereat Sotimus, one of the young nobles who attended him, asked why he hesitated in so dangerous a crisis, and pointed out the Lucanians, who were looking for a chance to waylay him. With a backward glance the king perceived them at a little distance coming towards him in a body, and drawing his sword, urged his horse through the middle of the stream. He had already gained the shallow water, when a Lucanian exile cast a javelin that transfixed him. He fell with the javelin in his lifeless body, and the current carried him down to the enemy's guard. By them his corpse was barbarously mangled, for they cut it in two through the middle, and sending a half to Consentia, kept the other half to make sport for themselves. They were standing off and pelting it with javelins and stones, when a solitary woman, exposing herself to the inhuman savagery of the raging crowd, besought them to forbear a little, and with many tears declared that her husband and children were prisoners in the hands of the enemy, and that she hoped that with the body of the king, however much disfigured, she might redeem them. This ended the mutilation. What was left of the corpse was cremated at Consentia by the care of none other than the woman, and the bones sent back to Metapontum,[2] to the enemy ; whence they were conveyed by ship to Epirus, to his wife Cleopatra and his sister

A.U.C.
428

sororemque Olympiadem, quarum mater magni
18 Alexandri altera, soror altera fuit. Haec de Alexandri Epirensis tristi eventu, quamquam Romano
bello fortuna eum abstinuit, tamen, quia in Italia
bella gessit, paucis dixisse satis sit.

XXV. Eodem anno lectisternium Romae, quintum
post conditam urbem, iisdem quibus ante placandis
2 habitum est deis.   Novi deinde consules iussu populi
cum misissent qui indicerent Samnitibus bellum,
ipsi maiore conatu quam adversus Graecos cuncta
parabant ; et alia nova nihil tum animo tale agitanti-
3 bus accesserunt auxilia.   Lucani atque Apuli, quibus
gentibus nihil ad eam diem cum Romano populo
fuerat, in fidem venerunt, arma virosque ad bellum
pollicentes ; foedere ergo in amicitiam accepti.
Eodem tempore etiam in Samnio res prospere
4 gesta.   Tria oppida in potestatem venerunt, Allifae
Callifae Rufrium, aliusque ager primo adventu
consulum longe lateque est pervastatus.

5   Hoc bello tam prospere [1] commisso, alteri quoque
bello, quo Graeci obsidebantur, iam finis aderat.
Nam praeterquam quod intersaeptis munimentis
hostium pars parti abscisa erat, foediora aliquanto
6 intra muros iis [2] quibus hostis territabat fiebant,[3] et
velut capti a suismet ipsi [4] praesidiis indigna in [5] liberis

---

[1] prospere Ω : propere *HT* : prope (*for* prope = propere) *M*.
[2] iis ⌐ : his Ω.
[3] fiebant *Luterbacher* : patiebant Ω.
[4] ipsi *Perizonius Gronovius* : *ipsis* Ω.
[5] in *Gronovius* : iam Ω.

---

[1] The first of these banquets for the gods took place in 399
B.C., the others in 392, 364, and 348.

Olympias, of whom the latter was mother, the B.C. 326
former sister, to Alexander the Great. This brief
account of the sad end of Alexander may be excused on the score of his having warred in Italy,
albeit Fortune held him back from attacking the
Romans.

XXV. A *lectisternium*, the fifth since the founding
of the City, was held this year, to propitiate the
same deities as before.[1] Then the new consuls,
having sent fetials, as commanded by the people, to
declare war on the Samnites, not only began themselves to make ready for it, on a much greater scale in
every respect than they had done against the Greeks,
but received new and at that time quite unlooked-
for help. For the Lucanians and Apulians, nations
which until then had had no dealings with the
Roman People, put themselves under their protection
and promised arms and men for the war, and were
accordingly received into a treaty of friendship. At
the same time, the Romans conducted a successful
campaign in Samnium. Three towns—Allifae,
Callifae, and Rufrium—fell into their hands, and the
rest of the country was devastated far and wide at
the first coming of the consuls.

While this war was beginning in so prosperous a
fashion, the other, against the Greeks, was in a fair
way to be concluded. For not only were a part of
the besieged cut off from the rest by the intervening
entrenchments of the Romans, but things were
going on within their walls much more dreadful
than the perils with which the enemy threatened
them ; and as though the inhabitants had been
made prisoners by their own defenders, they were
subjected to outrage even in the persons of their

quoque ac coniugibus et quae captarum urbium

7 extrema sunt patiebantur. Itaque cum et a Tarento
et a Samnitibus fama esset nova auxilia ventura,
Samnitium plus quam vellent intra moenia esse

8 rebantur, Tarentinorum iuventutem, Graeci Graecos,
haud minus per quos Samniti Nolanoque quam ut
Romanis hostibus resisterent, exspectabant; postremo levissimum malorum deditio ad Romanos visa:

9 Charilaus et Nymphius, principes civitatis, communi-
cato inter se consilio partes ad rem agendam
divisere, ut alter ad imperatorem Romanorum
transfugeret, alter subsisteret ad praebendam

10 opportunam consilio urbem. Charilaus fuit qui ad
Publilium Philonem venit, et quod bonum faustum
felix Palaepolitanis populoque Romano esset, tradere

11 se ait moenia statuisse; eo facto, utrum ab se prodita
an servata patria videatur, in fide Romana positum
esse; sibi privatim nec pacisci quicquam nec petere;

12 publice petere quam pacisci magis ut, si successisset
inceptum, cogitaret populus Romanus potius cum
quanto studio periculoque reditum in amicitiam
suam esset, quam qua[1] stultitia et temeritate de

13 officio decessum. Conlaudatus ab imperatore tria
milia militum ad occupandam eam partem urbis

---

[1] quam qua U^2 (*or* U^1) $T^2 A^3$: quamquam (quemquam *M ?*)
Ω (*including* M^1).

children and their wives, and suffered all the horrors
of captured cities. And so, on a report that rein-
forcements were on their way, both from Tarentum
and from the Samnites, they felt that they had
within their city more Samnites than they wanted,
but being Greeks, looked forward to the coming of
their fellow Greeks, the young men of Tarentum, to
enable them to resist the Samnites and the Nolani,
no less than their enemies, the Romans. In the end
it appeared to them that surrender to the Romans
was the least intolerable evil. Charilaus and
Nymphius, their principal citizens, took counsel
together, and arranged the part that each should
play in order to bring this about. One was to go
over to the Roman general, the other to remain
behind and make the city ready for the accomplish-
ment of their design. It was Charilaus who went to
Publilius Philo, and praying that it might turn out a
good and favourable and fortunate thing for Palaepolis and for the Roman People, announced that he
had resolved to deliver up the walls. It depended,
he said, upon the honour of the Romans whether,
having accomplished his intention, he should appear
to have betrayed his country or to have saved it.
For himself in particular he neither stipulated nor
requested anything; for his people he requested—
though he did not stipulate—that if the enterprise
succeeded, the Roman People should consider with
what eagerness they had resumed the friendship, and
the hazard which they ran, rather than the folly and
temerity which had led them to forget their duty.
The general commended him, and gave him three
thousand soldiers to seize that part of the city
where the Samnites were established, appointing

quam Samnites insidebant accepit; praesidio ei L.
Quinctius tribunus militum praepositus.

XXVI. Eodem tempore et Nymphius praetorem
Samnitium arte adgressus perpulerat, ut, quoniam
omnis Romanus exercitus aut circa Palaepolim aut
in Samnio esset, sineret se classe circumvehi ad
Romanum agrum, non oram modo maris sed ipsi
2 urbi propinqua loca depopulaturum. Sed ut falleret,
nocte proficiscendum esse extemploque naves dedu-
cendas. Quod quo maturius fieret, omnis iuventus
Samnitium praeter necessarium urbis praesidium
3 ad litus missa. Ubi dum Nymphius in tenebris
et multitudine semet ipsa impediente, sedulo aliis
alia imperia turbans, terit tempus, Charilaus ex
composito ab sociis in urbem receptus, cum summa
urbis Romano milite implesset, tolli clamorem iussit:
ad quem Graeci signo accepto a principibus quievere,
4 Nolani per aversam partem urbis via Nolam ferente [1]
effugiunt. Samnitibus exclusis ab urbe, ut expeditior
in praesentia fuga, ita foedior, postquam periculo
5 evaserunt, visa, quippe qui inermes nulla rerum
suarum non relicta inter hostes, ludibrium non
externis modo sed etiam popularibus, spoliati atque

---

[1] via Nolam ferente T^2A^x: uiam nolam ferentem (-tes O) Ω.

---

[1] This shows that the Samnite general was in control in the
city.

Lucius Quinctius, a military tribune, to command the force.

XXVI. At the same time Nymphius for his part had gone craftily to work with the Samnite commander, and pointing out that all the forces of the Romans were either about Palaepolis or in Samnium, got him to consent [1] that he should take a fleet and sail round them to the Roman seaboard, where he proposed, so he said, to ravage not only the coastal region, but the vicinity of Rome itself; it would however be necessary, in order to slip past the enemy unobserved, to put out at night, and the ships must be drawn down at once. That this might be accomplished the more expeditiously, all the Samnite soldiers, except the few who were needed to mount guard in the city, were sent down to the shore. While Nymphius was killing time there in the darkness, purposely issuing contradictory orders to confuse the throng, which was so large as to get in its own way, Charilaus, having been received into the city, as agreed upon by the conspirators, had occupied the highest part of it with Roman soldiers, whom he now commanded to give a cheer. On hearing this, the Greeks, who had received a signal from their leaders, remained still, but the Nolani fled through the opposite quarter of the city by the road that leads to Nola. The Samnites, being shut out from the town, enjoyed a momentary advantage in the ease with which they fled, but appeared in a more disgraceful light, when the danger had been left behind. Unarmed—for they had abandoned everything to the enemy—they returned to their homes despoiled and destitute, a laughing-stock not only to strangers but to their own

6 egentes domos rediere. Haud ignarus opinionis
alterius, qua haec proditio ab Samnitibus facta
traditur, cum auctoribus hoc dedi quibus dignius
credi est, tum foedus Neapolitanum—eo enim
deinde summa rei Graecorum venit—similius vero
7 facit ipsos in amicitiam redisse. Publilio triumphus
decretus, quod satis credebatur obsidione domitos
hostes in fidem venisse. Duo singularia haec ei viro
primum contigere, prorogatio imperii non ante in
ullo facta et acto honore triumphus.

XXVII. Aliud subinde bellum cum alterius orae
2 Graecis exortum. Namque Tarentini, cum rem
Palaepolitanam vana spe auxilii aliquamdiu sustinuissent, postquam Romanos urbe potitos accepere,
velut destituti ac non qui ipsi destituissent, increpare Palaepolitanos, ira atque invidia in Romanos
furere, eo etiam magis, quod Lucanos et Apulos—
nam utraque eo anno societas coepta est—in fidem
3 populi Romani venisse allatum est : quippe propemo-
dum perventum ad se esse, iamque in eo rem fore,
ut Romani aut hostes aut domini habendi sint.
4 Discrimen profecto rerum suarum in bello Samnitium
eventuque eius verti ; eam solam gentem restare, nec
eam ipsam satis validam, quando Lucanus defecerit ;

---

¹ The treaty secured advantages to the inhabitants of
Palaepolis-Neapolis—of which combination Neapolis now
became the head—which would hardly have been granted
them if they had been subdued, and had not voluntarily
surrendered.

countrymen. I am not unaware of the other tradition which ascribes the capture to betrayal by the Samnites, but have followed the authorities who are more deserving of credence; moreover, the treaty with Neapolis—to which place the Greeks now transferred the seat of government —makes it more likely that they renewed the friendship voluntarily.[1] Publilius was decreed a triumph, in consequence of a belief that the enemy had surrendered because they were forced to do so by the siege. He was the first to enjoy these two distinctions: an extension of his command, never before granted to any, and a triumph after the expiration of his term.

XXVII. This war was immediately followed by the outbreak of another, with the Greeks of the eastern coast. For the Tarentines, after sustaining the people of Palaepolis for some time with delusive hopes of succour, when they learned that the Romans had got possession of the city, inveighed against the Palaepolitans, as though, instead of deserting them, they themselves had been deserted, and were raging with hatred and envy against the Romans: the more so, because they learnt that the Lucanians and Apulians had made their submission to the Roman People—for an alliance was formed that year with both these nations. The Romans, they said, were almost at the gates of Tarentum, and matters would soon be come to such a pass, that they must needs have them for enemies or masters; it was clear that their own future hinged on the outcome of the war then being waged by the Samnites; this was the only nation that continued to hold out, and indeed that nation was none too strong since the defection

5 quem revocari adhuc impellique ad abolendam societatem Romanam posse, si qua ars serendis discordiis
adhibeatur.

6   Haec consilia cum apud cupidos rerum novan-
darum valuissent, ex iuventute quidam Lucanorum
pretio adsciti, clari magis inter populares quam
honesti, inter se mulcati ipsi virgis, cum corpora
7 nuda intulissent in civium coetum, vociferati sunt
se, quod castra Romana ingredi ausi essent, a consulibus virgis caesos ac prope securi percussos esse.
8 Deformis suapte natura res cum speciem iniuriae
magis quam doli prae se ferret, concitati homines
9 cogunt clamore suo magistratus senatum vocare; et
alii circumstantes concilium bellum in Romanos
poscunt, alii ad concitandam in arma multitudinem
agrestium discurrunt, tumultuque etiam sanos
consternante animos decernitur ut societas cum
Samnitibus renovaretur, legatique ad eam rem
10 mittuntur.[1] Repentina res quia quam causam nullam
tam ne fidem quidem habebat, coacti a Samnitibus
et obsides dare et praesidia in loca munita accipere,
11 caeci fraude et ira nihil recusarunt.   Dilucere deinde
brevi fraus coepit, postquam criminum falsorum
auctores Tarentum commigravere; sed amissa omni [2]
de se potestate, nihil ultra quam ut paeniteret
frustra restabat.

   XXVIII. Eo anno plebei Romanae velut aliud

---

   [1] mittuntur *HT?LA¹R* : remittuntur *DA* : mittantur
PFUOT² : mitteantur *M* : mitterentur *Frigell.*
   [2] omni *UOHT²A¹* : omnia *MPFTDLA* : omni iam *Alschefski.*

of the Lucanians; but the latter might even yet be B.C. 326 brought back and induced to repudiate the Roman alliance, if a little art were employed in sowing discord

These counsels having prevailed—for they were eager to fall in with novel schemes—they bribed certain young Lucanians, of greater prominence among their countrymen than respectability, who lacerated one another with rods and then exhibited their naked bodies before a concourse of their fellow citizens, crying out that for having dared to enter the Roman camp they had been ordered by the consuls to be scourged, and had narrowly escaped losing their heads. This spectacle, so hideous in itself, pointed clearly to injury and not to guile. In an uproar of excitement, the people obliged their magistrates to convoke the senate. At the meeting some crowded round and clamoured for war against the Romans, while others hurriedly departed this way and that, to rouse the inhabitants of the countryside to arms, till even the prudent lost their heads in the tumult, and it was voted to renew the alliance with the Samnites; and ambassadors were sent off to arrange it. This impulsive action, as it had no cause, so it carried no conviction; they were forced by the Samnites both to give hostages and also to admit garrisons within their strongholds; but, blinded by the cheat and by resentment, they stuck at nothing. A little later, when the false witnesses had retired to Tarentum, they began to see through the imposition; but having lost all power of independent action, they could only indulge in vain regrets.

XXVIII. In that year the liberty of the Roman

LIVY

initium libertatis factum est, quod necti desierunt;
mutatum autem ius ob unius feneratoris simul libi-
2 dinem simul crudelitatem insignem. L. Papirius
is fuit, cui cum se C. Publilius ob aes alienum
paternum nexum dedisset, quae aetas formaque
misericordiam elicere poterant, ad libidinem et con-
3 tumeliam animum accenderunt. Florem [1] aetatis
eius fructum adventicium crediti ratus, primo perlicere adulescentem sermone incesto est conatus;
dein, postquam aspernabantur flagitium aures, minis
4 territare atque identidem admonere fortunae; postremo, cum ingenuitatis magis quam praesentis
condicionis memorem videret, nudari iubet ver-
5 beraque adferri. Quibus laceratus iuvenis cum se
in publicum proripuisset, libidinem crudelitatemque
6 conquerens feneratoris, ingens vis hominum cum
aetatis miseratione atque indignitate iniuriae accensa, tum suae condicionis liberumque suorum
respectu, in forum atque inde agmine facto ad
7 curiam concurrit; et cum consules tumultu repentino coacti senatum vocarent, introeuntibus in
curiam patribus laceratum iuvenis tergum, pro-
cumbentes ad singulorum pedes, ostentabant.
8 Victum eo die ob impotentem iniuriam unius
ingens vinculum fidei; iussique consules ferre ad
populum ne quis, nisi qui noxam meruisset, donec
poenam lueret, in compedibus aut in nervo tene-

---

[1] Florem *Madvig*: ut florem Ω: et florem ς.

---

[1] The plebs had gained *political* liberty on the expulsion
of the kings and the adoption of the republican government.
Now they were assured of *personal* liberty as well. The
reform is put by Valerius Maximus (VI. i. 9) and Dionysius
of Halicarnassus (XVI. 9) after the disaster at the Caudine
Forks in 321 B.C.

plebs had as it were a new beginning; for men B.C. 326 ceased to be imprisoned for debt.[1] The change in the law was occasioned by the notable lust and cruelty of a single usurer, Lucius Papirius, to whom Gaius Publilius had given himself up for a debt owed by his father. The debtor's youth and beauty, which might well have stirred the creditor's compassion, did but inflame his heart to lust and contumely. Regarding the lad's youthful prime as additional compensation for the loan, he sought at first to seduce him with lewd conversation; later, finding he turned a deaf ear to the base proposal, he began to threaten him and now and again to remind him of his condition; at last, when he saw that the youth had more regard to his honourable birth than to his present plight, he had him stripped and scourged. The boy, all mangled with the stripes, broke forth into the street, crying out upon the money-lender's lust and cruelty; and a great throng of people, burning with pity for his tender years, and with rage for the shameful wrong he had undergone, and considering, too, their own condition and their children's, rushed down into the Forum, and from there in a solid throng to the Curia. The consuls were forced by the sudden tumult to convene the senate; and as the Fathers entered the Curia, the people threw themselves at the feet of each, and pointed to the young lad's mutilated back. On that day, owing to one man's outrageous injury, was broken a strong bond of credit, and the consuls were ordered to carry a proposal to the people that none should be confined in shackles or in the stocks, save those who, having been guilty of some crime, were waiting to pay the penalty;

9 retur; pecuniae creditae bona debitoris, non corpus
obnoxium esset. Ita nexi soluti, cautumque in
posterum ne necterentur.

XXIX. Eodem anno, cum satis per se ipsum
Samnitium bellum et defectio repens Lucanorum
auctoresque defectionis, Tarentini, sollicitos haberent
patres, accessit ut et Vestinus populus Samnitibus
2 sese coniungeret. Quae res sicut eo anno sermonibus magis passim hominum iactata quam in
publico ullo concilio est, ita insequentis anni consulibus, L. Furio Camillo iterum Iunio Bruto Scaevae,
nulla prior potiorque visa est, de qua ad senatum
3 referrent. Et quamquam non nova[1] res erat, tamen
tanta cura patres incessit, ut pariter eam susceptam
neglectamque timerent, ne aut impunitas eorum
lascivia superbiaque aut bello poenae expetitae
metu propinquo atque ira concirent finitimos populos;
4 et erat genus omne abunde bello Samnitibus par,
Marsi Paelignique et Marrucini, quos, si Vestinus
5 attingeretur, omnes habendos hostes. Vicit tamen
pars quae in praesentia videri potuit maioris animi
quam consilii; sed eventus docuit fortes fortunam
6 iuvare. Bellum ex auctoritate patrum populus adversus Vestinos iussit. Provincia ea Bruto, Samnium

---

[1] non nova (*or* nota) *Duker* : noua Ω.

and that for money lent, the debtor's goods, but
not his person, should be distrainable. So those
in confinement were released, and it was forbidden
that any should be confined thereafter.

XXIX. In that same year, though the Samnite
war and the sudden revolt of the Lucanians, together
with the Tarentines their abettors, were enough of
themselves to fill the senators with concern, yet the
Vestini added to their cares by uniting with the
Samnites. This action was widely discussed in
private conversations, without being made the subject, in that year, of any public deliberations; but
the consuls of the following year, Lucius Furius
Camillus (for the second time) and Junius Brutus
Scaeva, deemed it a matter that should take precedence over all other business to come before the
senate. There, notwithstanding it was no news to
them, the situation occasioned the Fathers so great
anxiety as to make them equally afraid to deal with
it or to let it alone, lest the impunity of the
Vestini might inspire the neighbouring tribes with
licence and insolence, or a punitive war inflame
them with apprehensions of imminent danger and
with resentment; moreover the race as a whole was
fully equal to the Samnites in military power, comprising, as it did, the Marsi, and the Paeligni and
Marrucini,—all of whom must be had for enemies,
should the Vestini be molested. The day, however,
was carried by that party which might have seemed
at the moment to have on its side a greater share of
courage than of wisdom; but the sequel showed
that Fortune favours the brave. Being authorized
by the senate, the people voted a war against the
Vestini. This command was assigned by lot to

LIVY

7 Camillo sorte evenit. Exercitus utroque ducti, et
cura tuendorum finium hostes prohibiti coniungere
8 arma. Ceterum alterum consulem L. Furium, cui
maior moles rerum imposita erat, morbo gravi im-
9 plicitum fortuna bello subtraxit; iussusque dictatorem dicere rei gerendae causa, longe clarissimum
bello ea tempestate dixit, L. Papirium Cursorem,
a quo Q.[1] Fabius Maximus Rullianus[2] magister
10 equitum est dictus, par nobile rebus in eo magistratu
gestis, discordia tamen, qua prope ad ultimum
dimicationis ventum est, nobilius.

11 Ab altero consule in Vestinis multiplex bellum
nec usquam vario eventu gestum est. Nam et
pervastavit agros et populando atque urendo tecta
12 hostium sataque in aciem invitos extraxit, et ita
proelio uno accidit Vestinorum res, haudquaquam
tamen incruento milite suo, ut non in castra solum
refugerent hostes, sed iam ne vallo quidem ac fossis
freti dilaberentur in oppida, situ urbium moeni-
13 busque se defensuri. Postremo oppida quoque vi
expugnare adortus, primo Cutinam ingenti ardore
militum a volnerum ira,[3] quod haud fere quisquam
integer proelio excesserat, scalis cepit, deinde
14 Cingiliam. Utriusque urbis praedam militibus, quod

---

[1] a quo Q. $F^2F^3T^2$: a quo que (*or* a quoq.) Ω: amquoq. *M*:
a quo D^x: abeoquo A^2.
[2] Rullianus *Sigon.* (*C.I.L.* i^2, *p.* 45. *a.u.c.* 432. 445;
Plin. N.H. VII. xli. 42): rutilanus *O*: rutilianus *MPFUHT*:
rutulianus *DLA*.
[3] a vol (vul-)nerum ira *Madvig* (*cf.* XXIV. XXX. 1): aut vol
(uul-)nerum ira Ω: ac uulnerum ira ς: aut uulneratum ira *M*.

---

[1] Since the Vestini were not supported by their neighbours,
as men had feared they would be.   [2] Cf. p. 156, note.
[3] Also called Rullus (XXIV. IX. 8). He was the grandfather
of Fabius Cunctator, who opposed Hannibal.

B.C.
325–324

Brutus, that against the Samnites to Camillus. Armies were dispatched in both directions, and the enemy, concerned to protect their borders, were kept from joining forces. But one of the consuls, Lucius Furius, on whom the heavier burden had been laid,[1] had the misfortune to fall dangerously ill and was compelled to relinquish his command; being ordered to nominate a dictator[2] for the purpose of carrying on the war, he named by far the most distinguished soldier of that time, Lucius Papirius Cursor, by whom Quintus Fabius Maximus Rullianus[3] was appointed master of the horse. They were a pair famous for the victories won while they were magistrates; but their quarrelling, which almost went the length of a mortal feud, made them more famous still.

The other consul, in the country of the Vestini, carried on a war of many phases, but of unvarying success at every point. For he ravaged their farms, and by pillaging and burning their houses and their crops, compelled them against their will to take the field; and then in a single battle wrought such havoc with the Vestinian power—though his own troops came off by no means scatheless—that the enemy not only retreated to their camp, but, no longer trusting to their parapet and trenches, slipped away to their several towns, seeking protection in the situation of the places and their walls. Finally, the consul addressed himself to the capture of these towns. The soldiers fought with great fury to revenge their wounds, for hardly a man had come unhurt out of the battle; and first Cutina was carried by escalade, and then Cingilia. The consul gave the booty of both these cities to his men,

eos neque portae nec muri hostium arcuerant, con-
cessit.

XXX. In Samnium incertis itum auspiciis est;
cuius rei vitium non in belli eventum, quod prospere
gestum est, sed in rabiem atque iras imperatorum
2 vertit. Namque Papirius dictator a pullario monitus,
cum ad auspicium repetendum Romam proficisce-
retur, magistro equitum denuntiavit ut sese loco
teneret, neu absente se cum hoste manum conse-
3 reret. Q.[1] Fabius cum post profectionem dictatoris
per exploratores comperisset perinde omnia soluta
apud hostes esse ac si nemo Romanus in Samnio
4 esset, seu ferox adulescens indignitate accensus,
quod omnia in dictatore viderentur reposita esse,
seu occasione bene gerendae rei inductus, exercitu
instructo paratoque profectus ad Imbrinium—ita
5 vocant locum—acie cum Samnitibus conflixit. Ea
fortuna pugnae fuit ut nihil relictum sit quo, si
adfuisset dictator, res melius geri potuerit; non dux
6 militi, non miles duci defuit; eques etiam auctore
L. Cominio tribuno militum, qui aliquotiens impetu
capto perrumpere non poterat[2] hostium agmen,[3]
detraxit frenos equis, atque ita concitatos calcaribus
permisit ut sustinere eos nulla vis posset; per
7 arma, per viros late stragem dedere; secutus pedes
impetum equitum turbatis hostibus intulit signa.

---

[1] Q. A^2 (or A^1) : que M : omitted by Ω.
[2] poterat Ω : potuerat Weissenborn.
[3] agmen Ω : aciem Weissenborn (but cf., with Walters and
Conway, Hor. Carm. IV. xiv. 29 and III. ii. 9).

because neither the gates nor the walls of the enemy had held them back.

XXX. The expedition into Samnium was attended with ambiguous auspices; but the flaw in them took effect, not in the outcome of the war, which was waged successfully, but in the animosities and madness of the generals. For Papirius, the dictator, as he was setting out for Rome, on the advice of the keeper of the sacred chickens, to take the auspices afresh, warned the master of the horse to remain in his position, and not to engage in battle with the enemy while he himself was absent. When Quintus Fabius had ascertained from his scouts—after the departure of the dictator—that the enemy were in all respects as careless and unguarded as if there had been not a single Roman in Samnium, whether it was that the spirited young man felt aggrieved that all power should seem to be vested in the dictator, or that he was tempted by the opportunity of striking a successful blow, he put the army in fighting trim, and advancing upon a place they call Imbrinium, engaged in a pitched battle with the Samnites. This engagement was so fortunate that no greater success could have been gained, had the dictator been present; the general failed not his men, nor the men their general. The cavalry, too—at the suggestion of Lucius Cominius, a tribune of the soldiers—after charging a number of times without being able to break the enemy's lines, pulled the bridles off their horses and spurred them on so hotly that nothing could resist the shock, and arms and men went down before them over a wide front. The foot-soldiers, following up the cavalry charge, advanced on the disordered enemy,

Viginti milia hostium caesa eo die traduntur. Auctores habeo bis cum hoste signa conlata dictatore
absente, bis rem egregie gestam ; apud antiquissimos
scriptores una haec pugna invenitur ; in quibusdam
annalibus tota res praetermissa est.

8   Magister equitum, ut ex tanta caede multis potitus spoliis, congesta in ingentem acervum hostilia
arma subdito igne concremavit, seu votum id deorum

9 cuipiam fuit, seu credere libet Fabio auctori eo
factum, ne suae gloriae fructum dictator caperet
nomenque ibi scriberet aut spolia in triumpho ferret.

10 Litterae quoque de re prospere gesta ad senatum,
non ad dictatorem, missae argumentum fuere minime
cum eo communicantis laudes. Ita certe dictator
id factum accepit, ut laetis aliis victoria parta prae

11 se ferret iram tristitiamque. Misso itaque repente
senatu se ex curia proripuit, tum vero non Samnitium
magis legiones quam maiestatem dictatoriam et
disciplinam militarem a magistro equitum victam et
eversam dictitans, si illi impune spretum imperium

12 fuisset. Itaque plenus minarum iraeque profectus
in castra, cum maximis itineribus isset, non tamen

13 praevenire famam adventus sui potuit ; praecucur-
rerant enim ab urbe qui nuntiarent dictatorem

B.C.
325–324

of whom it is said that twenty thousand were slain
that day. I find it stated by certain writers that
Quintus Fabius twice fought the enemy while the
dictator was absent, and twice gained a brilliant
victory. The oldest historians give but this one
battle, and in certain annals the story is omitted
altogether.

The master of the horse found himself, after so
great a slaughter, in possession of extensive spoils.
He piled the enemy's arms in a great heap, applied
a torch to them, and burnt them. This may have
been done in fulfilment of a vow to one of the gods,
or—if one chooses to accept the account of Fabius
—to prevent the dictator reaping the harvest of his
glory and inscribing his name on the arms, or having
them carried in his triumph. A dispatch, too,
reporting the victory, which Fabius sent to the
senate and not to the dictator, argues that he
had no mind to share the credit with him. At all
events, the dictator so received the news, that
while everyone else was rejoicing at the victory, he
showed no uncertain signs of anger and discontent.
And so, having hastily dismissed the senate, he
rushed out of the Curia, repeatedly asserting that
in that battle the master of the horse had defeated
and overthrown the prestige of the dictatorship
and military discipline not less decisively than the
Samnite legions, should it end in his having flouted
orders with impunity. And so he set out for the
camp, breathing wrath and menaces; but though
he travelled by exceedingly long stages, he was unable to arrive before the report of his being on
the way. For couriers had hastened from the City,
bringing word that the dictator was coming, athirst

avidum poenae venire, alternis paene verbis T.
Manli factum laudantem.

XXXI. Fabius contione extemplo advocata ob-
testatus milites est ut, qua virtute rem publicam
ab infestissimis hostibus defendissent, eadem se,
cuius ductu auspicioque vicissent, ab impotenti
2 crudelitate dictatoris tutarentur : venire amentem
invidia, iratum virtuti alienae felicitatique; furere
quod se absente res publica egregie gesta esset;
malle, si mutare fortunam posset, apud Samnites
3 quam Romanos victoriam esse; imperium dictitare
spretum, tamquam non eadem mente pugnari ve-
tuerit qua pugnatum doleat. Et tunc invidia impedire virtutem alienam voluisse cupidissimisque
arma ablaturum fuisse militibus, ne se absente
4 moveri possent; et nunc[1] id furere, id aegre pati,
quod sine L. Papirio non inermes, non manci milites
fuerint, quod se Q. Fabius magistrum equitum
5 duxerit ac non accensum dictatoris. Quid illum
facturum fuisse, si, quod belli casus ferunt Marsque
communis, adversa pugna evenisset, qui sibi devictis
hostibus, re publica bene gesta, ita ut non ab illo
unico duce melius geri potuerit, supplicium magistro
6 equitum tunc victori minetur? Neque illum magi-

---

[1] nunc Ω : tunc M.

---

[1] See chapter vii.

for vengeance and praising with almost every other
word the deed of Titus Manlius.[1]

B.C.
325–324

XXXI. Fabius at once convened an assembly of
the soldiers, and reminding them how their bravery
had saved the state from the most determined of
enemies, conjured them to be no less brave in
defending him—under whose command and auspices
they had gained the victory—from the ungovernable
wrath of the dictator. He was coming, said Fabius,
crazed with jealousy, and exasperated that another
should have been both brave and fortunate; it
enraged him that the state should have won a
glorious victory in his absence; he would prefer—
could he effect a change of fortune—that the
Samnites and not the Romans had been the victors;
he repeatedly declared that his authority had been
despised, as though his orders against fighting had
not been inspired by the same motive as was his grief
over the battle! On the former occasion envy had
made him wish to thwart the bravery of others; he
would have stripped the most willing of soldiers of
their arms, that they might be unable to use them in
his absence. At present his rage and resentment
were due to this, that his troops, though lacking the
help of Lucius Papirius, had lacked neither swords nor
hands to wield them, and that Quintus Fabius had
regarded himself as master of the horse, and not as
the dictator's orderly. What would he have done, had
the chances of war and the common lot of armies
resulted in defeat? Despite the conquest of the
enemy and a campaign so well directed that not even
his own peerless leadership could have bettered it,
he was now threatening the master of the horse with
punishment, victorious though he was. For that

LIVY

stro equitum infestiorem [1] quam tribunis militum,
quam centurionibus, quam militibus esse. Si posset,
7 in omnes saeviturum fuisse: quia id nequeat, in
unum saevire; etenim [2] invidiam tamquam ignem
summa petere; in caput consilii, in ducem incur-
rere; si se simul cum gloria rei gestae exstinxisset,
tunc victorem velut in capto exercitu dominantem,
quidquid licuerit in magistro equitum, in militibus
8 ausurum. Proinde adessent in sua causa omnium
libertati. Si consensum exercitus eundem qui in
proelio fuerit in tuenda victoria videat et salutem
unius omnibus curae esse, inclinaturum ad clemen-
9 tiorem sententiam animum. Postremo se vitam
fortunasque suas illorum fidei virtutique permittere.

XXXII. Clamor e tota contione ortus, uti bonum
animum haberet: neminem illi vim allaturum salvis
legionibus Romanis.

Haud multo post dictator advenit classicoque
2 extemplo ad contionem advocavit. Tum silentio
facto praeco Q. Fabium magistrum equitum citavit.
Qui simul ex inferiore loco ad tribunal accessit, tum
3 dictator "Quaero" inquit, "de te, Q. Fabi, cum
summum imperium dictatoris sit pareantque ei consules, regia potestas, praetores, iisdem [3] auspiciis

[1] tunc victori minetur? Neque illum magistro equitum
infestiorem *O* (*but with a stop after* victori): et tunc victori
minetur? neque illum magistro equitum infestiorem *edd.
before Gronov.*: tunc uictorem uelut in capto exercitu infestiorem *MPFU*: minetur (minuetur *H*) neque illum magistro
equitum infestiorem *HTDLA*.

[2] etenim *Boot*: etiam (et iam *A*) Ω.

[3] iisdem *A*ˣ: isdem *H*⸢*T*²: hisdem *MPFT* is de *D?L*:
wanting in O: *illegible in A*.

---

[1] cf. II. i. 8. All the rights of the kings and all their
insignia were possessed by the earliest consuls.

matter, he was no angrier with the master of the
horse than with the tribunes of the soldiers, the
centurions, and the men. Had he been able, he
would have vented his rage upon them all: this being
imposible, he was pouring it out on one. The truth
is that envy, like lightning, seeks out the highest
places; he was hurling himself upon the head of
their counsels, upon their general; should he succeed
in destroying Fabius, and with him the glory of their
achievement, he would then follow up his victory—as
though lording it over a captured army—and would
visit upon the soldiers all the cruelty he had been
permitted to inflict upon the master of the horse.
Let them defend, he cried, the liberty of all by
defending him. If that same singleness of purpose
which the army had displayed in battle should
appear in the way they stood up for their victory and
made one man's safety the safety of them all, the
dictator would incline his heart to a more merciful
determination. He ended by committing himself,
his life, and his fortunes to their loyalty and valour.

XXXII. A shout arose from the whole concourse,
bidding him be of good courage; no one, they cried,
should do him violence, while the Roman legions
were safe.

Not long after came the dictator, and forthwith by
sound of trumpet summoned an assembly. Then a
herald, having obtained silence, cited Quintus Fabius
the master of the horse, who was no sooner come up
from below to the tribunal, than the dictator cried
out: "I ask you, Quintus Fabius, seeing that the
dictator's authority is paramount, and the consuls
obey him, though they possess the might of kings,[1]
and the praetors, too, who have been elected under

A.U.C.
429

4 quibus consules creati, aequum censeas necne, ei [1]
magistrum equitum dicto audientem esse; itemque
illud interrogo, cum me incertis auspiciis profectum
ab domo scirem, utrum mihi turbatis religionibus
res publica in discrimen committenda fuerit an
auspicia repetenda, ne quid dubiis dis agerem?
5 Simul illud, quae dictatori religio impedimento ad
rem gerendam fuerit, num ea magister equitum
solutus ac liber potuerit esse? Sed quid ego haec
interrogo, cum, si ego tacitus abissem, tamen tibi
ad voluntatis interpretationem meae dirigenda tua
6 sententia fuerit? Quin tu respondes, vetuerimne te
quicquam rei me absente agere, vetuerimne signa
7 cum hostibus conferre? Quo tu imperio meo spreto,
incertis auspiciis, turbatis religionibus adversus morem militarem disciplinamque maiorum et numen
8 deorum ausus es cum hoste confligere. Ad haec
quae interrogatus es responde; at [2] extra ea cave
vocem mittas.[3] Accede, lictor."

9 Adversus singula cum respondere haud facile esset,
et nunc quereretur eundem accusatorem capitis sui
ac iudicem esse, modo vitam sibi eripi citius quam
10 gloriam rerum gestarum posse vociferaretur purga-
retque se in vicem atque ultro accusaret, tunc [4]
Papirius redintegrata ira spoliari magistrum equitum
11 ac virgas et secures expediri iussit. Fabius fidem

---

[1] necne ei *Madvig* : necne Ω.

[2] responde; at F^x : respondeat Ω : responde A^3.

[3] vocem mittas A^2 (*or* A^1) ς : uocem emittas F^3 (-itas) A^3
(*or* A^2) : uocem mittat Ω : uoce mittat M : uox nece mittat[2]
(*i.e.* mittatur) H : uocem mittatur T (*or* T^1) D^3A (*or* A^1) :
uoce mittatur DL (*and* TA^{t2}).

[4] tunc Ω : tum L *Madvig*.

the same auspices with the consuls, whether or no
you deem it to be reasonable that the master of the
horse should hearken to his word; and I put this
further question to you—whether, when I knew that
I had set out from home with uncertain auspices, it
was my duty, in view of our troubled relations with
the gods, to jeopardize the public safety, or to seek
auspices again, that I might take no steps while the will
of Heaven was in doubt; and I likewise ask whether
that which a religious scruple has prevented the
dictator from doing can be freely and unrestrainedly
undertaken by the master of the horse. But why do
I put these questions, since, had I gone off without a
word, nevertheless your thoughts should have been
directed to the interpretation of my will? Come,
answer me: Did I forbid you to take any measures in
my absence? Did I forbid you to engage the enemy?
But you spurned this order; and notwithstanding the
uncertainty of the auspices and our uneasy scruples,
you had the hardihood, against all military precedent,
and the discipline of our fathers, and the divine will
of the gods, to encounter with the enemy. Answer
these questions I have put to you; but have a care
that you utter no word besides! Stand ready,
lictor."

To answer the separate indictments was far from
easy. Now complaining that the same man was his
accuser and his judge in a matter of life and death,
and again crying out that he could more easily be
robbed of his life than of the glory of his deeds, he
defended himself and accused the general by turns,
until Papirius in a fresh burst of anger bade them
strip the master of the horse and make ready rods
and axes. Then Fabius, imploring the protection of

militum implorans lacerantibus vestem lictoribus ad triarios tumultum ultima[1] in contione miscentes sese recepit.

12 Inde clamor in totam contionem est perlatus; alibi preces, alibi minae audiebantur. Qui proximi forte tribunali steterant, quia subiecti oculis imperatoris noscitari poterant, orabant ut parceret magistro equitum, neu cum eo exercitum damnaret;

13 extrema contio et circa Fabium globus increpabant inclementem dictatorem nec procul seditione aberant. Ne tribunal quidem satis quietum erat;

14 legati circumstantes sellam orabant ut rem in posterum diem differret et irae suae spatium et con-

15 silio tempus daret: satis castigatam adulescentiam Fabi esse, satis deformatam victoriam; ne ad extremum finem supplicii tenderet, neu unico iuveni neu patri eius, clarissimo viro, neu Fabiae genti eam

16 iniungeret ignominiam. Cum parum precibus, parum causa proficerent, intueri saevientem contionem iubebant: ita inritatis militum animis subdere ignem ac materiam seditioni non esse aetatis, non prudentiae

17 eius; neminem id Q. Fabio poenam deprecanti suam vitio versurum, sed dictatori, si occaecatus ira infestam multitudinem in se pravo certamine mo-

18 visset. Postremo, ne id se gratiae dare Q. Fabi

---

[1] ultima *Wesenberg*: iam Ω.

---

[1] For an assembly the soldiers stood in maniples, drawn up in the same order as for a battle. See chapter viii.

124

B.C.
325-324

the soldiers, escaped from the clutches of the lictors with his clothes in tatters, and sought refuge in the midst of the *triarii*, who were stirring up riot in the rear of the assembly.[1]

Thence the outcry spread to the entire host. In one place were heard entreaties, in another threats. Those who chanced to be standing next to the tribunal, and being under the general's eyes were able to be marked by him, implored him to spare the master of the horse, and not condemn the army with him. Those in the outskirts of the meeting, and the crowd that surrounded Fabius, railed at the dictator's cruelty, and were near to mutiny. Not even the tribunal itself was quiet; the lieutenants, standing about the dictator's chair, besought him to put the matter off until the morrow and allow time for consideration and for his anger to cool; he had sufficiently chastened the youth of Fabius, they said, and discredited his victory; it would not be well to carry out his punishment to the end, nor to fasten such humiliation upon a young man of extraordinary merit, nor on that most distinguished man, his father, and the Fabian family. Finding that neither prayers nor arguments did any good, they bade him look at the turmoil in the assembly; when the passions of the soldiers were so overwrought, it was not, they said, for one of his years and discretion to furnish fuel to the flames of mutiny; no one would ascribe the fault to Quintus Fabius—who was but deprecating his own punishment—but all would blame the dictator, if, blinded with resentment, he should bring down the angry multitude upon himself by an ill-judged contention. Finally, that he might not suppose that they argued thus out of any

crederet, se ius iurandum dare paratos esse non videri e re publica in Q. Fabium eo tempore animadverti.

XXXIII. His vocibus cum in se magis incitarent dictatorem quam magistro equitum placarent, iussi 2 de tribunali descendere legati; et silentio nequiquam per praeconem temptato, cum prae[1] strepitu ac tumultu nec ipsius dictatoris nec apparitorum eius vox audiretur, nox velut in proelio certamini finem fecit.

3 Magister equitum, iussus postero die adesse, cum omnes adfirmarent infestius Papirium exarsurum, agitatum contentione[2] ipsa exacerbatumque, clam 4 ex castris Romam profugit; et patre auctore M. Fabio, qui ter iam consul dictatorque fuerat, vocato extemplo senatu, cum maxime conquereretur apud patres vim atque iniuriam dictatoris, repente strepitus 5 ante curiam lictorum summoventium auditur, et ipse infensus aderat, postquam comperit profectum ex castris, cum expedito equitatu secutus. Iterata deinde contentio, et prendi Fabium Papirius iussit. 6 Ubi cum deprecantibus primoribus patrum atque universo senatu perstaret in incepto immitis animus,

---

[1] cum prae $T^2 A^3$ (*or* A^2) ς : prae Ω.
[2] contentione ς : contione F^3 (*or* F^2) *over erasure* : conuentione Ω.

---

[1] It was not until 216 B.C. that the senate was a second time convened by a master of the horse (XXIII. xxv. 3).

B.C.
325–324

personal regard for Fabius, they were ready, they said, to take an oath that it appeared to be inconsistent with the interests of the state that Quintus Fabius should then be punished.

XXXIII. But the lieutenants by these words rather stirred up the wrath of the dictator against themselves than lessened his rancour against the master of the horse, and he ordered them to go down from the tribunal. He then sought by the mouth of a herald to procure silence, but without success, for the din and uproar were so great that it was impossible for the dictator himself or his attendants to be heard ; and it was left for darkness, as though descending on a battle-field, to end the struggle.

The master of the horse was commanded to appear next day ; but since everyone assured him that Papirius would be more violent than ever, aroused as he was and exasperated by the opposition he had met with, he slipped out of the camp and fled to Rome. There, with the approval of his father, who had thrice been consul, and dictator to boot, he at once assembled the senate,[1] and had reached, in his speech to the senators, the very point where he was complaining of the violence and injury offered him by the dictator, when a sudden noise was heard outside the Curia, as the lictors cleared the way, and Papirius himself, in high dudgeon, appeared before them ; for he had learned of the other's departure from the camp, and taking a troop of light horse had pursued him. The dispute was now renewed, and the dictator ordered Fabius to be seized. Both the leading members and the senate as a body sought to pacify his wrath ; but he would not relent, and persisted in his pur-

7 tum pater M. Fabius "Quando quidem" inquit,
"apud te nec auctoritas senatus nec aetas mea, cui
orbitatem paras, nec virtus nobilitasque magistri
equitum a te ipso nominati valet nec preces, quae
saepe hostem mitigavere, quae deorum iras placant,
tribunos plebis appello et provoco ad populum eum-
8 que tibi, fugienti exercitus tui, fugienti senatus
iudicium, iudicem fero, qui certe unus plus quam
tua dictatura potest polletque. Videro, cessurusne
provocationi sis, cui rex Romanus Tullus Hostilius
cessit."

9 Ex curia in contionem itur. Quo cum paucis
dictator, cum omni agmine principum magister
equitum cum escendisset,[1] deduci eum de rostris
10 Papirius in partem inferiorem iussit. Secutus pater
"Bene agis" inquit, "cum eo ros deduci iussisti,
unde et privati vocem mittere possemus." Ibi primo
non tam perpetuae orationes quam altercatio exaudie-
11 batur[2]; vicit deinde strepitum vox et indignatio
Fabi senis increpantis superbiam crudelitatemque
12 Papiri: se quoque dictatorem Romae fuisse, nec a
se quemquam, ne plebis quidem hominem, non
13 centurionem, non militem violatum; Papirium tamquam ex hostium ducibus, sic ex Romano imperatore

---

[1] cum escendisset ς: escendisset *MPOHT*: ascendisset
M⁴P²FUDLA.
[2] exaudiebatur *Gronov.*: exaudiebantur Ω.

---

[1] See Book I., chap. xxvi.

pose. Then the father of the young man said: B.C. 325-324
"Inasmuch as neither the senate's authority nor
my old age—which you are going about to bereave
—nor the merits and noble lineage of a master of
the horse whom you yourself appointed, are of any
weight with you, nor yet entreaties, which have
often moved an enemy to mercy, which can persuade
the gods to put away their anger,—I invoke the
tribunes of the plebs, and appeal to the people ; and
since you would shun the judgment of your own
army and shun the judgment of the senate, I propose to you a judge that singly has more might and
power—be well assured—than has your dictatorship.
We shall see whether you will submit to an appeal to
which a Roman king, Tullus Hostilius, submitted ! " [1]

Leaving the senate-house, they repaired to an
assembly ; here the dictator mounted with only
a few attendants, while the master of the horse
was accompanied thither by the whole body of the
leading men. Then Papirius bade Fabius be removed from the Rostra to the ground below; and
his father followed him, exclaiming, "You do well
to bid us be removed to a place where even as
private citizens we can say our say ! " At first there
were not so much set speeches to be heard above
the tumult as an interchange of angry words. But
presently the strong voice and the indignation of
the elder Fabius prevailed over the din, as he
inveighed against the pride and cruelty of Papirius.
He reminded him that he too had been dictator at
Rome, and that no man—not even a plebeian, a
centurion, or a common soldier—had been misused
by him ; but Papirius was seeking a victory and
triumph over a Roman general, as if over com-

victoriam et triumphum petere. Quantum interesse [1]
inter moderationem antiquorum et novam superbiam
14 crudelitatemque! Dictatorem Quinctium Cincin-
natum in L. Minucium consulem ex obsidione a se
ereptum non ultra saevisse quam ut legatum eum
15 ad exercitum pro consule relinqueret. M. Furium
Camillum in L. Furio, qui contempta sua senectute
et auctoritate foedissimo cum eventu pugnasset, non
solum in praesentia moderatum irae esse, ne quid
16 de collega secus populo aut senatui scriberet, sed
cum revertisset, potissimum ex tribunis consularibus
habuisse quem ex collegis optione ab senatu data
17 socium sibi imperii deligeret. Nam populi quidem,
penes quem potestas omnium rerum esset, ne iram
quidem unquam atrociorem fuisse in eos qui temeritate atque inscitia exercitus amisissent quam ut
pecunia eos multaret: capite anquisitum ob rem
bello male gestam de imperatore nullo [2] ad eam
18 diem esse. Nunc ducibus populi Romani, quae ne
victis quidem bello fas fuerit, virgas et secures
victoribus et iustissimos meritis triumphos intentari.
19 Quid enim tandem passurum fuisse filium suum, si
exercitum amisisset, si fusus, fugatus, castris exutus
fuisset? Quo ultra iram violentiamque eius exces-
20 suram fuisse, quam ut verberaret necaretque? Quam
conveniens esse, propter Q. Fabium civitatem in

---

[1] interesse *Gronov.* : interesset (-ent *?* *F*) Ω : interest *L*
[2] nullo *A*²ϛ : nullum (nulum *T*) Ω : nullam *M*.

---

[1] The story is related at length, III. xxvi.–xxix.
[2] See VI. xxii.–xxv.

manders of the enemy. How great was the
difference betwixt the moderation of the ancients
and this new-fangled arrogance and ruthlessness!
When Quinctius Cincinnatus had been dictator, and
had rescued the consul Lucius Minucius from the
toils of the enemy, his anger had gone no further
than to leave Minucius in command of the army as
his lieutenant, in place of being consul.[1] Marcus
Furius Camillus, when Lucius Furius, in contempt
of his great age and his authority, had fought a
battle, with the direst results, not only controlled
his indignation at the moment and made no animad-
versions upon his colleague in writing to the senate
or the people, but, on being permitted by the
senate, after his return, to choose a partner in
command, selected Lucius Furius in preference to
all the other consular tribunes, his associates.[2] As
to the people, who had all power in their hands,
their indignation against those who by recklessness or
lack of skill had lost their armies had never burned
so fiercely that they punished them with anything
worse than a fine; a capital charge on account of a
defeat had never until that day been lodged against
a general. But now the generals of the Roman
People, who even if beaten might not be so dealt
with without sin, were, despite their victories and
their well-earned title to a triumph, being threatened with scourging and decapitation. What, pray,
would his son have suffered, if he had lost his army,
if he had been discomfited, routed, and driven
from his camp? To what higher pitch could the
passionate violence of Papirius have mounted than
to scourge him and put him to death? How proper
it was that because of Quintus Fabius the citizens

LIVY

laetitia victoria supplicationibus ac gratulationibus
21 esse, eum propter quem deum delubra pateant, arae
sacrificiis fument, honore donis cumulentur, nudatum
virgis lacerari in conspectu populi Romani, intuentem
Capitolium atque arcem deosque ab se duobus proeliis
22 haud frustra advocatos! Quo id animo exercitum,
qui eius ductu auspiciisque vicisset, laturum? Quem
luctum in castris Romanis, quam laetitiam inter
hostes fore!
23 Haec simul iurgans, querens, deum hominumque
fidem obtestans et complexus filium, plurimis cum
lacrimis agebat.

XXXIV. Stabat cum eo senatus maiestas, favor
populi, tribunicium auxilium, memoria absentis exer-
2 citus; ex parte altera imperium invictum populi
Romani et disciplina rei militaris et dictatoris edictum
pro numine semper observatum et Manliana imperia
et posthabita filii caritas publicae utilitati iactabantur:
3 hoc etiam L. Brutum, conditorem Romanae libertatis,
antea in duobus liberis fecisse; nunc patres comes
et senes faciles de alieno imperio spreto, tamquam
rei parvae, disciplinae militaris eversae iuventuti
4 gratiam facere. Se tamen perstaturum in incepto,
nec ei qui adversus dictum suum turbatis religionibus
ac dubiis auspiciis pugnasset quicquam ex iusta poena

---

[1] Chap. vii. § 22.   [2] ii. v. 5.

B.C.
325–324

should exult in victory with thanksgivings and
rejoicings; while he on whose account the shrines
of the gods were open, and the altars smoked with
sacrifices and were heaped high with incense and
with offerings, should be stripped and mangled with
rods in full sight of the Roman People, as he looked
up to the Capitol and the Citadel and the gods
whose help in battle he had twice invoked, and not
in vain! In what spirit would this be taken by the
army, which under his conduct and his auspices had
gained the victory? What grief would there be in the
Roman camp, what rejoicings amongst their enemies!

So he made his plea, now chiding and now complaining, now calling on gods and men to help him,
now bursting into tears, as he embraced his son.

XXXIV. On his side were ranged the countenance
of the senate, the favour of the populace, the assistance of the tribunes, the remembrance of the
absent army. His opponent urged the invincible
authority of the Roman People, and military discipline, and the edict of a dictator—which had ever
been revered as the will of Heaven—and the severity
of Manlius,[1] who had preferred the general good to
the love he bore his son, even as Lucius Brutus,[2]
the founder of Roman liberty, had done before, in
the case of his two children. But nowadays—the
dictator proceeded—fathers were indulgent; and
the older generation, little caring if another man's
authority were flouted, excused the young for
overturning military discipline, as a thing of no
importance. He should nevertheless persist in his
undertaking, nor remit an iota of his due punishment to one who had fought against his orders,
while the rites of religion were confused and the

5 remissurum. Maiestas imperii perpetuane esset non
6 esse in sua potestate: L. Papirium nihil de eius
iure[1] deminuturum[2]; optare ne potestas tribunicia,
inviolata ipsa, violet intercessione sua Romanum
imperium, neu populus in se potissimum dictatore
7 vim et ius[3] dictaturae exstinguat. Quod si fecisset,
non L. Papirium sed tribunos, sed pravum populi
iudicium nequiquam posteros accusaturos, cum polluta
semel militari disciplina non miles centurionis, non
centurio tribuni, non tribunus legati, non legatus
consulis, non magister equitum dictatoris pareat
8 imperio, nemo hominum, nemo deorum verecundiam
habeat, non edicta imperatorum, non auspicia obser-
ventur, sine commeatu vagi milites in pacato, in
9 hostico errent,[4] immemores sacramenti licentia sua
10 se[5] ubi velint exauctorent, infrequentia deserantur
signa neque conveniatur ad edictum nec discernatur
interdiu nocte, aequo iniquo loco, iussu iniussu[6]
imperatoris pugnent, et non signa, non ordines
servent, latrocinii modo caeca et fortuita pro sollemni
11 et sacrata militia sit;—" Horum criminum vos reos
in omnia saecula offerte, tribuni plebi, vestra obnoxia
capita pro licentia Q. Fabi obicite."

---

[1] nihil de eius iure ς: nihil eius iure Ω: nihil eius
MHTDLAς.

[2] deminuturum ς: diminuturum Ω: diminutum A^3M.

[3] dictatore vim et ius *Kreyssig*: dictatorem ius ς: dictatorem et ius Ω: dictatore ius *Duker*: dictatore et ius *H. J.
Mueller* (and P?).

[4] errent F^3A^2: errarent Ω.

[5] sua se *Walters and Conway*: sola uase HTDLA: sola se
MA^2 *Gelenius*: sola PFUT[2]: *lacuna between* sacramenti *and*
uelint O: sola sua se *Alschefski*: soluta se *Madvig*: sola
qua se D^3.

[6] iussu iniussu *Gelenius* ς: iniussu Ω.

B.C.
325-324

auspices uncertain. Whether the majesty of the
supreme authority were to endure or not was
beyond his power to determine; but Lucius
Papirius would do nothing to diminish it. He
prayed that the tribunes might not employ their
power—itself inviolate—to violate by their interference the authority of Rome; that the people
might not single out the very time of his holding
that office to extinguish the lawful might of the
dictatorship. Should they do so, it would not be
Lucius Papirius, but the tribunes and the crooked
judgment of the people, that posterity would censure,
and censure without avail. For let military discipline be once broken, and soldier would not
obey centurion, nor centurion tribune, nor tribune
lieutenant, nor lieutenant consul, nor master of the
horse dictator—none would have respect for men,
none reverence for the gods; neither edicts of
generals nor auspices would be regarded; the
soldiers, without leave, would roam in hostile as
in peaceful territory; with no thought of their
oath they would quit the service by their own permission, when they pleased; the standards would
be deserted, the men would not come together at
command; they would fight without reference to
night or day, to the advantage or disadvantage of
the ground, to the orders or prohibition of the
general; they would neither wait for the word nor
keep to their ranks; blind and haphazard brigan-
dage would supplant the time-honoured and hallowed
ways of war.—"On such charges, tribunes of the
plebs, expose yourselves to be arraigned through
all the ages! Let your own heads bear the guilt
of the licence of Quintus Fabius!"

XXXV. Stupentes tribunos et suam iam vicem magis anxios quam eius cui auxilium ab se petebatur, liberavit onere consensus populi Romani, ad preces et obtestationem versus, ut sibi poenam magistri 2 equitum dictator remitteret. Tribuni quoque inclinatam rem in preces subsecuti orare dictatorem insistunt ut veniam errori humano, veniam adulescentiae Q. Fabi daret; satis eum poenarum dedisse. 3 Iam ipse adulescens, iam pater M. Fabius, contentionis obliti procumbere ad genua et iram deprecari dicta- 4 toris. Tum dictator silentio facto "Bene habet" inquit, "Quirites. Vicit disciplina militaris, vicit imperii maiestas, quae in discrimine fuerunt an ulla 5 post hanc diem essent. Non noxae eximitur Q. Fabius, qui contra edictum imperatoris pugnavit, sed noxae damnatus donatur populo Romano, donatur tribuniciae potestati precarium non iustum auxilium 6 ferenti. Vive, Q. Fabi, felicior hoc consensu civitatis ad tuendum te quam qua paulo ante exsultabas victoria; vive, id facinus ausus cuius tibi ne parens quidem, si eodem loco fuisset quo fuit L. Papirius, 7 veniam dedisset. Mecum, ut voles, reverteris in gratiam; populo Romano, cui vitam debes, nihil maius praestiteris quam si hic tibi dies satis documenti dederit ut bello ac pace pati legitima imperia

XXXV. The tribunes were dumbfounded, more B.C.
troubled now on their own account than on his, for 325–324
whom their help was being solicited; but the
Roman People relieved them of their burden of
responsibility, when they turned as one man to the
dictator, and entreated and adjured him to remit for
their sake the punishment of the master of the horse.
The tribunes, too, fell in with the prevailing mood,
and earnestly besought Papirius to allow for human
frailty, to allow for the youth of Quintus Fabius,
who had suffered punishment enough. Now the
young man himself, now his father Marcus Fabius,
forgetting all contention, threw themselves down at
the dictator's knees and attempted to avert his
anger. Then said the dictator, when silence was
obtained, " It is well, Quirites. The discipline of
war, the majesty of government, have got the
victory, despite the danger that this day would see
the end of them. Quintus Fabius is not found
guiltless, seeing that he fought against the orders of
his general; but, convicted of that guilt, is granted
as a boon to the Roman People, is granted to the
authority of the tribunes, who plead for him but can
bring him no legal relief. Live, Quintus Fabius,
more blest in this consent of your fellow citizens to
save you, than in the victory over which, a little
while ago, you were exulting! Live, though you
dared a deed which not even your sire would have
pardoned, had he been in the place of Lucius
Papirius! With me you shall again be on good
terms when you will; for the Roman People, to
whom you owe your life, you can do nothing greater
than to show that you have learned what this day
clearly teaches—to submit in war and in peace

A.U.C.
429

8 possis." Cum se nihil morari magistrum equitum pronuntiasset, degressum[1] eum templo laetus senatus, laetior populus, circumfusi ac gratulantes hinc
9 magistro equitum, hinc dictatori, prosecuti sunt, firmatumque imperium militare haud minus periculo Q. Fabi quam supplicio miserabili adulescentis Manli videbatur.

10   Forte ita eo anno evenit ut quotienscumque dictator ab exercitu recessisset,[2] hostes in Samnio moverentur. Ceterum in oculis exemplum erat Q. Fabius M. Valerio legato, qui castris praeerat, ne quam vim hostium magis quam trucem dictatoris
11 iram timeret. Itaque frumentatores cum circumventi ex insidiis caesi loco iniquo essent, creditum volgo est subveniri eis ab legato potuisse, ni tristia edicta
12 exhorruisset. Ea quoque ira alienavit a dictatore militum animos, iam ante infensos, quod implacabilis Q. Fabio fuisset et, quod suis precibus negasset, eius populo Romano veniam dedisset.

XXXVI. Postquam dictator praeposito in urbe L. Papirio Crasso, magistro equitum Q. Fabio vetito quicquam pro magistratu agere, in castra rediit,
2 neque civibus satis laetus adventus eius fuit nec hostibus quicquam attulit terroris. Namque postero die, seu ignari venisse dictatorem seu adesset an

---

[1] degressum *Gronovius* : digressum Ω.
[2] recessisset D^3A^3 (*or* A^2) ς *Muretus* : recessit Ω.

B.C.
325–324

to lawful authority." Then, declaring that the master of the horse was free to depart, he descended from the platform, and the joyful senators and yet more joyful people thronged about them and attended them, congratulating now the master of the horse and now the dictator. It seemed that the peril of Fabius had been not less efficacious than the pitiful punishment of young Manlius in the establishment of military authority.

It so fell out that year, that as often as the dictator left the army, there was a rising of the enemy in Samnium. But with the example of Quintus Fabius before his eyes, Marcus Valerius, the lieutenant who commanded in the camp, could not fear any violence of the enemy more than the dread displeasure of the dictator. And so when a party of foragers had fallen into an ambush and fighting at a disadvantage had been slain, it was commonly believed that the lieutenant might have rescued them, had he not quailed at the thought of those harsh orders. Their resentment of this still further estranged the soldiers from the dictator, angry as they already were at his unwillingness to pardon Quintus Fabius, and his having granted to the Roman People a boon he had denied to their own entreaties.

XXXVI. When the dictator had set Lucius Papirius Crassus over the City and had forbidden Quintus Fabius, the master of the horse, to exercise his magistracy in any way, he returned to the camp, where his arrival occasioned no great satisfaction to the Romans nor the slightest apprehension to their enemies. For on the following day, whether unaware that the dictator was come or caring little

abesset parvi facientes, instructa acie ad castra
3 accesserunt. Ceterum tantum momenti in uno viro
L. Papirio fuit ut, si ducis consilia favor subsecutus
militum foret, debellari eo die cum Samnitibus
4 potuisse pro haud dubio habitum sit; ita instruxit
aciem, ita loco[1] ac subsidiis, ita omni arte bellica
firmavit; cessatum a milite ac de industria, ut obtrec-
taretur laudibus ducis, impedita victoria est. Plures
Samnitium cecidere, plures Romani volnerati sunt.
5 Sensit peritus dux quae res victoriae obstaret:
temperandum ingenium suum esse et severitatem
6 miscendam comitati. Itaque adhibitis legatis ipse
circuit[2] saucios milites, inserens in tentoria caput,
singulosque ut sese haberent rogitans curam eorum
nominatim legatis tribunisque et praefectis de-
7 mandabat. Rem per se popularem ita dextere[3]
egit ut medendis corporibus animi multo prius
militum imperatori reconciliarentur, nec quicquam
ad salubritatem efficacius fuerit quam quod grato
8 animo ea cura accepta est. Refecto exercitu cum
hoste congressus, haud dubia spe sua militumque, ita
fudit fugavitque Samnites, ut ille ultimus eis dies
9 conferendi signa cum dictatore fuerit. Incessit
deinde qua duxit praedae spes victor exercitus per-

---

[1] ita loco *Madvig* : loco Ω.
[2] circuit *Walters* (*cf. chap.* xxxvii § 9): circū *POHD*:
circum *MFTLA* : circumiens *U*.
[3] dextere *Frag. Haverk.* ς: dexter (*or* dexŧ) Ω: sedulo
F[3] (*over erasure*).

whether he were there or not, the Samnites formed
in order of battle and approached the camp. So
great however was the importance of one man,
Lucius Papirius, that if the goodwill of the soldiers
had seconded the measures taken by their general,
it was held as certain that the war with Samnium
might that day have been brought to a successful
termination—so skilfully did he dispose his army, so
well secure it with every advantage of position and
reserves, and with every military art. But the men
were listless, and, on purpose to discredit their
commander, threw away the victory. There were
more Samnites killed, more Romans wounded. The
experienced general perceived what stood in the
way of his success : he must qualify his native disposition, and mingle geniality with his sternness.
So, calling together his lieutenants, he made the
round of his wounded soldiers in person, and putting
his head into their tents and asking each how he
was doing, he commended them by name to the
care of the lieutenants, the tribunes, and the prefects.
This of itself was a popular thing to do, and
Papirius managed it with such tact, that in healing
their bodies he gained their affections much more
rapidly ; and indeed there was nothing that more
promoted their recovery than the pleasurable feelings with which they accepted these attentions.
When the army was restored, he met the enemy,
with no doubt as to the result, either on his own
part or on that of his soldiers, and so routed and
dispersed the Samnites that this was the last time
they joined battle with the dictator. The victorious
army then marched on where the prospect of booty
beckoned them, and traversed the territories of the

LIVY

lustravitque hostium agros, nulla arma, nullam vim
10 nec apertam nec ex insidiis expertus. Addebat ala-
critatem quod dictator praedam omnem edixerat
militibus; nec ira magis publica quam privatum
11 compendium in hostem acuebat. His cladibus subacti
Samnites pacem a dictatore petiere; cum quo pacti,
ut singula vestimenta militibus et annuum stipen-
12 dium darent, cum ire ad senatum iussi essent, secu-
turos se dictatorem responderunt, unius eius fidei
virtutique causam suam commendantes. Ita deductus
ex Samnitibus exercitus.

XXXVII. Dictator triumphans urbem est ingressus; et cum se dictatura abdicare vellet, iussu
patrum, priusquam abdicaret, consules creavit C. Sulpicium Longum iterum Q. Aemilium Cerretanum.
2 Samnites infecta pace, quia de condicionibus ambigebatur,[1] indutias annuas ab urbe rettulerunt. Nec
earum ipsarum sancta fides fuit; adeo, postquam
Papirium abisse magistratu nuntiatum est, arrecti ad
bellandum animi sunt.
3   C. Sulpicio Q. Aemilio—Aulium[2] quidam annales
habent—consulibus ad defectionem Samnitium Apu-
lum novum bellum accessit. Utroque exercitus
missi. Sulpicio Samnites, Apuli Aemilio sorte
4 evenerunt. Sunt qui non ipsis Apulis bellum in-
latum, sed socios eius gentis populos ab Samnitium
5 vi atque iniuriis defensos scribant; ceterum fortuna
Samnitium, vix a se ipsis eo tempore propulsantium

---

[1] ambigebatur *Drakenborch*: agebatur Ω.
[2] Aulium *Gelenius and Sigonius*: aulum Ω.

enemy without encountering any armed resistance whatsoever, either face to face or from an ambush. The dictator had increased the alacrity of his troops by proclaiming that the booty should all be theirs, and private gain did as much as the public resentment to whet their zeal against the enemy. Discouraged by these reverses, the Samnites sought peace of Papirius, and agreed with him to give every soldier a garment and a year's pay. He directed them to go before the senate, but they replied that they would attend him thither, committing their cause wholly to his honour and integrity. So the army was withdrawn from Samnium.

XXXVII. The dictator, having entered the City in triumph, would have laid down his office, but was commanded by the senate first to hold a consular election; he announced that Gaius Sulpicius Longus had been chosen for the second time, together with Quintus Aemilius Cerretanus. The treaty was not completed, owing to a disagreement over terms, and the Samnites left the City with a truce for a year; nor did they scrupulously hold even to that; so encouraged were they to make war, on learning that Papirius had resigned.

In the consulship of Gaius Sulpicius and Quintus Aemilius—some annals have Aulius—the defection of the Samnites was followed by a new war with Apulia. Armies were sent out in both directions. The lots assigned the Samnites to Sulpicius, the Apulians to Aemilius. Some say that the war was not waged against the Apulians, but in defence of some of the allies of that people whom the Samnites had wantonly invaded; but the circumstances of the Samnites, who at that time could hardly ward off

LIVY

bellum, propius ut sit vero facit non Apulis ab
Samnitibus arma inlata, sed cum utraque simul
6 gente bellum Romanis fuisse. Nec tamen res ulla
memorabilis acta; ager Apulus Samniumque eva-
statum; hostes nec hic nec illic inventi.

Romae nocturnus terror ita ex somno trepidam
repente civitatem excivit ut Capitolium atque arx
7 moeniaque et portae plena armatorum fuerint; et
cum concursatum clamatumque ad arma omnibus
locis esset, prima luce nec auctor nec causa terroris
comparuit.

8 Eodem anno de Tusculanis Flavia rogatione populi
fuit iudicium. M. Flavius[1] tribunus plebis tulit ad
populum ut in Tusculanos animadverteretur, quod
eorum[2] ope ac consilio Veliterni Privernatesque
9 populo Romano bellum fecissent. Populus Tusculanus cum coniugibus ac liberis Romam venit. Ea
multitudo veste mutata et specie reorum tribus
10 circuit, genibus se omnium advolvens; plus itaque
misericordia ad poenae veniam impetrandam quam
11 causa ad crimen purgandum valuit. Tribus omnes
praeter Polliam antiquarunt legem. Polliae sententia
fuit puberes verberatos necari, coniuges liberosque
12 sub corona lege belli venire. Memoriam eius irae
Tusculanis in poenae tam atrocis auctores mansisse
ad patrum aetatem constat, nec quemquam ferme ex
Pollia tribu candidatum Papiriam ferre solitum.

---

[1] Flavius ς: fabius Ω.
[2] quod eorum ς: quō eorum O: quorum A: quorum
eorum Ω: quoniam eorum A²ς.

---

[1] The Tusculans, upon gaining Roman citizenship, were
enrolled in the Papirian tribe, and were so numerous as to
control its vote.

invasion from themselves, render it more probable that they did not attack the Apulians but that they and the Apulians were at war with Rome simultaneously. There was, however, no memorable engagement. The Romans laid waste Apulia and Samnium, without encountering the enemy in either country.

At Rome a nocturnal alarm awoke the sleeping citizens with such a fright that Capitol and Citadel, walls and gates, were crowded with armed men; and after all the hurrying to posts and crying "to arms!" in every quarter, day broke and discovered neither author nor occasion of the panic.

In the same year, the Tusculans were tried before the people in accordance with the Flavian rogation. Marcus Flavius, a plebeian tribune, had proposed to the people that the Tusculans be punished for having lent their countenance and aid to the Veliterni and Privernates in their war with the Roman People. The citizens of Tusculum, with their wives and children, came to Rome; and the great throng, putting on the sordid raiment of defendants, went about amongst the tribes and clasped the knees of the citizens in supplication. And so it happened that pity was more effective in gaining them remission of their punishment than were their arguments in clearing away the charges. All the tribes rejected the proposal, save only the Pollian, which voted that the grown men should be scourged and put to death, and their wives and children sold at auction under the laws of war. It seems that the resentment engendered in the Tusculans by so cruel a proposal lasted down to our fathers' time, and that a candidate of the Pollian tribe almost never got the vote of the Papirian.[1]

A.U.C.
432

XXXVIII. Insequenti anno, Q. Fabio L. Fulvio consulibus, A. Cornelius Arvina dictator et M. Fabius Ambustus magister equitum metu gravioris in Samnio belli—conducta enim pretio a finitimis iuventus dicebatur—intentiore dilectu habito egregium exer-
2 citum adversus Samnites duxerunt. Castra in hostico incuriose ita posita tamquam procul abesset hostis, cum subito advenere Samnitium legiones tanta ferocia ut vallum usque ad stationem Romanam inferrent.
3 Nox iam appetebat; id prohibuit munimenta adoriri; nec dissimulabant orta luce postero die facturos.
4 Dictator ubi propiorem spe dimicationem vidit, ne militum virtuti damno locus esset, ignibus crebris relictis, qui conspectum hostium frustrarentur, silentio legiones educit; nec tamen fallere propter propin-
5 quitatem castrorum potuit. Eques extemplo in-secutus ita institit agmini ut, donec lucesceret, proelio abstineret; ne [1] pedestres quidem copiae
6 ante lucem castris egressae. Eques luce demum ausus incursare in hostem, carpendo novissimos pre-mendoque iniquis ad transitum locis, agmen detinuit. Interim pedes equitem adsecutus, et totis iam copiis
7 Samnis urgebat. Tum dictator, postquam sine

[1] ne Ω : nec Uς.

XXXVIII. In the following year, when Quintus B.C. 322 Fabius and Lucius Fulvius were consuls, the dread of a serious war with the Samnites—who were said to have gathered an army of mercenaries from neighbouring tribes—occasioned the appointment of Aulus Cornelius Arvina as dictator and Marcus Fabius Ambustus as master of the horse. By a vigorous levy these men raised an excellent army, and marching against the Samnites, went into camp on hostile soil with as little regard to their position as if the enemy had been far away. Suddenly the Samnite legions appeared, and advancing with great hardihood entrenched themselves close to the Roman outposts. Night was now drawing on, which prevented them from assaulting the Roman works; but they made no secret of their intention to do so with the morrow's earliest light. The dictator saw that the battle was coming sooner than he had anticipated, and feared that the courage of his men would be affected by their cramped position. So, leaving behind him numerous fires to deceive the enemy, he silently led the legions out. But the camps were so near each other that he could not elude their observation. Their cavalry at once pursued him, but though they hung upon the fringe of his column, they refrained from attacking until the day began to break; as for the infantry, they did not even leave their stockade before the dawn. Finally, when it was light, the cavalry ventured to charge the Romans, and by harassing their rear and pressing them when they came to places that were difficult to cross, delayed their march. Meanwhile the foot had caught up with the horse, and the Samnites were throwing all their forces into the assault. Then the

magno incommodo progredi non poterat, eum ipsum
in quo constiterat locum castris dimetari iussit.
Id[1] vero circumfuso undique equitatu—ut vallum
peteretur opusque inciperet—fieri non poterat.

8 Itaque ubi neque eundi neque manendi copiam
esse videt, instruit aciem, impedimentis ex agmine
remotis. Instruunt contra et hostes, et animis et
9 viribus pares. Auxerat id maxime animos quod
ignari loco iniquo, non hosti cessum, velut fugientes
10 ac territos terribiles ipsi secuti fuerant. Id aliquamdiu aequavit pugnam, iam pridem desueto
Samnite clamorem Romani exercitus pati; et
hercule[2] illo die ab hora diei tertia ad octavam
ita anceps dicitur certamen stetisse, ut neque clamor,
ut primo semel concursu est sublatus, iteratus sit,
neque signa promota loco retrove recepta, neque
11 recursum ab ulla sit parte. In suo quisque gradu
obnixi,[3] urgentes scutis, sine respiratione ac respectu
pugnabant; fremitus aequalis tenorque idem pugnae
in defatigationem ultimam aut noctem spectabat.
12 Iam viris vires, iam ferro sua vis, iam consilia
ducibus deerant, cum subito Samnitium equites, cum
turma una longius provecta accepissent impedimenta

---

[1] id Ω: ibi *Weissenborn.*
[2] Et hercule (-lae *T*) Ω *Aldus*: at hercule *O Gelenius.*
[3] obnixi *A*[2]: obnixis *U*: obnoxi *T*[2](*or T*[1]): obnoxio *O*:
obnoxii *MPHDLA*: ab obnoxii *F*: obnoxiis *F*[3]*T.*

dictator, finding that he could make no headway without great distress, gave orders to lay out a camp on the very spot where he had halted. But enveloped, as they were, by the enemy's horse, it was impossible to gather stakes and begin the work.

And so, when he saw that he could neither advance nor encamp, he removed the baggage from his column and formed a line of battle. The enemy then formed up against him, being inferior neither in spirit nor in strength. Their encouragement was due chiefly to ignorance that their enemies had retreated from an awkward position, and not from them; for they assumed that their own doughty appearance had driven the Romans before them in a panic. This held the fighting in balance for a while, though the Samnites had now for some time been unused to abide the battle-cry of a Roman army. Indeed it is said that on that day from the third hour to the eighth the outcome was so much in doubt, that there was never a second cheer after that which was once given when the armies rushed together; nor were standards either moved forward or withdrawn; nor did the combatants anywhere give ground. Facing each other with every man squarely in his place, they pressed forward with their shields and fought without stopping to breathe or to look behind. The monotonous din and changeless tenor of the battle made it seem probable that sheer exhaustion or the night would put an end to it. And now men's strength was ebbing, and the sword was forgetting its keenness and the generals their strategy;—when the Samnite horsemen, learning from one of their squadrons that had pushed on ahead how the

Romanorum procul ab armatis sine praesidio, sine
munimento stare, aviditate praedae impetum faciunt.
13 Quod ubi dictatori trepidus nuntius attulit, "Sine
modo" inquit, "sese praeda praepediant." Alii
deinde super alios diripi passim ferrique fortunas
14 militum vociferabantur. Tum magistro equitum
accito "Vides tu" inquit, " M. Fabi, ab hostium
equite omissam pugnam? Haerent impediti impedi-
15 mentis nostris. Adgredere, quod inter praedandum
omni multitudini evenit, dissipatos; raros equis
insidentes, raros, quibus ferrum in manu sit, invenies;
sese equosque[1] dum praeda onerant, caede inermes
16 cruentamque illis praedam redde. Mihi legiones
peditumque pugna curae erunt; penes te equestre
sit decus."

XXXIX. Equitum acies, qualis quae esse instruc-
tissima potest, invecta in dissipatos impeditosque
2 hostes caede omnia replet. Inter sarcinas omissas
repente, obiacentes pedibus fugientium consterna-
torumque equorum, neque pugnae neque fugae satis
3 potentes caeduntur. Tum deleto prope equitatu
hostium M. Fabius circumductis paulum alis[2] ab
4 tergo pedestrem aciem adoritur. Clamor inde novus
accidens et Samnitium terruit animos, et dictator,
ubi respectantes hostium antesignanos turbataque

---

[1] sese equosque *Luterbacher* (se equosque *Madvig*): equosque
(*or* aequosq.) *PFUHT²D*: et quosque *MTLA*ς.
[2] alis *T³*: aliis (*omitted by UA*) Ω.

baggage of the Romans lay remote from their fighting men, without defenders or a rampart to protect it, were seized with the lust of pillaging, and made a sudden dash for it. But when a frightened messenger brought word of this to the dictator, he said, " Only let them cumber themselves with spoil!" After that came others and still others, crying aloud that the soldiers' possessions were being plundered and carried clean away. Then Cornelius called the master of the horse and said, " Do you not see, Marcus Fabius, how the enemy's cavalry have ceased to fight ? They are caught fast and entangled in our baggage. Have at them while they are dispersed, as any body of men will be in pillaging ! You shall find few in the saddle, few sword in hand ; while they are loading themselves and their horses with spoils, cut them down unarmed and make it a bloody booty for them. I will see to the legions and the battle of the infantry ; be yours the glory of the cavalry fight."

XXXIX. The cavalry, drawn up in the most perfect order, charged their scattered and embarrassed enemies and cut them down on every hand. They had hastily flung aside their packs—which lay all about and impeded the terrified horses as they tried to run away—and, powerless either to resist or to escape, were massacred where they stood. Then Marcus Fabius, having almost annihilated the enemy's cavalry, fetched a short compass with his squadrons and attacked from behind their line of infantry. The shouts that were now heard in that quarter struck terror into the hearts of the Samnites; and the dictator, seeing the men in their fighting line glance nervously behind them, and their standards

LIVY

signa et fluctuantem aciem vidit, tum appellare,
tum adhortari milites, tribunos principesque ordinum
nominatim ad iterandam secum pugnam vocare.
5 Novato clamore signa inferuntur; et quidquid pro-
grediebantur, magis magisque turbatos, hostes cernebant. Eques ipse iam primis erat in conspectu, et
6 Cornelius respiciens ad manipulos militum, quod
manu, quod voce poterat, monstrabat vexilla se
7 suorum parmasque cernere equitum. Quod ubi
auditum simul visumque est, adeo repente laboris
per diem paene totum tolerati volnerumque obliti
sunt, ut haud secus quam si tum integri e castris
signum pugnae accepissent concitaverint se in hostem.
8 Nec ultra Samnis tolerare terrorem equitum peditumque vim potuit; partim in medio caesi, partim
9 in fugam dissipati sunt. Pedes[1] restantes ac cir-
cumventos cecidit: ab equite fugientium strages est
facta, inter quos et ipse imperator cecidit.
10   Hoc demum proelium Samnitium res ita infregit,
ut omnibus conciliis fremerent minime id quidem
mirum esse, si impio bello et contra foedus suscepto,
infestioribus merito deis quam hominibus nihil
prospere agerent; expiandum id bellum magna
11 mercede luendumque esse; id referre tantum, utrum
supplicia noxio paucorum an omnium innoxio prae-

---

[1] pedes *Gelenius* ("*scriptura vetus*") ⸂: pedes res *M* :
pedestres (pedestris *U*) Ω.

---

[1] That of 341 B.C. See chap. ii § 4, and (for the violation)
chap. xxii. § 7 and chap. xxiii. § 1.

become disordered, and their line begin to waver, B.C. 322
then cried out to his men, then urged them on, and
called by name on tribunes and company-commanders
to join him in a new attack. With a fresh cheer
the ranks pressed forward, and at each advance
perceived the Samnites to be more and more confused. The horse themselves could now be seen by
those in the van ; and Cornelius, looking back on the
maniples of soldiers, made them understand as best
he could with hand and voice that he saw the
banners and round shields of their comrades. On
hearing and at the same time seeing them, they
straightway forgot the toil they had endured for
well-nigh the entire day, and forgot their wounds,
and, like troops who were but that moment fresh
from camp and had received the battle-signal, they
flung themselves upon the enemy. The Samnites
could support no longer the fury of the cavalry and
the violent onset of the foot; some were slaughtered
in the midst, others were scattered abroad in flight.
The foot-soldiers surrounded those who resisted
and put them to the sword ; the cavalry made havoc
of the fugitives, amongst whom perished their
general himself.

This defeat, after all that had gone before, so
broke the spirit of the Samnites, that in all their
councils they began to murmur that it was no
wonder if they met with no success in an impious
war, undertaken in violation of a treaty,[1] for the
gods had even more right than men to be incensed
with them. They would have to pay a heavy price
to expiate this war and atone for it; the only
question was, should they offer atonement with the
blood of the guilty few or with that of the innocent

LIVY

beant sanguine; audebantque iam quidam nominare
12 auctores armorum. Unum maxime nomen per consensum clamantium Brutuli Papi exaudiebatur. Vir
nobilis potensque erat, haud dubie proximarum in-
13 dutiarum ruptor. De eo coacti referre, praetores
decretum fecerunt, ut Brutulus Papius Romanis
dederetur et cum eo praeda omnis Romana capti-
vique ut Romam mitterentur, quaeque res per fetiales
ex foedere repetitae essent secundum ius fasque
14 restituerentur. Fetiales Romam, ut censuerunt,
missi, et corpus Brutuli exanime; ipse morte volun-
15 taria ignominiae se ac supplicio subtraxit. Placuit
cum corpore bona quoque eius dedi. Nihil tamen
earum rerum praeter captivos ac si qua cognita
ex praeda sunt acceptum est; ceterarum rerum
inrita fuit deditio. Dictator ex senatus consulto
triumphavit.

XL. Hoc bellum a consulibus bellatum quidam
auctores sunt, eosque de Samnitibus triumphasse;
Fabium etiam in Apuliam processisse atque inde
2 magnas praedas egisse. Nec discrepat quin dictator
eo anno A. Cornelius fuerit; id ambigitur, belline
gerendi causa creatus sit, an ut esset qui ludis
Romanis, quia L. Plautius praetor gravi morbo forte
3 implicitus erat, signum mittendis quadrigis daret

---

¹ *i.e.* the Romans would not accept the tardy compliance
of the Samnites with the old terms, being resolved to impose
harder ones.
² Instituted by Tarquinius Priscus (I. xxxv. 9).

multitude? Some ventured at this juncture to name
those who had been responsible for the war. One
name in particular could be distinguished; for all
agreed in denouncing Papius Brutulus, a powerful
noble who had without question been the breaker of
the latest truce. The praetors were compelled to
refer his case to the council, which decreed that
Papius Brutulus should be surrendered to the
Romans, and that all the Roman booty and all the
prisoners should be sent with him to Rome; and
further, that all the property which the fetials had
sought to recover under the provisions of the treaty
should be restored in compliance with law and with
religion. The fetials proceeded to Rome, in accordance with this resolution, taking with them the
lifeless body of Brutulus, who had escaped the
humiliation and punishment by a voluntary death.
It was voted to surrender his goods also with his
body. But of all these things the Romans would
accept none but the prisoners and such articles of
booty as they recognized as theirs; the surrender
of all the rest was of no effect.[1] The dictator
triumphed by resolution of the senate.

XL. Some writers hold that this war was waged
by the consuls, and that it was they who triumphed
over the Samnites; they say that Fabius even
advanced into Apulia and thence drove off much
booty. But that Aulus Cornelius was dictator in
that year is not disputed, and the doubt is only
whether he was appointed to administer the war, or
in order that there might be somebody to give the
signal to the chariots at the Roman Games [2]—since
the praetor, Lucius Plautius, happened to be very
sick—and whether, having discharged this office,

LIVY

functusque eo haud sane memorandi imperii mini-
sterio se dictatura abdicaret. Nec facile est aut
4 rem rei aut auctorem auctori praeferre. Vitiatam
memoriam funebribus laudibus reor falsisque ima-
ginum titulis, dum familiae [1] ad se quaeque famam
rerum gestarum honorumque fallenti mendacio tra-
5 hunt; inde certe et singulorum gesta et publica
monumenta rerum confusa. Nec quisquam aequalis
temporibus illis scriptor exstat, quo satis certo auctore
stetur.

[1] familiae ς *Madvig*: familia Ω.

NOTE ON THE " DICTATOR YEARS ".
See pp. 67, 113, 369.

The years 333 B.C., 324 B.C., 309 B.C., and 301 B.C. are
" dictator years ". In each case the Fasti Cap. assign a whole
year to a dictator whom Livy names as serving under the
consuls of the year preceding. Our conventional system of
chronology counts these " dictator years ".

which is, to be sure, no very noteworthy exercise of B.C. 322
power, he resigned the dictatorship. It is not easy
to choose between the accounts or the authorities.
The records have been vitiated, I think, by funeral
eulogies and by lying inscriptions under portraits,
every family endeavouring mendaciously to appro-
priate victories and magistracies to itself—a practice
which has certainly wrought confusion in the
achievements of individuals and in the public
memorials of events. Nor is there extant any
writer contemporary with that period, on whose
authority we may safely take our stand.

LIBRI VIII PERIOCHA

Latini cum Campanis defecere et missis legatis ad senatum condicionem tulerunt ut si pacem habere vellent alterum ex Latinis consulem facerent. Qua legatione perlata praetor eorum Annius de Capitolio ita lapsus est ut exanimaretur. T. Manlius consul filium, quod contra edictum eius adversus Latinos pugnaverat, quamvis prospere pugnasset, securi percussit. Laborantibus in acie Romanis P. Decius, tunc consul cum Manlio, devovit se pro exercitu, et concitato equo cum in medios hostes se intulisset, interfectus morte sua Romanis victoriam restituit. Latini in deditionem venerunt. T. Manlio in urbem reverso nemo ex iuventute obviam processit. Minucia virgo Vestalis incesti damnata est. Ausonibus victis et oppido ex is capto Cales[1] item[2] Fregellae coloniae deductae sunt. Veneficium complurium matronarum deprehensum est, ex quibus plurimae statim epotis medicaminibus perierunt. Lex de veneficio tunc primum constituta est. Privernatibus, cum bellassent, victis civitas data est. Neapolitani bello et obsidione victi in deditionem venerunt. Q. Publilio, qui eos obsederat, primo et imperium prolatum est et pro cos. triumphus decretus. Plebs nexu liberata est propter L. Papiri creditoris libidinem, qui C. Publilio debitori suo stuprum inferre voluerat. Cum L. Papirius Cursor dictator reversus in urbem ab exercitu esset propter auspicia repetenda, Q. Fabius magister equitum, occasione bene gerendae rei invitatus, contra edictum eius prospere adversus Samnites pugnavit. Ob eam causam cum dictator de magistro equitum supplicium sumpturus videretur, Fabius Romam profugit, et cum parum causa proficeret, populi precibus donatus est. Res praeterea contra Samnites prospere gestas continet.

---

[1] et oppido ex is capto Cales *Rossbach*: in oppido exis cales capto cales (*or* in oppido ex his capto cales) *MSS.*

[2] item *Gronovius*: item colonia deducta est *MSS.*

SUMMARY OF BOOK VIII.

The Latins and Campanians revolted, and sending envoys to the senate proposed as a condition of peace that one of the two consuls should be chosen from the Latins. After delivering these terms, their praetor Annius fell from the Capitol, and so lost consciousness. Titus Manlius the consul had his son beheaded, because he had fought—albeit successfully—against the Latins in defiance of his edict. In a battle which was going against the Romans, Publius Decius, who was then consul, along with Manlius, devoted himself in behalf of the army, and having spurred his horse among the enemy, was slain, and by his death restored the victory to the Romans. The Latins surrendered. Titus Manlius, returning to the City, was met by none of the young men. Minucia, a Vestal virgin, was convicted of unchastity. The Ausonians were defeated; and their town being taken from them, the colonies of Cales and Fregellae were established. A number of matrons were discovered to be guilty of poisoning, of whom very many drank off at once the drugs they had prepared, and died. A law about poisoning was then for the first time enacted. The Privernates, having gone to war, were defeated and given citizenship. The Neapolitans were beaten in war and in a siege, and made submission. Quintus Publilius, who had besieged them, was the first to have his authority extended and to be granted a triumph as proconsul. The plebs were relieved of imprisonment for debt on account of the lust of Lucius Papirius, a creditor, who had sought to violate the chastity of his debtor, Gaius Publilius. When Lucius Papirius Cursor the dictator had returned from the army to the City in order to renew the auspices, Quintus Fabius, the master of the horse, tempted by the opportunity for a successful action, fought the Samnites, against orders, and gained a victory. For this reason it appeared that the dictator would punish the master of the horse; but Fabius fled to Rome, and though his cause was weak, was begged off by the people. The book also contains victories over the Samnites.

BOOK IX

LIBER IX

I. Sequitur hunc annum nobilis clade Romana Caudina pax T. Veturio Calvino Sp. Postumio con-
2 sulibus. Samnites eo anno imperatorem C. Pontium Herenni filium habuerunt, patre longe prudentissimo natum, primum ipsum bellatorem ducemque.
3 Is, ubi legati qui ad dedendas res missi erant pace infecta redierunt, "Ne nihil actum" inquit "hac legatione censeatis, expiatum est quidquid ex foedere
4 rupto irarum in nos caelestium fuit. Satis scio quibuscumque dis cordi fuit subigi nos ad necessitatem dedendi res quae ab nobis ex foedere repetitae fuerant, iis non fuisse cordi tam superbe ab Romanis
5 foederis expiationem spretam. Quid enim ultra fieri ad placandos deos mitigandosque homines potuit quam quod nos fecimus? Res hostium in praeda captas, quae belli iure nostrae videbantur, remisimus;
6 auctores belli, quia vivos non potuimus, perfunctos iam fato dedidimus; bona eorum, ne quid ex contagione noxae remaneret penes nos, Romam porta-
7 vimus. Quid ultra tibi, Romane, quid foederi, quid dis arbitris foederis debeo? Quem tibi tuarum

---

[1] For the second time, having held the office together thirteen years before.

[2] The reference is to events described at VIII. xxxvii. 3.

I. In the following year came the Caudine Peace, B.C. 321 the notorious sequel of a disaster to the Roman arms. Titus Veturius Calvinus and Spurius Postumius were consuls.[1] The Samnites had that year for their general Gaius Pontius, whose father Herennius far excelled them all in wisdom, while the son was their foremost warrior and captain. When the envoys who had been dispatched to make restitution returned without having achieved a peace, Pontius said: "You must not think that this embassy has been of no avail: whatever divine resentment we incurred by breaking the treaty[2] has been appeased. Well do I know that whatever gods desired that we might be compelled to restore the spoils which had been demanded again of us in accordance with the treaty did not desire that our expiation of the treaty should be so scornfully rejected by the Romans. For what more could have been done to mollify the gods and to placate men than we have done? The goods of the enemy which we had taken as booty, and regarded as our own by the laws of war, we restored to them; the authors of the war, whom we could not surrender living, we surrendered dead; their possessions—that no guilt might remain with us from touching them—we carried to Rome. What more do I owe to you, Romans, or to the treaty, or to the gods, its witnesses? Whom can I proffer as umpire betwixt

irarum, quem meorum suppliciorum iudicem feram?
Neminem neque populum neque privatum fugio.

8 Quod si nihil cum potentiore iuris humani relinquitur
inopi, at ego ad deos vindices intolerandae superbiae

9 confugiam et precabor ut iras suas vertant in eos
quibus non suae redditae res, non alienae accumu-
latae satis sint; quorum saevitiam non mors noxiorum,
non deditio exanimatorum corporum, non bona
sequentia domini deditionem exsatient,[1] nisi hauri-
endum sanguinem laniandaque viscera nostra prae-

10 buerimus.   Iustum est bellum, Samnites, quibus
necessarium, et pia arma quibus nulla nisi in armis

11 relinquitur spes.   Proinde, cum rerum humanarum
maximum momentum sit, quam propitiis rem, quam
adversis agant dis, pro certo habete priora bella
adversus deos magis quam homines gessisse, hoc
quod instat ducibus ipsis dis gesturos."

II. Haec non laeta magis quam vera vaticinatus
exercitu educto circa Caudium castra quam potest

2 occultissime locat.   Inde ad Calatiam, ubi iam consules Romanos castraque esse audiebat, milites decem
pastorum habitu mittit pecoraque diversos, alium
alibi, haud procul Romanis pascere iubet praesidiis;

3 ubi inciderint in praedatores, ut idem omnibus sermo
constet, legiones Samnitium in Apulia esse, Luceriam
omnibus copiis circumsedere nec procul abesse quin

---

[1] exsatient *Walters*: exsatient placari nequeant (-unt *F³*)
Ω: exsatient placari qui nequeant *Drakenborch*: exsatient;
qui placari nequeant *Gronovius*.

your anger and my punishment? I refuse no nation, B.C. 321 no private citizen. But if, in dealing with the mighty, the weak are left no human rights, yet will I seek protection of the gods, who visit retribution on intolerable pride, and will beseech them that they turn their anger against those who are not content with the restitution of their own possessions, nor the heaping up in addition of other men's; whose rage is not sated with the death of the guilty, nor with the surrender of their lifeless bodies, nor with the master's goods going with that surrender—unless we yield them our blood to drink and our flesh to rend. Samnites, that war is just which is necessary, and righteous are their arms to whom, save only in arms, no hope is left. Since, therefore, it is of the utmost moment in the affairs of men whether what they undertake be pleasing in the sight of Heaven or whether it be offensive, be well assured that you waged your former war rather against gods than men, but that you will wage this war now threatening with the gods themselves for your leaders."

II. Having pronounced these words, as prophetic as they were encouraging, he led his army out and encamped with all possible secrecy in the vicinity of Caudium. Thence he dispatched in the direction of Calatia, where he heard that the Roman consuls were already in camp, ten soldiers in the guise of shepherds, with orders to graze their flocks—dispersed one here another there—at no great distance from the Romans. On encountering pillagers, they were all to tell one story; namely, that the Samnite levies were in Apulia, where they were laying siege with all their forces to Luceria, and were on the

A.U.C.
433

4 vi capiant. Iam is rumor et ante[1] de industria
volgatus venerat ad Romanos, sed fidem auxere
captivi eo maxime quod sermo inter omnes con-
5 gruebat. Haud erat dubium quin Lucerinis opem
Romanus ferret, bonis ac fidelibus sociis, simul ne
Apulia omnis ad praesentem terrorem deficeret: ea
modo qua irent consultatio fuit.

6 Duae ad Luceriam ferebant viae, altera praeter
oram superi maris, patens apertaque sed quanto
tutior tanto fere longior, altera per furculas Caudinas,
7 brevior; sed ita natus locus est: saltus duo alti
angusti silvosique sunt montibus circa perpetuis
inter se iuncti; iacet inter eos satis patens clausus
in medio campus herbidus aquosusque, per quem
8 medium iter est; sed antequam venias ad eum,
intrandae primae angustiae sunt, et aut eadem qua
te insinuaveris retro via repetenda aut, si ire porro
pergas, per alium saltum artiorem impeditioremque,
evadendum.

9 In eum campum via alia per cavam rupem Romani
demisso[2] agmine cum ad[3] alias angustias protinus
pergerent, saeptas deiectu arborum saxorumque
ingentium obiacente mole[4] invenere. Cum fraus
hostilis apparuisset, praesidium etiam in summo
10 saltu conspicitur. Citati inde retro, qua venerant
pergunt repetere viam; eam quoque clausam sua

---

[1] iam is rumor et ante *H. J. Mueller*: iam is n (*or* 7 *i.e.* et)
rumor ante *P*: iam et is rumor ante P^1F^1U: iam is $\propto$
rumor ante *M*.

[2] demisso ς: remisso Ω.

[3] cum ad $T^1\varsigma$: quō ad *U*: qm̄ ad *PFT*[2] (*marg.*): quad *M*:
ad *TDLA*: quo ad A^x.

[4] obiacente mole ς *Sigonius*: obiacente molem *D*: obia-
centem molem Ω.

point of taking it by assault. This rumour, which B.C. 321 had designedly been given out before, had already come to the ears of the Romans, but the prisoners strengthened their belief in it, especially since they all gave the same account. The Romans did not hesitate about helping the Lucerini, their good and faithful allies, and preventing Apulia at the same time from a general defection in the face of instant peril: the only subject of deliberation was by what route they should march.

There were two roads to Luceria. One skirted the Adriatic, and though open and unobstructed, was long almost in proportion to its safety. The other led through the Caudine Forks,[1] and was shorter, but this is the nature of the place: two deep defiles, narrow and wooded, are connected by an unbroken range of mountains on either hand; shut in between them lies a rather extensive plain, grassy and well-watered, with the road running through the middle of it; but before you come to it, you must enter the first defile, and afterwards either retrace the steps by which you made your way into the place, or else —should you go forward—pass out by another ravine, which is even narrower and more difficult.

Into this plain the Romans debouched from the rocky gorge of one of the two passes; and advancing forthwith to the other pass, found it blocked with a barrier of felled trees and huge boulders. The enemy's stratagem now stood revealed, and indeed a body of troops was descried at the head of the defile. The Romans thereupon hastened back to regain the road by which they had come, but found that this was likewise closed with its own

---

[1] See map at the end of the volume.

obice armisque inveniunt. Sistunt inde gradum
sine ullius imperio, stuporque omnium animos ac
11 velut torpor quidam insolitus membra tenet, intu-
entesque alii alios, cum alterum quisque compotem
magis mentis ac consilii ducerent, diu immobiles
12 silent; deinde, ubi praetoria consulum erigi videre
et expedire quosdam utilia operi, quamquam ludibrio
13 fore munientes perditis rebus ac spe omni adempta
cernebant, tamen, ne culpam malis adderent, pro
se quisque nec hortante ullo nec imperante ad
muniendum versi castra propter aquam vallo circum-
14 dant, sua ipsi opera laboremque inritum, praeterquam
quod hostes superbe increpabant, cum miserabili
15 confessione eludentes. Ad consules maestos, ne
advocantes quidem in consilium, quando nec consilio
nec auxilio locus esset, sua sponte legati ac tribuni
conveniunt, militesque ad praetorium versi opem,
quam vix di immortales ferre poterant, ab ducibus
exposcunt.

III. Querentes magis quam consultantes nox
oppressit, cum pro ingenio quisque fremerent: "Per
obices viarum," alius,[1] "per adversa montium, per
2 silvas, qua ferri arma poterunt, eamus, modo ad
hostem pervenire liceat, quem per annos iam prope
triginta vincimus; omnia aequa et plana erunt

---

[1] "per obices viarum," alius *Walters*: alius (alium *M*)
per obices uiarum alius Ω: alius "per obi es viarum ς *Sigon.
Mu etus.*

---

[1] The speaker disregards the interval of peace (341–328).

barricade and armed men. At this they came to a
halt, without any command, and a stupor came over
the minds of all, and a strange kind of numbness
over their bodies; and looking at one another—
for every man supposed his neighbour more capable
of thinking and planning than himself—they stood
for a long time motionless and silent. Afterwards,
when they saw the tents of the consuls going up
and some of the men getting out entrenching tools,
although they perceived that in their desperate
plight, deprived of every hope, it would be ridicu-
lous for them to entrench themselves, nevertheless,
that they might not add a fault to their misfortunes,
they fell to digging—each for himself with no
encouragement or command from anyone—and fortified a camp close to the water; meanwhile not only
did their enemies insolently scoff at them, but they
jested themselves, with pathetic candour, at the
futility of their works and the pains they took.
The dejected consuls did not even call a council,
for the situation admitted neither of discussion nor
of help, but the lieutenants and tribunes assembled
of their own accord, and the soldiers, turning to
the headquarters tent, called on their generals for
help, which the immortal gods could scarce have
given them.

III. Night came, and found them not so much
consulting as lamenting, while each murmured as
his nature prompted him. "Let us force the barriers
of the road," said one, "let us scale the mountains,
penetrate the forests, go wherever we can carry
arms, if only we may come at the enemy, whom we
have now been conquering for close upon thirty
years[1]; any field will be smooth and level to a

Romano in perfidum Samnitem pugnanti"; alius:
3 "Quo aut qua eamus? Num montes moliri sede
sua paramus? Dum haec imminebunt iuga, qua tu
ad hostem venias?[1] Armati inermes, fortes ignavi,
pariter omnes capti atque victi sumus; ne ferrum
quidem ad bene moriendum oblaturus est hostis;
4 sedens bellum conficiet." His in vicem sermonibus
qua cibi qua quietis immemor nox traducta est.

Ne Samnitibus quidem consilium in tam laetis
suppetebat rebus; itaque universi Herennium
Pontium, patrem imperatoris, per litteras consu-
5 lendum censent. Iam is gravis annis non militaribus
solum sed civilibus quoque abscesserat muneribus;
in corpore tamen adfecto vigebat vis animi con-
6 siliique. Is ubi accepit ad furculas Caudinas inter
duos saltus clausos esse exercitus Romanos, consultus
ab nuntio filii censuit omnes inde quam primum
7 inviolatos dimittendos. Quae ubi spreta sententia
est iterumque eodem remeante nuntio consulebatur,
8 censuit ad unum omnes interficiendos. Quae ubi
tam discordia inter se velut ex ancipiti oraculo
responsa data sunt, quamquam filius ipse in primis
iam animum quoque patris consenuisse in adfecto
corpore rebatur, tamen consensu omnium victus est
9 ut ipsum in consilium acciret. Nec gravatus senex

---

[1] venias A (*Madvig*) : uenies Ω.

Roman who fights against a treacherous Samnite!" _{B.C. 321} Another would ask: "Where or by what way can we go? Do we think to remove the mountains from their seat? So long as these ridges tower over you, how shall you come at the enemy? Armed and unarmed, the brave and the cowardly, we are all alike captured and beaten men. The foe will not even draw his sword on us, that we may die with honour; he will end the war by sitting still." With such-like exchange of talk the night wore on, neither was there any thought of food or sleep.

Even the Samnites were at a loss what course to follow in such happy circumstances; and accordingly they agreed unanimously to dispatch a letter to Herennius Pontius, the father of their general, asking his advice. This man, bowed down with years, had already withdrawn not only from military but even from civic duties; yet, despite his bodily infirmity, his mind and judgment retained their vigour. When he learned that the Roman armies had been hemmed in between two defiles at the Caudine Forks, and was asked by his son's messenger for his opinion, he advised that they should all be dismissed unscathed, at the earliest possible moment. This policy having been rejected, and the messenger returning a second time to seek his counsel, he recommended that all, to the last man, be slain. Having received these answers, as inconsistent as the riddling responses of an oracle, the younger Pontius was among the first to conclude that his father's mind had now given way along with his failing body, but yielded to the general desire and sent for him to advise with them in person. The old man made no objection; he was

plaustro in castra dicitur advectus vocatusque in
consilium ita ferme locutus esse ut nihil sententiae
10 suae mutaret, causas tantum adiceret: priore se
consilio, quod optimum duceret, cum potentissimo
populo per ingens beneficium perpetuam firmare
pacem amicitiamque; altero consilio in multas aetates,
quibus amissis duobus exercitibus haud facile recep-
tura vires Romana res esset, bellum differre; tertium
11 nullum consilium esse. Cum filius aliique principes
percontando [1] exsequerentur, quid si media via
consilii caperetur, ut et dimitterentur incolumes et
12 leges iis iure belli victis imponerentur, "Ista quidem
sententia" inquit "ea est, quae neque amicos parat
nec inimicos tollit. Servate modo quos ignominia
inritaveritis: ea est Romana gens quae victa quiescere
13 nesciat. Vivet semper in pectoribus illorum quidquid istuc praesens necessitas inusserit, nec eos ante
multiplices poenas expetitas a vobis quiescere sinet."
Neutra sententia accepta Herennius domum e castris
est avectus.

IV. Et in castris Romanis cum frustra multi
conatus ad erumpendum capti essent et iam omnium
2 rerum inopia esset, victi necessitate legatos mittunt
qui primum pacem aequam peterent; si pacem non
3 impetrarent, uti provocarent ad pugnam. Tum
Pontius debellatum esse respondit; et, quoniam ne

---

[1] percontando *A*: percunctando Ω.

brought to the camp in a waggon—so the story _{B.C. 321} runs—and being invited to join the council of war, spoke to such purpose as merely, without changing his opinion, to add thereto his reasons: If, he said, they adopted his first proposal—which he held to be the best—they would establish lasting peace and friendship with a very powerful people by conferring an enormous benefit upon them; by adopting the other plan they would postpone the war for many generations, in which time the Roman State, having lost two armies, would not easily regain its strength; there was no third plan. When his son and the other leading men pressed him to say what would happen if they took a middle course, and while letting them go unhurt imposed terms upon them by the rights of war, as upon the vanquished, "That," he answered, "is in sooth a policy that neither wins men friends nor rids them of their enemies. Spare, if you will, those whom you have stung to anger with humiliation; the Roman race is one that knows not how to be still under defeat. Whatever shame you brand them with in their present necessity, the wound will ever rankle in their bosoms, nor will it suffer them to rest until they have exacted many times as heavy a penalty of you." Neither proposal was accepted, and Herennius was carried home from the camp.

IV. In the other camp the Romans, finding themselves now, after many fruitless efforts to break out, in want of everything, were reduced to the necessity of sending envoys; who were first to treat for an equal peace, and, if peace could not be had, to provoke the enemy to fight. To them Pontius made answer, that the war was

A.U.C.
433

victi quidem ac capti fortunam fateri scirent, inermes
cum singulis vestimentis sub iugum missurum; alias

4 condiciones pacis aequas victis ac victoribus fore : si
agro Samnitium decederetur, coloniae abducerentur,
suis inde legibus Romanum ac Samnitem aequo

5 foedere victurum ; his condicionibus paratum se esse
foedus cum consulibus ferire; si quid eorum dis-

6 pliceat, legatos redire ad se vetuit.   Haec cum
legatio renuntiaretur, tantus gemitus omnium subito
exortus est tantaque maestitia incessit ut non gravius
accepturi viderentur si nuntiaretur omnibus eo loco
mortem oppetendam [1] esse.

7   Cum diu silentium fuisset nec consules aut pro
foedere tam turpi aut contra foedus tam necessarium
hiscere possent, tum L. Lentulus, qui princeps [2]

8 legatorum virtute atque honoribus erat : " Patrem
meum " inquit, " consules, saepe audivi memorantem
se in Capitolio unum non fuisse auctorem senatui
redimendae auro a Gallis civitatis, quando nec fossa
valloque ab ignavissimo ad opera ac muniendum
hoste clausi essent et erumpere, si non sine magno

9 periculo tamen sine certa pernicie, possent.   Quod
si, ut illis [3] decurrere ex Capitolio armatis in hostem
licuit, quo saepe modo obsessi in obsidentes eru-

---

[1] oppetendam *F ? A*[1]: appetendam *UA* : adpetendam
MPOTDL.
[2] princeps *Drakenborch* : tum princeps Ω.
[3] ut illis *Aldus* : illis ut Ω.

---

[1] He had been consul 327 B.C. (VIII. xxii. 8).   His descend-
ants assumed the surname of Caudini and a P. Cornelius
Caudinus is mentioned at XXVI. xlviii. 9 and a L. Cornelius
Caudinus at XXVII. xxi. 9.

already fought and won; and since they knew B.C. 321
not how to admit their plight, even when beaten
and made prisoners, he intended to send them
unarmed and with a single garment each under the
yoke; in all else the peace should be one of equal
terms to the vanquished and the victors; for if the
Romans would evacuate the Samnite territory and
withdraw their colonies, Romans and Samnites should
thenceforward live by their own laws in an equal
alliance. On these terms he was ready to conclude
a treaty with the consuls; if they were any of them
unacceptable, he forbade the envoys to return to
him. When the upshot of this embassy was made
known to the Romans, they all straightway fell to
groaning, and so overcome were they with sorrow
that it seemed as though they could not possibly take
it more to heart if they should be told that they
must all die in that place.

Finally, after a long silence—for the consuls were
incapable of uttering a word, either for a treaty
so disgraceful or against a treaty so necessary—
Lucius Lentulus, at that time first of the lieutenants
both for his valour and his dignities,[1] spoke as
follows: "Consuls, I have often heard my father
say that on the Capitol he was the only man who
would not have the senate ransom the City from
the Gauls with gold, since their enemies, who were
most indolent besiegers, had not shut them in with
trench and rampart, and they were able to make
a sortie, if not without great danger, yet without
certain destruction. But if, in like manner as they
had it in their power to run down from the Capitol,
sword in hand, against their enemy, even as the
besieged have often sallied out against the besiegers,

175

perunt, ita nobis aequo aut iniquo loco dimicandi
tantummodo cum hoste copia esset, non mihi paterni
10 animi indoles in consilio dando deesset. Equidem
mortem pro patria praeclaram esse fateor et me vel
devovere pro populo Romano legionibusque vel in
11 medios immittere hostes[1] paratus sum; sed hic
patriam video, hic quidquid Romanarum legionum
est, quae nisi pro se ipsis ad mortem ruere volunt,
12 quid habent quod morte sua servent? 'Tecta urbis'
dicat aliquis 'et moenia et eam turbam a qua urbs
incolitur.' Immo hercule produntur ea omnia deleto
13 hoc exercitu, non servantur. Quis enim ea tuebitur?
Imbellis videlicet atque inermis multitudo. Tam
14 hercule quam a Gallorum impetu defendit. An a
Veiis exercitum Camillumque ducem implorabunt?
Hic omnes spes opesque sunt, quas servando patriam
servamus, dedendo ad necem patriam deserimus ac
15 prodimus. 'At foeda atque ignominiosa deditio est.'
Sed ea caritas patriae est ut tam ignominia eam quam
16 morte nostra, si opus sit, servemus. Subeatur ergo
ista, quantacumque est, indignitas et pareatur neces-
sitati, quam ne di quidem superant. Ite, consules,
redimite armis civitatem quam auro maiores vestri
redemerunt."

V. Consules profecti ad Pontium in conloquium,
cum de foedere victor agitaret, negarunt iniussu
populi foedus fieri posse nec sine fetialibus caeri-
2 moniaque alia sollemni. Itaque non, ut volgo

---

[1] in medios immittere hostes *Gronovius*: in medios hostes
me inmittere *O*: in medios me immittere hostes Ω.

so we were able, whether on favourable ground or B.C. 321
no, only to come to grips with our antagonist, I
should not lack my father's spirit in advising you.
I do indeed confess that it is glorious to die for
one's country, and I am ready to devote myself
for the Roman People and the legions, or to throw
myself into the midst of the enemy ; but it is here
I see my country, here all the legions Rome
possesses, and unless they would rush on death to
please themselves, what have they to save by
dying ? ' The roof-trees of the City,' someone may
say, ' and its walls, and the multitude by whom
it is inhabited.' Nay, not so ! For all these are
betrayed, not saved, if this army is wiped out ! For
who shall preserve them ? The unwarlike, unarmed
rabble ? Ay, even as it preserved them from the
onset of the Gauls ! Or will they pray perhaps
that an army may be sent from Veii, and a Camillus
to command it ? Here are all our hopes and our
resources, which if we save we save our country ;
whereas if we give these up to die, we abandon our
country and betray it. ' But surrender is shameful
and humiliating.' True, but our country is so dear
that we would save it by enduring shame, as we
would, if need were, by our death. Let us submit
then to that indignity, however great, and obey
necessity, to which even gods are not superior.
Go, consuls, at the cost of arms redeem the City
which your sires paid gold to redeem."

V. The consuls then went to confer with Pontius.
The victor proposed a treaty, but they declared that
a treaty could not be made without the authorization
of the people, nor without fetials and the rest of the
customary ceremonial. Consequently the Caudine

LIVY

credunt Claudiusque etiam scribit, foedere pax Cau-
3 dina, sed per sponsionem facta est. Quid enim aut
sponsoribus in foedere opus esset aut obsidibus, ubi
precatione res transigitur, per quem populum fiat
quo minus legibus dictis stetur, ut eum ita Iuppiter
feriat quemadmodum a fetialibus porcus feriatur?
4 Spoponderunt consules, legati, quaestores, tribuni
militum, nominaque omnium qui spoponderunt ex-
stant, ubi, si ex foedere acta res esset, praeterquam
5 duorum fetialium non exstarent; et propter necessariam foederis dilationem obsides etiam sescenti
equites imperati, qui capite luerent, si pacto non
6 staretur. Tempus inde statutum tradendis obsidibus
exercituque inermi mittendo.

Redintegravit luctum in castris consulum adventus,
ut vix ab iis abstinerent manus quorum temeritate
in eum locum deducti essent, quorum ignavia foedius
7 inde quam venissent abituri : illis non ducem locorum, non exploratorem fuisse ; beluarum modo caecos
8 in foveam missos. Alii alios intueri, contemplari
arma mox tradenda et inermes futuras dextras
obnoxiaque corpora hosti ; proponere sibimet ipsi
ante oculos iugum hostile et ludibria victoris et

---

[1] Q. Claudius Quadrigarius (Introduction, Vol. I. p. xxx).

[2] "The *sponsio* was a verbal engagement or pledge made
by those in authority (the generals and, if required, their
officers) in answer to a formal question from the other
party."—Anderson.

[3] See I. xxiv. 8.

Peace was not entered into by means of a treaty, as B.C. 321 people in general believe and as Claudius[1] actually states, but by a guarantee.[2] For what need would there have been for guarantors or for hostages in a treaty, where the agreement is concluded with a prayer that the nation responsible for any departure from the recited terms may be smitten by Jupiter even as the swine is smitten by the fetials?[3] The guarantors were the consuls, the lieutenants, the quaestors, and the tribunes of the soldiers, and the names of all who gave the guarantee are extant, whereas, if the agreement had been entered into as in making a treaty, none would be preserved except those of the two fetials; and because of the inevitable postponement of the treaty, hostages were also required to the number of six hundred knights, whose lives were to be forfeit if the Romans should fail to keep the terms. A time was then set for the delivery of the hostages and the dismissal of the army without their arms.

Fresh lamentations broke out in the camp when the consuls returned; and the men could hardly keep from laying violent hands on those through whose rashness they had been led into that place, and through whose cowardice they were now to depart more shamefully than they had come. They bethought them how they had been unprovided either with guides or with patrols, but had been driven blindly, like wild beasts, into a trap. They looked at one another; they gazed on the arms that they must presently surrender, on the right hands that would be helpless and the bodies that would be at the mercy of the foe. They pictured to their mind's eye the hostile yoke, the victor's taunts,

9 voltus superbos et per armatos inermium iter, inde
foedi agminis miserabilem viam per sociorum urbes,
reditum in patriam ad parentes, quo saepe ipsi
10 maioresque eorum triumphantes venissent : se solos
sine volnere, sine ferro, sine acie victos ; sibi non
stringere licuisse gladios, non manum cum hoste
conferre ; sibi nequiquam arma, nequiquam vires,
nequiquam [1] animos datos.

11   Haec frementibus hora fatalis ignominiae advenit,
omnia tristiora experiundo factura quam quae prae-
12 ceperant animis. Iam primum cum singulis vestimentis inermes extra vallum exire iussi, et primi
13 traditi obsides atque in custodiam abducti. Tum a
consulibus abire lictores iussi paludamentaque de-
tracta : id tantam [2] inter ipsos, qui paulo ante eos
exsecrantes dedendos lacerandosque censuerant,
14 miserationem fecit, ut suae quisque condicionis
oblitus ab illa deformatione tantae maiestatis velut
ab nefando spectaculo averteret oculos.

VI. Primi consules prope seminudi sub iugum
missi ; tum ut quisque gradu proximus erat ita
2 ignominiae obiectus ; tum deinceps singulae legiones.
Circumstabant armati hostes, exprobrantes eluden-
tesque ; gladii etiam plerisque intentati, et volnerati

---

[1] sibi nequiquam arma, nequiquam vires, nequiquam
Gelenius : sibe (*and in marg.* uires nequiquam) nequiquam
M : sibi nequiquam Ω.
[2] tantam id *Drakenborch* : tantam Ω.

and fleering countenance; and how they must pass unarmed between the ranks of their armed enemies, and then wend their wretched way, a pitiful band, through the cities of their allies; and finally the return to their own city and their parents, whither they themselves and their ancestors had often returned in triumph. They alone had been defeated without a wound, without a weapon, without a battle; to them it had not been granted to draw the sword, nor to join in combat with the enemy; on them in vain had arms, in vain had strength, in vain had bravery been bestowed.

As they uttered these complaints, the fateful hour of their humiliation came, an hour destined to transcend all anticipations in the bitterness of its reality. To begin with, they were ordered to pass outside the rampart, clad in their tunics and unarmed, and the hostages were at once handed over and led off into custody. Next, the lictors were commanded to forsake the consuls, who then were stripped of their generals' cloaks,—a thing which inspired such compassion in those very men who a little while before had cursed them and had declared that they deserved to be given up and put to torture, that every man, forgetting his own evil case, averted his eyes from that degradation of so majestic an office, as from a spectacle of horror.

VI. First the consuls, little better than half-naked, were sent under the yoke, then their subordinates were humbled, each in the order of his rank; and then, one after another, the several legions. The enemy under arms stood on either side, reviling them and mocking them; many they actually threatened with the sword, and some, whose

A.U.C.
433 quidam necatique, si voltus eorum indignitate rerum
acrior victorem offendisset.

3   Ita traducti sub iugum, et quod paene gravius
erat, per hostium oculos, cum e saltu evasissent,
etsi velut ab inferis extracti tum primum lucem
aspicere visi sunt, tamen ipsa lux ita deforme
4 intuentibus agmen omni morte tristior fuit.   Itaque
cum ante noctem Capuam pervenire possent, incerti
de fide sociorum et quod pudor praepediebat, circa
viam haud procul Capua omnium egena corpora
5 humi prostraverunt.   Quod ubi est Capuam nuntiatum, evicit miseratio iusta sociorum superbiam in-
6 genitam Campanis.   Confestim insignia sua consulibus,[1] arma equos vestimenta commeatus militibus,
7 benigne mittunt; et venientibus Capuam cunctus
senatus populusque obviam egressus iustis omnibus
hospitalibus privatisque et publicis fungitur officiis.
8 Neque illis sociorum comitas voltusque benigni et
adloquia non modo sermonem elicere sed ne ut
oculos quidem attollerent aut consolantes amicos
9 contra intuerentur efficere poterant: adeo super
maerorem pudor quidam fugere conloquia et coetus
hominum cogebat.

10   Postero die cum iuvenes nobiles missi a Capua ut
proficiscentes ad finem Campanum prosequerentur

----

[1] consulibus *Hertz*: consulibus fasces lictores Ω.

resentment of the outrage showing too plainly in their B.C. 321
faces gave their conquerors offence, they wounded
or slew outright.

Thus they were sent under the yoke, and, what
was almost harder to bear, while their enemies looked
on. On emerging from the pass, although they
seemed like men raised from the dead, who beheld
for the first time the light of day, yet the very light
itself, which allowed them to see that dismal throng,
was gloomier than any death. And so, although it
was in their power to have made Capua before nightfall, yet, questioning the loyalty of their allies, and
withheld also by shame, they threw themselves upon
the ground along the roadside, not far from the city,
with nothing to supply their wants. When tidings of
this were brought to Capua, a feeling of pity, natural
to allies, overcame the ingrained arrogance of the Campanians. Ungrudgingly, without an instant's hesitation, they dispatched the insignia of their office to the
consuls, together with arms, horses, clothing, and provisions, for the men; and as they drew near Capua, the
whole senate and people going forth to meet them
used towards them all the rites of hospitality and
every public and private courtesy. Yet the kindness
of their allies and their friendly looks and words
were so far from drawing the Romans into talk that
they could not even be got to raise their eyes or
look their friends and comforters in the face; so
constrained were they by a kind of humiliation—
over and above their grief—to avoid the speech and
assemblages of men.

On the following day, when the young nobles sent
from Capua to attend them to the borders of Campania had returned, and were called into the senate-

A.U.C.
433 11 revertissent vocatique in curiam percontantibus
maioribus natu multo sibi maestiores et abiectiores
animi visos referrent : adeo silens ac prope mutum
12 agmen incessisse ; iacere [1] indolem illam Romanam,
ablatosque cum armis animos ; non reddere salutem
salutantibus, non dare responsum,[2] non hiscere
quemquam prae metu potuisse, tamquam ferentibus
adhuc cervicibus iugum sub quod missi [3] essent ;
13 habere Samnites victoriam non praeclaram solum
sed etiam perpetuam, cepisse enim eos non Romam,
sicut ante Gallos, sed, quod multo bellicosius fuerit,
A.U.C.
434 Romanam virtutem ferociamque.—VII. cum haec
dicerentur audirenturque et deploratum paene
Romanum nomen in concilio sociorum fidelium esset,
2 dicitur A. Calavius,[4] Ovi filius, clarus genere
factisque, tum etiam aetate verendus, longe aliter
3 se habere rem dixisse : silentium illud obstinatum
fixosque in terram oculos et surdas ad omnia solacia
aures et pudorem intuendae lucis ingentem molem
4 irarum ex alto animi [5] cientis indicia esse. Aut
Romana se ignorare ingenia, aut silentium illud
Samnitibus flebiles brevi clamores gemitusque exci-
taturum, Caudinaeque pacis aliquanto Samnitibus
5 quam Romanis tristiorem memoriam fore ; quippe
suos quemque eorum animos habiturum, ubicumque
congressuri sint ; saltus Caudinos non ubique
Samnitibus fore.
6 Iam Romae etiam [6] sua infamis clades erat. Ob-

---

[1] iacere ς : tacere Ω.
[2] salutantibus, non dare responsum *Madvig* : non salutan
tibus dare responsum Ω : *bracketed by Conway.*
[3] quod missi *ⱶˣAˣς* : quod emissi (*or* quo demissi) Ω.
[4] A. Calavius *Conway* : Ofillius (*or* Ofilius) A. Calauius (*or*
acalauius *or* accilauius *or other corruptions*) Ω.
[5] animi Uς : animo Ω.

house and questioned by the elders, they reported
that they had seemed to be much more sorrowful
and dejected than before : their column had marched
on in silence and almost as though dumb ; the old
Roman spirit was quite dashed ; they had lost their
courage with their arms ; being saluted, they returned
not the salutation ; they responded to no questions ;
not a man of them had been able to open his mouth
for shame, as if they still bore on their necks the
yoke under which they had been sent ; the Samnites
had won not only a famous but a lasting victory, for
they had conquered, not Rome—as the Gauls had
done before—but a thing which demanded far
greater prowess—the Roman valour and independ-
ence. VII. Such were the opinions that were spoken
and listened to, and the Roman name had well-nigh
been given up for lost in the council of Rome's
faithful allies, when Aulus Calavius, son of Ovius, a
man of famous birth and achievements and at that
time venerable also for his age, asserted that the
case was very different : that obstinate silence, those
eyes fixed on the ground and ears deaf to every consolation, that shame at looking on the light, were
signs, he argued, of bosoms bursting with passionate
resentment ; either he knew nothing of the Roman
character, or that silence was destined ere long to
draw from the Samnites cries and groans of anguish,
and the Caudine Peace to become a far more bitter
memory to Samnites than to Romans ; for each
people would have its own native spirit wherever
they might encounter, but the Samnites would not
everywhere have a Caudine Pass.

By this time Rome, too, had heard of her shameful

---

[6] Romae etiam *Drakenborch* : Romae et Ω. Romae ϰ *M.*

sessos primum audierunt; tristior deinde ignominiosae
7 pacis magis quam periculi nuntius fuit. Ad famam
obsidionis dilectus haberi coeptus erat; dimissus
deinde auxiliorum apparatus, postquam deditionem
tam foede factam acceperunt, extemploque sine ulla
publica auctoritate consensum in omnem formam
8 luctus est. Tabernae circa forum clausae, iustitium-
que in foro sua sponte coeptum prius quam indictum ;
9 lati clavi, anuli aurei positi ; paene maestior exercitu
ipso civitas esse ; nec ducibus solum atque auctoribus
sponsoribusque pacis irasci sed innoxios etiam milites
10 odisse et negare urbe tectisve accipiendos. Quam
concitationem animorum fregit adventus exercitus
etiam iratis miserabilis. Non enim tamquam in patriam revertentes ex insperato incolumes sed capto-
11 rum habitu voltuque ingressi sero in urbem ita se in
suis quisque tectis abdiderunt ut postero atque
insequentibus diebus nemo eorum forum aut publi-
12 cum aspicere vellet. Consules in privato abditi nihil
pro magistratu agere, nisi quod expressum senatus
consulto est ut dictatorem dicerent comitiorum
13 causa. Q. Fabium Ambustum dixerunt et P. Aelium
14 Paetum [1] magistrum equitum ; quibus vitio creatis

<hr/>

[1] Aelium Paetum ς : ae (e-) milium paetum Ω.

<hr/>

[1] The *latus clavus*, a broad (purple) stripe in the tunic
marked the senator. Both senators and knights wore golden
rings, though these later became the distinguishing badge of
the knights.

calamity. The first news was that the army was B.C. 320
entrapped; then came a gloomier report, more by
reason of the disgraceful peace than because of the
peril. On the rumour of a blockade they had begun
to hold a levy; but they afterwards gave over their
measures for relief, when they learned that there
had been so infamous a capitulation, and immediately,
without official sanction of any sort, betook themselves with one mind to every form of mourning.
The booths round about the Forum were shut up,
and ere proclamation could be made, all business was
suspended; tunics with the broad stripe of purple
were discarded, as were golden rings.[1] The citizens
were almost more dejected than the army; and not
only were they enraged against their generals and
those who had favoured and guaranteed the peace,
but they even visited their hate upon the innocent
soldiers and proposed to exclude them from the
City and from their homes. But this flurry of resentment was dispelled by the arrival of the army, which
even angry men could not but pity. For they came
not like men returning in safety to their homes, after
all hope of them had been abandoned; but entering
the City late in the day, with the bearing and looks
of prisoners, they slipped away every man to his own
house, and on the next and the succeeding days not
one of them would look into the Forum or the
streets. The consuls shut themselves up in their
houses and would transact no public business, except
that they were forced by a senatorial decree to name
a dictator to preside at the election. They designated Quintus Fabius Ambustus, with Publius Aelius
Paetus to be master of the horse. A flaw in their
appointment occasioned the substitution in their

A.U.C.
484

suffecti M. Aemilius Papus dictator. L. Valerius
Flaccus magister equitum. Nec per eos comitia
habita; et quia taedebat populum omnium magis-
15 tratuum eius anni, res ad interregnum rediit. Interreges Q. Fabius Maximus M. Valerius Corvus. Is
consules creavit Q. Publilium Philonem tertium[1] et
L. Papirium Cursorem iterum haud dubio consensu
civitatis, quod nulli ea tempestate duces clariores
essent.

VIII. Quo creati sunt die, eo—sic enim placuerat
patribus—magistratum inierunt sollemnibusque senatus consultis perfectis de pace Caudina rettulerunt;
2 et Publilius, penes quem fasces erant, " Dic, Sp. Postumi," inquit. Qui ubi surrexit, eodem illo vultu
3 quo sub iugum missus erat, " Haud sum ignarus "
inquit, " consules, ignominiae non honoris causa me
primum excitatum iussumque dicere, non tamquam
senatorem, sed tamquam reum qua infelicis belli, qua
4 ignominiosae pacis. Ego tamen, quando neque de
noxa nostra neque de poena rettulistis, omissa defen-
sione, quae non difficillima esset apud haud ignaros
fortunarum humanarum necessitatiumque, sententiam de eo de quo rettulistis paucis peragam; quae
sententia testis erit mihine an legionibus vestris
pepercerim, cum me seu turpi seu necessaria spon-

---

[1] Q. Publilium Philonem tertium *Glareanus*: Q. Publilium
Philonem Ω.

---

[1] The *fasces* (bundles of rods, symbolic of supreme authority
were borne by the lictors in alternate attendance on the two
consuls. The elder had them first.

room of Marcus Aemilius Papus, as dictator, and B.C. 32
Lucius Valerius Flaccus, as master of the horse.
However, even they did not hold an election; and
because the people were dissatisfied with all the
magistrates of that year, the state reverted to an
interregnum. The interreges were Quintus Fabius
Maximus and Marcus Valerius Corvus. The latter
announced the election to the consulship of Quintus
Publilius Philo (for the third time) and Lucius
Papirius Cursor (for the second) with the unmistakable approval of the citizens, for there were at
that time no leaders more distinguished.

VIII. On the day of their election—for so the
Fathers had ordained—they entered upon the duties
of their magistracy, and having disposed of the
routine resolutions, raised the question of the
Caudine Peace. Publilius had the fasces,[1] and
called on Spurius Postumius to speak. Having
risen to his feet, he said, with the same expression
on his countenance as when he had been sent under
the yoke, "I am not ignorant, consuls, that I have
been called on first and bidden to speak because
of my disgrace, and not to honour me; not as a
senator, but as one charged with the guilt not only
of an unlucky war but of a shameful peace. However, you have not raised the question of our wrong-
doing or our punishment; I will therefore attempt
no defence—though it should be no difficult cause
to plead before judges not unacquainted with the
fortunes of men and their necessities—but will
briefly formulate a motion concerning the subject
you have asked us to consider. My motion will bear
witness whether it was myself or your legions that I
spared, when I bound myself by a base, or, perhaps,

189

5 sione obstrinxi; qua tamen, quando iniussu populi
facta est, non tenetur populus Romanus, nec quicquam ex ea praeterquam corpora nostra debentur
6 Samnitibus. Dedamur per fetiales nudi vinctique;
exsolvamus religione populum, si qua obligavimus,
ne quid divini humanive obstet quo minus iustum
7 piumque de integro ineatur bellum. Interea consules exercitum scribere, armare, educere placet,
nec prius ingredi hostium fines, quam omnia iusta
8 in deditionem nostram[1] perfecta erunt. Vos, di
immortales, precor quaesoque, si vobis non fuit cordi
Sp. Postumium T. Veturium consules cum Samnitibus
9 prospere bellum gerere, at vos satis habeatis vidisse
nos sub iugum missos, vidisse sponsione infami
obligatos, videre nudos vinctosque hostibus deditos,
omnem iram hostium nostris capitibus excipientes;
10 novos consules legionesque Romanas ita cum Samnite
gerere bellum velitis ut omnia ante nos consules
bella gesta sunt."

11 Quae ubi dixit, tanta simul admiratio miseratioque
viri incessit homines ut modo vix crederent illum
eundem esse Sp. Postumium qui auctor tam foedae
12 pacis fuisset; modo miserarentur quod vir talis etiam
praecipuum apud hostes supplicium passurus esset
13 ob iram diremptae pacis. Cum omnes laudibus modo

---

[1] deditionem nostram Ω: deditionem nostra *TDA*: didi-
tione nostra *Lς*.

a necessary pledge,—by which, however, the Roman B.C. 320
People is not held, since it was given without the
people's authorization ; nor by its terms is aught but
our own persons due to the Samnites. Let us be
given up, I propose, by the fetials, stripped and
bound ; let us release the people from their religious
obligation, if in any such we have involved them,
that no obstacle, divine or human, may block the
way to a just and righteous renewal of the war.
Meantime I move that the consuls enroll an army
and arm it and lead it forth, yet without crossing the
borders of the enemy, until all the ceremonies
incident to our surrender shall have been completed.
Do you, immortal gods, I beseech and pray you, if
you were not pleased that the consuls Spurius
Postumius and Titus Veturius should wage a successful war with the Samnites, yet deem it enough to
have seen us sent beneath the yoke, to have seen us
bound by an infamous agreement, to behold us,
naked and in bonds, delivered to the enemy, receiving on our own heads all the resentment of our
foes ; and vouchsafe to the new consuls and the
Roman legions so to wage war with the Samnites,
as, until our consulship, all Rome's wars were
waged."

When he had finished speaking, such a thrill of
astonishment, and at the same time of pity for the
man, ran through the senate, that at first men could
hardly believe it was the same Spurius Postumius
who had been the author of a peace so shameful;
and presently they were all compassion, to think
that such a man should suffer what would be no
ordinary punishment at the hands of enemies
enraged by the rupture of the peace. As they

prosequentes virum in sententiam eius pedibus irent,
14 temptata paulisper intercessio est ab L. Livio et Q.
Maelio tribunis plebis, qui neque exsolvi religione
populum aiebant deditione sua, nisi omnia Samnitibus, qualia apud Caudium fuissent, restituerentur;
15 neque se pro eo quod spondendo pacem servassent
exercitum populi Romani poenam ullam meritos esse;
neque ad extremum, cum sacrosancti essent, dedi
hostibus violarive posse.[1]

IX. Tum Postumius " Interea dedite " inquit " pro-
fanos nos, quos salva religione potestis; dedetis
deinde et istos sacrosanctos, cum primum magistratu
2 abierint, sed, si me audiatis, priusquam dedantur, hic
in comitio virgis caesos, hanc iam ut intercalatae
3 poenae usuram habeant. Nam quod deditione nostra negant exsolvi religione populum, id istos magis
ne dedantur quam quia ita se res habeat dicere, quis
4 adeo iuris fetialium expers est qui ignoret? Neque
ego infitias eo, patres conscripti, tam sponsiones[2]
quam foedera sancta esse apud eos homines apud
quos iuxta divinas religiones fides humana coli-
tur; sed iniussu populi nego quicquam sanciri posse
5 quod populum teneat. An, si eadem superbia qua
sponsionem istam expresserunt nobis Samnites coegis-

---

[1] posse ς : posset MPT : possent Ω.
[2] sponsiones ς : sponsores Ω.

---

[1] Livius and Maelius are apparently thought of as having
been among the guarantors and as having afterwards been
elected plebeian tribunes.

were all crossing over to support his motion, with nothing but praises for his heroism, Lucius Livius and Quintus Maelius, tribunes of the plebs, endeavoured for a moment to interpose their veto. The people, they said, could not be freed from their obligation by surrendering *them*, unless every advantage which the Samnites had possessed at Caudium were restored to them; moreover, they had merited no punishment for having preserved by their pledge of peace the army of the Roman People; nor, finally, seeing that they were sacrosanct, could they be surrendered to the enemy or violated.[1]

IX. Then said Postumius: "Meanwhile, surrender us, who are unconsecrate, as you may do without offence to Heaven; afterwards you shall surrender also those sacrosanct ones, when once they have retired from their magistracy; but, if you should listen to me, before surrendering them you would have them scourged here in the Comitium, that they might receive in advance this extra punishment, by way of interest. For when they deny that the people can be freed of their obligation by surrendering us, who is so unacquainted with the fetial law as not to be aware that they say this, more that they may not be surrendered than because the case is so? And yet, Conscript Fathers, I do not dispute the fact that guarantees as well as treaties are sacred in the eyes of those who cherish honour among men on an equal footing with obligations due to the gods; but I deny that without the people's authorization any sanction can be given which shall be binding on the people. What! If the Samnites with that same arrogance with which they extorted this capitulation from us had com-

A.U.C.
434

sent nos verba legitima dedentium urbes nuncupare,
deditum populum Romanum vos tribuni diceretis et
hanc urbem templa delubra fines aquas Samnitium
6 esse? Omitto deditionem, quoniam de sponsione
agitur; quid tandem si spopondissemus urbem hanc
relicturum populum Romanum? si incensurum? si
magistratus, si senatum, si leges non habiturum? si
7 sub regibus futurum? Di meliora, inquis. Atqui
non indignitas rerum sponsionis vinculum levat: si
quid est in quod [1] obligari populus possit, in omnia
potest. Et ne illud quidem, quod quosdam forsitan
moveat, refert, consul an dictator an praetor spopon-
8 derit. Et hoc ipsi etiam Samnites iudicaverunt,
quibus non fuit satis consules spondere, sed legatos,
quaestores, tribunos militum spondere coegerunt.

9 "Nec a me nunc quisquam quaesiverit quid ita
spopo.. erim, cum id nec consulis ius esset nec illis
spondere pacem quae mei non erat arbitrii, nec pro
10 vobis qui nihil mandaveratis possem. Nihil ad Caudium, patres conscripti, humanis consiliis gestum est
di immortales et vestris et hostium imperatoribus
11 mentem ademerunt. Nec nos in bello satis cavimus,
et illi male partam victoriam male perdiderunt, dum
vix locis quibus vicerant credunt, dum quacumque

---

[1] quod ς: quo Ω.

pelled us to pronounce the solemn form of words B.C. 320
of those who surrender cities, would you tribunes
assert that the Roman People had been surrendered,
and that this City, with its temples, its holy places,
its bounds and waters, was become the property of
the Samnites? But enough of *surrender;* we are
talking of a *guarantee.* How, pray, if we had
guaranteed that the Roman People should forsake
this City? that they should burn it? that it should
cease to have magistrates, a senate, laws? that it
should be subject to the rule of kings? 'The gods
forbid!' you say. And yet the unworthiness of
the conditions cannot lessen the force of a guarantee;
if there is anything for which the people can be
bound, it can be bound for everything. Nor does
it matter, either, as some are perhaps inclined to
think, whether consul or dictator or praetor have
given the guarantee. And this the very Samnites
themselves deemed to be true, for not content
with the guarantee of consuls, they obliged the
lieutenants, the quaestors, and the tribunes of the
soldiers to add theirs.

"And let no man now demand of me why I gave
this guarantee, seeing that a consul has no right so
to do and that I could not pledge them a peace
which was not mine to grant, nor in your behalf,
who had given me no mandate. There was nothing
done at Caudium, Conscript Fathers, by man's
wisdom: the immortal gods deprived of understanding both your commanders and the enemy's. We,
on our part, took no sufficient precautions in the
war: while, as for them, they threw away their ill-
got victory by their ill-guided conduct, for they
hardly trusted the very ground that had given them

LIVY

condicione arma viris in arma natis auferre festinant.

12 An, si sana mens fuisset, difficile illis fuit, dum senes ab domo ad consultandum accersunt, mittere Romam legatos? cum senatu, cum populo de pace ac foedere

13 agere? Tridui iter expeditis erat; interea in indutiis res fuisset, donec ab Roma legati aut victoriam illis certam aut pacem adferrent. Ea demum sponsio

14 esset quam populi iussu spopondissemus. Sed neque vos tullissetis nec nos spopondissemus; nec fas fuit alium rerum exitum esse quam ut illi velut somnio laetiore quam quod mentes eorum capere possent

15 nequiquam eluderentur et nostrum exercitum eadem quae impedierat fortuna expediret, vanam victoriam vanior inritam faceret pax, sponsio interponeretur

16 quae neminem praeter sponsorem obligaret. Quid enim vobiscum, patres conscripti, quid cum populo Romano actum est? Quis vos appellare potest, quis se a vobis dicere deceptum? Hostis an civis? Hosti nihil spopondistis, civem[1] neminem spondere pro

17 vobis iussistis. Nihil ergo vobis nec nobiscum est, quibus nihil mandastis, nec cum Samnitibus, cum

18 quibus nihil egistis. Samnitibus sponsores nos sumus rei satis locupletes in id quod nostrum est, in id quod praestare possumus, corpora nostra et animos;

---

[1] civem A^3: quem Ω: quin U: qui F^3.

---

[1] Victory, in case the Roman People declined to accept terms for the ransom of their army; peace, if they acceded to those terms.

their conquest, in their haste to deprive of arms, on
any terms, men born to the use of arms. Why, had
they had their wits about them, would it have been
hard, while summoning old men from home for con-
sultation, to dispatch envoys to Rome? to treat
with senate and with people for a peace and
covenant? It was only three days' journey to those
who travel light; meantime hostilities would have
been suspended, until their envoys should return
from Rome with either certain victory or a peace.[1]
Then, and then only, would there have been a
guarantee in which our pledge was backed by the
mandate of the people. But neither would you
have voted one, nor should we have given it; nor
was it Heaven's will that the affair should have any
other ending, but that they should be beguiled with
a dream too joyful for their comprehension, and that
our army should be extricated by the same fortune
which had entrapped it; that their idle victory
should evaporate in a yet idler peace, and a guarantee
be proffered that should bind none but the guarantor.
For what negotiation, Conscript Fathers, has there
been with you or with the Roman People? Who
can appeal to you, who can say that he has been
deceived by you? Can the enemy, can a fellow-
citizen? You have pledged nothing to the enemy,
you have given no authority to make a pledge to
any fellow-citizen. You have therefore naught to
do with us, to whom you gave no mandate, or with
the Samnites, with whom you have had no dealings
The Samnites have in us guarantors who are responsible and quite competent, so far as concerns what
belongs to ourselves and what we are able to deliver,
namely, our persons and our lives; against these let

A.U.C.
434

in haec saeviant, in haec ferrum, in haec iras acuant.
19 Quod ad tribunos attinet, consulite utrum praesens
deditio eorum fieri possit an in diem differatur; nos
interim, T. Veturi vosque ceteri, vilia haec capita
luendae sponsionis[1] feramus et nostro supplicio
liberemus Romana arma."

X. Movit patres conscriptos cum causa tum auctor
nec ceteros solum sed tribunos etiam plebei, ut se
2 in senatus dicerent fore potestate. Magistratu inde
se extemplo abdicaverunt traditique fetialibus cum
ceteris Caudium ducendi. Hoc senatus consulto
3 facto lux quaedam adfulsisse civitati visa est. Postumius in ore erat; eum laudibus ad caelum ferebant,
devotioni P. Deci consulis, aliis claris facinoribus
4 aequabant: emersisse civitatem ex obnoxia pace
illius consilio et opera; ipsum se cruciatibus et
hostium irae offerre piaculaque pro populo Romano
5 dare. Arma cuncti spectant et bellum: en unquam
futurum ut congredi armatis cum Samnite liceat?
6 In civitate ira odioque ardente dilectus prope
omnium voluntariorum fuit. Rescriptae ex eodem
milite novae legiones ductusque ad Caudium exer-
7 citus. Praegressi fetiales ubi ad portam venere,
vestem detrahi pacis sponsoribus iubent, manus post
tergum vinciri. Cum apparitor verecundia maiestatis
Postumi laxe vinciret, "Quin tu" inquit "adduces[2]

---

[1] sponsionis Ω : sponsioni 𝒄 edd.
[2] adduces Ω : adducis (or adduce) 𝒄.

---

[1] VIII. ix. 4 f.

them storm, against these direct their swords, against B.C. 320
these make sharp their anger. As for the tribunes,
you must determine whether their surrender can
take place at once or had better be deferred; meantime, Titus Veturius, let us, and you others, offer
these caitiff heads of ours in satisfaction of our pledge,
and by our suffering liberate the Roman arms."

X. Both the cause itself and the speaker greatly
stirred the Conscript Fathers and the others present,
including even the tribunes of the plebs, who declared
that they would obey the senate, and having forthwith resigned their office were delivered over to the
fetials to be led with the rest to Caudium. When
the senate had acted on this motion, it somehow
seemed as though day had dawned upon the State.
Postumius was on all men's lips; they extolled him
to the skies, and compared his conduct to the
devotion of Publius Decius, the consul,[1] and to other
glorious deeds. The state, they said, had emerged
—thanks to his wisdom and his services—from a
slavish peace; he was freely giving himself up to
the tortures of a resentful foe, that he might make
expiation for the Roman People. Men thought of
nothing but war and arms. Would ever the hour
come, they asked, when they might encounter the
Samnites, sword in hand?

In a city ablaze with wrath and hate, the levy was
almost wholly made up with volunteers. The same
soldiers were enrolled into new legions, and the army
marched on Caudium. Before them went the fetials,
who, when they had come to the gate, bade the
guarantors of peace be stripped and their hands be
bound behind their backs. As the officer, awed by
the dignity of Postumius, would have left him loosely

8 lorum, ut iusta fiat deditio!" Tum ubi in coetum
Samnitium et ad tribunal ventum Ponti est, A. Cor-
9 nelius Arvina fetialis ita verba fecit: "Quandoque
hisce homines iniussu populi Romani Quiritium
foedus ictum iri spoponderunt atque ob eam rem
noxam nocuerunt, ob eam rem quo populus Romanus
scelere impio sit solutus hosce homines vobis dedo."
10 Haec dicenti fetiali Postumius genu femur quanta
maxime poterat vi perculit et clara voce ait se
Samnitem civem esse, illum legatum[1] a se contra
ius gentium violatum : eo iustius bellum gesturos.

XI. Tum Pontius "Nec ego istam deditionem
accipiam" inquit, "nec Samnites ratam habebunt.
2 Quin tu, Spuri Postumi, si deos esse censes, aut
omnia inrita facis aut pacto stas? Samniti populo
omnes quos in potestate habuit aut pro iis pax
3 debetur. Sed quid ego te appello, qui te captum
victori cum qua potes fide restituis? Populum
Romanum appello ; quem si sponsionis ad furculas
Caudinas factae paenitet, restituat legiones intra
4 saltum quo saeptae fuerunt. Nemo quemquam de-
ceperit ; omnia pro infecto sint ; recipiant arma,
quae per pactionem tradiderunt ; redeant in castra
sua ; quidquid pridie habuerunt quam in conloquium
est ventum habeant : tum bellum et fortia consilia
5 placeant, tum sponsio et pax repudietur. Ea fortuna,

---

[1] legatum *Walters and Conway* : legatum fetialem Ω.

---

[1] *i.e.* the *pater patratus*, see I. xxiv. 6.

bound, " Nay, draw the thong tight," he exclaimed, B.C. 320
" that the surrender may be duly carried out." Then,
on arriving at the assembly of the Samnites and the
tribunal of Pontius, Aulus Cornelius Arvina the
fetial[1] spoke as follows: "Whereas these men,
unbidden by the Roman People of the Quirites, have
guaranteed that a treaty should be ratified, and by so
doing have committed an injury; to the end that
the Roman People may be absolved of heinous guilt,
I deliver up these men to you." As the fetial spoke
these words, Postumius thrust his knee into the
other's thigh, with all the force he could summon
up, and proclaimed in a loud voice that he was a
Samnite citizen, who had maltreated the envoy in
violation of the law of nations, whereby the Romans
would make war with the better right.

XI. Then said Pontius, " I will not receive this
surrender, nor will the Samnites hold it valid. And
you, Spurius Postumius, if you believe in the existence
of the gods, why not either reject the whole negotiation or abide by your agreement? The Samnite
People is entitled to all whom it had in its power,
or to peace in place of them. But why do I
appeal to you, who yield yourself a prisoner as
honourably as you can? I appeal to the Roman
People; if they repent them of the pledge that was
given at the Caudine Forks, let them replace their
legions in the defile where they were surrounded.
Let no one deceive anybody; let all be as though it
had not happened; let them resume the arms they
laid down in accordance with the compact; let them
go back to their camp; whatever they had on the
day before the conference, let them have again; *then*
let them vote for war and warlike measures, *then* let

iis [1] locis, quae ante pacis mentionem habuimus,
geramus bellum, nec populus Romanus consulum
sponsionem nec nos fidem populi Romani accusemus.

6 Nunquamne causa defiet cur victi pacto non stetis? Obsides Porsinnae dedistis : furto eos subduxistis ; auro civitatem a Gallis redemistis : inter accipiendum

7 aurum caesi sunt ; pacem nobiscum pepigistis, ut legiones vobis captas restitueremus : eam pacem inritam facitis. Et semper aliquam fraudi speciem

8 iuris imponitis. Non probat populus Romanus igno-miniosa pace legiones servatas? Pacem sibi habeat, legiones captas victori restituat ; hoc fide, hoc foederibus, hoc fetialibus caerimoniis dignum erat.

9 Ut quidem tu quod petisti per pactionem habeas, tot cives incolumes, ego pacem quam hos tibi re-mittendo pactus sum non habeam, hoc tu, A. Corneli, hoc vos, fetiales, iuris gentibus dicitis?

10 "Ego vero istos quos dedi simulatis nec accipio nec dedi arbitror, nec moror quo minus in civitatem obligatam [2] sponsione commissa iratis omnibus dis,

11 quorum eluditur numen, redeant. Gerite bellum, quando Sp. Postumius modo legatum [3] genu perculit. Ita di credent Samnitem civem Postumium, non ci-

---

[1] iis ⲥ: his (hiis *A*) Ω.
[2] obligatam *F³A*: obluctam (*or other corruptions*) Ω : convictam *Walters.*
[3] legatum *Walters and Conway*: legatum fetialem (*or fec-*) Ω.

---

[1] An allusion to the Cloelia episode, II. xiii. 6-11.
[2] v. xlviii–xlix.

them reject the guarantee and the peace! Let us B.C. 320
fight it out in those circumstances, and in those
positions, which were ours before peace was
mentioned; let the Roman People not blame the
pledge given by the consuls, nor let us blame the
honour of the Roman People. Will you never, when
you have been beaten, lack excuses for not holding
to your covenants? You gave hostages to Porsinna
—and withdrew them by a trick.[1] You ransomed
your City from the Gauls with gold—and cut them
down as they were receiving the gold.[2] You pledged
us peace, on condition that we gave you back your
captured legions—and you nullify the peace. And
always you contrive to give the fraud some colour of
legality. Does the Roman People not approve the
preservation of its legions by a disgraceful peace?
Let it keep its peace, and give back the captured
legions to the victor; that would be conduct worthy
of its promise, its covenants, its fetial ceremonies.
That you, on your side, should have what you aimed
at in your compact, the safety of these many citizens,
but that I should not have the peace I stipulated for,
when I released them,—is this the judgment which
you, Aulus Cornelius, and you, fetials, render to the
nations?

"As for me, I will none of these whom you
pretend to be surrendering, nor do I deem them to
be surrendered, neither do I stand in the way of
their returning, despite the wrath of all the gods,
whose divinity they have made a mock, to the City
which is committed by their guarantee. Aye, go to
war, since Spurius Postumius has just now jostled
the envoy with his knee! So shall the gods believe
that Postumius is a Samnite—not a Roman—citizen,

vem Romanum esse, et a Samnite legatum Romanum
violatum : eo vobis iustum in nos factum esse bellum.
12 Haec ludibria religionum non pudere in lucem proferre et vix pueris dignas ambages senes ac consu-
13 lares fallendae fidei exquirere ! I, lictor, deme vincla
Romanis ; moratus sit nemo, quo minus ubi visum
fuerit abeant." Et illi quidem, forsitan et publica,
sua certe liberata fide ab Caudio in castra Romana
inviolati redierunt.

XII. Samnitibus pro superba pace infestissimum
cernentibus renatum bellum, omnia[1] quae deinde
evenerunt non in animis solum sed prope in oculis
2 esse ; et sero ac nequiquam laudare senis Ponti
utraque consilia, inter quae se media lapsos via[2]
victoriae possessionem pace incerta mutasse ; et
beneficii et maleficii occasione amissa pugnaturos
cum eis quos potuerint in perpetuum vel inimicos
3 tollere vel amicos facere. Adeoque nullodum certamine inclinatis viribus post Caudinam pacem animi
mutaverant, ut clariorem inter Romanos deditio
Postumium quam Pontium incruenta victoria inter
4 Samnites faceret, et geri posse bellum Romani pro
victoria certa haberent, Samnites simul rebellasse et
vicisse crederent Romanum.

[1] omnia ς : omniaque Ω.
[2] media lapsos via *Doujat* (*Madvig*) : media lapsos Ω :
medio lapsos *Perizonius*.

and that a Roman envoy has been maltreated by a B.C. 320 Samnite, and that you, in consequence of this, have justly made war on us! Does it not shame you to bring forth into the light of day these mockeries of religion, and, old men and consulars as you are, to devise such quibbles to evade your promise as were scarce worthy of children? Go, lictor, strike their fetters from the Romans; let no man hinder them from departing when they list." And the guarantors, released it may be from the nation's pledge, but at all events from their own, returned from Caudium, inviolate, to the Roman camp.

XII. The Samnites now perceived that instead of their domineering peace they were confronted with the renewal of a most bitter war, and not only imagined but almost saw all the consequences which afterwards proceeded from it. Too late and all in vain did they praise the alternative policies suggested by the aged Pontius, between which they had fallen, and exchanged a victory already in their possession for an uncertain peace; they had let slip the opportunity both of doing good and of doing harm, and were going to fight with men whom they might permanently have removed from their path, as enemies, or have made their permanent friends. And though there had so far been no battle since the Caudine Peace to give an advantage to either side, yet such a change of feeling had come about that Postumius enjoyed more fame among the Romans for his surrender than did Pontius among the Samnites for his bloodless victory; and while the Romans regarded their being able to make war as certain victory, the Samnites felt that the Romans had at one and the same moment renewed the war and won it.

LIVY

5 Inter haec Satricani ad Samnites defecerunt, et
Fregellae colonia necopinato adventu Samnitium—
fuisse et Satricanos cum iis satis constat—nocte
occupata est. Timor inde mutuus utrosque usque
6 ad lucem quietos tenuit; lux pugnae initium fuit,
quam aliquamdiu aequam et quia pro aris ac focis
dimicabatur et quia ex tectis adiuvabat imbellis
7 multitudo tamen [1] Fregellani sustinuerunt. Fraus
deinde rem inclinavit, quod vocem audiri praeconis
passi sunt, incolumem abiturum qui arma posuisset.
Ea spes remisit a certamine animos, et passim arma
8 iactari coepta. Pertinacior pars armata per aversam
portam erupit, tutiorque eis audacia fuit quam in-
cautus ad credendum ceteris pavor, quos circumdatos
igni nequiquam deos fidemque invocantes Samnites
concremaverunt.

9 Consules inter se partiti provincias, Papirius in
Apuliam ad Luceriam pergit, ubi equites Romani
obsides ad Caudium dati custodiebantur, Publilius
in Samnio substitit adversus Caudinas legiones.
10 Distendit ea res Samnitium animos, quod nec ad
Luceriam ire, ne ab tergo instaret hostis, nec
manere, ne Luceria interim amitteretur, satis aude-
11 bant. Optimum visum est committere rem fortunae

---

[1] multitudo tamen Ω: multitudo certamen (*or* multitudo)
Madvig.

206

Meanwhile the Satricans revolted to the Samnites, B.C. 320 and the colony of Fregellae, in a surprise attack by the Samnites—accompanied, it would seem, by people from Satricum—was seized during the night. Mutual fear then caused both sides to remain quiet until the morning, when the light ushered in a battle which for a long time was equally sustained —for the townsfolk were fighting for their hearths and altars and a throng of those unfit for arms gave them assistance from the housetops,—still, the people of Fregellae held their own, until presently a ruse decided the victory; for they permitted a herald to be heard, who promised safety to any who laid down his arms. The hope of this relaxed the tension of their courage and on every side they began throwing their arms away. The more determined portion of them retained their weapons and burst out by the opposite gate, and their boldness stood them in better stead than did their too credulous timidity the others; for these the Samnites compassed about with fire, and, despite their appeals to Heaven and to the promise of their captors, burnt them alive.

The consuls having divided the provinces between them, Papirius took his way into Apulia towards Luceria, where the Roman knights given up at Caudium for hostages were being guarded, while Publilius stopped behind in Samnium to oppose the Caudine legions. This plan distracted the minds of the Samnites, since they neither dared move towards Luceria, lest they should bring the enemy down upon their rear, nor remain where they were, for fear that Luceria would meanwhile be lost. The best course seemed to be to entrust their cause to

et transigere cum Publilio certamen; itaque in aciem copias educunt.

XIII. Adversus quos Publilius consul cum dimicaturus esset, prius adloquendos milites ratus contionem advocari iussit. Ceterum sicut ingenti alacritate ad praetorium concursum est, ita prae clamore poscentium pugnam nulla adhortatio im-2 peratoris audita est: suus cuique animus memor ignominiae adhortator aderat. Vadunt igitur in proelium urgentes signiferos, et ne mora in concursu pilis emittendis stringendisque inde gladiis esset, pila velut dato ad id signo abiciunt strictisque gladiis 3 cursu in hostem feruntur. Nihil illic imperatoriae artis ordinibus aut subsidiis locandis fuit: omnia ira 4 militaris prope vesano impetu egit. Itaque non fusi modo hostes sunt, sed ne castris quidem suis fugam impedire[1] ausi Apuliam dissipati petiere; Luceriam tamen coacto rursus in unum agmine est perventum. 5 Romanos ira eadem quae per mediam aciem hostium tulerat et in castra pertulit. Ibi plus quam in acie sanguinis ac caedis factum praedaeque pars maior ira corrupta.

6 Exercitus alter cum Papirio consule locis maritimis pervenerat Arpos per omnia pacata Samnitium magis iniuriis et odio quam beneficio ullo populi Romani;

---

[1] impedire Ω: inhibere *Madvig.*

Fortune and fight it out with Publilius. They accordingly formed up in line of battle.

XIII. Publilius the consul was ready to engage them, but thinking it best to encourage his soldiers first, he bade summon them to an assembly. But though they came running to the praetorium with vast alacrity, yet the outcry of those who demanded battle was so loud that the general's exhortation could not be heard; still, every man's own heart, remembering the late humiliation, was there to exhort him. So they went forward into battle, urging on their standard-bearers; and, that there might be no delay in coming to grips while they were discharging their javelins and drawing their swords, they threw away their javelins, as if a signal had been given them, and, sword in hand, pushed forward at the double against the enemy. No tactical skill was there employed in ranging centuries or reserves: the wrath of the soldiers swept everything along in its mad rush. And so not only were the Samnites routed, but not daring to interrupt their flight even at their camp, they dispersed and struck out for Apulia; yet they afterwards rallied again and came to Luceria in one body. The same fury that took the Romans through their enemy's battle-line, carried them also into his camp. There was more bloodshed and carnage there than in the battle, and the greater part of the booty was destroyed in anger.

The other army, under the consul Papirius, marching along the coast as far as Arpi, had found all peaceably disposed, more because of the wrongs done by the Samnites and the hatred they had engendered than owing to any favour shown by the

7 nam Samnites, ea tempestate in montibus vicatim habitantes, campestria et maritima loca contempto [1] cultorum molliore atque, ut evenit fere, locis simili genere ipsi montani atque agrestes depopulabantur.

8 Quae regio si fida Samnitibus fuisset, aut pervenire Arpos exercitus Romanus nequisset, aut interiecta penuria [2] rerum omnium exclusos a commeatibus

9 absumpsisset. Tum quoque profectos inde ad Luceriam, iuxta obsidentes obsessosque, inopia vexavit. Omnia ab Arpis Romanis suppeditabantur, ceterum adeo exigue ut militi occupato stationibus vigiliisque et opere eques folliculis in castra ab

10 Arpis frumentum veheret, interdum occursu hostium cogeretur abiecto ex equo frumento pugnare. Obsessis priusquam alter consul victore exercitu advenit, et commeatus ex montibus Samnitium invecti

11 erant et auxilia intromissa. Artiora omnia adventus Publili fecit, qui obsidione delegata in curam collegae vacuus [3] per agros cuncta infesta commeatibus hostium

12 fecerat. Itaque cum spes nulla esset diutius obsessos inopiam laturos, coacti Samnites, qui ad Luceriam castra habebant, undique contractis viribus signa cum Papirio conferre.

XIV. Per id tempus parantibus utrisque se ad

---

[1] contempto A^5₋ : contempta M : contemptu Ω.
[2] interiecta penuria *Tan. Faber* (*Walters and Conway*) : interiecta inter Romam et Arpos penuria Ω.
[3] vacuus Ω : uacuos A^1 (*or* A^2) : uacuis U : uagus *Duker* (*Madvig*).

Roman People. For the Samnites, who in those days dwelt in villages among the mountains, used to ravage the regions of the plain and coast, despising their cultivators, who were of a softer character, and one that—as often happens—resembled their country, while they themselves were rude highlanders. If this district had been faithful to the Samnites, it would either have been impossible for a Roman army to have got as far as Arpi, or the utterly barren nature of the intervening country would have destroyed them, cut off as they would have been from their supplies. Even as it was, when they had proceeded to the vicinity of Luceria, besiegers and besieged suffered alike from scarcity of food: everything was carried up from Arpi for the Romans, but so precarious were their supplies, that while the foot-soldiers were busy with outpost-duty, guard-mounting, and entrenching, the cavalry brought up corn for them from Arpi in leather pouches, and, now and then, encountering the enemy, were forced to throw off the corn from their horses and fight; the besieged, until the arrival of the other consul with his victorious army, had got in their provisions —and auxiliary forces too—from the mountains of the Samnites. The coming of Publilius tightened up the lines; for, turning the siege over to his colleague, he was free to range the country-side, where he made things difficult for the supply-trains of the enemy. The Samnites, therefore, who were encamped about Luceria, in despair of being able to endure the scarcity, if the siege continued, were obliged to gather up their forces from every quarter and give battle to Papirius.

XIV. At this juncture, while both sides were

A.U.C.
434

proelium legati Tarentini interveniunt denuntiantes
Samnitibus Romanisque ut bellum omitterent: per
utros stetisset quo minus discederetur ab armis,
2 adversus eos se pro alteris pugnaturos. Ea legatione Papirius audita perinde ac motus dictis eorum
cum collega se communicaturum respondit; acci-
toque eo, cum tempus omne in apparatu pugnae
consumpsisset, conlocutus de re haud dubia signum
3 pugnae proposuit. Agentibus divina humanaque
quae adsolent cum acie dimicandum est consulibus
Tarentini legati occursare responsum exspectantes;
4 quibus Papirius ait: "Auspicia secunda esse, Tarentini, pullarius nuntiat; litatum praeterea est egregie;
auctoribus dis, ut videtis, ad rem gerendam pro-
5 ficiscimur." Signa inde ferre[1] iussit et copias
eduxit, vanissimam increpans gentem quae, suarum
impotens rerum prae domesticis seditionibus dis-
cordiisque, aliis modum pacis ac belli facere aequum
censeret.
6 Samnites ex parte altera, cum omnem curam belli
remisissent, quia aut pacem vere cupiebant aut
expediebat simulare, ut Tarentinos sibi conciliarent,
cum instructos repente ad pugnam Romanos con-
7 spexissent, vociferari se in auctoritate Tarentinorum
manere nec descendere in aciem nec extra vallum
arma ferre; deceptos potius quodcumque casus ferat

---

[1] ferre Ω : ferri ⸂ *Gronovius*.

---

[1] *i.e.* a red flag hung out in front of the general's tent.
[2] Two kinds of divination are alluded to: (1) by observing
the feeding of the sacred chickens, (2) by inspecting the
entrails of a victim.

making ready for the struggle, came ambassadors B.C. 320
from Tarentum, admonishing both Samnites and
Romans to desist from war. Whichever party should
oppose the cessation of hostilities, against that they
proposed to fight in behalf of the other. After
listening to these envoys, Papirius, as though moved
by what they said, replied that he would consult his
colleague. Having sent for Publilius, he employed
every moment of the interval in making his preparations, and when he had conferred with him about
a matter which admitted of no doubt, displayed the
battle-signal.[1] The consuls were busy with matters
pertaining to gods and to men, as they are wont to
to be on the eve of an engagement, when the envoys
from Tarentum approached them to receive their
answer; to whom Papirius replied, "Tarentines, the
keeper of the chickens reports that the signs are
favourable; the sacrifice too has been exceedingly
auspicious;[2] as you see, the gods are with us at our
going into action." He then commanded to advance
the standards, and marshalled his troops, with exclama-
tions on the folly of a nation which, powerless to
manage its own affairs, because of domestic strife
and discord, presumed to lay down the limits of
peace and war for others.

The Samnites, on their side, having dismissed from
their minds every anxiety regarding the war, either
because they sincerely wished for peace, or because
it was expedient for them to pretend that they
wished it, in order to gain the support of the Tarentines, when they beheld the Romans suddenly
arrayed for battle, cried out that they would abide
by the will of the Tarentines and would neither take
the field nor advance beyond the rampart; they had

LIVY

passuros quam ut sprevisse pacis auctores Tarentinos
8 videantur. Accipere se omen consules aiunt et eam
precari mentem hostibus ut ne vallum quidem
9 defendant. Ipsi inter se partitis copiis succedunt
hostium munimentis et simul undique adorti, cum
pars fossas explerent, pars vellerent vallum atque
in fossas proruerent nec virtus modo insita sed ira
etiam exulceratos ignominia stimularet animos, castra
10 invasere; et pro se quisque, non haec Furculas nec
Caudium nec saltus invios esse, ubi errorem fraus
superbe vicisset, sed Romanam virtutem, quam nec
11 vallum nec fossae arcerent memorantes, caedunt
pariter resistentes fusosque, inermes atque armatos,
servos liberos, puberes impubes, homines iumentaque ;
12 nec ullum superfuisset animal, ni consules receptui
signum dedissent avidosque caedis milites e castris
13 hostium imperio ac minis[1] expulissent. Itaque
apud infensos ob interpellatam dulcedinem irae confestim oratio habita est, ut doceretur miles minime
cuiquam militum consules odio in hostes cessisse
14 aut cessuros ; quin duces sicut belli ita insatiabilis
supplicii futuros fuisse, ni respectus equitum sescen-
torum qui Luceriae obsides tenerentur praepedisset[2]
15 animos, ne desperata venia hostes caecos in sup-

---

[1] ac minis D^3⸗ : agminis Ω.
[2] praepedisset (pre-) ⸗ : praepedissent Ω.

---

[1] The omen lay in the Samnites' expressed purpose to offer
no resistance.

been deceived, but they chose rather to endure
whatever Fortune might have in store for them than
be thought to have spurned the peaceful advice of the
Tarentines. The consuls declared that they embraced
the omen,[1] praying that the enemy might be so minded
as not even to defend his rampart. They themselves,
dividing their troops between them, marched up to
the earthworks of the Samnites, and attacked them
at once from every side. Some began to fill the
trenches, others to pull up the palings and fling
them into the trenches; besides their native courage
they were goaded on by anger at the disgrace that
rankled in their hearts. Forcing their way into the
camp, while every man repeated that here were no
Forks, no Caudium, no trackless passes, where guile
had arrogantly triumphed over error, but Roman
manhood, which neither rampart nor trenches could
keep out, they cut down without distinction those
who resisted and those who fled, the armed and the
unarmed, slaves and freemen, adults and children,
men and beasts; nor would anything living have
survived, had not the consuls bade sound the recall
and expelled the bloodthirsty soldiers from the
enemy's camp with commands and threats. The
men were incensed at the interruption of their sweet
revenge, and accordingly the consuls at once addressed
them and explained that they had neither yielded
nor meant to yield to any of the soldiers in hatred
of the enemy; on the contrary, they would have
led the way, as in war, so in the exaction of end-
less vengeance, had their indignation not been
checked by thoughts of the six hundred knights
who were being held as hostages in Luceria; but
they feared that the enemy, if they despaired of

plicia eorum ageret, perdere prius quam perire
16 optantes.   Laudare ea milites laetarique obviam
itum irae suae esse ac fateri omnia patienda potius
quam proderetur salus tot principum Romanae
iuventutis.

XV. Dimissa contione consilium habitum omni-
busne copiis Luceriam premerent an altero exercitu
et duce Apuli circa, gens dubiae ad id voluntatis,
2 temptarentur.   Publilius consul ad peragrandam
profectus Apuliam aliquot expeditione una populos
aut vi subegit aut condicionibus in societatem accepit.
3 Papirio quoque, qui obsessor Luceriae restiterat,
brevi ad spem eventus respondit.   Nam insessis
omnibus viis per quas commeatus ex Samnio sub-
vehebantur, fame domiti Samnites qui Luceriae in
praesidio erant legatos misere ad consulem Romanum,
ut receptis equitibus qui causa belli essent absisteret
4 obsidione.   Iis Papirius ita respondit: debuisse eos
Pontium Herenni filium, quo auctore Romanos sub
iugum misissent, consulere quid victis patiendum
5 censeret; ceterum quoniam ab hostibus in se aequa
statui quam in se ipsi ferre maluerint, nuntiare
Luceriam iussit, arma sarcinas iumenta multitudinem omnem imbellem intra moenia relinquerent

quarter, might be driven blindly to put their prisoners to death, choosing to slay before they were slain themselves. These arguments the men applauded, and rejoiced that their wrath had been restrained; they confessed that it was better that they should suffer anything than betray the lives of so many distinguished young Romans.

XV. The assembly was dismissed, and a council of war was held to determine whether they should press the siege with all their forces, or should employ one army and its general to test the dispositions of the Apulians around them—a people whose sympathies were still in doubt. The consul Publilius set out on a march through Apulia and in a single expedition either subjugated, or by granting terms, received into alliance, a goodly number of states. Papirius, too, who had remained behind at Luceria to conduct the siege, soon found the outcome answerable to his hopes; for all the roads by which supplies were wont to be brought in from Samnium were blocked, and the Samnite garrison were reduced by hunger to send a deputation to the Roman consul with an offer to release the horsemen who were the cause of the war, on condition that he would raise the siege. Papirius replied that they ought to have gone to Pontius, the son of Herennius, at whose instance they had sent the Romans under the yoke, to find out what the vanquished deserved to suffer; however, since they preferred that their enemies should decide on a just penalty for them, rather than propose one for themselves, he bade them take word to Luceria that they should leave their arms, packs, sumpter animals, and all the non-combatants, within the walls; the soldiers he in-

217

A.U.C.
435 6 militem se cum singulis vestimentis sub iugum
missurum, ulciscentem inlatam, non novam infe-
7 rentem ignominiam. Nihil recusatum. Septem
milia militum sub iugum missa, praedaque ingens
Luceriae capta receptis omnibus signis armisque
quae ad Caudium amissa erant, et quod omnia
superabat gaudia, equitibus reciperatis[1] quos pignora
pacis custodiendos Luceriam Samnites dederant.
8 Haud ferme alia mutatione subita rerum clarior
victoria populi Romani est, si quidem etiam, quod
quibusdam in annalibus invenio, Pontius Herenni
filius, Samnitium imperator, ut expiaret consulum
ignominiam, sub iugum cum ceteris est missus.

9 Ceterum id minus miror obscurum esse de hostium
duce dedito missoque; id magis mirabile est ambigi
Luciusne Cornelius dictator cum L. Papirio Cursore
10 magistro equitum eas res ad Caudium atque inde
Luceriam gesserit ultorque unicus Romanae ignominiae haud sciam an iustissimo triumpho ad eam
aetatem secundum Furium Camillum triumphaverit,
an consulum—Papirique praecipuum—id decus sit.
11 Sequitur hunc errorem alius error, Cursorne Papirius
proximis comitiis cum Q. Aulio Cerretano iterum ob
rem bene gestam Luceriae continuato magistratu

---

[1] reciperatis *Walters and Conway* (*passim*): recuperatis Ω

218

tended to send under the yoke, clad only in their B.C. 319
tunics, inflicting on them no new disgrace, but
requiting that which had first been put upon
the Romans. They made no objection, and seven
thousand men were sent under the yoke. Huge
spoils were captured in Luceria, and all the standards
and arms which had been lost at Caudium were
retaken, and, to cap the climax of their joy, the
horsemen were recovered whom the Samnites had
assigned, as pledges of peace, to be guarded at
Luceria. There is scarce any other Roman victory
more glorious for its sudden reversal of fortune,
especially if it is true, as I find in certain annals,
that Pontius the son of Herennius, the Samnite
general-in-chief, was sent with the rest under the
yoke, to expiate the humiliation of the consuls.

Be that as it may, I am not greatly surprised that
there should be some doubt as to the general of the
enemy who was surrendered and disgraced; the
amazing thing is the uncertainty whether it was
Lucius Cornelius, as dictator—with Lucius Papirius
Cursor, as master of the horse—who won these
victories at Caudium and subsequently at Luceria,
and, because of the signal vengeance that he exacted
for Rome's shame, enjoyed a triumph which I should
be inclined to rate as the best-deserved of all down
to that time, next after that of Furius Camillus; or
whether that honour belongs to the consuls—and
particularly to Papirius. This doubt is attended with
another—whether at the ensuing election Papirius
Cursor was retained in office in recognition of his
victory at Luceria, being returned for a third time
to the consulship, together with Quintus Aulius
Cerretanus— then chosen for the second time—or

LIVY

consul tertium creatus sit an L. Papirius Mugillanus [1]
et in cognomine erratum sit.

XVI. Convenit iam inde per consules reliqua belli
perfecta. Aulius cum Ferentanis [2] uno secundo
proelio debellavit urbemque ipsam, quo se fusa
contulerat acies, obsidibus imperatis in deditionem
2 accepit. Pari fortuna consul alter cum Satricanis,
qui cives Romani post Caudinam cladem ad Samnites
defecerant praesidiumque eorum in urbem acce-
3 perant, rem gessit. Nam cum ad moenia Satrici [3]
admotus esset exercitus legatisque missis ad pacem
cum precibus petendam triste responsum ab consule
redditum esset, nisi praesidio Samnitium interfecto
aut tradito ne ad se remearent, plus ea voce quam
4 armis inlatis terroris colonis iniectum. Itaque subinde exsequuntur quaerendo a consule legati quonam
se pacto paucos et infirmos crederet praesidio tam
valido et armato vim allaturos. Ab iisdem consilium
petere iussi, quibus auctoribus praesidium in urbem
accepissent, discedunt aegreque impetrato ut de ea
5 re consuli senatum responsaque ad se referri sineret
6 ad suos redeunt. Duae factiones senatum distine-
bant, una cuius principes erant defectionis a populo
Romano auctores, altera fidelium civium; certatum
ab utrisque tamen est ut ad reconciliandam pacem
7 consuli opera navaretur. Pars altera, cum praesidium

---

[1] Mugillanus *PFUO* : mugilanus *MTDLA*.
[2] Ferentanis *M²P²FUOT²* : frentanis *MTDLA* : frentranis
P : Forentanis *Gronovius.*
[3] Satrici *ς* : Satricae (*or* -ce) Ω.

---

[1] Their town has been conjecturally identified with
Horace's "low-lying Forentum," *Odes*, III. iv. 16.

whether it was Lucius Papirius Mugillanus, and the
mistake was a matter of the surname.

XVI. It is agreed that from this point onwards
the war was brought to a conclusion by the consuls.
Aulius finished in one successful battle the campaign
against the Ferentani,[1] and having exacted hostages,
received the surrender of the city itself, in which
their defeated army had taken refuge. With no less
good fortune the other consul overcame the Satricans,
who—though Roman citizens—had revolted, after
the Caudine misfortune, to the Samnites, of whom
they had admitted a garrison into their city. For
when the Roman army had drawn near the walls of
Satricum, the townspeople sent ambassadors to sue
humbly for peace ; but the consul returned them a
harsh answer: that unless they put to death the
Samnite garrison or delivered it up, they must come
back to him no more—a saying which struck more
terror into their hearts than the threatened assault.
And so the envoys persisted in demanding of the
consul how he supposed that they, being few and
weak, could force so strong and well-armed a garrison.
But he bade them seek advice from those same men
at whose instigation they had received the garrison
into their city ; and after they had with no small
difficulty persuaded him to suffer them to consult
their senate in the matter and report to him its
decision, they went back to their people. Two
factions kept the senate divided : one of these had
for leaders the men who had inspired the revolt from
Rome, the other was composed of loyal citizens ;
both, however, were equally anxious to accommodate
the consul, so that they might be granted peace. One
party, seeing that the Samnite garrison was intend-

Samnitium, quia nihil satis praeparati erat ad obsidionem tolerandam, excessurum proxima nocte
esset,[1] enuntiare consuli satis habuit, qua noctis
hora quaque porta et quam in viam egressurus hostis
8 foret; altera, quibus invitis descitum ad Samnites
erat, eadem nocte portam etiam consuli[2] aperuerunt
9 armatosque clam hoste[3] in urbem acceperunt. Ita
duplici proditione et praesidium Samnitium insessis
circa viam silvestribus locis necopinato oppressum
est, et ab urbe plena hostium clamor sublatus;
momentoque unius horae caesus Samnis, Satricanus
10 captus, et omnia in potestate consulis erant. Qui
quaestione habita quorum opera defectio esset facta,
quos sontes comperit virgis caesos securi percussit
praesidioque valido imposito arma Satricanis ademit.
11 Inde ad triumphum decessisse Romam Papirium
Cursorem scribunt, qui eo duce Luceriam receptam
12 Samnitesque sub iugum missos auctores sunt. Et
fuit vir haud dubie dignus omni bellica laude, non
animi solum vigore sed etiam corporis viribus
13 excellens. Praecipua pedum pernicitas inerat, quae
cognomen etiam dedit; victoremque[4] cursu omnium
aetatis suae fuisse ferunt,[5] seu crurum[6] vi seu exer-

---

[1] esset D^3A^3: esse $MTDLA$: *omitted* by $PFUO$.
[2] consuli ς: consulibus Ω.
[3] clam hoste *Gelenius*: clam nocte Ω: clam *Weissenborn*.
[4] victoremque M^3F^1 (*or* F^3) A^x (*over erasure*) Frag. Hav.[2]:
uictorisque Ω.
[5] ferunt *Madvig*: ferunt et Ω.
[6] crurum *Madvig*: uirium Ω.

ing to escape on the following night—for they had B.C. 319
made no preparations for enduring a siege—deemed
it sufficient to let the consul know at what hour and
by what gate the enemy meant to leave, and what
road he planned to take. The others, who had
opposed going over to the Samnites, that same night
also opened a gate to the consul, and without letting
the Samnites know, admitted his soldiers into the
city. In consequence of this double betrayal, the
Samnite garrison was surprised and overpowered by
an ambush laid in the woods about their road, while
a shout went up in the city, which was filled with
enemies. Thus, in one crowded hour, the Samnites
were slain and the Satricans captured, and all things
brought under the power of the consul; who conducted an investigation, and, having ascertained who
were responsible for the defection, had the guilty
parties scourged and beheaded; after which he
imposed a strong garrison upon the Satricans and
deprived them of their arms.

Papirius Cursor then departed for Rome to celebrate his triumph, as those writers state who name
him as the commander who recovered Luceria and
sent the Samnites under the yoke. No question, he
was a man deserving of all praise as a soldier,
excelling, as he did, not only in the vigour of his
spirit, but in physical strength. He possessed
remarkable fleetness of foot, which was even the
source of his surname.[1] It is said that he vanquished
all his mates at running, whether owing to the

---

[1] *Cursor* means "runner," but the name seems really to
have been an inheritance in the present case, for at chap.
xxxiv. § 20 we read of it as belonging to the grandfather of
our Papirius.

LIVY

citatione multa; cibi vinique eundem capacissimum;
14 nec cum ullo asperiorem, quia ipse invicti ad laborem
corporis esset, fuisse militiam pediti pariter equi-
15 tique; equites etiam aliquando ausos ab eo petere
ut sibi pro re bene gesta laxaret aliquid laboris;
16 quibus ille "Ne nihil remissum dicatis, remitto,"
inquit, "ne utique dorsum demulceatis, cum ex
equis descendetis." Et vis erat in eo viro imperii
17 ingens pariter in socios civesque. Praenestinus
praetor per timorem segnius ex subsidiis suos duxerat
in primam aciem; quem cum inambulans ante taber-
18 naculum vocari iussisset, lictorem expedire securem
iussit, ad quam vocem exanimi stante Praenestino:
"Agedum, lictor, excide radicem hanc" inquit "in-
commodam ambulantibus," perfusumque ultimi sup-
19 plicii metu multa dicta dimisit. Haud dubie illa
aetate, qua nulla virtutum feracior fuit, nemo unus
erat vir quo magis innixa res Romana staret. Quin
eum parem destinant animis magno Alexandro ducem,
si arma Asia perdomita in Europam vertisset.

XVII. Nihil minus quaesitum a principio huius
operis videri potest quam ut plus iusto ab rerum
ordine declinarem varietatibusque distinguendo opere
et legentibus velut deverticula amoena et requiem

strength of his legs or to much exercise; that he B.C. 319 had also the greatest capacity for food and wine; and that no general was harder on his men, whether horse or foot, for his own constitution could never be overcome by toil. It is related how his cavalrymen ventured once to ask him if in view of their good conduct he would not excuse them from some portion of their duties; to whom he answered, "That you may not say that I have excused you nothing, I excuse you from rubbing your horses' backs in any way when you dismount." And the man possessed a power of command which was equally effective with citizens and allies. A Praenestine praetor had, through timidity, been somewhat slow in bringing his men up from the supports to the fighting line. Papirius strolled over to the praetor's tent and having bidden them call him out, commanded a lictor to prepare his axe. Hearing this the praetor stood aghast, but Papirius said to the lictor, "Come, cut out this root; it is a nuisance to those who walk." He then fined the man and let him go, half-dead with the fear of capital punishment. There can be no doubt that in his generation, than which none was ever more fruitful of great qualities, there was no single man who did more to uphold the Roman State. Indeed people regard him as one who might have been a match in generalship for Alexander the Great, if the latter, after subjugating Asia, had turned his arms against Europe.

XVII. Nothing can be thought to have been more remote from my intention, since I first set about this task, than to depart unduly from the order of events, and to aim, by the introduction of ornamental digressions, at providing as it were agreeable by-

LIVY

2 animo meo quaererem ; tamen tanti regis ac ducis
mentio, quibus saepe tacitus [1] cogitationibus volutavi [2]
animum, eas evocat in medium, ut quaerere libeat
quinam eventus Romanis rebus, si cum Alexandro
foret bellatum, futurus fuerit.

3   Plurimum in bello pollere videntur militum copia
et virtus, ingenia imperatorum, fortuna per omnia
4 humana, maxime in res bellicas potens : ea et singula
intuenti et universa, sicut ab aliis regibus genti-
busque ita ab hoc quoque, facile praestant invictum
5 Romanum imperium. Iam primum, ut ordiar ab
ducibus comparandis, haud equidem abnuo egregium
ducem fuisse Alexandrum ; sed clariorem tamen eum
facit quod unus fuit, quod adulescens in incremento
rerum, nondum alteram fortunam expertus, decessit.
6 Ut alios reges claros ducesque omittam, magna
exempla casuum humanorum, Cyrum, quem maxime
Graeci laudibus celebrant, quid nisi longa vita, sicut
Magnum modo Pompeium, vertenti praebuit fortunae ?
7 Recenseam duces Romanos, nec omnes omnium
aetatium, sed ipsos eos cum quibus consulibus aut
8 dictatoribus Alexandro fuit bellandum, M. Valerium
Corvum C. Marcium Rutulum [3] C. Sulpicium T.
Manlium Torquatum Q. Publilium Philonem L.
Papirium Cursorem Q. Fabium Maximum duos Decios

---

[1] tacitus *PF* : tacitis Ω.
[2] volutavi ς : uolutauit Ω.
[3] Rutulum *Conway* (*cf. his note on* III.·vii. 6) : Rutilium Ω.

---

[1] Professor Anderson argues that the following digression
(chap. xvii. § 3 through chap. xix) was a youthful exercise
in rhetoric written when Livy was a boy and later inserted
here without revision, but with the addition of an intro-
ductory section (§§ 1, 2). See his edition, *App.* III, and

paths for the reader, and mental relaxation for B.C. 319
myself. Nevertheless the mention of so great a
prince and captain evokes certain thoughts which
I have often silently pondered in my mind, and dis-
poses me to enquire how the Roman State would
have fared in a war with Alexander.[1]

It appears that in war the factors of chief importance are the numbers and valour of the soldiers,
the abilities of the commanders, and Fortune, which,
powerful in all the affairs of men, is especially so in
war. These factors, whether viewed separately or
conjointly, afford a ready assurance, that, even as
against other princes and nations, so also against this
one the might of Rome would have proved invincible.
First of all—to begin by comparing commanders—I
do not deny that Alexander was a remarkable general ;
still, his fame was enhanced by the fact that he was
a sole commander, and the further fact that he died
young, in the flood-tide of success, when as yet he
had experienced no other lot. Not to speak of other
distinguished kings and generals, illustrious proofs
of human vicissitude, what else was it but length of
days that exposed Cyrus, whom the Greeks exalt so
high in their panegyrics, to the fickleness of Fortune ?
And the same thing was lately seen in the case of
Pompey the Great. Need I repeat the names of the
Roman generals, not all nor of every age, but those
very ones with whom, as consuls or as dictators,
Alexander would have had to fight—Marcus Valerius
Corvus, Gaius Marcius Rutulus, Gaius Sulpicius,
Titus Manlius Torquatus, Quintus Publilius Philo,
Lucius Papirius Cursor, Quintus Fabius Maximus,

Transactions of the American Philological Association, XXXIX.
(1908), pp. 94–99.

LIVY

A.U.C.
435 9 L. Volumnium M'. Curium?[1] Deinceps ingentes
sequuntur viri, si Punicum Romano praevertisset
10 bellum seniorque in Italiam traiecisset. Horum in
quolibet cum indoles eadem quae in Alexandro erat
animi ingeniique; tum disciplina militaris, iam inde
ab initiis urbis tradita per manus, in artis[2] perpetuis
11 praeceptis ordinatae modum venerat. Ita reges
gesserant bella, ita deinde exactores regum Iunii
Valeriique, ita deinceps Fabii Quinctii Cornelii, ita
Furius Camillus, quem iuvenes ii quibus cum Alex-
12 andro dimicandum erat senem viderant. Militaria
opera pugnando obeunti Alexandro—nam ea quoque
haud minus clarum eum faciunt—cessisset videlicet
in acie oblatus par Manlius Torquatus aut Valerius
13 Corvus, insignes ante milites quam duces, cessissent
Decii, devotis corporibus in hostem ruentes, cessisset
Papirius Cursor illo corporis robore, illo animi!
14 Victus esset consiliis iuvenis unius, ne singulos
nominem, senatus ille, quem qui ex regibus constare
dixit unus veram speciem Romani senatus cepit!
15 Id vero erat periculum, ne sollertius quam quilibet
unus ex his quos nominavi castris locum caperet,
commeatus expediret, ab insidiis praecaveret, tempus

---

[1] M'. Curium? *Sigonius* (*C.I.L.* i², p. 46): marcum (*or* m̄)
Ω (*C.I.L.* i², pp. 135, 171): marcium O.
[2] artis *A*⁶ ϛ: artes Ω.

---

[1] Cineas, the ambassador of King Pyrrhus. *Cf.* Plut.
Pyrrhus, xix.

228

the two Decii, Lucius Volumnius, Manius Curius?
After these come some extraordinary men, if he
had turned his attention to war with Carthage
first and later with Rome, and had crossed into
Italy when somewhat old. Any one of these was
as highly endowed with courage and talents as
was Alexander; and military training, handed down
from the very beginning of the City, had taken
on the character of a profession, built up on com-
prehensive principles. So the kings had warred;
so after them the expellers of the kings, the Junii
and the Valerii, and so in succession the Fabii,
Quinctii, Cornelii, and Furius Camillus, whom in
his old age those had seen, as youths, who would
have had to fight with Alexander. But in the per-
formance of a soldier's work in battle—for which
Alexander was no less distinguished—Manlius Torquatus or Valerius Corvus would, forsooth, have
yielded to him, had they met him in a hand-to-hand
encounter, famous though they were as soldiers
before ever they won renown as captains! The
Decii, of course, would have yielded to him, who
hurled their devoted bodies upon the foe! Papirius
Cursor would have yielded, with that wondrous
strength of body and of spirit! The counsels of a
single youth would no doubt have got the better of
that senate—not to speak of individual members—
which was called an assembly of kings by him who
before all others had a true conception of the Roman
Senate! [1] And I suppose there was the danger that
Alexander would display more skill than any of
these whom I have named, in selecting a place for a
camp, in organizing his service of supply, in guarding
against ambuscades, in choosing a time for battle, in

LIVY

pugnae deligeret, aciem instrueret, subsidiis firmaret!
16 Non cum Dareo[1] rem esse dixisset, quem mulierum
ac spadonum agmen trahentem, inter purpuram atque
aurum oneratum fortunae apparatibus suae, praedam
verius quam hostem, nihil aliud quam bene ausus
17 vana contemnere incruentus devicit. Longe alius
Italiae quam Indiae, per quam temulento agmine
comisabundus incessit, visus illi habitus esset, saltus
Apuliae ac montes Lucanos cernenti et vestigia
recentia domesticae cladis ubi avunculus eius nuper,
Epiri rex Alexander, absumptus erat.

XVIII. Et loquimur de Alexandro nondum merso
secundis rebus, quarum nemo intolerantior fuit.
2 Qui si ex habitu novae fortunae novique, ut ita
3 dicam, ingenii quod sibi victor induerat spectetur,
Dareo magis similis quam Alexandro in Italiam
venisset et exercitum Macedoniae oblitum degene-
4 rantemque iam in Persarum mores adduxisset.
Referre in tanto rege piget superbam mutationem
vestis et desideratas humi iacentium adulationes,
etiam victis Macedonibus graves, nedum victoribus,
et foeda supplicia et inter vinum et epulas caedes
5 amicorum et vanitatem ementiendae stirpis. Quid

---

[1] Dareo *MPTDL* (*and chap.* xviii. § 3 *MPOT*): dario (darici
O) *P²FUA* (*and below* *P²FUDLA*).

---

[1] Darius III, defeated by Alexander in the battle of
Arbela, 331 B.C.

[2] VIII. xxiv.

[3] Philotas was examined under torture and confessed
participation in a plot against Alexander's life. He im-
plicated also his father Parmenio, the general, and both
were executed. Clitus, who had saved Alexander's life at
the Granicus, was killed by him at a banquet in a fit of

marshalling his troops, in providing strong reserves! B.C. 319 He would have said it was no Darius[1] whom he had to deal with, trailing women and eunuchs after him, and weighed down with the gold and purple trappings of his station. Him he found a booty rather than an enemy, and conquered without bloodshed, merely by daring to despise vain shows. Far different from India, through which he progressed at the head of a rout of drunken revellers, would Italy have appeared to him, as he gazed on the passes of Apulia and the Lucanian mountains, and the still fresh traces of that family disaster wherein his uncle, King Alexander of Epirus, had lost his life.[2]

XVIII. And we are speaking of an Alexander not yet overwhelmed with prosperity, which none has ever been less able to bear. For viewing him in the light of his new fortune and of the new character—if I may use the expression—which he had assumed as conqueror, he would evidently have come to Italy more like Darius than like Alexander, at the head of an army that had forgotten Macedonia and was already adopting the degenerate customs of the Persians. I am loath, in writing of so great a prince, to remind the reader of the ostentatious alteration in his dress, and of his desire that men should prostrate themselves in adulation, a thing which even conquered Macedonians would have found oppressive, much more then those who had been victorious; of his cruel punishments and the murder of his friends as they drank and feasted; of the boastful lie about his origin.[3] What if his love of wine had

---

drunken rage. The last clause alludes to Alexander's claim that Zeus, not Philip, was his father.

LIVY

si vini amor in dies fieret acrior? Quid si trux ac
praefervida ira?—Nec quicquam dubium inter scriptores refero—, nullane haec damna imperatoriis
6 virtutibus ducimus? Id vero periculum erat, quod
levissimi ex Graecis, qui Parthorum quoque contra
nomen Romanum gloriae favent, dictitare solent,
ne maiestatem nominis Alexandri, quem ne fama
7 quidem illis notum arbitror fuisse, sustinere non
potuerit populus Romanus; et adversus quem
Athenis, in civitate fracta Macedonum armis,
cernentes[1] tum maxime prope fumantes Thebarum
ruinas, contionari libere ausi sunt homines—id
quod ex monumentis orationum patet—adversus
eum nemo ex tot proceribus Romanis vocem liberam
missurus fuerit!

8   Quantalibet magnitudo hominis concipiatur animo;
unius tamen ea magnitudo hominis erit collecta
9 paulo plus decem annorum felicitate; quam qui eo
extollunt quod populus Romanus etsi nullo bello
multis tamen proeliis victus sit, Alexandro nullius
pugnae non secunda fortuna fuerit, non intellegunt
se hominis res gestas, et eius iuvenis, cum populi
iam quadringentesimum[2] bellantis annum rebus
10 conferre. Miremur si, cum ex hac parte saecula
plura numerentur quam ex illa anni, plus in tam

---

[1] cernentes *UD*ˣ (*Madvig*): cernente Ω.
[2] quadringentesimum (*i.e.* CCCC) *Tan. Faber*: octingente
simum (*i.e.* DCCC) Ω.

---

[1] This is supposed to refer to Timagenes, an historian o
a notoriously anti-Roman bias.

every day grown stronger? and his truculent and B.O. 319
fiery anger? I mention only things which historians
regard as certain. Can we deem such vices to be
no detraction from a general's good qualities? But
there was forsooth the danger—as the silliest of the
Greeks,[1] who exalt the reputation even of the
Parthians against the Romans, are fond of alleging—
that the Roman People would have been unable to
withstand the majesty of Alexander's name, though
I think that they had not so much as heard of him;
and that out of all the Roman nobles not one would
have dared to lift up his voice against him, although
in Athens, a city crushed by the arms of Macedonia,
at the very moment when men had before their
eyes the reeking ruins of the neighbouring Thebes,
they dared inveigh against him freely, as witness
the records of their speeches.[2]

However imposing the greatness of the man may
appear to us, still this greatness will be that of one
man only, and the fruits of little more than ten
years of success. Those who magnify it for this
reason, that the Roman People, albeit never in any
war, have yet suffered defeat in a number of battles,
whereas Alexander's fortune was never aught but
prosperous in any battle, fail to perceive that they
are comparing the achievements of a man—and a
young man too—with those of a people that was
now in its four hundredth year of warfare. Should
it occasion us surprise if, seeing that upon the one
side are counted more generations than are years

---

[2] An allusion, more rhetorical than exact, to the famous
Philippics of Demosthenes, the latest of which was probably
delivered some six years before the destruction of Thebes in
335 B.C.

longo spatio quam in aetate tredecim annorum
11 fortuna variaverit? Quin tu hominis cum homine
12 et ducis cum duce fortunam confers?[1] Quot Romanos duces nominem quibus nunquam adversa
fortuna pugnae fuit! Paginas in annalibus magistratuumque fastis[2] percurrere licet consulum dic-
tatorumque quorum nec virtutis nec fortunae ullo
13 die populum Romanum paenituit. Et quo sint
mirabiliores quam Alexander aut quisquam rex,
denos vicenosque dies quidam dictaturam, nemo
14 plus quam annum consulatum gessit; ab tribunis
plebis dilectus impediti sunt; post tempus ad bella
ierunt, ante tempus comitiorum causa revocati sunt;
15 in ipso conatu rerum circumegit se annus; collegae
nunc temeritas nunc pravitas impedimento aut damno
fuit; male gestis rebus alterius successum est; tironem
aut mala disciplina institutum exercitum acceperunt.
16 At hercule reges non liberi solum impedimentis
omnibus sed domini rerum temporumque trahunt
17 consiliis cuncta, non sequuntur. Invictus ergo
Alexander cum invictis ducibus bella gessisset et
eadem fortunae pignora in discrimen detulisset;
18 immo etiam eo plus periculi subisset quod Macedones
unum Alexandrum habuissent, multis casibus non

---

[1] hominis cum homine et ducis cum duce fortunam confers?
Madvig: hominis cum homine et ducis (duces *F*) cum fortunam cum fortuna (cum fortuna fortunam *T*) confers Ω:
homines cum homine, [et] duces cum duce, fortunam cum
fortuna confers *Walters and Conway*.

[2] magistratuumque fastis *Walters and Conway*: magistratuum fastisque Ω.

---

[1] If we reckon the *saeculum* or "generation" at thirty
three years, the Rome of Alexander's time would have

upon the other,[1] fortune should have varied more B.C. 319 in that long time than in a life of thirteen years? Why not compare a man's fortune with a man's, and a general's with a general's? How many Roman generals could I name who never suffered a reverse in battle! In our annals and lists of magistrates you may run through pages of consuls and dictators of whom it never on any day repented the Roman People, whether of their generalship or fortune. And what makes them more wonderful than Alexander or any king is this: some were dictators of ten or twenty days, and none held the consulship above a year; their levies were obstructed by the tribunes of the plebs; they were late in going to war, and were called back early to conduct elections; in the midst of their undertakings the year rolled round; now the rashness, now the frowardness of a colleague occasioned them losses or difficulties; they succeeded to affairs which others had mismanaged, they received an army of raw recruits, or one badly disciplined. Now consider kings: not only are they free from all impediments, but they are lords of time and circumstance, and in their counsels carry all things with them, instead of following in their train. So then, an undefeated Alexander would have warred against undefeated generals, and would have brought the same pledges of Fortune to the crisis. Nay, he would have run a greater risk than they, inasmuch as the Macedonians would have had but a single Alexander, not only exposed to many dangers, but

endured a little over thirteen *saecula*. Livy says that people are really comparing these thirteen generations with the thirteen years of Alexander's (effective) life, *i.e.* his reign (336–323 B.C.).

235

19 solum obnoxium sed etiam offerentem se, Romani multi fuissent Alexandro vel gloria vel rerum magnitudine pares, quorum suo quisque fato sine publico discrimine viveret morereturque.

XIX. Restat ut copiae copiis comparentur vel numero vel militum genere vel multitudine auxiliorum. Censebantur eius aetatis lustris ducena 2 quinquagena milia capitum. Itaque in omni defectione sociorum Latini nominis urbano prope dilectu 3 decem scribebantur legiones; quaterni quinique exercitus saepe per eos annos in Etruria, in Umbria Gallis hostibus adiunctis, in Samnio, in Lucanis 4 gerebant bellum. Latium deinde omne cum Sabinis et Volscis et Aequis et omni Campania et parte umbriae Etruriaeque et Picentibus et Marsis Paelignisque ac Vestinis atque Apulis, adiuncta omni ora [1] Graecorum inferi maris a Thuriis [2] Neapolim et Cumas et inde Antio atque Ostiis tenus aut [3] socios validos Romanis aut fractos bello invenisset hostes. 5 Ipse traiecisset mare cum veteranis Macedonibus, non plus triginta milibus hominum et quattuor milibus equitum, maxime Thessalorum; hoc enim roboris erat. Persas Indos aliasque si adiunxisset gentes, impedimentum maius quam auxilium traheret.

[1] omni ora $O^1 A^x$ (or A^1) *Aldus*: omnis ora Ω.
[2] a Thuriis ς: a Thuris (or athuris) Ω: authuris F: a brutiis *Gronovius*.
[3] aut *Dobree*: Samnites aut Ω.

---

[1] In the last census which Livy had recorded (459 B.C.) were enrolled 117,321 persons (III. xxiv. 10). Livy seems to have consulted the records of the censors, at least occasionally.
[2] Or possibly: at every revolt of the Latin allies.

incurring them voluntarily, while there would have B.C. 319
been many Romans a match for Alexander, whether
for glory or for the greatness of their deeds, of
whom each several one would have lived and died
as his own fate commanded, without endangering
the State.

XIX. It remains to compare the forces on both
sides, whether for numbers, or types of soldiers, or
size of their contingents of auxiliaries. The quin-
quennial enumerations of that period put the population at 250,000.[1] And so at the time when all the
Latin allies were in revolt[2] it was the custom to
enroll ten legions, by a levy which was virtually
limited to the City. In those years frequently four
and five armies at a time would take the field, in
Etruria, in Umbria (where they also fought the
Gauls), in Samnium, and in Lucania. Later on
Alexander would have found all Latium, with the
Sabines, the Volsci and the Aequi, all Campania,
and a portion of Umbria and Etruria, the Picentes
and the Marsi and Paeligni, the Vestini and the
Apulians, together with the whole coast of the
Lower Sea, held by the Greeks, from Thurii as
far as Naples and Cumae, and thence all the way
to Antium and Ostia—all these, I say, he would
have found either powerful friends of the Romans
or their defeated enemies. He himself would have
crossed the sea with veteran Macedonians to the
number of not more than thirty thousand foot and
four thousand horse—mostly Thessalians—for this
was his main strength. If to these he had added
Persians and Indians and other nations, he would
have found them a greater burden to have dragged
about than a help.

LIVY

6 Adde, quod Romanis ad manum domi supplementum esset, Alexandro, quod postea Hannibali accidit, alieno in agro bellanti exercitus consenu-
7 isset. Arma clipei essent illis sarisaeque [1]: Romano scutum, maius corpori tegumentum, et pilum, haud paulo quam hasta vehementius ictu missuque [2] telum.
8 Statarius uterque miles, ordines servans; sed illa phalanx immobilis et unius generis, Romana acies distinctior, ex pluribus partibus constans, facilis partienti, quacumque opus esset, facilis iungenti.
9 Iam in opere quis par Romano miles, quis ad tolerandum laborem melior? Uno proelio victus Alexander bello victus esset: Romanum, quem Caudium, quem Cannae non fregerunt, quae fregisset acies?
10 Ne ille saepe, etiam si prima prospere evenissent, Persas et Indos et imbellem Asiam quaesisset et
11 cum feminis sibi bellum fuisse dixisset, quod Epiri regem Alexandrum mortifero volnere ictum dixisse ferunt, sortem bellorum in Asia gestorum ab hoc ipso iuvene cum sua conferentem.
12 Equidem cum per annos quattuor et viginti primo Punico bello classibus certatum cum Poenis recordor,

[1] Arma clipei essent illis sarisaeque *Madvig*: arma cluisset arma cluisset sarisaeque illis id est hastae *M*: arma cluisset sarisaeque *etc.* M[1] *or* M̄[2]: arma clipeus (*or* clupeus) sarisaeque (*or* -eque) illis (*or* illis portare *or* illis. at *or* illis id est hastae) Ω.

[2] ictu missuque ς: ictu missumque *PTA*[2]: ictum missumque Ω.

[1] The *sarisa* was a pike 21 feet long.
[2] The *hasta* was ordinarily used as a pike or lance, but was sometimes thrown, by means of a thong.
[3] Aulus Gellius, XVII. xxi. 33, says that Alexander, as he

238

Add to this, that the Romans would have had recruits B.C. 319
ready to call upon, but Alexander, as happened afterwards to Hannibal, would have found his army wear
away, while he warred in a foreign land. His men
would have been armed with targets and spears: [1]
the Romans with an oblong shield, affording more
protection to the body, and the Roman javelin,
which strikes, on being thrown, with a much harder
impact than the lance.[2] Both armies were formed
of heavy troops, keeping to their ranks; but their
phalanx was immobile and consisted of soldiers of a
single type; the Roman line was opener and comprised more separate units; it was easy to divide,
wherever necessary, and easy to unite. Moreover,
what soldier can match the Roman in entrenching?
Who is better at enduring toil? Alexander would,
if beaten in a single battle, have been beaten in the
war; but what battle could have overthrown the
Romans, whom Caudium could not overthrow, nor
Cannae? Nay, many a time—however prosperous
the outset of his enterprise might have been—would
he have wished for Persians and Indians and unwarlike Asiatics, and would have owned that he had
before made war upon women, as Alexander, King
of Epirus, is reported to have said, when mortally
wounded, contrasting the type of war waged by this
very youth in Asia, with that which had fallen to
his own share.[3]
Indeed when I remember that we contended
against the Carthaginians on the seas for four-and-

was setting sail for Italy, remarked that he was going to the
Romans, as it were to the men's quarters (*andronitin*);
whereas the Macedonian had gone to the Persians, as to the
quarters of the women (*gynaeconitin*).

LIVY

vix aetatem Alexandri suffecturam fuisse reor ad
13 unum bellum; et forsitan, cum et foederibus vetustis
iuncta res Punica Romanae esset et timor par
adversus communem hostem duas potentissimas
armis virisque urbes armaret, simul[1] Punico Roma-
14 noque obrutus bello esset. Non quidem Alexandro
duce nec integris Macedonum rebus sed experti
tamen sunt Romani Macedonem hostem adversus
Antiochum Philippum Persen non modo cum clade
15 ulla sed ne cum periculo quidem suo. Absit invidia
verbo et civilia bella sileant : nunquam[2] a pedite,
nunquam aperta acie, nunquam aequis, utique
16 nunquam nostris locis laboravimus; equitem sagittas,
saltus impeditos, avia commeatibus loca gravis armis
17 miles timere potest. Mille acies graviores quam
Macedonum atque Alexandri avertit avertetque,
modo sit perpetuus huius qua vivimus pacis amor
et civilis cura concordiae.—

XX. M. Folius[3] Flaccina inde et L. Plautius
2 Venox consules facti. Eo anno ab frequentibus
Samnitium populis de foedere renovando legati cum
senatum humi strati movissent, reiecti ad populum
3 haudquaquam tam efficaces habebant preces. Itaque
de foedere negatum; indutiae biennii, cum per
aliquot dies fatigassent singulos precibus, impetratae.

---

[1] simul ς: et simul Ω.
[2] nunquam *Dobree and Madvig*: nunquam ab equite hoste
nunquam Ω.
[3] Folius ς: follius (*or* ollius) Ω: Foslius *Sigonius* (*C.I.L.*
i², *p.* 130).

---

[1] The earliest treaty was said to have been made in
509 B.C. (Livy does not mention it, but Polybius does, at
III. xxii.); and another in 348. See VII. xxvii. 2, and
note.

twenty years, I think that the whole life of Alexander would hardly have sufficed for this single
war; and perchance, inasmuch as the Punic State
had been by ancient treaties leagued with the
Roman,[1] and the two cities most powerful in men
and arms might well have made common cause
against the foe whom both dreaded, he had been
crushed beneath the simultaneous attacks of Rome
and Carthage. The Romans have been at war with
the Macedonians—not, to be sure, when Alexander
led them or their prosperity was unimpaired, but
against Antiochus, Philippus, and Perses—and not
only without ever suffering defeat, but even without
incurring any danger. Proud word I would not
speak, but never—and may civil wars be silent!—
never have we been beaten by infantry, never in
open battle, never on even, or at all events on
favourable ground : cavalry and arrows, impassable
defiles, regions that afford no road to convoys, may
well occasion fear in heavy-armed troops. A thousand battle-arrays more formidable than those of
Alexander and the Macedonians have the Romans
beaten off—and shall do—if only our present love
of domestic peace endure and our concern to maintain concord.

XX. Marcus Folius Flaccina and Lucius Plautius
Venox were the next consuls. In that year came
ambassadors from many Samnite states to seek a
renewal of the treaty. Prostrating themselves before the senate, they aroused the pity of that order,
but on being referred to the people found their
prayers by no means so efficacious. Accordingly
they were refused the treaty, but after some days
spent in importuning individual citizens, they suc-

LIVY

4 Et ex Apulia Teanenses Canusinique populationibus
fessi obsidibus L. Plautio consuli datis in deditionem
5 venerunt. Eodem anno primum praefecti Capuam
creari coepti legibus ab L. Furio praetore datis, cum
utrumque ipsi pro remedio aegris rebus discordia
6 intestina petissent; et duae Romae additae tribus,
Ufentina ac Falerna.

7 Inclinatis semel in Apulia rebus Teates quoque
Apuli ad novos consules, C. Iunium Bubulcum Q.
Aemilium Barbulam, foedus petitum venerunt, pacis
per omnem Apuliam praestandae populo Romano
8 auctores. Id audacter spondendo impetravere, ut
foedus daretur neque ut aequo tamen foedere sed ut
9 in dicione populi Romani essent. Apulia perdomita
—nam Forento [1] quoque, valido oppido, Iunius potitus
erat—in Lucanos perrectum; inde repentino adventu
10 Aemili consulis Nerulum vi captum. Et postquam
res Capuae stabilitas Romana disciplina fama per
socios volgavit, Antiatibus quoque, qui se sine legibus
certis, sine magistratibus agere querebantur, dati ab
senatu ad iura statuenda ipsius coloniae patroni; nec
arma modo sed iura etiam Romana late pollebant.

XXI. C. Iunius Bubulcus et Q. Aemilius Barbula

---

[1] nam Forento *Gronovius* Iam Iorento *M*: nam florento
PFOT[2] (*marg.*): nam florente *U*: nam Torento *TDLA*: iam
torento (*al.* laurento) *A*[2].

---

[1] Making the number now thirty-one.
[2] *Teate* was in reality only another name for *Teanum*.
Livy has been drawing upon two authorities, and their use
of different names for the same people has led him to make
two episodes out of one.
[3] Prominent Romans were often invited to act in a semi-
official relation of protectorship to Italian or even to foreign
towns.

B.C.
318–317

ceeded in obtaining a two years' truce. In Apulia,
likewise, the Teanenses and Canusini, exhausted by
the devastation of their lands, gave hostages to
Lucius Plautius the consul and made submission.
In the same year praefects began to be elected and
sent out to Capua, after Lucius Furius, the praetor,
had given them laws—both steps being taken at
the instance of the Capuans themselves, as a remedy
for the distress occasioned by internal discord. At
Rome two tribes were added, the Ufentina and the
Falerna.[1]

When affairs had once taken a turn in Apulia, the
Apulian Teates[2] also came to the new consuls, Gaius
Junius Bubulcus and Quintus Aemilius Barbula, to
sue for a treaty, engaging to insure the Roman
People peace throughout Apulia. By this bold
pledge they prevailed so far as to obtain a treaty—
not, however, on equal terms, but such as made
them subject to the Romans. After Apulia had
been thoroughly subdued—for Forentum, a strong
town, had also fallen into the hands of Junius—the
campaign was extended to the Lucanians, from
whom, on the sudden arrival of Aemilius the
consul, Nerulum was taken by assault. And once
t had been noised abroad amongst the allies how
the affairs of Capua were firmly established by Roman
discipline, the Antiates, too, complained that they
were living without fixed statutes and without magis-
rates, and the senate designated the colony's own
patrons to draw up laws for it.[3] Not Roman arms
alone but also Roman law began to exert a wide-
pread influence.

XXI. The consuls Gaius Junius Bubulcus and
Quintus Aemilius Barbula gave over their legions, at

B.C. 316

LIVY

consules exitu anni non consulibus ab se creatis, Sp.
Nautio et M. Popilio, ceterum dictatori L. Aemilio
2 legiones tradiderant. Is cum L. Fulvio magistro
equitum Saticulam[1] oppugnare adortus rebellandi
3 causam Samnitibus dedit. Duplex inde terror inlatus
Romanis: hinc Samnis magno exercitu coacto ad exi-
mendos obsidione socios haud procul castris Romanorum castra posuit; hinc Saticulani magno cum
tumultu patefactis repente portis in stationes hostium
4 incurrerunt. Inde pars utraque, spe alieni magis
auxilii quam viribus freta suis, iusto mox proelio inito
Romanos urgent, et quamquam anceps dimicatio
erat, tamen utrimque tutam aciem dictator habuit,
quia et locum haud facilem ad circumveniendum
5 cepit et diversa statuit signa. Infestior tamen in
erumpentes incessit nec magno certamine intra
moenia compulit, tum totam aciem in Samnites
6 obvertit. Ibi plus certaminis fuit; victoria sicut
sera ita nec dubia nec varia fuit. Fusi in castra
Samnites exstinctis nocte ignibus tacito agmine
abeunt et spe abiecta Saticulae tuendae Plisticam[2]
ipsi, socios Romanorum, ut parem dolorem hosti
redderent, circumsidunt.

XXII. Anno circumacto bellum deinceps ab dicta-

---

[1] Saticulam (*and in* § 3 Saticulani *and in* § 6 Saticulae)
Sigonius (Diod. xix. lxxii. 4): Satriculam (*and* Satriculan
and Satriculae *below*) Ω.

[2] Plisticam Sigonius (Diod. xix. lxxii. 3): plistiam $M^3D^4A^2$
plistiam postiam F: post iam philistiam O: postiam Ω.

---

[1] Saticula was probably on the border between Campani
and Samnium, and possibly occupied the same site as th
modern S. Agata dei Goti.

the conclusion of the year, not to Spurius Nautius B.C. 316 and Marcus Popilius, the consuls at whose election they had presided, but to a dictator—Lucius Aemilius. The latter, with Lucius Fulvius, his master of the horse, laid siege to Saticula,[1] and by so doing afforded the Samnites a pretext for renewing the war. The Romans were thus threatened in two quarters: on the one side the Samnites, with a large army which they had mustered to relieve their besieged allies, were encamped at no great distance from the Roman camp; on the other side the Saticulani suddenly threw their gates wide open and charged pell-mell against the outposts of the Romans. Both hostile armies—each relying rather on the other's help than on any strength of its own—then pressed home their attack, in what soon developed into a general engagement. But the dictator, despite the twofold struggle, was protected on both fronts, since he had chosen a position that was difficult to turn, and made his maniples face opposite ways. However, he attacked the sallying party with the greater fury, and, encountering no very sharp resistance, drove them back into the town. He then directed his entire line against the Samnites. There was more resistance here, but though the victory was slow in coming yet it was neither dubious nor partial. The Samnites fled in disorder to their camp, and in the night, putting out their fires, they silently stole away, and relinquishing all hope of saving Saticula, themselves laid siege to Plistica, an ally of Rome, that they might pay the enemy out in their own coin.

XXII. When the year had come round, the con- B.C. 315 duct of the war passed without a break into the

A.U.C.
439

tore Q. Fabio gestum est; consules novi, sicut superiores, Romae manserunt; Fabius ad accipiendum
ab Aemilio exercitum ad Saticulam cum supplemento
2 venit. Neque enim Samnites ad Plisticam [1] manse-
rant sed accitis ab domo novis militibus multitudine
freti castra eodem quo antea loco posuerunt lacessen-
tesque proelio Romanos avertere ab obsidione co-
3 nabantur. Eo intentius dictator in moenia hostium
versus id bellum tantum [2] ducere quod urbem
oppugnabat, securior ab Samnitibus agere stationibus
4 modo oppositis ne qua in castra vis fieret. Eo ferocius
adequitare Samnites vallo neque otium pati. Et
cum iam prope in portis castrorum esset hostis,
nihil consulto dictatore magister equitum Q. Aulius
Cerretanus magno tumultu cum omnibus turmis
5 equitum evectus summovit hostem. Tum in [3] minime pertinaci genere pugnae sic fortuna exercuit
opes ut insignes [4] utrimque clades et clara ipsorum
6 ducum ederet funera. Prior Samnitium imperator,
aegre patiens quo [5] tam ferociter adequitasset inde
se fundi fugarique, orando hortandoque equites
7 proelium iteravit; in quem insignem inter suos
cientem pugnam magister equitum Romanus infesta
cuspide ita permisit equum ut uno ictu exanimem

---

[1] plisticam *edd.* (*with* Ω *in* § 11): plistiam Ω.
[2] tantum (= tantummodo) *Gronovius*: tantum nitebatur
ς: tanti Ω.
[3] tum in ς: cum in Ω: cumq. *T.*
[4] insignes ς: insignis Ω.
[5] quo ς: quod Ω.

---

[1] The men whose names are by so strange an oversight
omitted here were L. Papirius Cursor and Q. Publilius Philo,
each of whom had thrice held the office.

hands of the dictator Quintus Fabius. The new
consuls,[1] as their predecessors had done, remained
in Rome ; Fabius took new forces to replace the old,
and proceeded to Saticula, to receive the army from
Aemilius. For the Samnites had not continued before Plistica, but, summoning fresh troops from home
and confiding in their numbers, had pitched their
camp on the same spot as before, and were trying to
provoke the Romans into giving battle, in the
endeavour to divert them from the siege. This
but intensified the dictator's concentration on the
enemy's walls, for he deemed the war to consist
solely in the attack upon the city, and treated the
Samnites with much indifference, save only that he
posted out-guards to prevent their making any inroad
upon his camp. But this only made the Samnites
the more audacious, and riding again and again up
to the rampart, they gave no respite to the Romans.
And now the enemy were almost in the gateway of
the camp, when Quintus Aulius Cerretanus, the
master of the horse, without consulting the dictator,
sallied out with all his squadrons in a furious charge
and drove them off. At this juncture—though in a
type of battle by no means marked by obstinacy—
Fortune so used her powers as to bring extraordinary
losses on both sides, and on the commanders themselves distinguished deaths. The Samnite general
first, indignant at being routed and put to flight from
a position he had so boldly occupied, prevailed with
his troopers by entreaties and encouragement to
renew the conflict ; against whom, conspicuous
amongst his followers as he urged them into battle,
the Roman master of the horse rode such a tilt with
levelled lance as at one lunge unhorsed and killed

equo praecipitaret. Nec, ut fit, ad ducis casum
8 perculsa magis quam inritata est multitudo; omnes
qui circa erant in Aulium temere invectum per
9 hostium turmas tela coniecerunt; fratri praecipuum
decus ulti Samnitium imperatoris di dederunt.[1] Is
victorem detractum ex equo magistrum equitum
plenus maeroris atque irae trucidavit, nec multum
afuit quin corpore etiam, quia inter hostilis cecide-
10 rat turmas, Samnites potirentur. Sed extemplo ad
pedes descensum ab Romanis est coactique idem
Samnites facere; et repentina acies circa corpora
ducum pedestre proelium iniit, quo haud dubie
superat Romanus, reciperatumque Auli corpus mixta
11 cum dolore laetitia victores in castra referunt. Samnites duce amisso et per equestre certamen temptatis
viribus omissa Saticula, quam nequiquam defendi
rebantur, ad Plisticae obsidionem redeunt, intraque
paucos dies Saticula Romanus per deditionem,
Plistica per vim Samnis potitur.

XXIII. Mutata inde belli sedes est; ad Soram
2 ex Samnio Apuliaque traductae legiones. Sora ad
Samnites defecerat interfectis colonis Romanorum.
Quo cum prior Romanus exercitus ad ulciscendam
civium necem reciperandamque coloniam magnis
itineribus pervenisset[2] et sparsi[3] per vias speculatores

---

[1] di (dii) dederunt *Walch* (*who also suggested* deditum):
dederunt Ω: dedere A^2.
[2] pervenisset ς: praeuenisset Ω.
[3] et sparsi ς: sparsi Ω: sparsiq. ς.

him.   Yet the rank and file were not more dismayed
by their leader's death—though it often happens so
—than they were angered ; and as Aulius rode reck-
lessly on through the enemy's squadrons, all those
about him darted their javelins at him.   But the
glory of avenging the Samnite general was given by
Heaven in largest measure to his brother, who, wild
with grief and rage, dragged down the victorious
Roman from his seat and slew him.   Indeed the
Samnites almost got possession of the body, which
had fallen in the midst of their troops.   But the
Romans at once dismounted, and the Samnites were
forced to do the same ; and hurriedly forming up
their lines, they began a battle on foot around the
bodies of their generals, in which the Romans had
easily the better.   So they rescued the body of
Aulius, which they bore back victoriously to their
camp, with mingled feelings of sorrow and satisfaction.
The Samnites, having lost their commander, and
having tried what they could do in a cavalry engagement, gave up Saticula, which they felt was holding
out in vain, and returned to the siege of Plistica.
Within a few days' time Saticula had surrendered
to the Romans and the Samnites had carried Plistica
by assault.

XXIII. The seat of war was now shifted, and the
legions were transferred from Samnium and Apulia
to Sora, which had gone over to the Samnites, after
putting to death the Roman colonists.   The Roman
army, by a series of forced marches, undertaken to
avenge their slaughtered fellow-citizens and regain
the colony, came first upon the ground.   But the
scouts who had scattered out along the roads reported one after the other that the Samnite legions

LIVY

3 sequi legiones Samnitium nec iam procul abesse alii
4 super alios nuntiarent, obviam itum hosti atque
ad Lautulas ancipiti proelio dimicatum est. Non
caedes non fuga alterius partis sed nox incertos
5 victi victoresne essent diremit. Invenio apud quosdam adversam eam pugnam Romanis fuisse atque
in ea cecidisse Q. Aulium magistrum equitum.
6 Suffectus in locum Auli C. Fabius magister equitum
cum exercitu novo ab Roma advenit et per prae-
missos nuntios consulto dictatore ubi subsisteret
quove tempore et qua ex parte hostem adgrederetur,
substitit occultus ad omnia satis exploratis consiliis.
7 Dictator cum per aliquot dies post pugnam con-
tinuisset suos intra vallum obsessi magis quam
8 obsidentis modo, signum repente pugnae proposuit
et efficacius ratus ad accendendos virorum fortium
animos nullam alibi quam in semet ipso cuiquam
relictam spem de magistro equitum novoque ex-
9 ercitu militem celavit, et tamquam nulla nisi in
eruptione spes esset, "Locis" inquit "angustis,
milites, deprehensi, nisi quam victoria patefecerimus
10 viam nullam habemus. Stativa nostra munimento
satis tuta sunt, sed inopia eadem infesta; nam et
circa omnia defecerunt unde subvehi commeatus
poterant, et si homines [1] iuvare velint, iniqua loca
11 sunt. Itaque non frustrabor ego vos castra hic

---

[1] homines ς: omnes Ω.

---

[1] Whom Diodorus follows (XIX. lxxii.).

[2] The *Fasti Capitolini* give his name in full as C. Fabius
M. f. N. n. Ambustus, which makes him a brother of the
dictator.

[3] *i.e.* down the valley of the Liris, through the Samnite
army, for the other way was blocked by the town of Sora.

were following and were already close at hand. B.C. 315
Whereupon the Romans marched to meet the enemy,
and an indecisive battle was fought near Lautulae.
It was not the losses nor the rout of either army
that put a stop to the engagement, but darkness,
which left them uncertain if they had lost or won.
I find in some authorities[1] that the Romans were
defeated in this battle, and that it was here that the
master of the horse, Quintus Aulius, lost his life.
To fill out the term of Aulius they appointed Gaius
Fabius,[2] who marched from Rome with a fresh army.
Sending messengers on ahead to the dictator, he
consulted him as to where he should halt, and when,
and from what quarter, attack the enemy. On
being accurately informed regarding every detail of
the dictator's plans, he halted where his army could
lie concealed. For some days after the battle the
dictator had kept his soldiers within their works,
more like one besieged than a besieger. Then,
suddenly, he displayed the battle-signal, and thinking it more efficacious for quickening the courage of
brave men to leave none of them any hope but in
himself, he concealed from his troops the arrival of
the master of the horse and his new army, and, as
though their only salvation lay in cutting their way
through, "Soldiers," he said, "we are trapped and
have no way of escape save such as victory shall open
to us.[3] Our standing camp is sufficiently protected
by its rampart, but for lack of provisions is unten-
able; for every place round about us from which
supplies could be brought up has revolted, and even
if men wished to help us, the character of the
country is against it. I will therefore not beguile
you by leaving the camp standing here for you to

relinquendo, in quae infecta victoria sicut pristino die vos recipiatis. Armis munimenta, non muni-
12 mentis arma tuta esse debent. Castra habeant repetantque quibus operae est trahere bellum : nos omnium rerum respectum praeterquam victoriae
13 nobis abscidamus. Ferte signa in hostem; ubi extra vallum agmen excesserit, castra quibus imperatum est incendant. Damna vestra, milites, omnium circa
14 qui defecerunt populorum praeda sarcientur." Et oratione dictatoris, quae necessitatis ultimae index erat, milites accensi vadunt in hostem, et respectus ipse ardentium castrorum, quamquam proximis tantum—ita enim iusserat dictator—ignis est subditus,
15 haud parvum fuit inritamentum. Itaque velut vecordes inlati signa primo impetu hostium turbant; et in tempore, postquam ardentia procul vidit castra, magister equitum—id convenerat signum—hostium terga invadit. Ita circumventi Samnites, qua potest
16 quisque, fugam per diversa petunt; ingens multitudo in unum metu conglobata ac semet ipsam turba
17 impediens in medio caesa. Castra hostium capta direptaque, quorum praeda onustum militem in Romana castra dictator reducit, haudquaquam tam victoria laetum, quam quod praeter exiguam deformatam incendio partem cetera contra spem salva invenit.

XXIV. Ad Soram inde reditum; novique consules M. Poetelius C. Sulpicius exercitum ab dictatore

make a refuge, if you fail of victory, as on the former B.C. 315
occasion. Entrenchments should be secured by
arms, not arms by entrenchments. Let those have
a camp, and retire to it, who have time to prolong
the war: as for us, let us shut out all regard for
everything but victory. Forward against the enemy!
When the column is outside the rampart, let those
who have been ordered to do so fire the camp!
Your losses, men, shall be made good with the spoils
of all the revolted peoples round about!" Inflamed
by the dictator's speech, which pointed to the direst
necessity, the soldiers advanced upon the foe; and
the mere sight of their blazing camp as they glanced
back, though only the nearest tents were set afire—
for so the dictator had commanded—was no small
whet to their resentment. And so, charging like
madmen, they threw the enemy's ranks into confusion at the first assault; and in the nick of time
the master of the horse, who had seen far away
the burning camp—which was the signal they had
agreed upon—assaulted the enemy from behind.
Being thus hemmed in, the Samnites fled, as each
best might, in different directions; a vast throng
huddled up together, in their terror, and blocking
each other's way in the confusion, were cut down
where they stood. The enemy's camp was seized
and plundered, and the soldiers, laden with the
spoils, were led back by the dictator to the Roman
camp, rejoicing not so greatly in their victory as
because, contrary to their expectation, they found
all safe there, except for a trifling part that had
been damaged by the flames.

XXIV. The Romans then returned to Sora; and B.C. 314
new consuls, Marcus Poetelius and Gaius Sulpicius,

A.U.C.
440

Fabio accipiunt magna parte veterum militum
dimissa novisque cohortibus in supplementum ad-
2 ductis. Ceterum cum propter difficilem urbis situm
nec oppugnandi satis certa ratio iniretur et aut
tempore longinqua aut praeceps periculo victoria
3 esset, Soranus transfuga clam ex oppido profectus,
cum ad vigiles Romanos penetrasset, duci se extemplo ad consules iubet deductusque traditurum
4 urbem promittit. Visus[1] inde, cum quonam modo
id praestaturus esset percontantes doceret, haud
vana adferre, perpulit prope adiuncta moenibus
Romana castra ut sex milia ab oppido removerentur:
5 fore ut minus intentae in custodiam urbis diurnae
stationes ac nocturnae vigiliae essent. Ipse insequenti nocte sub oppido silvestribus locis cohortibus
insidere iussis decem milites delectos secum per
ardua ac prope invia in arcem ducit, pluribus quam
6 pro numero virorum missilibus telis eo conlatis; ad
hoc saxa erant et temere iacentia, ut fit in aspretis,
et de industria etiam, quo locus tutior esset, ab
oppidanis congesta.
7   Ubi cum constituisset Romanos semitamque an-
gustam et arduam erectam ex oppido in arcem
ostendisset, "Hoc quidem ascensu" inquit "vel tres
8 armati quamlibet multitudinem arcuerint: vos et

---

[1] The legions had been three years in the field, although
some of the soldiers, who had been enlisted to replace those
killed or disabled, had not served so long. These latter
were retained with the colours and the others were discharged. The word "cohorts" is anachronistic; Livy has
perhaps forgotten that the organization by cohorts dated only
from the time of Marius.

[2] Apparently conceived of as merely an unfortified and
(for the time being) unoccupied height.

took over the army from Fabius the dictator, dismiss- B.C. 314
ing a great part of the veteran troops and bringing
in new cohorts to replace them.[1] But the city lay
in a troublesome position, where the Romans could
devise no very certain way of getting at it, and
it seemed that victory would either be long in
coming, or fraught with fearful risks; when a Soran
deserter stole out of the town, and picking his
way to the Roman sentinels, bade them bring him
immediately to the consuls. Arrived in their
presence, he offered to betray the city. On being
questioned how he could accomplish it, he satisfied
his interrogators that his plan was not unfeasible,
and induced them to withdraw the Roman camp—
which was almost in contact with the city walls—to
a distance of six miles from the town; for so, he
said, the sentinels would be less vigilant in guarding
the place, whether by night or day. He himself on
the following night, having directed certain cohorts
to seek cover in the woods below the town, took
with him ten picked men, whom he conducted over
steep and almost impassable ground up to the
citadel.[2] Here he had brought together a quantity
of missiles out of all proportion to the number of
men, besides which there were stones—both those
which happened to be lying there, as is usual in
rough country, and those which the townsmen had
piled up on purpose, for the better protection of the
place.

On this height he posted the Romans, and, indi-
cating to them a steep and narrow path which led
up from the town to the citadel, he said, "From an
ascent like this three men would be enough to keep
back a multitude, however numerous: you are not

decem numero, et quod plus est, Romani Romano-
rumque fortissimi viri estis. Et locus pro vobis et
nox erit, quae omnia ex incerto maiora territis
ostentat. Ego iam terrore omnia implebo: vos
9 arcem intenti tenete." Decurrit inde, quanto
maxime poterat cum tumultu, "Ad arma!" et "Pro
vestram fidem, cives!" clamitans; "arx ab hostibus
10 capta est; defendite!"[1] Haec incidens principum
foribus, haec obviis, haec excurrentibus in publicum
pavidis increpat. Acceptum ab uno pavorem plures
11 per urbem ferunt. Trepidi magistratus missis ad
arcem exploratoribus cum tela et armatos tenere
arcem multiplicato numero audirent, avertunt animos
12 a spe reciperandae arcis; fuga cuncta complentur
portaeque ab semisomnis ac maxima parte inermibus
refringuntur, quarum per unam praesidium Romanum
clamore excitatum inrumpit et concursantes per vias
13 pavidos caedit. Iam Sora capta erat, cum consules
prima luce advenere et quos reliquos fortuna ex
nocturna caede ac fuga fecerat in deditionem
14 accipiunt. Ex his ducentos viginti quinque, qui
omnium consensu destinabantur et infandae colonorum caedis et defectionis auctores, vinctos Romam
deducunt; ceteram multitudinem incolumem prae-
15 sidio imposito Sorae relinquunt. Omnes qui Romam
deducti erant virgis in foro caesi ac securi percussi,
summo gaudio plebis, cuius maxime intererat tutam

---

[1] defendite *A*[x] *Madvig*: defendite ite Ω: ite defendite ς.

only ten, but Romans, and of Romans the very
bravest. You will have the advantage of position
and of night, which makes everything loom greater
in the eyes of frightened men, because of the
obscurity. As for me, I will presently strike terror
into every heart: do you hold the citadel and
watch." He then ran down, making all the noise
he could, as he cried "To arms!" and "Help, help,
my countrymen! The citadel has been taken by
the enemy! Defend us!" These words he shouted
as he knocked at the doors of the great, the same
to all he met, the same to those who rushed out
terrified into the streets. The panic begun by one
man was spread by numbers through all the city.
Quaking with fear, the magistrates dispatched scouts
to investigate, and on hearing that armed men, in
exaggerated numbers, held the citadel, relinquished
all hope of regaining it. The city was thronged
with fugitives, and men who were hardly yet awake
and most of them unarmed, began battering down
the gates. Through one of them rushed in the band
of Romans, who had started up on hearing the outcry,
and now running through the streets, cut down the
frightened townsfolk. Sora was already taken, when
the consuls arrived at early dawn, and received the
surrender of such as Fortune had spared in the rout
and slaughter of the night. Of these, two hundred
and twenty-five, who were designated on all hands
as the authors of the revolt and the hideous massacre
of the colonists, they sent to Rome in chains; the
rest they left unharmed in Sora, only setting a
garrison over them. All those who were taken to
Rome were scourged and beheaded in the Forum,
to the great joy of the commons, whom it most

ubique quae passim in colonias mitteretur multitudinem esse.

XXV. Consules ab Sora profecti in agros atque
2 urbes Ausonum bellum intulerunt. Mota namque
omnia adventu Samnitium cum apud Lautulas
dimicatum est fuerant, coniurationesque circa Cam-
3 paniam passim factae; nec Capua ipsa crimine
caruit; quin Romam quoque et ad principum
quosdam inquirendo ventum est. Ceterum Ausonum gens proditione urbium sicut Sora in potestatem
4 venit. Ausona et Minturnae et Vescia [1] urbes erant
ex quibus principes iuventutis duodecim numero in
proditionem urbium suarum coniurati ad consules
5 veniunt. Docent suos iam pridem exoptantes
Samnitium adventum, simul ad Lautulas pugnatum
audierint,[2] pro victis Romanos habuisse, iuventute
6 armis Samnitem iuvisse: fugatis inde Samnitibus
incerta pace agere nec claudentes portas Romanis,
ne arcessant bellum, et obstinatos claudere, si
exercitus admoveatur; in ea fluctuatione animorum
7 opprimi incautos posse. His auctoribus mota propius
castra missique eodem tempore circa tria oppida
milites, partim armati, qui occulti propinqua moenibus insiderent loca, partim togati tectis veste gladiis
qui sub lucem apertis portis urbes ingrederentur.

---

[1] Vescia *Sigonius* (VIII. xi. 5): uescina (uestina *FAˣ*) Ω.
[2] audierint *Ruperti*: audierunt Ω.

---

[1] Ausones is the Greek name for the Aurunci.
[2] Site unknown.

nearly concerned that the people who were sent out B.C. 314
here and there to colonies should in every case be
protected.

XXV. The consuls on leaving Sora conducted a
campaign against the lands and cities of the Ausones.[1]
For everything had been disturbed by the coming
of the Samnites, when the battle was fought at
Lautulae, and conspiracies had been formed all about
Campania. Even Capua itself did not escape accusation; nay, the investigation actually led to Rome
and to some of the prominent men there. But the
Ausones were brought into subjection by the betrayal
of their cities, as had happened in the case of Sora.
From Ausona,[2] from Minturnae, and from Vescia,
twelve young nobles, having conspired to betray
their cities, came to the consuls, and explained to
them that their countrymen, after long looking
forward to the coming of the Samnites, had no
sooner heard of the battle at Lautulae than they had
concluded the Romans vanquished and had aided
the Samnites with men and arms; that since the
expulsion of the Samnites from that region, they
had been living in an uncertain kind of peace, not
closing their gates upon the Romans, lest to do so
should invite attack, but determined none the less
to close them in case an army should approach;
and that in that wavering state of mind they could
be surprised and overcome. By their advice the
camp was moved up nearer and soldiers were simultaneously sent round to the three towns. Some of
these, in armour, were to lie in ambush in places
near the walls, while others, wearing the toga and
concealing swords under their dress, were to enter
the cities, a little before day, by the open gates.

8 Ab his simul custodes trucidari coepti, simul datum
signum armatis ut ex insidiis concurrerent. Ita
portae occupatae triaque oppida eadem hora
eodemque consilio capta; sed quia absentibus duci-
9 bus impetus est factus, nullus modus caedibus fuit,
deletaque Ausonum gens vix certo defectionis crimine perinde ac si internecivo bello certasset.

XXVI. Eodem anno prodito hostibus Romano
2 praesidio Luceria Samnitium facta. Nec diu pro-
ditoribus impunita res fuit: haud procul inde exercitus Romanus erat, cuius primo impetu urbs sita
in plano capitur. Lucerini ac Samnites ad inter-
3 necionem caesi; eoque ira processit ut Romae
quoque, cum de colonis mittendis Luceriam con-
suleretur senatus, multi delendam urbem censerent.
4 Praeter odium, quod exsecrabile in bis captos erat,
longinquitas quoque abhorrere a relegandis tam
procul ab domo civibus inter tam infestas gentes
5 cogebat. Vicit tamen sententia ut mitterentur coloni.
Duo milia et quingenti missi.

Eodem anno, cum omnia infida Romanis essent,
Capuae quoque occultae principum coniurationes
6 factae. De quibus cum ad senatum relatum esset,
haudquaquam neglecta res: quaestiones decretae
dictatoremque quaestionibus exercendis dici placuit.

---

[1] With this sentence Livy resumes the narrative begun in
Chap. XXV. §§ 1 and 2.

B.C. 314

These latter fell upon the watchmen, at the same time making a signal to their fellows in armour to rush in from their ambuscade. Thus the gates were captured, and three towns were taken in one hour and by one device. But because the leaders were not present when the attack was made, there was no limit to the slaughter, and the Ausonian nation was wiped out—though it was not quite clear that it was guilty of defection—exactly as if it had contended in an internecine war.

XXVI. In the same year Luceria, betraying its Roman garrison to the enemy, passed into the possession of the Samnites; but the traitors did not long go unpunished for their deed. Not far away there was a Roman army, which captured the city— situated as it was in a plain—at the first attack. The Lucerini and Samnites were shown no quarter, and resentment ran so high that even in Rome, when the senate was debating the dispatch of colonists to Luceria, there were many who voted to destroy the town. Besides men's hate, which was very bitter against those whom they had twice subdued, there was also the remoteness of the place, which made them shrink from condemning fellow-citizens to an exile so far from home and surrounded by such hostile tribes. However, the proposal to send colonists prevailed, and twenty-five hundred were sent.

In that year also of general disloyalty to the Romans, there were secret conspiracies of the nobles, even at Capua.[1] On their being reported to the senate, the danger was by no means minimized, but tribunals of enquiry were voted and it was determined to appoint a dictator to conduct the

A.U.C.
440

7 C. Maenius dictus; is M. Folium magistrum equitum
dixit. Ingens erat magistratus eius terror. Itaque,
sive is timor seu conscientia fuit,[1] Calavios [2] Ovium [3]
Noviumque—ea capita coniurationis fuerant—priusquam nominarentur apud dictatorem, mors haud
dubie ab ipsis conscita iudicio subtraxit.

8 Deinde ut quaestioni Campanae materia decessit,
versa Romam interpretando res: non nominatim
qui Capuae sed in universum qui usquam coissent
coniurassentve adversus rem publicam quaeri sena-
9 tum iussisse; et coitiones honorum adipiscendorum
causa factas adversus rem publicam esse. Latiorque
et re et personis quaestio fieri haud abnuente dicta-
10 tore sine fine ulla quaestionis suae ius esse. Postu-
labantur ergo nobiles homines appellantibusque
tribunos nemo erat auxilio quin nomina reciperentur.
11 Inde nobilitas, nec ii [4] modo in quos crimen in-
tendebatur sed universi, simul negare nobilium id
crimen esse, quibus, si nulla obstetur fraude, pateat
12 via ad honorem, sed hominum novorum; ipsos adeo
dictatorem magistrumque equitum reos magis quam
quaesitores idoneos eius criminis esse intellectu-
rosque ita id esse, simul magistratu abissent.
13 Tum enimvero Maenius, iam famae magis quam
imperii memor, progressus in contionem [5] ita verba
14 fecit: " Et omnes ante actae vitae vos conscios habeo,

---

[1] sive is timor seu conscientia fuit *Madvig*: siue timor seu
conscientiae uis *PF* (*or* ius) *OTD* (*or* ius) *LA*[2] (*and* *A*[4] *over
erasure*): siuet (*or* siuei) timor seu conscientia eius *M* (*or* *M*[1]
or *M*[2] *over erasure*): siue is timor seu conscientiae uis *U*.
[2] Calavios ⚹: calabios Ω.
[3] Ovium ⚹: obium (*or* obuium) Ω.
[4] ii ⚹: hi (*or* hii) Ω: in *PF*: *omitted by* O.
[5] contionem *D*[4]⚹: contione Ω.

investigations. Gaius Maenius was nominated, and named Marcus Folius master of the horse. Great was the terror inspired by that magistracy ; and so, whether from fear or a guilty conscience, the Calavii, Ovius and Novius, who had headed the conspiracy, before informations could be lodged against them with the dictator, avoided trial by a death which was undoubtedly self-inflicted.

After that, the field of enquiry at Capua having been exhausted, the proceedings were transferred to Rome, on the theory that the senate had ordered an investigation, not of specified individuals in Capua, but, in general, of all who had anywhere combined or conspired against the State ; and that cabals for obtaining magistracies had been made against the common weal. The enquiry began to take a wider range, in respect both of charges and of persons, and the dictator was nothing loath that there should be no limit to the jurisdiction of his court. Certain nobles were accordingly impeached, and on appealing to the tribunes found none to help them by stopping the informations. The nobles then declared—not those alone at whom the charge was levelled, but all of them conjointly—that this accusation did not lie against the nobility, to whom, unless fraudulently obstructed, the road to office lay wide open, but rather against upstart politicians ; that in fact the dictator and the master of the horse themselves were fitter to be tried on such a charge than to act as judges, and they would find this to be so the moment they resigned their places.

Then indeed Maenius, more mindful now of his reputation than of his authority, came forward and addressed the assembly. "You are all of you," he

LIVY

Quirites, et hic ipse honos delatus ad me testis est
innocentiae meae; neque enim, quod saepe alias,
quia ita tempora postulabant rei publicae, qui bello
clarissimus esset, sed qui maxime procul ab his
coitionibus vitam egisset, dictator deligendus exer-
15 cendis quaestionibus fuit. Sed quoniam quidam nobiles homines—qua de causa vos existimare quam
me pro magistratu quicquam incompertum dicere
16 melius est—primum ipsas expugnare quaestiones
omni ope adnisi sunt, dein postquam ad id parum
potentes erant, ne causam dicerent, in praesidia
adversariorum, appellationem et tribunicium au-
17 xilium, patricii confugerunt; postremo repulsi inde
adeo omnia tutiora quam ut innocentiam suam
purgarent visa—in nos inruerunt et privatis dicta-
18 torem poscere reum verecundiae non fuit;—ut
omnes di hominesque sciant ab illis etiam quae
non possint temptari ne rationem vitae reddant, me
obviam ire crimini et offerre me inimicis reum,
19 dictatura me abdico. Vos quaeso, consules, si vobis
datum ab senatu negotium fuerit, in me primum et
hunc M. Folium quaestiones exerceatis, ut appareat
innocentia nostra nos non maiestate honoris tutos
20 a criminationibus istis esse." Abdicat inde se dictatura et post eum confestim Folius magisterio equi
264

said, "Quirites, aware of my past life, and this very B.C. 314
office which has been conferred upon me is witness
to my innocence; for it was necessary to select as
dictator for the administration of judicial investigations, not the most distinguished soldier—as has
often been done at other times, when some crisis in
the state required it—but the man who had lived a
life most aloof from these cabals. But since certain
noblemen—for what cause it is better that you
should form your own opinion than that I as magistrate should affirm anything not fully ascertained—
have in the first place striven with might and main
to defeat these very investigations; and then, finding themselves not strong enough to escape pleading
their cause in court, have sought refuge, patricians
though they are, in the safeguards of their adversaries
—the appeal, I mean, and the help of the tribunes;—
and since at last, repulsed in that quarter, they have
fallen upon us—so much safer does any course appear
to them than to try to vindicate their innocence—
and have not blushed, though private citizens, to
demand the impeachment of a dictator;—in order
that all gods and men may know that they are
attempting even impossibilities to avoid accounting
for their lives, whereas I am ready to face their charge
and to offer myself to my enemies to be tried, I hereby
resign the dictator's authority. You, consuls, I
beseech, if the task shall be devolved upon you by the
senate, that you begin your investigations with me and
with Marcus Folius here, that it may be seen that we
are safe from these accusations by reason of our
innocence, not by reason of the awe inspired by our
office." He then resigned as dictator, and so at
once did Folius as master of the horse. They were

A.U.C.
440 tum; primique apud consules—iis enim ab senatu
mandata res est—rei facti adversus nobilium testi-
21 monia egregie absolvuntur. Publilius etiam Philo
multiplicatis summis honoribus post res tot domi
belloque gestas, ceterum invisus nobilitati, causam
22 dixit absolutusque est. Nec diutius, ut fit, quam
dum recens erat quaestio per clara nomina reorum
viguit; inde labi coepit ad viliora capita, donec
coitionibus factionibusque adversus quas comparata
erat oppressa est.

XXVII. Earum fama rerum, magis tamen spes
Campanae defectionis, in quam coniuratum erat,
Samnites in Apuliam versos rursus ad Caudium re-
2 vocavit, ut inde ex propinquo, si qui motus occasio-
3 nem aperiret, Capuam Romanis eriperent. Eo
consules cum valido exercitu venerunt. Et primo
circa saltus, cum utrimque ad hostem iniqua via
4 esset, cunctati sunt; deinde Samnites per aperta
loca brevi circuitu in loca plana, Campanos campos,
agmen demittunt,[1] ibique primum castra in con-
5 spectum[2] hostibus data, deinde levibus proeliis
equitum saepius quam peditum utrimque periculum
factum; nec aut eventus eorum Romanum aut
6 morae, qua trahebant bellum, paenitebat. Samni-

---

[1] demittunt ⌐: dimittunt Ω: dimatant (?) F.
[2] in conspectum *Gronovius*: in conspectu Ω: conspectu F.

---

[1] In 339 B.C. Philo had proposed three democratic laws,
which won him the enmity of the patricians. See VIII. xii.
14–16.

the first to go to trial before the consuls—for to
these the senate had given the matter in charge—
and, against the testimony of the nobles, were
gloriously acquitted. Publilius Philo, too, after all
his famous achievements at home and in war, and
after having repeatedly held the highest offices, had
incurred the hate of the nobility, and was brought
to trial and acquitted.[1] But the inquisition, as often
happens, had the vigour to deal with illustrious
defendants no longer than while its novelty lasted;
after that it began to descend to the baser sort,
until it was finally put down by the cabals and
factions which it had been instituted to oppose.

XXVII. The rumour of these events, and still
more the hope of a Campanian insurrection, which
had been the aim of the conspirators, recalled the
Samnites from Apulia, on which their attention had
been fixed, to Caudium; in the hope that, being
there so near, they might, if any disturbance should
afford the opportunity, seize Capua from the
Romans; and to Caudium came the consuls, with
a powerful force. Both armies at first held back,
each on its own side of the pass, for either would
have been at a disadvantage in advancing against
the other. Then the Samnites made a short detour
over open ground, and brought their army down
to the plain, where the hostile forces were, for
the first time, encamped in sight of one another.
Some skirmishing followed, in which both sides
made trial more often of their cavalry than their
foot. The Romans were not dissatisfied either with
the outcome of these brushes or with the delays
by which the campaign was protracted. To the
Samnite leaders, on the contrary, it appeared that

LIVY

tium contra ducibus et carpi parvis cottidie damnis
et senescere dilatione belli vires suae videbantur.

7 Itaque in aciem procedunt equitibus in cornua
divisis, quibus praeceptum erat intentiores ad respectum castrorum, ne qua eo vis fieret, quam[1] ad
8 proelium starent: aciem pedite[2] tutam fore. Consulum Sulpicius in dextro, Poetelius[3] in laevo cornu
consistunt. Dextra pars, qua et Samnites raris
ordinibus aut ad circumeundos hostes aut ne ipsi
9 circumirentur constiterant, latius patefacta stetit:
sinistris, praeterquam quod confertiores steterant,
repentino consilio Poeteli consulis additae vires, qui
subsidiarias cohortes, quae integrae ad longioris
pugnae casus reservabantur, in primam aciem extemplo emisit universisque hostem primo impetu
10 viribus impulit. Commota pedestri acie Samnitium
eques in pugnam succedit. In hunc transverso
agmine inter duas acies se inferentem Romanus
equitatus concitat equos signaque et ordines peditum atque equitum confundit, donec universam ab
11 ea parte avertit aciem. In eo cornu non Poetelius
solus sed Sulpicius etiam hortator adfuerat, avectus
ab suis nondum conserentibus manus ad clamorem

---

[1] quam *Gelenius* ς : cum Ω: et cum *F*.
[2] pedite *U* (*anticipating Gronovius*) : pediti Ω : peditum
*Ax*ς.
[3] Poetelius *edd.* (*cf. chap.* xxiv. § 1) : potelius *MPF*:
petilius *O*: poetellius *TD*: petellius *LA* (*similar corruptions
in* §§ 9 *and* 11, *and at chap.* xxviii. §§ 2, 5, 6).

---

[1] *i.e.* the Samnite right.

their forces were daily diminishing with petty B.C. 314
losses, and were wasting away with the prolongation
of the war.

They accordingly made ready for a general engagement, dividing their cavalry between the wings,
with orders to pay more attention to the camp,
to prevent any attack upon it, than to the battle;
for the infantry would sufficiently safeguard the
line. Of the consuls, Sulpicius took up his post
on the right wing, Poetelius on the left. The
formation on the right was spread out over a
considerable distance, and on that wing the Samnites, too, were drawn up in ranks of little depth,
either meaning to turn the Romans' flank, or to
keep their own from being turned. The troops on
the left, besides being drawn up in closer order,
had received an accession to their strength from
a plan conceived on the spur of the moment by
Poetelius. For those subsidiary cohorts which were
wont to be kept fresh in reserve, to meet the
chance needs of a long engagement, he sent immediately into the fighting line; and by using all
his strength at once, he forced the enemy back
at the first assault. As the Samnite infantry
wavered, their cavalry moved up to support them.
But while they came obliquely onward, in the
interval between the armies, the Roman cavalry
charged them at the gallop, confounding the ranks
and the formations of horse and foot, until they
had routed the entire army at that point.[1] On
that wing Sulpicius was present, as well as Poetelius,
to animate the soldiers, for when the shouting arose
upon the left, he had ridden over there, leaving
his own men, who were not yet come to grips with

LIVY

12 a sinistra parte prius exortum. Unde haud dubiam
victoriam cernens cum ad suum cornu tenderet cum
mille ducentis viris, dissimilem ibi fortunam invenit,
Romanos loco pulsos, victorem hostem signa in
13 perculsos inferentem. Ceterum omnia mutavit repente consulis adventus; nam et conspectu ducis
refectus militum est animus, et maius quam pro
numero auxilium advenerant fortes viri, et partis
alterius victoria audita mox visa etiam proelium
14 restituit. Tota deinde iam vincere acie Romanus
et omisso certamine caedi capique Samnites, nisi
qui Maleventum, cui nunc urbi Beneventum nomen
est, perfugerunt. Ad triginta milia caesa aut capta
Samnitium proditum memoiiae est.

XXVIII. Consules egregia victoria parta protinus
2 inde ad Bovianum oppugnandum legiones ducunt;
ibique hiberna egerunt, donec ab novis consulibus,
L. Papirio Cursore quintum C. Iunio Bubulco iterum
nominatus dictator C. Poetelius cum M. Folio
3 magistro equitum exercitum accepit. Is cum audisset arcem Fregellanam ab Samnitibus captam,
omisso Boviano ad Fregellas pergit. Unde nocturna
Samnitium fuga sine certamine receptis Fregellis
praesidioque valido imposito in Campaniam reditum
4 maxime ad Nolam armis repetendam. Eo se intra

---

¹ The city, which was a Greek colony, was called Μαλοϝείς,
which meant "Sheeptown" (or, perhaps, "Appletown").
The Romans corrupted the accusative case, Μαλοϝέντα, to
Maleventum, which they regarded as derived from *male* and
venire, and then, to avoid the omen, changed it to *Beneventum* when they planted a colony there, 268 B.C.

the enemy. But perceiving his colleague's victory B.C. 314 to be safe, he left him and rode off with twelve hundred men to his own wing. There he found affairs in a different posture; the Romans had been driven out of their position, and the victorious enemy were charging their disordered ranks. But all was quickly changed by the arrival of the consul. For the sight of their general revived the spirits of the soldiers, and the brave men who followed him were a greater succour than their numbers indicated; and the tidings of their comrades' victory, which they soon saw for themselves, restored the battle. Presently the Romans had begun to conquer all along the line, while the Samnites, giving up the struggle, were massacred or made prisoners, except those who fled to Maleventum, the city which is now called Beneventum.[1] Tradition avers that some thirty thousand Samnites were slain or captured.

XXVIII. The consuls, who had won a brilliant B.C. 313 victory, at once marched away to lay siege to Bovianum, where they remained in winter quarters, until the new consuls, Lucius Papirius Cursor (for the fifth time) and Gaius Junius Bubulcus (for the second) appointed Gaius Poetelius dictator, who, with Marcus Folius as master of horse, took over the command. Poetelius, hearing that the citadel of Fregellae was captured by the Samnites, raised the siege of Bovianum and proceeded to Fregellae. Having got possession of the place without a struggle—for the Samnites fled from it in the night—he installed a strong garrison there, and leaving Fregellae, marched back into Campania, for the purpose, chiefly, of winning back Nola by force of

LIVY

moenia sub adventum dictatoris et Samnitium omnis
multitudo et Nolana agrestis contulerat.[1] Dictator
5 urbis situ circumspecto, quo apertior aditus ad
moenia esset, omnia aedificia—et frequenter ibi
habitabatur—circumiecta muris incendit; nec ita
multo post, sive a Poetelio dictatore sive ab C.
Iunio consule—nam utrumque traditur,—Nola est
6 capta. Qui captae decus Nolae ad consulem trahunt,
adiciunt Atinam et Calatiam ab eodem captas,
Poetelium autem pestilentia orta clavi figendi causa
dictatorem dictum.
7   Suessa et Pontiae eodem anno coloniae deductae
sunt. Suessa Auruncorum fuerat; Volsci Pontias,
insulam sitam in conspectu litoris sui, incoluerant.
8 Et Interamnam Sucasinam[2] ut deduceretur colonia,
senati consultum[3] factum est; sed triumviros cre-
avere ac misere colonorum quattuor milia insequentes
consules M. Valerius P. Decius.

XXIX. Profligato[4] fere Samnitium bello, priusquam ea cura decederet patribus Romanis, Etrusci
2 belli fama exorta est. Nec erat ea tempestate gens
alia cuius secundum Gallicos tumultus arma terri-

---

[1] et Nolana agrestis contulerat *codd. Gelen.*: et nolani
agrestes (agrestis *O* agrestas *PFD? LA*) contulerat (-et *F*,
-ant *AM*[3] or *M*[4]*T*[1] or *T*[2]*D*[3]) Ω.

[2] Sucasinam *Mommsen (Plin. N.H.* III. v. 64): casinam
MT: casinum Ω.

[3] senati consultum *Alschefski*: sic (*or* sic.) Ω: sicut *U*:
senatus consultum ς.

[4] profligato ς: M. Valerio P. Decio coss. (*or* cōs *or* coñs.)
profligato Ω: p̄ decio coss profligato *TDLA.*

---

[1] For the practice of driving a nail in the wall of the
shrine of Minerva in the great temple of Jupiter on the
Capitol, see VII. iii. But the writers referred to in
the present passage are probably mistaken, as the *Fasti*

arms. Within its walls, as the dictator drew near, B.C. 313 the whole Samnite population and the Nolani of the country-side had taken refuge. After examining the position of the city, the dictator, in order to open up approaches to the walls, caused all the buildings round them—and the tract was densely inhabited—to be burnt. Not very long after this Nola was captured, whether by Poetelius the dictator or the consul Gaius Junius—for the story is told both ways. Those who ascribe the honour of capturing Nola to the consul, add that Atina and Calatia were won by the same man, but that Poetelius was made dictator on the outbreak of a pestilence, that he might drive the nail.[1]

Colonies were planted in that same year at Suessa and Pontiae. Suessa had belonged to the Aurunci; Volscians had inhabited Pontiae, an island which lay within sight of their own coast. The senate also passed a resolution that a colony be sent out to Interamna Sucasina,[2] but it was left for the next consuls, Marcus Valerius and Publius Decius, to appoint the three commissioners and send out four thousand settlers.

XXIX. The war with the Samnites was practically B.C. 312 ended, but the Roman senators had not yet ceased to be concerned about it, when the rumour of an Etruscan war sprang up. In those days there was no other race—setting apart the risings of the Gauls

Capitolini say that Poetelius was made dictator *rei gerundae causa.*
[2] So called (or sometimes Lirenas) to distinguish it from two other towns called Interamna—a name which is derived from the two streams (in this case the Casinus and the Liris) at whose confluence the town was situated.

A.U.C.
442

biliora essent cum propinquitate agri tum multi-
3 tudine hominum. Itaque altero consule in Samnio
reliquias belli persequente P. Decius, qui graviter
aeger Romae restiterat, auctore senatu dictatorem
C. Sulpicium Longum, is magistrum equitum C.
4 Iunium Bubulcum [1] dixit. Is, prout rei magnitudo
postulabat, omnes iuniores sacramento adigit, arma
quaeque alia res poscit summa industria parat; nec
tantis apparatibus elatus de inferendo bello agitat,
quieturus haud dubie, nisi ultro arma Etrusci infer-
5 rent. Eadem in comparando cohibendoque bello
consilia et apud Etruscos fuere: neutri finibus
egressi.

Et censura clara eo anno Ap. Claudi et C. Plauti
fuit; memoriae tamen felicioris ad posteros nomen
6 Appi, quod viam munivit et aquam in urbem duxit;
7 eaque unus perfecit, quia ob infamem atque invi-
diosam senatus lectionem verecundia victus collega
8 magistratu se abdicaverat; Appius iam inde antiquitus insitam pertinaciam familiae gerendo solus
9 censuram obtinuit. Eodem Appio auctore Potitia
gens, cuius ad aram maximam Herculis familiare
sacerdotium fuerat, servos publicos ministerii dele-

---

[1] dictatorem C. Sulpicium Longum, is magistrum equitum
C. Bubulcum *Sigonius and Pighius* (*from the Fasti Capitolini*):
dictatorem C. Iunium Bubulcum Ω.

---

[1] The road was the Via Appia, which ran from Rome to
Capua, and was later extended to Beneventum and, finally,
to Brundisium. The aqueduct brought water from a point
between seven and eight miles out, on the road to Gabii, and
supplied the Circus Maximus and other low-lying parts of
the City.
[2] An ancient altar erected in honour of Hercules. The
origin of the cult is described at i. vii. 3–15.

—whose arms were more dreaded, not only because B.C. 312 their territory lay so near, but also because of their numbers. Accordingly, while the other consul was in Samnium, dispatching the last remnants of the war, Publius Decius, who was very sick and had stopped behind in Rome, in pursuance of a senatorial resolution named Gaius Sulpicius Longus dictator, who appointed Gaius Junius Bubulcus to be his master of the horse. Sulpicius, as the gravity of the circumstances required, administered the oath to all those of military age, and made ready arms and whatever else the situation called for, with the utmost assiduity. Yet he was not so carried away with these great preparations as to plan for an offensive war, clearly intending to remain inactive, unless the Etruscans should first take the field. But the Etruscans followed the same policy, preparing for war but preventing it from breaking out. Neither side went beyond their own frontiers.

Noteworthy, too, in that year was the censorship of Appius Claudius and Gaius Plautius; but the name of Appius was of happier memory with succeeding generations, because he built a road, and conveyed a stream of water into the City.[1] These undertakings he carried out by himself, since his colleague had resigned, overcome with shame at the disgraceful and invidious manner in which Appius revised the list of senators; and Appius, exhibiting the obstinacy which had marked his family from the earliest days, exercised the censorship alone. It was Appius, too, by whose warranty the Potitian clan, with whom the priesthood of Hercules at the Ara Maxima[2] was hereditary, taught the ritual of that sacrifice to public slaves,

LIVY

A.U.C.
442 10 gandi causa sollemnia eius sacri docuerat. Traditur
inde, dictu mirabile et quod dimovendis statu suo
sacris religionem facere posset, cum duodecim familiae
ea tempestate Potitiorum essent, puberes ad triginta,
11 omnes intra annum cum stirpe exstinctos; nec nomen
tantum Potitiorum interisse sed censorem etiam
memori deum ira post aliquot annos luminibus
captum.

A.U.C.
443 XXX. Itaque consules qui eum annum secuti
sunt, C. Iunius Bubulcus tertium et Q. Aemilius
Barbula iterum, initio anni questi apud populum
2 deformatum ordinem prava lectione senatus, qua
potiores aliquot lectis praeteriti essent, negaverunt
eam lectionem se, quae sine recti pravique discrimine ad gratiam ac libidinem facta esset, obser-
vaturos et senatum extemplo citaverunt eo ordine
qui ante censores Ap. Claudium et C. Plautium
3 fuerat. Et duo imperia[1] eo anno dari coepta per
populum, utraque pertinentia ad rem militarem:
unum, ut tribuni militum seni deni in quattuor
legiones a populo crearentur, quae antea perquam
paucis suffragio populi relictis locis dictatorum et
consulum ferme fuerant beneficia—tulere eam rogationem tribuni plebei L. Atilius C. Marcius;—
4 alterum, ut duumviros navales classis ornandae

---

[1] imperia Ω: feria M: ministeria Madvig.

---

[1] For an instance of the popular election of *tribuni militum*
cf. VII. v. 9. The plan adopted in 311 seems to have given the
people the right to elect four of the six tribunes assigned to
each legion, or sixteen in all. Soon after Livy wrote these
words another change was made and the emperor thenceforth
appointed all military tribunes.

in order to devolve the service upon them. Tradition B.C. 312 relates that after this a strange thing happened, and one that might well give men pause ere they disturb the established order of religious ceremonies. For whereas at that time there were twelve families of the Potitii, and grown men to the number of thirty, within the year they had perished, every man, and the stock had become extinct; and not only did the name of the Potitii die out, but even the censor, by the unforgetting ire of the gods, was a few years later stricken blind.

XXX. And so the consuls of the following year, B.C. 311 Gaius Junius Bubulcus (for the third time) and Quintus Aemilius Barbula (for the second), complained to the people, at the outset of their administration, that the senatorial order had been depraved by the improper choice of members, in which better men had been passed over than some that had been appointed. They then gave notice that they should ignore that list, which had been drawn up with no distinction of right and wrong, in a spirit of favouritism and caprice; and proceeded to call the roll of the senate in the order which had been in use before Appius Claudius and Gaius Plautius were censors. In that year, also, two commands—both military—began to be conferred by the people; for it was enacted, first, that sixteen tribunes of the soldiers should be chosen by popular vote for the four legions, whereas previously these places had been for the most part in the gift of dictators and consuls, very few being left to popular suffrage[1]; secondly, that the people should likewise elect two naval commissioners to have charge of equipping and refitting the fleet. The former of

A.U.C.
443 reficiendaeque causa idem populus iuberet; latoi
huius plebi sciti fuit M. Decius tribunus plebis.

5   Eiusdem anni rem dictu parvam praeterirem, ni
ad religionem visa esset pertinere. Tibicines, quia
prohibiti a proximis censoribus erant in aede Iovis
vesci quod traditum antiquitus erat, aegre passi
Tibur uno agmine abierunt, adeo ut nemo in urbe
6 esset qui sacrificiis praecineret. Eius rei religio
tenuit senatum, legatosque Tibur miserunt darent[1]
operam, ut ii[2] homines Romanis restituerentur.
7 Tiburtini benigne polliciti primum accitos eos in
curiam hortati sunt uti reverterentur Romam;
postquam perpelli nequibant, consilio haud abhor-
8 rente ab ingeniis hominum eos adgrediuntur. Die
festo alii alios per speciem celebrandarum cantu
epularum invitant[3] et vino, cuius avidum ferme id
9 genus[4] est, oneratos sopiunt atque ita in plaustra
somno vinctos coniciunt ac Romam deportant. Nec
prius sensere quam plaustris in foro relictis plenos
10 crapulae eos lux oppressit. Tunc concursus populi
factus, impetratoque ut manerent, datum ut triduum
quotannis ornati cum cantu atque hac quae nunc
sollemnis est licentia per urbem vagarentur, restitu-

---

[1] darent *Gronovius*: ut darent Ω.
[2] ut ii *A*[2] *Alschefski Madvig*: ut hii *M*: ut hi *PF*: ut id
OTDLA.
[3] invitant ς: causa inuitant Ω.
[4] id gen s ς: genus Ω.

these measures was proposed by the tribunes of the B.C. 311
plebs Lucius Atilius and Gaius Marcius; the latter
by Marcus Decius, another tribune of the plebs.

I should omit, as an incident hardly worth
narrating, a little thing that happened in that same
year, but that it seemed to concern religion. The
flute-players, angry at having been forbidden by
the last censors to hold their feast, according to
old custom, in the temple of Jupiter, went off to
Tibur in a body, so that there was no one in the
City to pipe at sacrifices. Troubled by the religious
aspect of the case, the senate dispatched repre-
sentatives to the Tiburtines, requesting them to
use their best endeavours to restore these men to
Rome. The Tiburtines courteously undertook to do
so; and sending for the pipers to their senate-house,
urged them to return. When they found it impossible to persuade them, they employed a ruse,
not ill-adapted to the nature of the men. On a
holiday various citizens invited parties of the pipers
to their houses, on the pretext of celebrating the
feast with music. There they plied them with
wine, which people of that profession are generally
greedy of, until they got them stupefied. In this
condition they threw them, fast asleep, into waggons
and carried them away to Rome; nor did the pipers
perceive what had taken place until daylight found
them—still suffering from the debauch—in the
waggons, which had been left standing in the
Forum. The people then flocked about them and
prevailed with them to remain. They were permitted on three days in every year to roam the
City in festal robes, making music and enjoying
the licence that is now customary, and to such

279

LIVY

tumque in aede vescendi ius iis [1] qui sacris prae-
cinerent. Haec inter duorum ingentium bellorum
curam gerebantur.

XXXI. Consules inter se provincias partiti : Iunio
Samnites, Aemilio novum bellum Etruria sorte
2 obvenit. In Samnio Cluviarum [2] praesidium Romanum, quia nequiverat vi capi, obsessum fame in
deditionem acceperant Samnites verberibusque foe-
3 dum in modum laceratos occiderant deditos. Huic
infensus crudelitati Iunius, nihil antiquius oppugna-
tione Cluviana ratus, quo die adgressus est moenia
4 vi cepit atque omnes puberes interfecit. Inde victor
exercitus Bovianum ductus. Caput hoc erat Pentro-
rum Samnitium, longe ditissimum atque opulentissi-
5 mum armis virisque. Ibi quia haud tantum irarum
erat, spe praedae milites accensi oppido potiuntur.
Minus itaque saevitum in hostes est ; praedae plus
paene quam ex omni Samnio unquam egestum
benigneque omnis militi concessa.

6 Et postquam praepotentem armis Romanum nec
acies subsistere ullae nec castra nec urbes poterant,
omnium principum in Samnio eo curae sunt intentae
ut insidiis quaereretur locus, si qua licentia populando effusus exercitus excipi ac circumveniri posset.
7 Transfugae agrestes et captivi quidam, pars forte,
pars consilio oblati, congruentia ad consulem adfe-

---

[1] iis ϛ : his Ω : in (or iu) hiis A hiis A².
[2] Cluviarum *Walters* : cluuiaru (?) O : cluuiani (cluiani P)
Ω : duliiani T : duuiani T¹.

---

[1] The story of the secession of the flute-players is found
also in Ovid, *Fasti*, VI. 651 ff., and Plutarch, *Quaestiones
Romanae*, 55. The three days (the so-called "lesser Quin
quatrus") were June 13th, 14th, 15th, and were a festival
peculiar to the guild of pipers.
[2] The site of Cluviae is not known.

as should play at sacrifices was given again the B.C. 311
privilege of banqueting in the temple.[1] These
incidents occurred while men were preoccupied with
two mighty wars.

XXXI. The consuls divided the commands between
them : to Junius the lot assigned the Samnites, to
Aemilius the new war with Etruria. In Samnium
the Roman garrison at Cluviae,[2] which had defended
itself successfully against assault, was starved into
submission. The Samnites, having scourged their
prisoners in brutal fashion, put them to death,
although they had surrendered. Incensed by this
act of cruelty, Junius felt that nothing should take
precedence over an attack on Cluviae. He carried
the place by storm on the day he arrived before it,
and slew all the grown-up males. From there he
led his victorious army to Bovianum. This was the
capital of the Pentrian Samnites, a very wealthy
city and very rich in arms and men. Against this
town the soldiers were not so exasperated, but the
hope of plunder spurred them on to capture it. And
so there was less severity shown to the enemy, but
there was almost more booty carried out than was
ever collected from all the rest of Samnium, and the
whole of it was generously made over to the soldiers.

When the conquering arms of the Romans might
now no longer be withstood by any embattled host or
camp or city, the leaders of the Samnites all eagerly
directed their attention to the seeking out a place
for an ambush, on the chance that the army might
somehow be permitted to disperse for plundering,
and so be surprised and surrounded. Certain rustic
deserters and prisoners, some falling into the
consul's hands by accident and some on purpose,

LIVY

A.U.C.
443

rentes—quae et vera erant—pecoris vim ingentem
in saltum avium compulsam esse, perpulerunt ut
8 praedatum eo expeditae ducerentur legiones. Ibi
ingens hostium exercitus itinera occultus insederat,
et postquam intrasse Romanos vidit saltum, repente
exortus cum clamore ac tumultu incautos invadit.
9 Et primo nova res trepidationem fecit, dum arma
capiunt, sarcinas congerunt in medium; dein postquam, ut quisque liberaverat se onere aptaveratque
arma,[1] ad signa undique coibant et notis ordinibus
in vetere disciplina militiae iam sine praecepto
10 ullius sua sponte struebatur acies, consul ad anci-
pitem maxime pugnam advectus desilit ex equo
et Iovem Martemque atque alios testatur deos se
nullam suam gloriam inde sed praedam militi
11 quaerentem in eum locum devenisse neque in se
aliud quam nimiam ditandi ex hoste militis curam
reprehendi posse; ab eo se dedecore nullam rem
12 aliam quam virtutem militum vindicaturam. Coni-
terentur modo uno animo omnes invadere hostem
victum acie, castris exutum, nudatum urbibus,
ultimam spem furto insidiarum temptantem et loco
13 non armis fretum. Sed quem esse iam virtuti
Romanae inexpugnabilem locum? Fregellana arx
Soranaque et ubicumque iniquo successum erat loco
memorabantur.

***

[1] arma *Gronovius*: armis Ω.

by giving all the same account—and a true one, B.C. 311 too—of enormous flocks that had been brought together in an out of the way mountain meadow, persuaded him to lead thither his legions in light marching order to seize the booty. There a great army of the enemy had secretly beset the ways, and seeing that the Romans had entered the pass, rose up suddenly with much din and shouting and fell upon them unawares. At first the unexpectedness of the attack occasioned some trepidation, while the soldiers were putting on their armour and piling their packs in the midst. Afterwards, when everyone had got rid of his encumbrance and had armed himself, they began to assemble from every side about their standards. In the course of a long training in the army they had become familiar with their places, and formed a line of their own accord, without anyone's direction. The consul, riding up to the place where the fighting was most critical, leaped down from his horse, and called on Jupiter and Mars and the other gods to witness that he had come there seeking no glory for himself, but only booty for his soldiers : his sole fault, he said, was a too great desire to enrich his men ; from this disgrace nothing could save him but their courage. Only let them all unite in singleness of purpose to assail an enemy conquered in battle, stripped of his camp, deprived of his cities, and pinning his last hopes to the treachery of an ambuscade, where his trust was in his position, not in arms. But what position was there now, he demanded, too strong for Roman valour to overwhelm? He reminded them of Fregellae's citadel and Sora's, and all the places where they had triumphed over disadvantage of ground.

LIVY

14 His accensus miles, omnium immemor difficultatium, vadit adversus imminentem hostium aciem. Ibi paulum laboris fuit, dum in adversum clivum 15 erigitur agmen; ceterum postquam prima signa planitiem summam ceperunt sensitque acies aequo se iam institisse loco, versus extemplo est terror in insidiatores easdemque latebras quibus se paulo ante texerant palati atque inermes fuga repetebant. 16 Sed loca difficilia hosti quaesita ipsos tum sua fraude impediebant. Itaque ergo perpaucis effugium patuit; caesa ad viginti milia hominum victorque Romanus ad oblatam ab hoste praedam pecorum discurrit.

XXXII. Dum haec geruntur in Samnio, iam omnes Etruriae populi praeter Arretinos ad arma ierant, ab oppugnando Sutrio, quae urbs socia Romanis 2 velut claustra Etruriae erat, ingens orsi bellum. Eo alter consul Aemilius cum exercitu ad liberandos obsidione socios venit. Advenientibus Romanis Sutrini commeatus benigne in castra ante urbem 3 posita advexere. Etrusci diem primum consultando maturarent traherentne bellum traduxerunt. Postero die, ubi celeriora quam tutiora consilia magis pla-

---

1 The *Fasti Capitolini* record that Junius triumphed over the Samnites on August 5th (*C.I L.*, I², p. 45).

Roused by these words, the soldiers disregarded B.C. 311 every obstacle and advanced against the battle-line which their enemies had formed above them. There was a little hard fighting there, while the column was mounting the slope; but as soon as the foremost companies had reached the plateau at the top, and the soldiers perceived that their line was now established on level ground, the panic was straightway turned upon the waylayers, who fled, dispersing and throwing down their arms, in search of those very lurking-places where a little while before they had concealed themselves. But the ground which they had sought out for the difficulties it presented to an enemy caught the Samnites themselves in a trap of their own devising. And so, very few were able to get off; about twenty thousand men were slain; and the victorious Romans struck out this way and that to collect the booty of cattle which the enemy had thrown in their way.[1]

XXXII. While these events were taking place in Samnium, all the peoples of Etruria, except the Arretini, had already armed, and beginning with the siege of Sutrium, a city in alliance with the Romans, and forming as it were the key to Etruria, had set on foot a tremendous war. Thither the other consul, Aemilius, came with an army, to relieve the blockade of the allies. As the Romans came up, the Sutrini obligingly brought provisions to their camp, which was formed before the city. The Etruscans spent the first day in deliberating whether to accelerate the war or to draw it out. On the following day, their generals having decided on the swifter plan in preference to the safer, the

cuere ducibus, sole orto signum pugnae propositum
4 est armatique in aciem procedunt. Quod postquam
consuli nuntiatum est, extemplo tesseram dari iubet
ut prandeat miles firmatisque cibo viribus arma
5 capiat. Dicto paretur. Consul ubi armatos para-
tosque vidit, signa extra vallum proferri iussit et
haud procul hoste instruxit aciem. Aliquamdiu
intenti utrimque steterunt exspectantes, ut ab ad-
6 versariis clamor et pugna inciperet; et prius sol
meridie se inclinavit quam telum hinc aut illinc
emissum est. Inde, ne infecta re abiretur, clamor
ab Etruscis oritur concinuntque tubae et signa
inferuntur. Nec segnius a Romanis pugna initur.
7 Concurrunt infensis animis; numero hostis, virtute
8 Romanus superat; anceps proelium multos utrimque
et fortissimum quemque absumit, nec prius inclinata
res est quam secunda acies Romana ad prima signa,
9 integri fessis, successerunt, Etrusci,[1] quia nullis
recentibus subsidiis fulta prima acies fuit, ante signa
circaque omnes ceciderunt. Nullo unquam proelio
fugae minus nec plus caedis fuisset, ni obstinatos
10 mori Tuscos nox texisset, ita ut victores prius quam
victi pugnandi finem facerent. Post occasum solis
signum receptui datum est; nocte utroque[2] in
castra reditum.

[1] successerunt, Etrusci *Walters and Conway*: successerunt.
Etrusci *edd.*

[2] utroque *Madvig*: ab utroque Ω: utrobique *Walters and
Conway* (*note*).

signal for battle was displayed at sunrise and their B.C. 311 men in fighting array marched out upon the field. When this was reported to the consul, he at once commanded the word to be passed round that the men should breakfast, and having recruited their strength with food, should then arm. The order was obeyed; and the consul, seeing them equipped and ready, bade advance the standards beyond the rampart, and drew up his troops a little way off from the enemy. For some time both sides stood fast, observing one another closely, each waiting for the other to give a cheer and begin to fight, and the sun had begun his downward course in the heavens ere a missile was hurled on either side. Then the Etruscans, that they might not withdraw without accomplishing their purpose, set up a shout, and with sound of trumpets advanced their ensigns. The Romans were equally prompt to begin the battle. The two armies rushed together with great fury, the enemy having a superiority in numbers, the Romans in bravery. Victory hung in the balance and many perished on both sides, including all the bravest, and the event was not decided until the Roman second line came up with undiminished vigour to relieve their exhausted comrades in the first; and the Etruscans, whose fighting line was supported by no fresh reserves, all fell in front of their standards and around them. There would never in any battle have been more bloodshed or less running away, but when the Etruscans were resolved to die, the darkness shielded them, so that the victors gave over fighting before the vanquished. The sun had set when the recall was sounded, and in the night both armies retired to their camps.

LIVY

11 Nec deinde quicquam eo anno rei memoria dignae
apud Sutrium gestum est, quia et ex hostium
exercitu prima tota acies deleta uno proelio fuerat
subsidiariis modo relictis, vix quod satis esset ad
12 castrorum praesidium, et apud Romanos tantum
volnerum fuit ut plures post proelium saucii de-

cesserint quam ceciderant in acie. XXXIII. Q.
Fabius, insequentis anni consul, bellum ad Sutrium
excepit, collega Fabio C. Marcius Rutulus [1] datus
2 est. Ceterum et Fabius supplementum ab Roma ad-
duxit et novus exercitus domo accitus Etruscis venit.
3 Permulti anni iam erant cum inter patricios
magistratus tribunosque nulla certamina fuerant,
cum ex ea familia cui velut fato lis [2] cum tribunis
4 ac plebe erat certamen oritur. Ap. Claudius censor
circumactis decem et octo mensibus quod Aemilia
lege finitum censurae spatium temporis erat, cum C.
Plautius collega eius magistratu se abdicasset, nulla
5 vi compelli ut abdicaret potuit. P. Sempronius erat
tribunus plebis, qui finiendae censurae intra legiti-
mum tempus actionem susceperat, non popularem
magis quam iustam nec in volgus quam optimo
6 cuique gratiorem. Is cum identidem legem Aemi-
liam recitaret auctoremque eius Mam. Aemilium
dictatorem laudibus ferret, qui quinquennalem ante
censuram et longinquitate potestatis [3] dominantem
7 intra sex mensum et anni coegisset spatium, "Dic
agedum" inquit, "Appi Claudi, quidnam facturus

---

[1] Rutulus *Conway*: rutilius (rutilius *T*?) Ω.
[2] cui velut fato lis *M. Seyffert*: quae uelut fatalis Ω: quae
uelut fatales *MPTDL*.
[3] potestatis *Crévier*: potestatem Ω.

---

[1] 434 B.C. (IV. xxiv. 5).

Thereafter there was nothing done that year at B.C. 311
Sutrium worth recording. The enemy had lost
their whole first line in a single engagement, and
had only their reserves remaining, who barely
sufficed to garrison their camp; whilst the Romans
had so many wounded that more died of their
hurts after the battle than had fallen on the field.
XXXIII. Quintus Fabius, consul in the following B.C. 310
year, took over the campaign at Sutrium. For
colleague he was given Gaius Marcius Rutulus.
Fabius brought up replacements from Rome, and
a new army came from Etruria to reinforce the
enemy.

For a great many years now there had been no
contests between the patrician magistrates and the
tribunes, when a dispute arose through that family
which was fated, as it seemed, to wrangle with the
tribunes and with the plebs. Appius Claudius the
censor, on the expiration of the eighteen months
which had been fixed by the Aemilian law [1] as the
limit of the censorship, although his colleague Gaius
Plautius had abdicated, could himself by no compulsion be prevailed upon to do likewise. It was
Publius Sempronius, a tribune of the people, who
commenced an action to confine the censorship to
its legal limits—an action no less just than popular,
and as welcome to every aristocrat as to the common
people. Having repeatedly read out the Aemilian
law, and praised its author, Mamercus Aemilius the
dictator, for confining the censorship—which had
until then been tenable for five years and was
proving despotic by reason of the long continuance
of its authority—within the space of a year and a
half, he said, " Come, tell us, Appius Claudius, what

A.U.C.
444

fueris, si eo tempore quo C. Furius et M. Geganius
8 censores fuerunt censor fuisses." Negare Appius
interrogationem tribuni magno opere ad causam
9 pertinere suam; nam etsi tenuerit lex Aemilia eos
censores quorum in magistratu lata esset, quia post
illos censores creatos eam legem populus iussisset
quodque postremum iussisset id ius ratumque esset,
non tamen aut se aut eorum quemquam qui post
eam legem latam creati censores essent teneri ea
lege potuisse.

XXXIV. Haec sine ullius adsensu cavillante Appio
" En " [1] inquit, " Quirites, illius Appi progenies, qui
decemvir in annum creatus altero anno se ipse
creavit, tertio nec ab se nec ab ullo creatus privatus
2 fasces et imperium obtinuit, nec ante continuando
abstitit magistratu quam obruerent eum male parta,
3 male gesta, male retenta imperia. Haec est eadem
familia, Quirites, cuius vi atque iniuriis compulsi
extorres patria Sacrum montem cepistis; haec adversus quam tribunicium auxilium vobis comparas-
4 tis; haec propter quam duo exercitus Aventinum
insedistis; haec quae fenebres leges, haec quae
5 agrarias semper impugnavit. Haec conubia patrum

---

[1] "En" *Aldus* : ē *FO* : est Ω.

---

[1] Appius held that, whereas the election of Furius and
Geganius for a period of five years had been set aside by
the Aemilian law, which was then the latest enactment on
the subject and so replaced any earlier one, nevertheless all
those who were elected subsequently derived their powers
from still later enactments, by which in its turn the Aemilian
law was superseded.

[2] For the story of the Decemvir, see III. xxxiii–lviii.

[3] II. xxxii. 2.

you would have done had you been censor at the B.C. 310
time when Gaius Furius and Marcus Geganius were
censors." Appius replied that the tribune's question had no particular bearing upon his own case;
for even though the Aemilian law had bound those
censors in whose term of office it had been passed,
because the people had enacted the law after their
election to the censorship and their latest enactment
was always the effective law, yet neither himself nor
any one of those who had been chosen censors subsequently to the passage of that law could have
been bound by it.[1]

XXXIV. While Appius raised these quibbles, but
found no one to support him, "Behold, Quirites,"
said Sempronius, "the descendant of that Appius,
who having been elected decemvir for one year,
himself declared his own election for a second year,
and in the third, although a private citizen, with
neither his own nor another's warrant of election,
retained the fasces and authority, and relinquished
not his hold on the magistracy until he was overwhelmed by his ill-gotten, ill-administered, and
ill-continued powers.[2] It was this same family,
Quirites, under compulsion of whose violence and
abuse you banished yourselves from your native City
and occupied the Sacred Mount [3]; the same against
which you provided yourselves with the help of
tribunes [4]; the same, because of which two armies
of you encamped upon the Aventine [5]; the same
that has ever attacked the laws restricting usury
and throwing open the public lands.[6] This same

---

[4] II. xxxiii. 1–3.   [5] III. l. 13, and li. 10.
[6] II. xxix. 9; xliv. 1; lxi. 1; VI. xl. 11.

LIVY

et plebis interrupit; haec plebi ad curules magistratus iter obsaepsit. Hoc est nomen multo quam Tarquiniorum infestius vestrae libertati. Itane 6 tandem, Appi Claudi? Cum centesimus iam annus sit ab Mam. Aemilio dictatore, tot censores fuerunt,[1] nobilissimi fortissimique viri, nemo eorum duodecim tabulas legit? Nemo id ius esse, quod postremo 7 populus iussisset, sciit? Immo vero omnes scierunt[2] et ideo Aemiliae potius legi paruerunt quam illi antiquae qua primum censores creati erant, quia hanc postremam iusserat populus, et quia, ubi duae contrariae leges sunt, semper antiquae obrogat nova.

8   "An hoc dicis, Appi, non teneri Aemilia lege 9 populum? An populum teneri, te unum exlegem esse? Tenuit Aemilia lex violentos illos censores C. Furium[3] et M. Geganium, qui quid iste magistratus in re publica mali[4] facere posset indicarunt, cum ira finitae potestatis Mam. Aemilium, principem 10 aetatis suae belli domique, aerarium fecerunt; tenuit deinceps omnes censores intra centum annorum spatium; tenet C. Plautium, collegam tuum iisdem[5] 11 auspiciis, eodem iure creatum. An hunc non ut qui optimo iure censor creatus esset populus creavit? Tu unus eximius es in quo hoc praecipuum ac singu-

---

[1] fuerunt (fueȓ) *F*: fuerin Ω.
[2] scierunt *H. J. Mueller*: sciuerunt Ω: sciuerint *DA*.
[3] C. Furium ς: m̄. furium Ω.
[4] mali *A²* (*or A¹*): male Ω: mala *M*.
[5] iisdem ς: isdem *T²*: hiisdem *A*: hisdem Ω.

---

[1] IV. i. vi.   [2] *e.g.* IV. vi. 7.

family broke off marriages between patricians and B.C. 310
plebeians¹; this same family blocked the path of
the plebeians to curule offices.² It is a name that
is far more hostile to your liberty than that of
the Tarquinii. So, Appius Claudius! Though it is
now a hundred years since Mamercus Aemilius was
dictator, and in that time we have had all these
censors, high-born and valiant men, has never one
of them inspected the Twelve Tables? Has none
of them known that the law was that which the
people had last enacted? Nay, all of them knew
it; and they obeyed the Aemilian law in preference
to that ancient ordinance which governed the first
elections of censors, precisely because it was the
latest which the people had enacted, and because
in a conflict of two laws the old is ever superseded
by the new.

"Or will this be your contention, Appius, that the
people is not bound by the Aemilian law? Or that
the people is bound, but that you alone are exempt?
The Aemilian law bound those violent censors
Gaius Furius and Marcus Geganius, who showed what
mischief that magistracy could accomplish in the
state, when, in their rage at the abridgment of their
powers, they reduced Mamercus Aemilius, the foremost man of his time in war and peace, to the lowest
class of citizens; it bound all the censors who
succeeded them, for the period of a hundred years;
it binds Gaius Plautius, your colleague, who was
given the office under the same auspices and with
the same rights as yourself. Or did the people not
make Plautius censor as one who had been elected
with the fullest rights? Are you the sole exception
in whose case this holds, as a unique and peculiar

A.U.C.
444

12 lare valeat? Quem tu regem sacrificiorum crees?
Amplexus regni nomen, ut qui optimo iure rex
Romae creatus sit, creatum se dicet. Quem semestri
dictatura, quem interregno quinque dierum con-
tentum fore putes? Quem clavi figendi aut ludorum
13 causa dictatorem audacter crees? Quam isti stolidos
ac socordes videri creditis eos qui intra vicesimum
diem ingentibus rebus gestis dictatura se abdicave-
14 runt aut qui vitio creati abierunt magistratu! Quid
ego antiqua repetam? Nuper intra decem[1] annos
C. Maenius dictator, quia, cum quaestiones severius
quam quibusdam potentibus tutum erat exerceret,
contagio eius quod quaerebat ipse criminis obiectata
ab inimicis est, ut privatus obviam iret crimini,
15 dictatura se abdicavit. Nolo ego istam in te modes-
tiam; ne degeneraveris a familia imperiosissima et
superbissima; non die, non hora citius quam necesse
est magistratu abieris, modo ne excedas finitum
16 tempus. Satis est aut diem aut mensem censurae
adicere? Triennium, inquit, et sex menses ultra
quam licet Aemilia lege censuram geram et solus
geram. Hoc quidem iam regno simile est.
17 "An collegam subrogabis, quem ne in demortui
18 quidem locum subrogari fas est? Paenitet enim,
quod antiquissimum sollemne et solum ab ipso cui

---

[1] decem Ω^1: quinque *Klockius Iac. Gronovius* (*chap.* xxvi.
§ 7).

---

[1] II. ii. 1–2
[2] Livy has himself put the dictatorship of Maenius in the
year 314. He is probably following another annalist here
whose account (like that of the *Fasti Capitolini*) assigned it to
320.

privilege? Whom, pray, could men elect as king
for sacrifice?[1] He will seize on the title of
sovereignty, and assert that he has been chosen as
one elected with fullest rights to be king at Rome.
Who, think you, will be content with six months
as dictator; who with five days as interrex? Whom
would you be so rash as to make dictator for the
purpose of driving the nail or celebrating games?
How dull and lumpish must those men seem to
Appius, who after accomplishing great feats resigned
the post of dictator within twenty days, or laid down
the reins of office because of a flaw in their election!
Why should I cite antiquity? Recently, within
these ten years,[2] Gaius Maenius the dictator, for
conducting an inquisition with more severity than
was safe for certain great men, was accused by his
ill-wishers of being tainted with that very felony
which he was searching out, and abdicated the dictatorship, that he might face the charge as a private
citizen. Far be it from me to require such self-
denial of you! Fall not away from the most imperious
and proud of families; quit not your magistracy one
day, one hour, sooner than you must; only see that
you overstep not the appointed limit. Is it enough
to add a day, or a month, to his censorship? 'Three
years,' quoth he, 'and six months beyond the time
permitted by the Aemilian law will I administer
the censorship, and administer it alone.' Surely this
begins to look like monarchy!

"Or will you substitute a colleague for the other,
though even in a dead man's place such substitution
is forbidden by religion? You are not satisfied forsooth with having in your scrupulous exercise of a
censor's powers diverted the service of our most

A.U.C.
444

fit institutum deo ab nobilissimis antistitibus eius
19 sacri ad servorum ministerium religiosus censor
deduxisti, gens antiquior originibus urbis huius,
hospitio deorum immortalium sancta, propter te ac
tuam censuram intra annum ab stirpe exstincta est,
nisi universam rem publicam eo nefario obstrinxeris
20 quod ominari etiam reformidat animus. Urbs eo
lustro capta est quo demortuo collega C. Iulio[1] L.
Papirius Cursor, ne abiret magistratu, M. Cornelium
21 Maluginensem collegam subrogavit. Et quanto
modestior illius cupiditas fuit quam tua, Appi! Nec
solus nec ultra finitum lege tempus L. Papirius
censuram gessit; tamen neminem invenit qui se
postea auctorem sequeretur; omnes deinceps censores post mortem collegae se magistratu abdicarunt.
22 Te nec quod dies exiit[2] censurae nec quod collega
magistratu abiit nec lex nec pudor coercet: virtutem
in superbia, in audacia, in contemptu deorum hominumque ponis.

23 " Ego te, Appi Claudi, pro istius magistratus maiestate ac verecundia quem gessisti non modo manu
violatum sed ne verbo quidem inclementiori a me
24 appellatum vellem; sed et haec quae adhuc egi
pervicacia tua et superbia coegit me loqui, et nisi
25 Aemiliae legi parueris, in vincula duci iubebo, nec
cum ita comparatum a maioribus sit ut comitiis

---

[1] C. Iulio *Walters and Conway*: C. Iulio censore Ω.
[2] exiit ς : exit Ω.

---

[1] The guilt of unlawfully prolonging his censorship.

ancient cult, the only one inaugurated by the god _{B.C. 310}
himself in whose honour it is observed, from the
priesthood of the most exalted nobles to the ministry
of slaves ; it was not enough that a family more
ancient than the beginnings of this City, and sanctified
by the entertainment of the immortal gods, should
through you and your censorship be within a year
uprooted and destroyed ; no, you must needs involve
the entire state in such heinous guilt[1] as even to
name is an omen that fills my mind with dread.
The city was captured in that lustrum when, on the
death of his colleague Gaius Julius, Lucius Papirius
Cursor, to avoid having to vacate his office, caused
Marcus Cornelius Maluginensis to be substituted in
the room of the dead man. And how much more
moderate, Appius, was his ambition than yours !
The censorship of Lucius Papirius was neither a sole
one nor one prolonged beyond the legally established
term ; yet he found none to follow his example ; all
succeeding censors have abdicated on the death of a
colleague. But you neither the expiration of your
time restrains nor the fact that your colleague has
resigned, nor the law, nor a sense of decency : you
reckon worth in terms of pride, of recklessness, of
contempt for gods and men.

" For my own part, Appius Claudius, when I think
of the dignity of that office you have held and the
reverence attaching to it, I could wish that I might
spare you not only personal violence but even an
ungentle word ; but your stubbornness and pride have
compelled me to say what I have so far said, and
unless you obey the Aemilian law, I shall order you
to prison ; nor, seeing that our forefathers have
ordained that in the election of censors, if either fall

A.U.C.
444

censoriis, nisi duo confecerint legitima suffragia, non renuntiato altero comitia differantur, ego te, qui solus censor creari non possis, solum censuram gerere nunc [1] patiar."

26 Haec taliaque cum dixisset, prendi censorem et in vincula duci iussit. Approbantibus sex tribunis actionem collegae tres appellanti Appio auxilio fuerunt; summaque invidia omnium ordinum solus censuram gessit.

XXXV. Dum ea Romae geruntur, iam Sutrium ab Etruscis obsidebatur consulique Fabio imis montibus ducenti ad ferendam opem sociis temptandasque munitiones, si qua posset, acies hostium instructa 2 occurrit; quorum ingentem multitudinem cum ostenderet subiecta late planities, consul, ut loco paucitatem suorum adiuvaret, flectit paululum in clivos agmen—aspreta erant strata saxis—inde signa 3 in hostem obvertit. Etrusci omnium praeterquam multitudinis suae, qua sola freti erant, immemores proelium ineunt adeo raptim et avide ut abiectis missilibus,quo celerius manus consererent,stringerent 4 gladios vadentes in hostem; Romanus contra nunc tela, nunc saxa, quibus eos adfatim locus ipse 5 armabat, ingerere. Igitur scuta galeaeque ictae cum etiam quos non volneraverant turbarent neque

---

[1] gerere nunc ς : gerere non Ω : gerere ς.

---

[1] No one was held to be elected unless he had received the votes of an absolute majority of the centuries.

short of the legal vote,[1] the election shall be put off and the other not be declared elected, will I now suffer you, who cannot be elected as sole censor, to administer the censorship alone."

Having uttered these and similar remonstrances, he ordered the censor to be arrested and carried off to prison. Six tribunes approved the action of their colleague: three protected Appius on his appeal, and, greatly to the indignation of all classes, he continued as sole censor.

XXXV. During the progress of this affair in Rome, the Etruscans were already laying siege to Sutrium; and the consul Fabius, leading his army along the foot of the mountains to relieve the allies, and, if in any way practicable, to attack the works of the besiegers, encountered the enemy drawn up in line of battle. The plain spreading out below him revealed to the consul their exceeding strength; and in order to make up for his own deficiency in numbers by the advantage of position, he altered slightly his line of march, so as to mount the hills—which were rough and covered with stones—and there turned and faced the enemy. The Etruscans, forgetting everything but their numbers, in which alone they trusted, entered the combat with such haste and eagerness that they cast away their missiles in order to come the sooner to close quarters, and drawing their swords rushed at the enemy. The Romans, on the contrary, fell to pelting them, now with javelins and now with stones, of which latter the ground itself provided a good supply; and even such of the Etruscans as were not wounded were confused by the blows that rattled down on their helms and shields. It was no easy matter to get close enough

LIVY

subire erat facile ad propiorem pugnam neque mis-
6 silia habebant, quibus eminus rem gererent—stantes
et expositos ad ictus cum iam satis nihil tegeret,
quosdam etiam pedem referentes fluctuantemque et
instabilem aciem redintegrato clamore strictis gladiis
7 hastati et principes invadunt. Eum impetum non
tulerunt Etrusci versisque signis fuga effusa castra
repetunt. Sed equites Romani praevecti per obliqua
campi cum se fugientibus obtulissent, omisso ad
8 castra itinere montes petunt; inde inermi paene
agmine ac vexato volneribus in silvam Ciminiam
penetratum. Romanus multis milibus Etruscorum
caesis, duodequadraginta signis militaribus captis,
castris etiam hostium cum praeda ingenti potitur.
Tum de persequendo hoste agitari coeptum.

XXXVI. Silva erat Ciminia magis tum invia atque
horrenda quam nuper fuere Germanici saltus, nulli
ad eam [1] diem ne mercatorum quidem adita. Eam
intrare haud fere quisquam praeter ducem ipsum
audebat; aliis omnibus cladis Caudinae nondum
2 memoria aboleverat. Tum ex iis [2] qui aderant,
consulis frater M. Fabius [3]—Caesonem alii, C.
Claudium quidam, matre eadem qua consulem geni-
tum, tradunt—speculatum se iturum professus bre-
3 vique omnia certa allaturum. Caere educatus apud
hospites, Etruscis inde litteris eruditus erat lin-

---

[1] eam $A\ \varsigma$: ea Ω.
[2] iis ς : hiis A : his Ω.
[3] frater M. Fabius—*Weissenborn* : fratrem m̄. fabium Ω.

---

[1] Livy is probably thinking of the German campaigns of
Caesar in 55 and 53, and of Agrippa in 38 B.C.

for fighting hand to hand, and they had no javelins B.C. 310
for long-range work.   There they stood, exposed to
missiles, with no adequate cover of any sort, and as
some of them gave ground and the line began to
waver and be unsteady, the Roman first and second
lines, giving a fresh cheer, charged them, sword in
hand.   Their onset was too much for the Etruscans,
who faced about and fled headlong towards their
camp.   But the Roman cavalry, riding obliquely
across the plain, presented themselves in front of the
fugitives, who then abandoned the attempt to reach
their camp and sought the mountains; from which
they made their way in a body, unarmed and suffering from their wounds, to the Ciminian Forest.   The
Romans, having slain many thousand Etruscans and
captured eight-and-thirty standards, took possession
also of the enemy's camp, with a very large booty.
They then began to consider the feasibility of a
pursuit.

XXXVI. In those days the Ciminian Forest was
more impassable and appalling than were lately the
wooded defiles of Germany,[1] and no one—not even a
trader—had up to that time visited it.   To enter it
was a thing that hardly anyone but the general
himself was bold enough to do : with all the rest the
recollection of the Caudine Forks was still too vivid.
Then one of those present, the consul's brother
Marcus Fabius,—some say that it was Caeso Fabius,
others Gaius Claudius, a son of the same mother as
the consul—offered to explore and return in a short
time with definite information about everything.
He had been educated at Caere in the house of
family friends, and from this circumstance was
learned in Etruscan writings and knew the Etruscan

guamque Etruscam probe noverat. Habeo auctores
volgo tum Romanos pueros, sicut nunc Graecis, ita
4 Etruscis litteris erudiri solitos; sed propius est vero
praecipuum aliquid fuisse in eo qui se tam audaci
simulatione hostibus immiscuerit. Servus ei dicitur
comes unus fuisse, nutritus una eoque haud ignarus
5 linguae eiusdem; nec quicquam aliud proficiscentes
quam summatim regionis quae intranda erat naturam
ac nomina principum in populis accepere, ne qua
inter conloquia insigni nota haesitantes deprendi
6 possent. Iere pastorali habitu, agrestibus telis,
falcibus gaesisque [1] binis, armati. Sed neque com-
mercium linguae nec vestis armorumve habitus sic
eos texit quam quod abhorrebat ab fide quemquam
7 externum Ciminios saltus intraturum. Usque ad
Camertes Umbros penetrasse dicuntur. Ibi qui
essent fateri Romanum ausum; introductumque in
senatum consulis verbis egisse de societate amici-
8 tiaque atque inde comi hospitio acceptum nuntiare
Romanis iussum commeatum exercitui dierum triginta praesto fore, si ea loca intrasset, iuventutemque
Camertium Umbrorum in armis paratam imperio
futuram.

9 Haec cum relata consuli essent, impedimentis
prima vigilia praemissis, legionibus post impedi-

---

[1] gaesisque A^5 ⌐ : caesisq. (gessis D^2 or D^1 in marg.) Ω.

language well.   I have authority for believing that
in that age Roman boys were regularly wont to be
schooled in Etruscan literature, as nowadays they are
trained in Greek ; but it seems more probable that
this man possessed some exceptional qualification to
induce him to venture amongst enemies in so daring
a disguise.   It is said that his only companion was a
slave, brought up with him, and hence acquainted,
like his master, with the language.   They set out,
after acquiring no more than a summary knowledge
of the nature of the region they must enter and the
names of the chief men in those tribes, to save them
from being detected in conversation by boggling
at any well-known fact.   They went dressed as
shepherds and armed with rustic weapons, namely
billhooks and a brace of javelins apiece. But neither
their familiarity with the tongue nor the fashion of
their dress and weapons was so great a protection to
them as the fact that it was repugnant to belief that
any stranger would enter the Ciminian defiles.
They are said to have penetrated as far as Camerinum
in Umbria, where the Roman, having ventured to
tell who they were, was introduced into the senate,
and treated with them in the consul's name for
friendship and an alliance.   Having then been
hospitably entertained, he was bidden to carry word
back to the Romans that thirty days' provisions for
their army would be waiting for them, if they came
into that region, and that the young men of the
Umbrian Camertes would be armed and ready to
obey their orders.

On their success being made known to the consul,
he sent the baggage ahead, in the first watch, and
directed the legions to follow the baggage.   He

A.U.C.
444 10 menta ire iussis ipse substitit cum equitatu et luce
orta postero die obequitavit stationibus hostium,
quae extra saltum dispositae erant; et cum satis
diu tenuisset hostem, in castra sese recepit portaque
altera egressus ante noctem agmen adsequitur.
11 Postero die luce prima iuga Ciminii montis tenebat;
inde contemplatus opulenta Etruriae arva milites
12 emittit. Ingenti iam abacta praeda tumultuariae
agrestium Etruscorum cohortes repente a principibus
regionis eius concitatae Romanis occurrunt, adeo
incompositae ut vindices praedarum prope ipsi
13 praedae fuerint. Caesis fugatisque his, late depopulato agro victor Romanus opulentusque rerum
14 omnium copia in castra rediit. Eo forte quinque
legati cum duobus tribunis plebis venerant denun-
tiatum Fabio senatus verbis ne saltum Ciminium
transiret. Laetati serius se quam ut impedire bellum
possent venisse, nuntii victoriae Romam revertuntur.

XXXVII. Hac expeditione consulis motum latius
erat quam profligatum bellum; vastationem namque
sub Ciminii montis radicibus iacens ora senserat,
conciveratque indignatione non Etruriae modo popu-
2 los sed Umbriae finitima. Itaque quantus non
unquam antea exercitus ad Sutrium venit; neque
e silvis tantummodo promota castra sed etiam avi-

---

[1] The tribunes were added to the embassy that they
might, if necessary, compel obedience to the senate by the
exercise of their sacrosanct authority. This was an unusual
procedure, as the powers of the tribunes were held to extend
no further than one mile from the City.

himself stopped behind with the cavalry, and at B.C. 310
dawn of the following day made a demonstration
against the enemy's outposts, which had been
stationed at the entrance to the pass. Having kept
the enemy in play for a sufficient time, he retired
within his camp, and emerging from it by the
opposite gate overtook the column before night.
Next day, with the first rays of light, he was on the
crest of the Ciminian mountain and, looking thence
over the rich ploughlands of Etruria, sent his soldiers
to plunder. The Romans had already brought away
out enormous booty when certain improvised bands
of Etruscan peasants, called together in hot haste by
the chief men of that country, encountered them, but
with so little discipline that in seeking to regain the
spoils they had nearly been made a spoil themselves.
Having slain or driven off these men and wasted the
country far and wide, the Romans returned to their
camp, victorious and enriched with all manner of
supplies. There, as it happened, they found five
legates, with two tribunes of the plebs,[1] who had
come to order Fabius in the name of the senate not
to cross the Ciminian Forest. Rejoicing that they
had come too late to be able to hinder the campaign,
they returned to Rome with tidings of victory.

XXXVII. This expedition of the consul's, instead
of putting an end to the war, only gave it a wider
range. For the district lying about the base of
Mount Ciminius had felt the devastation, and had
aroused not only Etruria to resentment but the
neighbouring parts of Umbria also. So an army
came to Sutrium that was larger than any they had
raised before; and not only did they move forward
their camp, out of the woods, but even, in their

LIVY

ditate dimicandi quam primum in campos delata
3 acies. Deinde instructa primo suo stare loco, relicto
hostibus [1] ad instruendum contra spatio; dein, postquam detractare [2] hostem sensere pugnam, ad vallum
4 subeunt. Ubi postquam stationes quoque receptas
intra munimenta sensere, clamor repente circa duces
ortus, ut eo sibi e castris cibaria eius diei deferri
iuberent: mansuros se sub armis et aut nocte aut
5 certe luce prima castra hostium invasuros. Nihilo
quietior Romanus exercitus imperio ducis continetur.
Decima erat fere diei hora, cum cibum capere consul
milites iubet; praecipit ut in armis sint quacumque
6 diei noctisve hora signum dederit; paucis milites
adloquitur, Samnitium bella extollit, elevat Etruscos;
nec hostem hosti nec multitudinem multitudini com-
parandam ait; esse praeterea telum aliud occultum;
7 scituros in tempore; interea taceri opus esse. His
ambagibus prodi simulabat hostes, quo animus militum
multitudine territus restitueretur; et, quod sine
munimento consederant,[3] veri similius erat quod
simulabatur.

Curati cibo corpora quieti dant et quarta fere
8 vigilia sine tumultu excitati arma capiunt. Dolabrae
calonibus dividuntur ad vallum proruendum fos-

---

[1] hostibus ς: hostio O: hostium Ω: hosti *Madvig*.
[2] detractare A²: detractare . . . pugnam *omitted by M*:
detrec (-traec- *or* -trac- P) tare Ω.
[3] consederant ς: considerant Ω: constiterant ς.

---

[1] Perhaps about six o'clock.

eagerness for combat, came down into the plain at
the earliest opportunity in battle formation. At
first, after forming up, they stood still in their
positions, having left their enemies room to draw up
opposite. Then, finding the Romans in no haste to
engage them, they advanced up to the rampart.
When they saw that even the outguards had retired
within the works, they began shouting to their
generals, to have their rations for the day sent out
to them from the camp; they would wait under
arms, they said, and either that night, or at daybreak
at the latest, attack the enemy's stockade. The
Roman army was every whit as restless, but was
restrained by the general's authority. It was about
the tenth hour of the day [1] when the consul bade
the soldiers sup, and commanded them to be armed
and ready at whatever hour of the day or night he
might give the signal. In a brief address he magni-
fied the Samnite wars and belittled the Etruscans :
there was no comparison, he said, between the two
enemies, or between their numbers ; moreover, he
had an additional weapon in concealment ; they
should know about it when the time came; until
then it must remain a secret. By these obscure
hints he sought to engender a belief that the enemy
were being betrayed, in order to revive the spirits of
his men, which were damped by the numbers of
their enemies ; and the fact that the Etruscans had
thrown up no breastworks where they lay lent
colour to the insinuation.

Refreshed with food, the soldiers gave themselves up
to sleep, and at about the fourth watch were awakened
without noise and put on their armour. Mattocks
were issued to the soldiers' servants, that they might

sasque implendas. Intra munimenta instruitur acies, delectae cohortes ad portarum exitus conlocantur.

9 Dato deinde signo paulo ante lucem, quod aestivis noctibus sopitae maxime quietis tempus est, proruto vallo erupit acies, stratos passim invadit hostes; alios immobiles, alios semisomnos in cubilibus suis, maximam partem ad arma trepidantes caedes oppressit;

10 paucis armandi se datum spatium est; eos ipsos non signum certum, non ducem sequentes fundit Romanus fugatosque persequitur. Ad castra, ad silvas diversi tendebant. Silvae tutius dedere refugium; nam castra in campis sita eodem die capiuntur. Aurum argentumque iussum referri ad consulem; cetera praeda militis fuit. Caesa aut capta eo die hostium milia ad sexaginta.

11 Eam tam claram pugnam trans Ciminiam silvam ad Perusiam pugnatam quidam auctores sunt metuque in magno civitatem fuisse ne interclusus exercitus tam infesto saltu coortis undique Tuscis Vmbrisque

12 opprimeretur.[1] Sed ubicumque pugnatum est, res Romana superior fuit. Itaque a Perusia et Cortona[2] et Arretio, quae ferme capita Etruriae populorum ea tempestate erant, legati pacem foedusque ab Romanis petentes indutias in triginta annos impetraverunt.

XXXVIII. Dum haec in Etruria geruntur, consul alter C. Marcius Rutulus[3] Allifas de Samnitibus vi

---

[1] opprimeretur A^2 ς: opprimerentur Ω: opprimentur M.
[2] Cortona A^2 (marg.) A^5 ς: cortone (?) A^1: crotone Ω.
[3] Rutulus Conway: rutulius or rutilius Ω.

level the rampart and fill up the trenches. The line B.C. 310 was drawn up inside the fortifications, and selected cohorts were posted at the exits. Then, on the signal being given a little before dawn, which on summer nights is the time of deepest sleep, the rampart was thrown down, and the Romans, rushing out in battle-formation, fell upon their enemies, who were lying all about the field. Some were slain without even stirring in their sleep, some were but half awake, the greatest number were reaching in terror for their weapons. Only a few were given time to arm themselves; and even these, with no definite standard to follow and no leader, the Romans routed and chased from the field. Some made for the camp and others for the mountains, as they fled this way and that. The forests afforded the surer refuge; for the camp, being situated in the plain, was captured the same day. Orders were issued that all gold and silver be brought to the consul; the rest of the booty went to the soldiers. On that day the enemy lost sixty thousand slain or captured.

Some historians relate that this famous battle was fought on the other side of the Ciminian Forest, near Perusia, and that Rome was in a panic lest the army should be surrounded and cut off in that dangerous defile by the Tuscans and Umbrians rising up on every hand. But, wherever it was fought, the Romans were the victors. And so from Perusia and Cortona and Arretium, which at that time might be the chief cities of the nations of Etruria, ambassadors came to Rome to sue for peace and an alliance. They obtained a truce for thirty years.

XXXVIII. While these things were going on in Etruria, the other consul, Gaius Marcius Rutulus,

LIVY

cepit. Multa alia castella vicique aut deleta hosti-
liter aut integra in potestatem venere.

2 Per idem tempus et classis Romana a P. Cornelio,
quem senatus maritimae orae praefecerat, in Campaniam acta cum adpulsa Pompeios esset, socii inde
navales ad depopulandum agrum Nucerinum profecti, proximis raptim vastatis unde reditus tutus ad
naves esset, dulcedine, ut fit, praedae longius pro-
3 gressi excivere hostes. Palatis per agros nemo
obvius fuit, cum occidione occidi possent; redeuntes
agmine incauto haud procul navibus adsecuti agrestes
exuerunt praeda, partem etiam occiderunt; quae
superfuit caedi trepida multitudo ad naves compulsa est.

4 Profectio Q. Fabi trans Ciminiam silvam quantum
Romae terrorem fecerat, tam laetam famam in
Samnium ad hostes tulerat interclusum Romanum
exercitum obsideri, cladisque imaginem Furculas
5 Caudinas memorabant: eadem temeritate avidam
ulteriorum semper gentem in saltus invios deductam,
saeptam non hostium magis armis quam locorum
6 iniquitatibus esse. Iam gaudium invidia quadam
miscebatur, quod belli Romani decus ab Samnitibus

---

[1] At VIII. xxv. 4, Livy mentioned the acquisition of
Allifae, but has nowhere spoken of its recapture by the
Samnites.

[2] Diod. (XIX. lxv.) tells us that Nuceria (formerly an ally
of Rome) had revolted to the Samnites.

captured Allifae from the Samnites by assault.[1] B.C. 310
Many forts and villages besides were either wiped
out in the course of hostilities or came intact into
the hands of the Romans.

At about this time a Roman fleet, commanded by
Publius Cornelius, whom the senate had placed in
charge of the coast, sailed for Campania and put
into Pompeii. From there the sailors and rowers
set out to pillage the territory of Nuceria.[2] Having
quickly ravaged the nearest fields, from which they
might have returned in safety to their ships, they
were lured on, as often happens, by the love of
booty, and going too far abroad aroused the enemy.
While they roamed through the fields, nobody inter-
fered with them, though they might have been utterly
annihilated; but as they came trooping back, without a thought of danger, the country-folk overtook
them not far from the ships, stripped them of their
plunder, and even slew a part of them; those who
escaped the massacre were driven, a disordered
rabble, to their ships.

Great as had been the fears excited in Rome when
Quintus Fabius marched through the Ciminian
Forest, the rejoicings that took place in Samnium
amongst the enemy were no less on their hearing a
report that the Roman army was intercepted and
besieged. They recalled the Caudine Forks as
showing what the disaster would be like; with the
same temerity, they said, a race that was ever reaching out for what lay beyond had been led into pathless
forests and there hemmed in, more by the difficulties
of the ground than by the arms of their enemy.
Soon their joy began to be mixed with a kind of
envy, that Fortune should have transferred the glory

7 fortuna ad Etruscos avertisset. Itaque armis virisque ad opprimendum [1] C. Marcium consulem concurrunt, protinus inde Etruriam per Marsos ac Sabinos
petituri, si Marcius dimicandi potestatem non faciat.

8 Obvius iis consul fuit. Dimicatum proelio utrimque
atroci atque incerto eventu est, et cum anceps caedes
fuisset, adversae tamen rei fama in Romanos vertit
ob amissos quosdam equestris ordinis tribunosque
militum atque unum legatum, et quod insigne
maxime fuit, consulis ipsius volnus.

9 Ob haec etiam aucta fama, ut solet, ingens terror
patres invasit dictatoremque dici placebat; nec quin
Cursor Papirius diceretur in quo tum summa rei
bellicae ponebatur, dubium cuiquam erat. Sed nec

10 in Samnium nuntium perferri omnibus infestis tuto
posse nec vivere Marcium consulem satis fidebant.
Alter consul Fabius infestus privatim Papirio erat;

11 quae ne ira obstaret bono publico, legatos ex con-
sularium numero mittendos ad eum senatus censuit,

12 qui sua quoque eum, non publica solum auctoritate
moverent ut memoriam simultatium patriae remit-

13 teret. Profecti legati ad Fabium cum senatus consultum tradidissent adiecissentque orationem convenientem mandatis, consul demissis in terram oculis
tacitus ab incertis quidnam acturus esset legatis

---

[1] opprimendum ς: optinendum (or ob-) Ω.

of the Roman war from Samnites to Etruscans. So they hastened to bring all their strength to bear upon crushing Gaius Marcius, the consul; and resolved, if Marcius should avoid an encounter, to march forthwith into Etruria, through the countries of the Marsi and the Sabines. The consul met them, and the battle was fiercely contested on both sides, but without a decision being reached. Yet, doubtful though it was which side had suffered most, the report gained ground that the Romans had been worsted: they had lost certain members of the equestrian order, certain military tribunes, and one lieutenant, and—most conspicuous of their misfortunes—the consul himself was wounded.

These reverses as usual were further exaggerated in the telling, and the senate in great dismay determined on the appointment of a dictator. Nobody could doubt that Papirius Cursor, who was regarded as the foremost soldier of his time, would be designated. But the senators were not certain that a messenger could be got through in safety to Samnium, where all was hostile, nor that the consul Marcius was alive. The other consul, Fabius, had a private grudge against Papirius; and lest this enmity might hinder the general welfare, the senate decided to send a deputation of former consuls, in the hope that their personal influence, when added to the wishes of the government, might induce him to forget those quarrels for the good of the country. The ambassadors went to Fabius and delivered the resolution of the senate, with a discourse that suited their instructions. The consul, his eyes fixed on the ground, retired without a word, leaving the ambassadors uncertain what he proposed to do. Then in the

A.U.O. 444

14 recessit; nocte deinde silentio, ut mos est, L. Papirium dictatorem dixit. Cui cum ob animum egregie victum legati gratias agerent, obstinatum silentium obtinuit ac sine responso ac mentione facti sui legatos dimisit, ut appareret insignem dolorem ingenti comprimi animo.

15 Papirius C. Iunium Bubulcum magistrum equitum dixit; atque ei legem curiatam de imperio ferenti triste omen diem diffidit, quod Faucia curia fuit principium, duabus insignis cladibus, captae urbis et Caudinae pacis, quod utroque anno eiusdem curiae

16 fuerat principium. Macer Licinius tertia etiam clade, quae ad Cremeram accepta est, abominandam eam curiam facit.

XXXIX. Dictator postero die auspiciis repetitis pertulit legem; et profectus cum legionibus ad terrorem traducti silvam Ciminiam exercitus nuper

2 scriptis ad Longulam pervenit acceptisque a Marcio consule veteribus militibus in aciem copias eduxit. Nec hostes detractare visi pugnam. Instructos deinde armatosque, cum ab neutris proelium in-

3 ciperet, nox oppressit. Quieti aliquamdiu nec suis

---

[1] In the Fasti Cap. the dictatorship of Papirius is placed between the term of Q. Fabius Maximus and C. Marcius Rutilus (310 B.C.) and that of Fabius and C. Decius Mus (308 B.C.). In Livy's account the campaign of the dictator runs parallel to those of the consuls of 310 B.C.

[2] Under the kings the curiate assembly had been the only formal assembly of the people (*cf.* I. xiii. 6 for the origin of the *curiae*), but in the time of the republic its functions had largely passed to the centuriate assembly. It was, however, still called upon to ratify the election of new magistrates by passing a *lex curiata de imperio*, and retained certain other ceremonial duties.

[3] This was determined each time by lot.

[4] 477 B.C. (Book II, chap. l.).

silence of the night, as the custom is, he appointed B.C. 310
Lucius Papirius dictator.[1]   When the envoys thanked
him for nobly conquering his feelings, he continued
obstinately silent, and dismissed them without
making any reply or alluding to what he had done,
so that it was clearly seen what agony his great
heart was suppressing.

Papirius named Gaius Junius Bubulcus master of
the horse.   When he began to lay before the curiate
assembly [2] a law confirming his authority, the proceedings were cut short by an evil omen, the first
vote to be counted being that of the ward called
Faucia, notorious for two calamities, the capture of
the City and the Caudine Peace, which had both
been incurred in years when this same curia had the
right of the first return.[3]   Licinius Macer makes
this ward unlucky also for a third disaster—that of
the Cremera.[4]

XXXIX. Next day the dictator sought the auspices B.C.
afresh and carried the law through.   Then, setting 310–309
out with the legions which had recently been
recruited on account of the fear occasioned by the
army's march through the Ciminian Forest, he came
to the vicinity of Longula,[5] and taking over from
Marcius the consul his veteran troops, marched out
and offered battle, which the enemy on their part
seemed willing to accept.   But while the two armies
stood armed and ready for the conflict, which neither
cared to begin, night overtook them.   For some
time after that they remained quietly in the camps

[5] Longula was a Volscian town, but was situated not far
from the Samnite border.   It is not necessary to assume,
with Weissenborn-Mueller, that Livy is referring to an
otherwise unknown Longula in Samnium.

LIVY

diffidentes viribus nec hostem spernentes, stativa in
5 propinquo habuere.[1] Interea Etrusci [2] lege sacrata
coacto exercitu, cum vir virum legisset, quantis
nunquam alias ante simul copiis simul animis dimi-
6 carunt; tantoque irarum certamine gesta res est ut
ab neutra parte emissa sint tela. Gladiis pugna
coepit et acerrime commissa ipso certamine, quod
aliquamdiu anceps fuit, accensa est, ut non cum
Etruscis totiens victis, sed cum aliqua nova gente
7 videretur dimicatio esse. Nihil ab ulla parte move-
tur fugae; cadunt antesignani, et ne nudentur
propugnatoribus signa, fit ex secunda prima acies.
8 Ab ultimis deinde subsidiis cietur miles; adeoque ad
ultimum laboris ac periculi ventum est ut equites
Romani omissis equis ad primos ordines peditum per
arma, per corpora evaserint. Ea velut nova inter fes-
9 sos exorta acies turbavit signa Etruscorum; secuta
deinde impetum eorum, utcumque adfecta erat, cetera
10 multitudo tandem perrumpit ordines hostium. Tunc
vinci pertinacia coepta et averti manipuli quidam, et,
ut semel dedere hi terga,[3] etiam ceteri item [4] capes-

---

[1] habuere *Anderson* (*ed. of Bk. IX. p.* 259): habuere. Nam
et cum umbrorum exercitu acie depugnatum est; fusi tamen
magis quam caesi hostes, quia coeptam acriter non tolerarunt
pugnam; et ad Vadimonis lacum *POTDLA*: *M has these
words and also* (*before* Nam) *the words* et rurae (?): *A⁴ the
words* interea res in etruria geste: *P²* (*or P³*) *F?* (*marg.*) *U
have them after* pugnam (*U adding* et *after* res): *F³ has after*
pugnam (*over erasure*) interim ab fabio cōs in etruria res
feliciter geste ad vadimonis lacum. *Anderson supposes that
we have here what was written as a comment on the first sentence
of* § 11.
[2] Interea Etrusci *Walters* (*note*): Et Etrusci *Anderson*:
Etrusci Ω.
[3] dedere hi terga *Walters and Conway*: dedere terga Ω:
dederunterga *O*: dederet terga *TD?*: dederet et terga *L?*:
dederet (*or* dederat *or* dedert) terga *D*.

they had established near one another, neither lacking
confidence in themselves nor yet making light of
their adversaries. Meanwhile the Etruscans, employ-
ing a *lex sacrata*,[1] had raised an army in which each
man had chosen his comrade, and joined battle, with
greater forces, and at the same time with greater
valour, than ever before. The field was contested
with such rivalry of rage that neither side discharged
a missile. The battle began with swords, and,
furious at the outset, waxed hotter as the struggle
continued, for the victory was long undecided. It
seemed as though the Romans were contending, not
with the so oft defeated Etruscans, but with some
new race. No sign of flight was visible in any
quarter. As the front-rankers fell, the second line
moved up to replace the first, that the standards
might not want defenders. After that the last
reserves were called upon; and to such extremity of
distress and danger did the Romans come that their
cavalry dismounted, and made their way over arms
and over bodies to the front ranks of the infantry.
Like a fresh line springing up amongst the exhausted
combatants, they wrought havoc in the companies of
the Etruscans. Then the rest of the soldiers, following up their charge, despite of weariness, at last
broke through the enemy's ranks. At this their
stubbornness began to be overcome, and certain
companies to face about; and when these had once
turned tail, the rest likewise took to flight. That

[1] One who violated the *lex sacrata* was forfeited to the
gods. See chap. xl. § 9, iv. xxvi. 3, xxxvi. xxxviii. 1, and
especially x. xxxviii. 3 ff.

---

[4] ceteri item *Harant*: certiorem Ω: tutiores *A*: certiores
A² *Koch*: ceteri certiorem *Walters and Conway*.

A.U.C.
444 11 sere fugam. Ille primum dies fortuna vetere abund-
antes Etruscorum fregit opes. Caesum in acie, quod
roboris fuit ; castra eodem impetu capta direptaque.

A.U.C.
446 XL. Pari subinde periculo gloriaeque eventu
bellum in Samnitibus erat, qui praeter cetoros belli
apparatus, ut acies sua fulgeret novis armorum
2 insignibus fecerunt. Duo exercitus erant ; scuta
alterius auro, alterius argento caelaverunt ; forma
erat scuti : summum latius, qua pectus atque umeri
teguntur, fastigio aequali ; ad imum cuneatior mobi-
3 litatis causa. Spongia pectori tegumentum et sinis-
trum crus ocrea tectum ; galeae cristatae, quae
speciem magnitudini corporum adderent. Tunicae
auratis militibus versicolores, argentatis linteae can-
didae. His vaginae argenteae, baltea argentea :
auratae vaginae, aurea baltea illis erant, et equorum
inaurata tapeta.[1] His dextrum cornu datum ; illi in
4 sinistro consistunt. Notus iam Romanis apparatus
insignium armorum fuerat doctique a ducibus erant
horridum militem esse debere, non caelatum auro et
5 argento sed ferro et animis fretum : quippe illa
praedam verius quam arma esse, nitentia ante rem,
6 deformia inter sanguinem et volnera. Virtutem

---

[1] *The words* his vaginae—tapeta *are not found in the MSS
of Livy.* Nonius (194, 20) *cites* (*as from Liv. IX*) auratae
vaginae, aurata baltea illis erant, *and* Auctor explan. in
Donatum, *and* Probus (*cf.* Keil, Gram, Lat. *IV* 542 *and* 129)
ascribe to Livy ("*Livy or Virgil,*" *Probus*) erant et equorum
inaurata tapeta. *Walters and Conway suggest placing them as
in the text, prefixing* his vaginae argenteae, baltea argentea
which they conjecture to have stood in the original (Class. Quart.
12 (1918) *p.* 103).

---

[1] Weissenborn-Mueller think a breastplate resembling a
sponge in appearance is intended. The translator follows

day for the first time broke the might of the B.C.
310–309
Etruscans, which had long flourished in prosperity.
Their strength was cut off in the battle, and their
camp was taken and plundered in the same attack.

XL. The war in Samnium, immediately afterwards,
was attended with equal danger and an equally
glorious conclusion. The enemy, besides their other
warlike preparations, had made their battle-line to
glitter with new and splendid arms. There were
two corps: the shields of the one were inlaid with
gold, of the other with silver. The shape of the
shield was this: the upper part, where it protected
the breast and shoulders, was rather broad, with a
level top; below it was somewhat tapering, to make
it easier to handle. They wore a sponge [1] to protect
the breast, and the left leg was covered with a
greave. Their helmets were crested, to make their
stature appear greater. The tunics of the gilded
warriors were parti-coloured; those of the silvern
ones were linen of a dazzling white. The latter
had silver sheaths and silver baldrics: the former
gilded sheaths and golden baldrics, and their horses
had gold-embroidered saddle-cloths. The right wing
was assigned to these: the others took up their post
on the left. The Romans had already learned of
these splendid accoutrements, and their generals
had taught them that a soldier should be rough to
look on, not adorned with gold and silver but putting
his trust in iron and in courage: indeed those other
things were more truly spoil than arms, shining
bright before a battle, but losing their beauty in
the midst of blood and wounds; manhood they said,

Professor Anderson in taking the expression literally, of a
corslet made of sponge.

A.U.C.
464

esse militis decus et omnia illa victoriam sequi et ditem hostem quamvis pauperis victoris praemium esse.

7   His Cursor vocibus instinctos milites in proelium ducit.   Dextro ipse cornu consistit, sinistro praefecit 8 magistrum equitum.   Simul est concursum, ingens fuit cum hoste certamen, non segnius inter dictatorem et magistrum equitum ab utra parte victoria 9 inciperet.   Prior forte Iunius commovit hostem, laevo dextrum cornu, sacratos more Samnitium milites eoque candida veste et paribus candore armis insignes; eos se Orco mactare Iunius dictitans [1] cum intulisset signa turbavit ordines et haud dubie impulit aciem. 10 Quod ubi sensit dictator, " Ab laevone cornu victoria incipiet" inquit, "et dextrum cornu, dictatoris acies, alienam pugnam sequetur, non partem maximam 11 victoriae trahet?" Concitat milites; nec peditum virtuti equites aut legatorum studia ducibus cedunt. 12 M. Valerius a dextro, P. Decius ab laevo cornu, ambo consulares, ad equites in cornibus positos evehuntur adhortatique eos ut partem secum capesserent decoris in transversa latera hostium incurrunt. 13 Is novus additus terror cum ex parte utraque circumvasisset aciem et ad terrorem hostium legiones Romanae redintegrato clamore intulissent gradum,

---

[1] intulisset T^2 (or T^1) ç: intulissent Ω.

---

[1] Orcus—the Greek Pluto—was god of the dead.

B.C.
310–309

was the adornment of a soldier; all those other things went with the victory, and a rich enemy was the prize of the victor, however poor.

Whilst his men were animated by these words, Cursor led them into battle. He took up his own post on the right, and committed the left to the master of the horse. From the moment of encountering, there was a mighty struggle with the enemy, and a struggle no less sharp between the dictator and the master of the horse, to decide which wing was to inaugurate the victory. It so happened that Junius was the first to make an impression on the Samnites. With the Roman left he faced the enemy's right, where they had consecrated themselves, as their custom was, and for that reason were resplendent in white coats and equally white armour. Declaring that he offered up these men in sacrifice to Orcus,[1] Junius charged, threw their ranks into disorder, and clearly made their line recoil. When the dictator saw this, he cried, "Shall the victory begin upon the left? Shall the right, the dictator's division, follow the attack of others? Shall it not carry off the honours of the victory?" This fired the soldiers with new energy; nor did the cavalry display less valour than the foot, or the lieutenants less enthusiasm than the generals. Marcus Valerius on the right and Publius Decius on the left, both men of consular rank, rode out to the cavalry, which was posted on the wings, and, exhorting them to join with themselves in seizing a share of glory, charged obliquely against the enemy's flanks. Thus a new and appalling danger enveloped their line on either side, and when the Roman legions, observing the terror of the Samnites, pressed forward with

A.U.C. 14 tum fuga ab Samnitibus coepta. Iam strage hominum
446 armorumque insignium campi repleri. Ac primo
pavidos Samnites castra sua accepere, deinde ne ea
quidem retenta; captis direptisque ante noctem
iniectus ignis.

15 Dictator ex senatus consulto triumphavit, cuius
triumpho longe maximam speciem captiva arma prae-
16 buere. Tantum magnificentiae visum in iis,[1] ut
aurata scuta dominis argentariarum[2] ad forum ornan-
dum dividerentur. Inde natum initium dicitur fori
17 ornandi ab aedilibus cum tensae ducerentur. Et
Romani quidem ad honorem deum insignibus armis
hostium usi sunt: Campani ab superbia et odio
Samnitium gladiatores, quod spectaculum inter epulas
erat, eo ornatu armarunt Samnitiumque nomine
compellarunt.

18 Eodem anno cum reliquiis[3] Etruscorum ad Perusiam, quae et ipsa indutiarum fidem ruperat, Fabius
19 consul nec dubia nec difficili victoria dimicat. Ipsum
oppidum—nam ad moenia victor accessit—cepisset,
20 ni legati dedentes urbem exissent. Praesidio Perusiae

---

[1] iis *ς*: hiis *A* : his Ω.
[2] argentariarum *Muretus*: argentariorum (-oriorum *O*) Ω.
[3] reliquiis *F*[3] *ς*: reliquis Ω.

---

[1] It was forty years later when the Romans began to
coin silver for themselves; but there would be much
coined silver in circulation by this time from Etruria and
Magna Graecia, to furnish employment for money-changers
(*argentarii*).

[2] A *tensa* is figured in Stuart Jones, *Companion to Roman
History*, Pl. xlix. It was used to carry the images of the
Capitoline gods in solemn procession to the Circus, at the
time of the *ludi circenses*.

[3] The Romans seem to have obtained from Capua the
idea of gladiators (Livy, *Per.* XVI.), and the "Samnite"

B.C.
310-309

redoubled shouts, the enemy began to flee. The
fields were soon heaped with slain and with glittering armour. At first the frightened Samnites found
a refuge in their camp, but presently even that had
to be abandoned, and ere nightfall it had been taken,
sacked, and set on fire.

The dictator, as decreed by the senate, celebrated
a triumph, in which by far the finest show was
afforded by the captured armour. So magnificent
was its appearance that the shields inlaid with gold
were divided up amongst the owners of the money-
changers' booths, to be used in decking out the
Forum.[1] From this is said to have come the custom
of the aediles adorning the Forum whenever the
tensae, or covered chariots of the gods, were conducted through it.[2] So the Romans made use of
the splendid armour of their enemies to do honour
to the gods; while the Campanians, in consequence
of their pride and in hatred of the Samnites, equipped
after this fashion the gladiators who furnished them
entertainment at their feasts, and bestowed on them
the name of Samnites.[3]

In the same year the consul Fabius fought a battle
with the remnants of the Etruscan forces near
Perusia—which, together with other cities, had
broken the truce [4]—and gained an easy and decisive
victory. He would have taken the town itself—for
after the battle he marched up to the walls—had
not ambassadors come out and surrendered the place.
Having placed a garrison in Perusia and having sent

was always one of the standard types. The sentence is
usually taken as implying that the Capuans had been present
as allies of the Romans in the battle.

[4] Chap, xxxvii. § 12.

LIVY

A.U.C.
446

imposito, legationibus Etruriae amicitiam petentibus
prae se Romam ad senatum missis consul praestantiore
etiam quam dictator victoria triumphans urbem est
21 invectus; quin etiam devictorum Samnitium decus
magna ex parte ad legatos, P. Decium et M. Valerium,
est versum; quos populus proximis comitiis ingenti
consensu consulem alterum, alterum praetorem de-
claravit.

XLI. Fabio ob egregie perdomitam Etruriam con-
tinuatur consulatus; Decius collega datur. Valerius
praetor quartum creatus. Consules partiti provincias:
2 Etruria Decio, Samnium Fabio evenit. Is profectus [1]
3 ad Nuceriam Alfaternam, cum pacem petentes, quod
uti ea cum daretur noluissent, aspernatus esset,[2]
4 oppugnando ad deditionem subegit. Cum Samnitibus
acie dimicatum. Haud magno certamine hostes
victi; neque eius pugnae memoria tradita foret, ni
Marsi eo primum proelio cum Romanis bellassent.
Secuti Marsorum defectionem Paeligni eandem fortunam habuerunt.
5 Decio quoque, alteri consuli, secunda belli fortuna
erat. Tarquiniensem metu subegerat frumentum
exercitui praebere atque indutias in quadraginta
6 annos petere. Volsiniensium castella aliquot vi
cepit; quaedam ex his diruit ne receptaculo hostibus
essent; circumferendoque passim bello tantum ter-

---

[1] Is profectus *Sigonius* : profectus Ω.
[2] esset *A⁴ (or A⁵) marg.* Madvig: êâ *L* : eā *DA* : est (*or* ē
Ω: *wanting in O.*

---

[1] The Marsi, though of Samnite stock, had hitherto been
on good terms with the Romans.

324

B.C.
310–309

on before him to the senate in Rome the Etruscan deputations which had come to him seeking friendship, the consul was borne in triumph into the City, after gaining a success more brilliant even than the dictator's; indeed the glory of conquering the Samnites was largely diverted upon the lieutenants, Publius Decius and Marcus Valerius, of whom, at the next election, the people with great enthusiasm made the one consul and the other praetor.

B.C. 308

XLI. In recognition of his remarkable conquest of Etruria, Fabius was continued in the consulship, and was given Decius for his colleague. Valerius was for the fourth time chosen praetor. The consuls cast lots for the commands, Etruria falling to Decius and Samnium to Fabius. The latter marched against Nuceria Alfaterna, and rejecting that city's overtures of peace because its people had declined it when it was offered them, laid siege to the place and forced it to surrender. A battle was fought with the Samnites, in which the enemy were defeated without much difficulty, nor would the engagement have been remembered but for the fact that it was the first time that the Marsi had made war against the Romans.[1] The Paeligni imitated the defection of the Marsi, and met with the same fate.

Decius, the other consul, was also successful in war. When he had frightened the Tarquinienses into furnishing corn for the army and seeking a truce for forty years, he captured by storm a number of strongholds belonging to the people of Volsinii. Some of these he dismantled, lest they should serve as a refuge for the enemy, and by devastating far and wide he made himself so feared that all who

A.U.C.
446

rorem sui fecit ut nomen omne Etruscum foedus ab
7 consule peteret. Ac de eo quidem nihil impetratum ;
indutiae annuae datae. Stipendium exercitu Romano
ab hoste in eum annum pensum et binae tunicae in
militem exactae ; ea merces indutiarum fuit.

8   Tranquillas res iam in ¹ Etruscis turbavit repentina
defectio Umbrorum, gentis integrae a cladibus belli,
9 nisi quod transitum exercitus ager senserat. Ii con-
citata omni iuventute sua et magna parte Etruscorum
ad rebellionem compulsa tantum exercitum fecerant
ut relicto post se in Etruria Decio ad oppugnandam
inde Romam ituros, magnifice de se ac contemptim
10 de Romanis loquentes, iactarent. Quod inceptum
eorum ubi ad Decium consulem perlatum est, ad
urbem ex Etruria magnis itineribus pergit et in agro
Pupiniensi ad famam intentus hostium consedit.
11 Nec Romae spernebatur Umbrorum bellum, et ipsae
minae metum fecerant expertis Gallica clade quam
12 intutam urbem incolerent. Itaque legati ad Fabium
consulem missi sunt, ut si quid laxamenti a bello
Samnitium esset, in Umbriam propere exercitum
13 duceret. Dicto paruit consul magnisque itineribus
ad Mevaniam, ubi tum copiae Umbrorum erant,
perrexit.
14   Repens adventus consulis, quem procul Umbria in
Samnio bello alio occupatum crediderant, ita exter-
ruit Umbros ut alii recedendum ad urbes munitas,

---

¹ iam in *Madvig* : iam Ω.

---

¹ Livy has not mentioned this before.
² South of the Anio not far from Gabii. See XXVI. ix. 12.
³ In the neighbourhood of Perugia and Assisi.

bore the Etruscan name begged the consul to grant B.C. 308 them a treaty. This privilege they were denied, but a truce for a year was granted them. They were required to furnish the Roman army with a year's pay and two tunics for each soldier ; such was the price they paid for a truce.

The tranquillity which now obtained in Etruria was disturbed by a sudden revolt of the Umbrians, a people which had escaped all the distress of war, except that an army had passed through their terri-tory.[1] Calling up all their fighting men, and in-ducing great part of the Etruscans to rebel, they mustered so large an army, that they boasted, with much glorifying of themselves and fleering at the Romans, that they would leave Decius behind them in Etruria and march off to the assault of Rome. When this purpose of theirs was reported to the consul Decius, he hastened by forced marches from Etruria towards the City, and encamped in the fields belonging to Pupinia,[2] eagerly waiting for word of their approach. At Rome no one made light of an Umbrian invasion. Their very threats had excited fear in those who had learnt from the Gallic disaster how unsafe was the City they inhabited. Accord-ingly envoys were dispatched to carry word to Fabius the consul, that if there were any slackening in the Samnite war he should with all speed lead his army into Umbria. The consul obeyed the order, and advanced by long marches to Mevania,[3] where the forces of the Umbrians at that time lay.

The sudden arrival of the consul, whom they had believed to have his hands full with another war in Samnium, a long way from Umbria, so dismayed the Umbrians that some were for falling back on their

15 quidam omittendum bellum censerent; plaga una
—Materinam ipsi appellant—non continuit modo
ceteros in armis sed confestim ad certamen egit.

16 Castra vallantem Fabium adorti sunt. Quos ubi
effusos ruere in munimenta consul vidit, revocatos
milites ab opere, prout loci natura tempusque patiebatur, ita instruxit; cohortatusque praedicatione vera
qua in Tuscis, qua in Samnio partorum decorum
exiguam appendicem Etrusci belli conficere iubet et
vocis impiae poenas expetere, qua se urbem Romanam

17 oppugnaturos minati sint.[1] Haec tanta sunt alacritate
militum audita ut clamor sua sponte ortus loquentem
interpellaverit ducem. Ante imperium, deinde concentu [2] tubarum ac cornuum cursu effuso in hostem

18 feruntur. Non tamquam in viros aut armatos incurrunt; mirabilia dictu, signa primo eripi coepta
signiferis, deinde ipsi signiferi trahi ad consulem,
armatique milites ex acie in aciem transferri, et
sicubi est certamen, scutis magis quam gladiis geritur
res; umbonibus incussaque ala sternuntur hostes.

19 Plus capitur hominum quam caeditur, atque una vox
ponere arma iubentium per totam fertur aciem

20 Itaque inter ipsum certamen facta deditio est ₂
primis auctoribus belli. Postero insequentibusqu₌

---

[1] sint *Modius* : sunt Ω.
[2] deinde concentu (contentu *PU* : concerta *F* : conuent₌
T) Ω : ante concentu *M* : ante concentum *M*[3].

fortified cities, and others for giving up the war;
but one canton—which they themselves call Materina
—not only kept the rest to their arms, but brought
them to an immediate engagement. Fabius was
entrenching his camp when they attacked him. As
soon as he saw them rushing madly upon his ramparts, he recalled the soldiers from their work and
drew them up, as time and the nature of the ground
permitted, and encouraging them with a true relation of the honours they had won, some in Etruria
and some in Samnium, bade them end this trivial
sequel to the Etruscan war, and revenge upon the
foe his impious threat that he would assault the
City of Rome. These words were received by
the soldiers with such alacrity that the speech of
the general was interrupted by a spontaneous cheer.
Then, before the command could be given, they
hurled themselves—to the blare of horns and
trumpets—with the wildest abandon against the
enemy. They fought not as though their opponents
had been men and armed; but—marvellous to relate
—began with tearing the standards out of the
bearers' hands, and then fell to dragging the bearers
themselves before the consul and to bringing armed
men over from the other line to their own; wherever they met with resistance, they did their work
more with shields than with swords, swinging them
from the shoulder and knocking down their enemies
with the bosses. The slain were outnumbered by
the prisoners, and all along the battle line one cry
was heard: that they should lay down their arms.
And so, while the battle was still going on, the
surrender was made, by the men who had first
advocated war. On the next and on succeeding

A.U.C.
446
diebus et ceteri Umbrorum populi deduntur; Ocriculani sponsione in amicitiam accepti.

A.U.C.
447–448
XLII. Fabius, alienae sortis victor belli, in suam
2 provinciam exercitum reduxit. Itaque ei ob res tam feliciter gestas, sicut priore anno populus continuaverat consulatum, ita senatus in insequentem annum, quo Ap. Claudius L. Volumnius consules fuerunt, prorogavit maxime Appio adversante imperium.

3 Appium censorem petisse consulatum comitiaque eius ab L. Furio tribuno plebis interpellata, donec se censura abdicarit,[1] in quibusdam annalibus invenio.

4 Creatus consul, cum collegae novum bellum, Sallentini[2] hostes decernerentur, Romae mansit ut urbanis artibus opes augeret quando belli decus penes alios esset.

5 Volumnium provinciae haud paenituit. Multa secunda proelia fecit, aliquot urbes hostium vi cepit. Praedae erat largitor et benignitatem per se gratam comitate adiuvabat militemque his artibus fecerat et periculi et laboris avidum.

6 Q. Fabius pro consule ad urbem Allifas cum Samnitium exercitu signis conlatis confligit. Minime ambigua res fuit; fusi hostes atque in castra compulsi. Nec castra forent retenta, ni exiguum superfuisset

---

[1] abdicarit *Ruperti*: abdicauit Ω.
[2] Sallentini *ς Sigonius*: salentini (-ne *F*) Ω.

---

[1] The senate had a grudge against Appius (see chap. xxx. § 1 f.), and so prolonged, unconstitutionally, the command of Fabius, and gave the other war to Volumnius.

days the other peoples of Umbria also capitulated: the men of Ocriculum were received into friendship under a stipulation.

XLII. Fabius, having won a war assigned by lot to another man, led his army back to his own province. Just as in the preceding year the people had rewarded his successful campaign by re-electing him to the consulship, so now the senate continued him in command for the year to follow. The new consuls were Appius Claudius and Lucius Volumnius, the former of whom had strongly opposed the resolution.[1]

I find in certain annals that Appius sought the consulship when censor, and that Lucius Furius, a tribune of the plebs, refused to let him stand until he should have resigned the censorship. The election over, his colleague was decreed the command in the new war—with the Sallentini—and Appius remained in Rome, to strengthen his power by civil arts, since the means of acquiring repute in war remained with others.

Volumnius had no cause to regret his assignment. He engaged in many successful battles and took several hostile towns by assault. Generous in his distribution of the spoil, he enhanced the effect of a liberality which was pleasing in itself by his friendly bearing—traits which had made his soldiers eager for toil and danger.

The proconsul Quintus Fabius fought near the city Allifae a pitched battle with the army of the Samnites. The result was anything but doubtful, for the enemy were routed and driven into their camp; and they could not have held the camp had there not been very little daylight left.

LIVY

diei; ante noctem tamen sunt circumsessa et nocte
7 custodita ne quis elabi posset. Postero die vixdum
luce certa deditio fieri coepta et pacti qui Samnitium
forent ut cum singulis vestimentis emitterentur;
8 ii omnes sub iugum missi. Sociis Samnitium nihil
cautum; ad septem milia sub corona veniere. Qui
se civem Hernicum dixerat seorsus in custodia
9 habitus. Eos omnes Fabius Romam ad senatum
misit; et cum quaesitum esset dilectu an voluntarii
10 pro Samnitibus adversus Romanos bellassent per
Latinos populos custodiendi dantur, iussique eam
integram rem novi consules P. Cornelius Arvina Q.
Marcius Tremulus—hi enim iam creati erant—ad
11 senatum referre. Id aegre passi Hernici; concilium
populorum omnium habentibus Anagninis in circo
quem Maritimum vocant praeter Aletrinatem Fer-
entinatemque et Verulanum omnes Hernici nominis
populo Romano bellum indixerunt.

XLIII. In Samnio quoque, quia decesserat inde
Fabius, novi motus exorti. Calatia et Sora praesidia-
que quae in his Romana erant expugnata et in
2 captivorum corpora militum foede saevitum. Itaque
eo P. Cornelius cum exercitu missus; Marcio novi
hostes—iam enim Anagninis Hernicisque aliis bellum
3 iussum erat—decernuntur. Primo ita omnia oppor-

---

[1] The Hernici had been at peace with the Romans ever
since their subjugation in 358 B.C. (VII. xv. 9).

[2] Calatia was mentioned in chap. ii. § 2 as a Samnite town,
and its capture by the Romans in 314 B.C. is noted in chap.
xxviii. § 6. Sora, on the borders of the Hernici, was taken
in the same year (chap. xxiv. § 14).

Even so they were invested before dark, and guards
were posted in the night to prevent anyone's escaping. Next day, before it was well light, they began to surrender. The Samnites among them bargained to be dismissed in their tunics; all these were sent under the yoke. The allies of the Samnites were protected by no guarantee, and were sold into slavery, to the number of seven thousand. Those who gave themselves out for Hernic citizens were detained apart in custody, and Fabius sent them all to the senate in Rome. There an enquiry was held as to whether they had been conscripted or had fought voluntarily for the Samnites against the Romans; after which they were parcelled out amongst the Latins to be guarded, and a resolution was passed directing the new consuls, Publius Cornelius Arvina and Quintus Marcius Tremulus— for these men had been elected—to refer the matter to the senate for fresh action. This the Hernici resented. The people of Anagnia assembled a council of all the states in the circus which they call the Maritime Circus, and all of the Hernic name, excepting the inhabitants of Aletrium, Ferentinum and Verulae, declared war on the Roman People.[1]

XLIII. In Samnium, too, the departure of Fabius was the cause of fresh disturbances. Calatia and Sora with their Roman garrisons were taken by assault, and the captured soldiers were treated with shameful rigour.[2] Accordingly Publius Cornelius was dispatched in that direction with an army. The new enemies—for by this time war had been declared on the men of Anagnia and the other Hernici—were allotted to Marcius. At the outset of the campaign the enemy were so successful in

tuna loca hostes inter consulum castra interceperunt
4 ut pervadere expeditus nuntius non posset et per
aliquot dies incerti rerum omnium suspensique de
statu alterius uterque consul ageret, Romamque is
metus manaret, adeo ut omnes iuniores sacramento
adigerentur atque ad subita rerum duo iusti scribe-
5 rentur exercitus. Ceterum Hernicum bellum nequaquam pro praesenti terrore ac vetusta[1] gentis gloria
6 fuit. Nihil usquam dictu dignum ausi, trinis castris
intra paucos dies exuti, triginta dierum indutias ita
ut ad senatum Romam legatos mitterent, pacti sunt
7 bimestri stipendio frumentoque et singulis in militem
tunicis. Ab senatu ad Marcium reiecti, cui senatus
consulto permissum de Hernicis erat, isque eam
gentem in deditionem accepit.

8 Et in Samnio alter consul superior viribus, locis
impeditior erat. Omnia itinera obsaepserant hostes
saltusque pervios ceperant, ne qua subvehi commeatus possent; neque eos, cum cottidie signa in
aciem consul proferret, elicere ad certamen poterat;
9 satisque apparebat neque Samnitem certamen prae-
10 sens nec Romanum dilationem belli laturum. Adventus Marci, qui Hernicis subactis maturavit collegae
11 venire auxilio, moram certaminis hosti exemit. Nam
ut qui ne alteri quidem exercitui se ad certamen

---

[1] vetusta *Gronovius* : vetustae *Klockius* : vetustate Ω.

seizing all the strategic points between the camps
of the consuls, that not even a nimble courier
could get through, and for some days the consuls
were kept in uncertainty regarding everything and
could only speculate about one another's state.
Fears for their safety even extended to Rome,
where all of military age were given the oath and
two full armies were enlisted, to meet any sudden
emergencies. But the war with the Hernici by
no means answered to the present panic or to the
nation's old renown. They ventured nothing to
speak of at any point, and having lost three camps
in the space of a few days they bargained for
a thirty days' truce, to enable them to send envoys
to the senate in Rome, and delivered up two
months' pay and corn, and a tunic for every soldier.
The senate sent them back to Marcius, having
passed a resolution empowering him to deal with
the Hernici as he saw fit. He received their
submission on terms of unconditional surrender.

In Samnium the other consul was also stronger
than the enemy, but was more embarrassed by the
character of the ground. The enemy had blockaded
all the roads and seized the practicable passes, to
prevent supplies being brought up anywhere. But
though the consul offered battle daily, he could
not entice them to fight. It was quite apparent
that the Samnites would not accept an immediate
engagement, nor the Romans endure any prolongation of the war. The arrival of Marcius, who,
having subdued the Hernici, made haste to come to
the assistance of his colleague, deprived the enemy
of any power to delay the struggle. For since
they had not considered themselves equal to a

credidissent pares, coniungi utique passi duos consulares exercitus nihil crederent superesse spei,
advenientem incomposito agmine Marcium adgredi-

12 untur. Raptim conlatae sarcinae in medium, et
prout tempus patiebatur instructa acies. Clamor
primum in stativa perlatus, dein conspectus procul
pulvis tumultum apud alterum consulem in castris

13 fecit; isque confestim arma capere iussis raptimque
eductis in aciem militibus transversam hostium aciem
atque alio certamine occupatam invadit, clamitans

14 summum flagitium fore si alterum exercitum utriusque victoriae compotem sinerent fieri nec ad se sui

15 belli vindicarent decus. Qua impetum dederat
perrumpit aciemque per mediam in castra hostium
tendit et vacua defensoribus capit atque incendit.

16 Quae ubi flagrantia Marcianus miles conspexit et
hostes respexere, tum passim fuga coepta Samnitium
fieri; sed omnia obtinet caedes, nec in ullam partem
tutum perfugium est.

17 Iam triginta milibus hostium caesis signum receptui consules dederant colligebantque in unum
copias in vicem inter se gratantes, cum repente
visae procul hostium novae cohortes, quae in supplementum scriptae fuerant, integravere caedem.

18 In quas nec iussu consulum nec signo accepto victores

---

[1] *i.e.* in a hollow square, as the words *in medium* show.

battle with even one army, and believed that, once B.C. 306
they had suffered two consular armies to unite,
there would be no hope for them, they made an
attack on Marcius as he was approaching in loose
marching order. Hastily throwing down their packs
in the midst, the Romans formed up[1] as well as
time permitted. The shouting was the first thing
that was noticed in the camp of Cornelius. Then,
far off, a cloud of dust was descried, and caused
a commotion in the camp. The consul ordered his
men to arm, and leading them quickly out into line
attacked the enemy in the flank, when their hands
were full with another struggle, crying out that
it would be a burning shame if they let the other
army win both victories, and failed to claim for
themselves the glory of their own campaign.
Bursting through at the point where he had
charged, he advanced through the enemy's line,
and capturing their camp, which was empty of
defenders, set fire to it. When the soldiers of
Marcius saw the blaze, and the enemy, looking over
their shoulders, saw it too, the flight of the Samnites
soon became general; but at every point death
blocked the way, and there was no escaping anywhere.

Thirty thousand of the enemy had already fallen,
and the consuls had sounded the recall and were
proceeding to assemble their forces in one body,
amid the mutual congratulations and rejoicings of
the men, when suddenly some new cohorts of the
Samnites, which had been levied as reliefs, were
made out in the distance, and occasioned a renewal
of the slaughter. The victors rushed upon them,
without orders from the consuls or receiving any

vadunt, malo tirocinio imbuendum Samnitem clami-
19 tantes.   Indulgent consules legionum ardori, ut qui
probe scirent novum militem hostium inter perculsos
fuga veteranos ne temptando quidem satis certamini
20 fore.   Nec eos opinio fefellit : omnes Samnitium
copiae, veteres novaeque, montes proximos fuga
capiunt.   Eo et Romana erigitur acies, nec quicquam
satis tuti loci victis est, et de iugis quae ceperant
funduntur ; iamque una voce omnes pacem petebant.
21 Tum trium mensum frumento imperato et annuo
stipendio ac singulis in militem tunicis ad senatum
pacis oratores missi.

22   Cornelius in Samnio relictus : Marcius de Hernicis
triumphans in urbem rediit, statuaque equestris in foro
decreta est, quae ante templum Castoris posita est.
23 Hernicorum tribus populis, Aletrinati Verulano Fe-
rentinati, qui id[1] maluerunt quam civitatem, suae leges
redditae, conubiumque inter ipsos, quod aliquamdiu
24 soli Hernicorum habuerunt, permissum.   Anagninis
quique alii[2] arma Romanis intulerant civitas sine
suffragii latione : data concilia conubiaque adempta et
magistratibus praeterquam sacrorum curatione inter-
dictum.
25   Eodem anno aedes Salutis a C. Iunio Bubulco

---

[1] qui id *Harant* : qui *FT*[2] *or T*[3] (*marg.*) : quia Ω.
[2] quinque alii *H. G. Mueller* : quique (quicque *D ? LA*) Ω.

---

[1] The temple of Castor and Pollux had been vowed at the
battle of Lake Regillus, 449 B.C., and dedicated fifteen years
later (II. xx. 12, and xlii. 5).

B.C. 306

signal, exclaiming that the Samnites must begin their soldiering with a bitter lesson. The consuls indulged the ardour of the legions, being well aware that the enemy's recruits, in the midst of routed veterans, would scarce be equal to so much as an attempt at fighting. They were not mistaken. All the forces of the Samnites, old and new, broke and fled to the nearest mountains, up which the Romans too advanced in pursuit of them. The conquered could find no refuge anywhere that afforded safety, but were driven pell-mell from the ridges where they had made a stand. And now with one voice they all begged for peace. They were required to furnish corn for three months, with a year's pay and a tunic for each Roman soldier, and envoys were then dispatched to the senate to sue for terms.

Cornelius was left in Samnium. Marcius returned to the City, which he entered in a triumph over the Hernici. An equestrian statue in the Forum was decreed him and was erected in front of the temple of Castor.[1] To the three Hernic peoples of Aletrium, Verulae, and Ferentinum their own laws were restored, because they preferred them to Roman citizenship, and they were given the right to intermarry with each other—a privilege which for some time they were the only Hernici to enjoy. The people of Anagnia and such others as had borne arms against the Romans were admitted to citizenship without the right of voting. They were prohibited from holding councils and from intermarrying, and were allowed no magistrates save those who had charge of religious rites.

In the same year the censor Gaius Junius

339

LIVY

censore locata est, quam consul bello Samnitium
voverat. Ab eodem collegaque eius M. Valerio
26 Maximo viae per agros publica impensa factae. Et
cum Carthaginiensibus eodem anno foedus tertio
renovatum, legatisque eorum, qui ad id venerant,
comiter munera missa.

XLIV. Dictatorem idem annus habuit P. Cornelium Scipionem cum magistro equitum P. Decio
2 Mure. Ab his, propter quae creati erant, comitia
consularia habita, quia neuter consulum potuerat[1]
3 bello abesse. Creati consules L. Postumius Ti.[2]
Minucius. Hos consules Piso Q. Fabio et P. Decio
suggerit biennio exempto quo Claudium Volumnium-
que et Cornelium cum Marcio consules factos tradidi-
4 mus. Memoriane fugerit[3] in annalibus digerendis,
an consulto binos consules, falsos ratus, transcenderit,
incertum est.
5 Eodem anno in campum Stellatem agri Campani
6 Samnitium incursiones factae. Itaque ambo consules
in Samnium missi cum diversas regiones, Tifernum
Postumius Bovianum Minucius petisset, Postum⟨io⟩
prius ductu ad Tifernum pugnatum. Alii haud
dubie Samnites victos ac viginti milia hominum
capta tradunt, alii Marte aequo discessum e⟨t⟩
8 Postumium metum simulantem nocturno itiner⟨e⟩

---

[1] potuerat A^x⟨: potuerant Ω : poterant F.
[2] Ti. *Sigonius* (Diod. xx. lxxxi. 1, *C.I.L.* i², *p.* 132) :
$MPUT^2A^2$: ·t P: ÷ (= et) F: et M^4: *wanting in OTDLA.*
[3] memoriane fugerit ⟨: memoriae (*or* -e)ne fugerit Ω
memorie ne fuerit U: *wanting in O.*

---

[1] On the Quirinal.
[2] VII. xxvii. 2 and note. *Per.* XIII., which speaks of a *fourt⟨h⟩*
treaty, would be in agreement with the present passage.
[3] Lucius Calpurnius Piso Frugi, the annalist, *cos.* 133 B.C.

Bubulcus let the contract for the temple of Safety,[1] B.C. 306
which he had vowed, while consul, during the
Samnite war. He and his colleague, Marcus
Valerius Maximus, built roads through the country-
side at the public costs. In this year also the
treaty with the Carthaginians was renewed for the
third time,[2] and their ambassadors, who had come
for the purpose of arranging it, were treated with
courtesy and given presents.

XLIV. The same year had a dictator in the B.C. 305
person of Publius Cornelius Scipio, the master of
the horse being Publius Decius Mus. These men
held a consular election—for to this end they had
been appointed, since neither consul had been able
to leave the seat of war. The consuls chosen were
Lucius Postumius and Tiberius Minucius. Piso[3]
makes these men follow Quintus Fabius and Publius
Decius, omitting the two years in which we have
placed the consulship of Claudius and Volumnius and
that of Cornelius and Marcius. Whether in the redac-
tion of his annals he forgot them, or omitted two sets
of consuls purposely, as not authentic, is uncertain.

In that year also the Samnites made forays upon
the Campus Stellatis[4] in Campania. Both consuls
were accordingly dispatched into Samnium in different
directions, Postumius marching on Tifernum, and
Minucius on Bovianum. The fighting began at
Tifernum, where Postumius commanded. Some relate
that the Samnites were decisively beaten and that
twenty thousand prisoners were taken; others that
the armies quitted the field on even terms, and that
Postumius, feigning fear, in the night withdrew his

---

[4] This was a tract forming part of the Ager Falernus, later
celebrated for its choice wine.

clam in montes copias abduxisse, hostes secutos duo milia inde locis munitis et ipsos consedisse.

9 Consul ut stativa tuta copiosaque—et ita erant— petisse videretur, postquam et munimentis castra firmavit et omni apparatu rerum utilium instruxit,

10 relicto firmo praesidio de vigilia tertia, qua duci proxime potest, expeditas legiones ad collegam, et

11 ipsum adversus alios sedentem, ducit. Ibi auctore Postumio Minucius cum hostibus signa confert, et, cum anceps proelium in multum diei processisset, tum Postumius integris legionibus defessam iam

12 aciem hostium improviso invadit. Itaque cum lassitudo ac volnera fugam quoque praepedissent, occidione occisi hostes, signa unum et viginti capta atque

13 inde ad castra Postumi perrectum. Ibi duo victores exercitus perculsum iam fama hostem adorti fundunt fugantque; signa militaria sex et viginti capta et imperator Samnitium Statius Gellius[1] multique alii

14 mortales et castra utraque capta. Et Bovianum urbs[2] postero die coepta oppugnari brevi capitur, magnaque gloria rerum gestarum consules triumpharunt.

15 Minucium consulem, cum volnere gravi relatum in castra, mortuum quidam auctores sunt, et M. Fulvium in locum eius consulem suffectum, et ab eo, cum ad exercitum Minuci missus esset, Bovianum captum.

[1] Gellius *Sigonius* (*Diod.* xx. xc. 4 Γέλλιος Γάιος): Cellius Ω.
[2] urbs *Crevier*: ubi Ω.

forces secretly to the mountains, where the enemy B.C. 305
followed him and themselves entrenched a camp, at
a distance of two miles from his. The consul, that
it might appear to have been his object to gain a
position at once secure and abounding in supplies,—
and such indeed it was—having fortified his camp
and equipped it with all manner of useful things,
left in it a strong garrison, and in the third watch led
his legions in light marching order by the most
direct route to his colleague, who likewise lay in
camp, facing another army. There, at the instigation of Postumius, Minucius gave battle to the
enemy; and when the doubtful struggle had been
prolonged until late in the afternoon, Postumius
with his fresh legions fell unexpectedly upon the
now jaded forces of their opponents. The Samnites,
debarred by their weariness and wounds even from
flight, were utterly annihilated, and the Romans,
having taken twenty-one standards, set out for the
camp of Postumius. There the two victorious armies
assailed the enemy, already dismayed by the tidings
of the other battle, and overwhelmingly routed them,
capturing six-and-twenty standards, the commander
of the Samnites—Statius Gellius—and many other
prisoners, besides both camps. On the following
day they began the siege of the city of Bovianum,
and on its capture, which quickly ensued, the consuls
crowned their glorious achievements with a triumph.
Some writers state that Minucius the consul was
severely wounded and expired after being carried
back to his camp. They add that Marcus Fulvius
was made consul suffect in his place, and that it was
he who, being sent out to the army of Minucius,
captured Bovianum.

LIVY

Eo anno Sora Arpinum Cesennia recepta ab Samnitibus.   Herculis magnum simulacrum in Capitolio
positum dedicatumque.

XLV. P. Sulpicio Saverrione [1] P. Sempronio Sopho
consulibus Samnites, seu finem seu dilationem belli
2 quaerentes, legatos de pace Roman misere.   Quibus
suppliciter agentibus responsum est, nisi saepe bellum
parantes pacem petissent Samnites, oratione ultro
citro habita de pace transigi potuisse ; nunc, quando
verba vana ad id locorum fuerint, rebus standum
3 esse.   P. Sempronium consulem cum exercitu brevi
in Samnio fore ; eum, ad bellum pacemne inclinent
animi, falli non posse ; comperta omnia senatui re-
laturum ; decedentem ex Samnio consulem legati
4 sequerentur.   Eo anno cum pacatum Samnium exercitus Romanus benigne praebito commeatu per-
agrasset, foedus antiquum Samnitibus redditum.
5   Ad Aequos inde, veteres hostes, ceterum per
multos annos sub specie infidae pacis quietos, versa
arma Romana, quod incolumi Hernico nomine missit-
6 averant simul cum iis Samniti auxilia et post Hernicos
subactos universa prope gens sine dissimulatione
consilii publici ad hostes desciverat ; et postquam

---

[1] Saverrione *Sigonius* (X. ix. 14, *C.I.L.* i², *p.* 45) : auerrione
(auerione *A*) Ω.

---

[1] Site unknown.
[2] Perhaps to appease the god for the indignity mentioned
in chap. xxix. § 9.
[3] In 354 B.C. the Samnites had sought and obtained a
treaty with the Romans, upon what terms is not known, but
they were doubtless liberal (VII. xix. 4)
[4] Since 388 B.C. (VI. iv. 8).
[5] Chap. xlii. § 8, where, however, the Aequi are not
specified.

In that year Sora, Arpinum, and Cesennia [1] were B.C. 305
won back from the Samnites. The great statue of
Hercules was set up and dedicated on the Capitol.[2]

XLV. In the consulship of Publius Sulpicius B.C. 304
Saverrio and Publius Sempronius Sophus, the Samnites, whether seeking to end or only to postpone
hostilities, sent envoys to Rome to treat for peace.
To their humble supplications the answer was returned, that if the Samnites had not frequently
sought peace while preparing for war, a treaty could
have been arranged by mutual discussion : as it was,
since words had hitherto proved of no effect, the
Romans must needs take their stand on facts.
Publius Sempronius, the consul, would shortly be in
Samnium with an army ; he was one whom they
would be unable to deceive as to whether their
hearts inclined to peace or war ; after a thorough
investigation he would report his findings to the
senate ; and on his leaving Samnium their envoys
might attend him. The Roman army marched all
over Samnium ; the people were peaceable and
furnished the army liberally with supplies ; accordingly their ancient treaty was in that year restored
again to the Samnites.[3]

The arms of Rome were then directed against the
Aequi, who had been her enemies of old, but for
many years past had remained quiet,[4] under colour
of a peace which they observed but treacherously.
The reason for making war on them was as follows :
before the overthrow of the Hernici they had repeatedly joined with them in sending assistance to
the Samnites,[5] and after the subjugation of the
Hernici, almost the entire nation had gone over to the
enemy, without attempting to disguise their policy ;

345

icto Romae cum Samnitibus foedere fetiales venerant
7 res repetitum, temptationem aiebant esse ut terrore
incusso belli Romanos se fieri paterentur; quod quanto
opere optandum foret Hernicos docuisse, cum quibus
licuerit suas leges Romanae civitati praeoptaverint:
8 quibus legendi quid mallent copia non fuerit pro
poena necessariam civitatem fore. Ob haec volgo in
conciliis iactata populus Romanus bellum fieri Aequis
9 iussit; consulesque ambo ad novum profecti bellum
quattuor milia a castris hostium consederunt.
10 Aequorum exercitus, ut qui suo nomine permultos
annos imbelles egissent, tumultuario similis, sine
11 ducibus certis, sine imperio, trepidare. Alii exeun-
dum in aciem, alii castra tuenda censent; movet
plerosque vastatio futura agrorum ac deinceps cum
12 levibus praesidiis urbium relictarum excidia. Itaque
postquam inter multas sententias una, quae omissa
cura communium ad respectum suarum quemque
13 rerum vertit, est [1] audita, ut prima vigilia diversi e
castris ad deportanda omnia tuendasque moenibus
urbes [2] abirent, cuncti eam sententiam ingenti ad-
14 sensu accepere. Palatis hostibus per agros prima
luce Romani signis prolatis in acie consistunt, et ubi

---

[1] vertit, est *Madvig*: uertisset (-ent *P*) Ω : auertisset *O*.
[2] tuendasque moenibus urbes *Madvig* ⌐ : tuendasque moenibus in urbes Ω: tuendasque in omnibus urbes *O* : tuendosque
moenibus se in urbes *H. J. Mueller.*

---

[1] *Cf.* chap. xliii. 23 f. for the two groups.
[2] *i.e.* while Aequians had volunteered for service in other
armies, they had engaged in no war as a nation—at any rate
with Rome—since 388 B.C. (VI. iv. 8).

and when fetials had applied to them for reparation, B.C. 304 after the adoption of the Samnite treaty at Rome, they had persistently asserted that the Romans were attempting under threats of war to intimidate them into becoming Roman citizens; and how little that was a thing to be desired had been shown, they said, by the Hernici, since those who had been permitted to do so had chosen their own laws in preference to Roman citizenship, while those who had not been given an option were to have citizenship thrust upon them as a punishment.[1] Because of such expressions, publicly uttered in their assemblies, the Roman People decreed that war should be made upon the Aequi. Both consuls set out for the new seat of operations, and took up a position four miles from the enemy's camp.

The army of the Aequi, who for many years had made no war on their own account,[2] like a hastily levied militia, under no definite commanders and subject to no supreme authority, were in a state of panic. Some were for offering battle, others for defending the camp. The consideration that affected most of them was the devastation which their farms would suffer and the subsequent destruction of their cities, which they had left inadequately garrisoned. And so when a proposal was heard—amongst many others—which disregarded the common welfare and made every one think of his own interest, to wit, that in the first watch they should leave the camp, and going their several ways, carry off all their possessions from the fields and defend their cities by means of their walls, they all with loud acclaim adopted it. The enemy were scattered over the countryside when at break of day the Romans came

nemo obvius ibat, pleno gradu ad castra hostium
15 tendunt.   Ceterum postquam ibi neque stationes
pro portis nec quemquam in vallo nec fremitum con-
suetum castrorum animadverterunt, insolito silentio
16 moti metu insidiarum subsistunt.   Transgressi deinde
vallum cum deserta omnia invenissent, pergunt hostem vestigiis sequi.   Sed vestigia in omnes aeque
ferentia partes, ut in dilapsis passim, primo errorem
17 faciebant; post per exploratores compertis hostium
consiliis ad singulas urbes circumferendo bello
unum et triginta oppida intra dies quinquaginta,
omnia oppugnando ceperunt, quorum pleraque diruta
atque incensa, nomenque Aequorum prope ad inter-
18 necionem deletum.   De Aequis triumphatum; ex-
emploque eorum clades fuit, ut Marrucini Marsi
Paeligni Frentani[1] mitterent Romam oratores pacis
petendae amicitiaeque.   His populis foedus petentibus datum.

XLVI.   Eodem anno Cn. Flavius Cn. filius[2] scriba,
patre libertino humili fortuna ortus, ceterum callidus vir
2 et facundus, aedilis curulis fuit.   Invenio in quibusdam
annalibus, cum appareret aedilibus fierique se pro
tribu aedilem videret neque accipi nomen quia scriptum faceret, tabulam posuisse et iurasse se scriptum

---

[1] Frentani *Sigonius* (*chap.* xvi. § 1 *and Conway, Ital. Dial.*
p. 212): feretani MA^2: feretrani Ω.
[2] Cn. filius A^2: cn̄ fil P^2: gn̄ fil̄ T: *various corruptions* Ω.

---

[1] The tribes were beginning to enter their votes in favour
of Flavius, but the aedile presiding at the election refused to
admit his candidacy, on the score that as an apparitor, a paid
civil servant, he might not hold a magistracy.   Flavius
thereupon renounced his position as secretary and declined to
serve as such at the election.   With Livy's narrative in this
chap. *cf.* Plin. *N. H.* xxxiii. i. 17-19, and Gellius, vii. (vi) 9,
who quotes Piso as his authority, and uses language so much

out and formed in order of battle, and encountering _{B.C. 304} nobody, advanced at a quick pace towards the Aequian camp. But not perceiving any outposts before the gates or anybody on the rampart, and missing the usual noises of a camp, they were troubled by the unaccustomed silence, and apprehending an ambush, halted. Later, when they had scaled the rampart and found everything deserted, they attempted to follow the enemy by his tracks; but the tracks, which led in all directions—as they would when an army had dispersed—at first bewildered them. Afterwards they found out through their scouts what the enemy designed to do; and attacking his cities in succession, one after another, they captured thirty-one of them within fifty days, in every instance by assault. Of these the greater number were dismantled and burnt, and the Aequian name was almost blotted out. A triumph was celebrated over the Aequi; and warned by the example of their downfall, the Marrucini, Marsi, Paeligni, and Frentani sent ambassadors to Rome to sue for peace and friendship. These nations, at their request, were granted a treaty of alliance.

XLVI. In the same year a government clerk, Gnaeus Flavius, the son of Gnaeus, was curule aedile. Born in humble circumstances—his father being a freedman—he was, for the rest, a man of shrewdness and eloquence. I find in certain annals that being in attendance upon the aediles, and perceiving that the tribes were supporting him for aedile, but that his name was thrown out because he was acting as a recorder, he put away his tablet and took an oath that he would keep no record.[1]

like Livy's as to suggest that this annalist was Livy's source also.

3 non facturum; quem aliquanto ante desisse scriptum
facere arguit Macer Licinius tribunatu ante gesto
triumviratibusque, nocturno altero, altero coloniae
4 deducendae. Ceterum, id quod haud discrepat, con-
tumacia adversus contemnentes humilitatem suam
5 nobiles certavit; civile ius, repositum in penetralibus
pontificum, evolgavit fastosque circa forum in albo
6 proposuit, ut quando lege agi posset sciretur; aedem
Concordiae in area Volcani summa invidia nobilium
dedicavit; coactusque consensu populi Cornelius
Barbatus pontifex maximus verba praeire, cum more
maiorum negaret nisi consulem aut imperatorem
7 posse templum dedicare. Itaque ex auctoritate senatus latum ad populum est ne quis templum aramve
iniussu senatus aut tribunorum plebei partis maioris
8 dedicaret. Haud memorabilem rem per se, nisi
documentum sit adversus superbiam nobilium plebeiae
9 libertatis, referam. Ad collegam aegrum visendi
causa Flavius cum venisset consensuque nobilium
adulescentium, qui ibi adsidebant, adsurrectum ei
non esset, curulem adferri sellam eo iussit ac de
sede¹ honoris sui anxios invidia inimicos spectavit.
10 Ceterum Flavium dixerat aedilem forensis factio, Ap.

¹ de sede *Siesbye*: sede Ω.

---

¹ These were commonly called *tresviri capitales*, and were
police commissioners, who besides the duty referred to in
the text, were charged with assisting the magistrates who
had criminal jurisdiction, and particularly with executing
sentences of death. Liv. *Per.* xi. would indicate that the
office was not introduced until about 289 B.C.

Licinius Macer alleges that he had ceased some time
before to act as secretary, having been already a
tribune, and on two occasions a triumvir, once on the
commission which had charge of the night-watch,[1]
and again on one appointed to found a colony. At
all events there is no difference of opinion about the
stubbornness of his contention with the nobles, who
despised his lowly birth. He published the formulae
of the civil law, which had been filed away in the
secret archives of the pontiffs, and posted up the
calendar on white notice-boards about the Forum,
that men might know when they could bring an
action. He dedicated a temple of Concord in the
precinct of Vulcan, greatly to the resentment of the
nobles; and Cornelius Barbatus, the chief pontiff,
was forced by the unanimous wishes of the people to
dictate the form of words to him, though he asserted
that by custom of the elders none but a consul or
commanding general might dedicate a temple. So,
in accordance with a senatorial resolution, a measure
was enacted by the people providing that no one
should dedicate a temple or an altar without the
authorization of the senate or a majority of the
tribunes of the plebs.—I will relate an incident, of
no importance in itself, which may serve to show
how the plebs asserted their liberties against the
arrogance of the nobles. Flavius had come to make
a call upon a colleague who was sick, and the young
nobles who were sitting by his bed with one consent
omitted to rise on his entering; whereupon he
ordered his curule chair to be fetched in, and from
his official seat gazed at his adversaries, who were
choking with resentment. Now Flavius had been
elected aedile by the faction of the market-place,

LIVY

11 Claudi censura vires nacta, qui senatum primus libertinorum filiis lectis inquinaverat, et posteaquam eam lectionem nemo ratam habuit nec in curia adeptus erat quas petierat opes, urbanis[1] humilibus per omnes tribus divisis forum et campum corrupit.

12 Tantumque Flavi comitia indignitatis habuerunt ut plerique nobilium anulos aureos et phaleras depone-

13 rent. Ex eo tempore in duas partes discessit civitas : aliud integer populus, fautor et cultor bonorum,

14 aliud forensis factio tendebat,[2] donec Q. Fabius et P. Decius censores facti, et Fabius simul concordiae causa, simul ne humillimorum in manu comitia essent, omnem forensem turbam excretam in quattuor tribus

15 coniecit urbanasque eas appellavit. Adeoque eam rem acceptam gratis animis ferunt ut Maximi cognomen, quod tot victoriis non pepererat, hac ordinum temperatione pareret. Ab eodem institutum dicitur ut equites idibus Quinctilibus transveherentur.

[1] urbanis *Gronovius* : urbanas Ω.
[2] tendebat *F ς Madvig*: tenebat Ω (*Walters and Conway cf. Cic. Par.* I. 14.)

---

[1] The centuriate comitia met in the Campus Martius, the tribal comitia in the Forum. Membership in the former assembly—now for the first time imparted to the tradesmen and artisans who were not freeholders—implied also membership in the latter. The result of this reform was to extend the franchise to a large class of citizens, many of whom were men of substance.

which had become powerful in consequence of the B.C. 304
censorship of Appius Claudius. Claudius had been
the first to debase the senate by the appointment of
the sons of freedmen, and afterwards, when no one
allowed the validity of his selection, and he had
failed to gain the influence in the senate-house which
had been his object, he had distributed the humble
denizens of the City amongst all the tribes, and had
thus corrupted the Forum and the Campus Martius.[1]
And so great was the indignation over the election
of Flavius that many of the nobles laid aside their
golden rings and medals. From that time the
citizens were divided into two parties; the men of
integrity, who favoured and cherished right principles, tended one way, the rabble of the market-
place another; until Quintus Fabius and Publius
Decius became censors, and Fabius, partly for the
sake of harmony, partly that the elections might not
be in the hands of the basest of the people, culled
out all the market-place mob and cast them into
four tribes, to which he gave the name of Urban.
The arrangement, they say, was so gratefully received, that by this regulation of the orders he
purchased the surname of the Great, which not all
his victories had been able to procure him. It was
Fabius too, so it is said, who instituted the parade of
the knights on the fifteenth of July.

LIBRI IX PERIOCHA

T. Veturius Spurius Postumius coss. apud furcas
Caudinas deducto in locum artum exercitu, cum spes nulla
esset evadendi, foedere cum Samnitibus facto et sescentis
equitibus Romanis obsidibus datis ita exercitum abdu-
xerunt ut omnes sub iugum mitterentur ; idemque auctore
Spurio Postumio cos. qui in senatu suaserat ut eorum
deditione quorum culpa tam deforme foedus ictum erat,
publica fides liberaretur, cum duobus trib. pl. et omnibus
qui foedus spoponderant dediti Samnitibus non sunt
recepti. nec multo post fusis a Papirio Cursore Samnitibus
et sub iugum missis receptisque sescentis equitibus
Romanis qui obsides dati erant, pudor flagitii prioris
abolitus est. tribus duae adiectae sunt, Oufentina [1] et
Falerna. Suessa et Pontia coloniae deductae sunt. Ap.
Claudius censor aquam perduxit ; viam stravit quae Appia
vocata est, libertinorum filios in senatum legit. ideoque,
quoniam is ordo indignis inquinatus videbatur, sequentis
anni coss. senatum observaverunt, quem ad modum ante
proximos censores fuerat. res praeterea contra Apulos et
Etruscos [2] et Umbros et Marsos et Paelignos et Aequos et
Samnites, quibus foedus restitutum est, prospere gestas continet. Cn. Flavius [3] scriba, libertino patre natus, aedilis
curulis fuit per forensem factionem creatus, quae, cum
comitia et campum turbaret et in his propter nimias vires
dominaretur, a Q. Fabio censore in quattuor tribus redacta

---

[1] Oufentina *Hertz* : ofentina (*or* osfentina) *MSS.*
[2] et Etruscos *cod. Bergianus :* Etruscos *MSS.*
[3] Cn. Flavius *edd :* C. Flavius *MSS.*

354

SUMMARY OF BOOK IX

TITUS VETURIUS and Spurius Postumius, the consuls, having led their army into a narrow place at the Caudine Forks, when there was no hope of escaping, made a treaty with the Samnites, and having given six hundred Roman knights as hostages, got their army off, on condition that all should be sent under the yoke. And these same men having been delivered up to the Samnites, together with two tribunes of the plebs and all those who had guaranteed the treaty—on the suggestion of Spurius Postumius the consul, who had advised the senate that the pledge of the State should be redeemed by the surrender of those by whose fault so disgraceful a treaty had been made —were by them rejected. Not long after, the Samnites were routed by Papirus Cursor and sent beneath the yoke, and the six hundred Roman knights who had been given as hostages were recovered, thus wiping out the shame of the earlier disgrace. Two tribes were added, the Oufentina and the Falerna. Colonies were planted at Suessa and Pontia. Appius Claudius the censor completed an aqueduct; paved the road which was called the Appian Way; and admitted the sons of freedmen to the senate, for which reason, since that order appeared to have been polluted with unworthy members, the consuls of the following year kept the senate as it had been before the last censors. The book also contains successful campaigns against the Apulians, the Etruscans, the Umbrians, the Marsi, the Paeligni, the Aequi, and the Samnites, to whom their treaty was restored. Gnaeus Flavius, a government clerk and a freedman's son, was elected curule aedile by the faction of the market-place, which since it threw into confusion the comitia and the Campus Martius, which it dominated by its overweening strength, was by Quintus Fabius the censor divided up into four tribes

355

est, quas urbanas appellavit;[1] eaque res Fabio Maximo nomen dedit. in hoc libro mentionem habet Alexandri, qui temporibus his fuit, et aestimatis populi R. viribus, quae tunc erant, colligit si Alexander in Italiam traiecisset, non tam ei victoriam de populo Romano fore quam de iis gentibus quas ad orientem imperio suo subiecerat.

[1] quas urbanas appellavit *cod. Guelferb.: omitted by best MSS.*

SUMMARY OF BOOK IX

which he called "urban"; and this circumstance procured Fabius his surname of Maximus. In this book the author mentions Alexander, who lived in those times, and, after appraising the strength of the Roman people in that age, gathers that if Alexander had crossed into Italy, he would not have gained the victory over the Roman People, as he had done over those races which he subjugated in the Orient.

BOOK X

LIBER X

I. L. Genucio Ser. Cornelio consulibus ab externis
ferme bellis otium fuit.   Soram atque Albam coloniae
deductae.   Albam in Aequos sex milia colonorum
2 scripta : Sora agri Volsci fuerat, sed possederant
3 Samnites ; eo quattuor milia hominum missa.   Eodem
anno Arpinatibus Trebulanisque civitas data.   Frusinates tertia parte agri damnati, quod Hernicos ab
eis sollicitatos compertum, capitaque coniurationis
eius quaestione ab consulibus ex senatus consulto [1]
4 habita virgis caesi ac securi percussi.   Tamen ne
prorsus imbellem agerent annum, parva expeditio in
Umbriam facta est, quod nuntiabatur ex spelunca qua-
5 dam excursiones armatorum in agros fieri.   In eam
speluncam penetratum cum signis est, et ex loco [2]
obscuro multa volnera accepta maximeque lapidum
ictu, donec altero specus eius ore—nam pervius erat—
invento utraeque fauces congestis lignis accensae.
6 Ita intus fumo ac vapore ad duo milia armatorum,
ruentia novissime in ipsas flammas, dum evadere
tendunt, absumpta.

---

[1] ex senatus consulto A^2 : ex sōc MPT : ex sc̄ $ODLA$? ex
sēc̄ P^2 : exe · c̄ · F.
[2] ex loco *Madvig*: ex eo (ea O) loco Ω.

BOOK X

I. In the consulship of Lucius Genucius and
Servius Cornelius there was in general a respite from
foreign wars. Colonies were established at Sora and
Alba. Six thousand settlers were enrolled for Alba,
in the Aequian country. Sora had belonged to the
territory of the Volsci, but the Samnites had got
possession of it; to this place were sent four
thousand men. In this year also the Arpinates and
Trebulani were granted citizenship. The Frusinates
were mulcted in one-third of their land, because it
was discovered that they had tampered with the
Hernici; the ringleaders of the conspiracy, after the
consuls, at the instance of the senate, had conducted
an investigation, were scourged and beheaded.
Nevertheless, that their year might not go by without
any war whatever, the consuls made a little expedition into Umbria, because of a report that armed
men issuing from a certain cave were making raids
upon the farms. The soldiers carried their standards
into the cave, and there in the murk received many
wounds, particularly from stones that were thrown at
them; until, having found the other mouth of the
cavern—for there was a way of going through it—
they heaped up faggots at both openings and set
them afire. In this way about two thousand armed
men perished in the cave from the smoke and heat,
for they finally rushed into the very flames in their
efforts to escape.

LIVY

7 M. Livio Dentre[1] M. Aemilio[2] consulibus re-
dintegratum Aequicum bellum. Coloniam aegre
patientes velut arcem suis finibus impositam summa
vi expugnare adorti ab ipsis colonis pelluntur.
8 Ceterum tantum Romae terrorem fecere, quia vix
credibile erat tam adfectis rebus solos per se Aequos
ad bellum coortos, ut tumultus eius causa dictator
9 diceretur C. Iunius Bubulcus. Cum M. Titinio
magistro equitum profectus primo congressu Aequos
subegit, ac die octavo triumphans in urbem cum
redisset, aedem Salutis, quam consul voverat censor
locaverat, dictator dedicavit.

II. Eodem anno classis Graecorum Cleonymo duce
Lacedaemonio ad Italiae litora adpulsa Thurias[3]
2 urbem in Sallentinis cepit. Adversus hunc hostem
consul Aemilius missus proelio uno fugatum compulit in naves. Thuriae redditae veteri cultori,
3 Sallentinoque agro pax parta. Iunium Bubulcum
dictatorem missum in Sallentinos in quibusdam
annalibus invenio et Cleonymum, priusquam confli-
gendum esset cum Romanis, Italia excessisse.
4 Circumvectus inde Brundisii promunturium medio-
que sinu Hadriatico ventis latus, cum laeva impor-
tuosa Italiae litora, dextra Illyrii Liburnique et
Histri, gentes ferae et magna ex parte latrociniis

---

[1] Dentre ⟨: dentrice (*or* -cae) Ω : dentice (*PFU* (*not in O*)
[2] M. Aemilio *Sigon.* (*Diod.* xx. cvi. 1, *CIL* i², *p.* 132)
ā *U*: c (*or* t) A² ⟨: *omitted by* Ω.
[3] Thurias ⟨: turias D³: thurios (trurios *T*, turios *A*) Ω
durior *D? L.*

---

[1] If *Thuriae* is what Livy wrote, it must have been an
otherwise unknown city in the heel of Italy, where the
Sallentini lived.

When Marcus Livius Denter and Marcus Aemilius were consuls, the Aequi resumed hostilities. Indignant that a colony had been established, like a citadel, within their borders, they attacked it with great fury. They were beaten off by the colonists themselves, but occasioned such dismay at Rome— since it was scarce to be believed that the Aequi when in so weakened a condition should have begun a war relying solely on their own resources—that a dictator was appointed to cope with the outbreak, in the person of Gaius Junius Bubulcus. Setting out with Marcus Titinius, his master of the horse, he reduced the Aequi to submission at the first encounter, and having returned in triumph to the City eight days later, dedicated as dictator the temple of Safety which he had vowed as consul and for which as censor he had let the contract.

II. During the same year a Greek fleet commanded by Cleonymus the Lacedaemonian put in to the shores of Italy and seized the city of Thuriae in the country of the Sallentini.[1] The consul Aemilius was dispatched against this enemy, whom he routed in a single engagement and drove to his ships. Thuriae was restored to its old inhabitants, and peace was established in the Sallentine territory. I find in some annals that Junius Bubulcus the dictator was sent among the Sallentini, and that Cleonymus withdrew from Italy before it became necessary to fight the Romans.

Rounding then the promontory of Brundisium, he was swept on by the winds in the mid gulf of the Adriatic, and dreading the harbourless coasts of Italy on his left and on his right the Illyrians, Liburnians, and Histrians,—savage tribes and

LIVY

maritimis infames, terrerent, penitus ad litora Vene-
5 torum pervenit. Expositis paucis qui loca explorarent,
cum audisset[1] tenue praetentum litus esse, quod
transgressis stagna ab tergo sint inrigua aestibus
maritimis; agros haud procul[2] capestres cerni,[3]
6 ulteriora colles videri; esse ostium fluminis praealti,
quo circumagi naves in stationem tutam possint[4]—
Meduacus amnis erat—: eo invectam classem subire
7 flumine adverso iussit. Gravissimas navium non pertulit alveus fluminis; in leviora navigia transgressa
multitudo armatorum ad frequentes agros, tribus
maritimis Patavinorum vicis colentibus eam oram,
8 pervenit. Ibi egressi praesidio levi navibus relicto
vicos expugnant, inflammant tecta, hominum pecudumque praedas agunt et dulcedine praedandi longius
usque a navibus procedunt.

9   Haec ubi Patavium sunt nuntiata—semper autem
eos in armis accolae Galli habebant—in duas partes
iuventutem dividunt. Altera[5] in regionem, qua
effusa populatio nuntiabatur, altera, ne cui praedonum
obvia fieret, alio[6] itinere ad stationem navium—milia
10 autem quattuordecim ab oppido aberat—ducta. In
naves ignaris[7] custodibus interemptis impetus factus,
territique nautae coguntur naves in alteram ripam
amnis traicere. Et in terra prosperum aeque in

[1] audisset A^2 or A^4 ς : audissent Ω.
[2] haud procul *Walters and Conway* : haud procul proximos
(proximus F) Ω : haut proximos A : haut procul agro pax . .
Salluntinos (*repeated from* § 3) proximos (*omitting* agros) O.
[3] cerni ς : cernit Ω.
[4] possint *Walters and Conway* : possint vidisse ς : possent
vidisse *Madvig* : vidisse Ω : vidisset $PFUOT^2$.
[5] altera A^2 or A^4 : alteram Ω : alterum F.
[6] alio *Gronovius* : altero (*wanting in O*) Ω.
[7] ignaris ς : paruis Ω : paruas Uς : paruas ignaris ς.

notorious most of them for their piracies—kept
straight on until he reached the coasts of the
Veneti. Having sent a small party ashore to explore
the country, and learning that it was a narrow beach
that extended in front of them, on crossing which one
found behind it lagoons which were flooded by the
tides; that not far off level fields could be made out,
and that hills were seen rising beyond them, and that
a river of great depth—the Mediacus—debouched
there, into which they could bring round their ships
to a safe anchorage—having learned all this, I say,
he ordered the fleet to sail in and make its way up
stream. But the channel would not admit the
heaviest ships, and the multitude of armed men,
passing over into the lighter vessels, kept on till
they came to thickly inhabited fields; for three
maritime villages of the Patavini were situated there
along the river-bank. Disembarking there they
left a small body of men to defend the boats, burnt
the houses, made spoil of men and cattle, and, lured
on by the sweets of pillage, advanced to a greater and
greater distance from their ships.

When word of these events was brought to the
Patavians, whom the vicinity of the Gauls kept
always under arms, they divided their young men
into two divisions. One of these marched into the
region where the scattered marauding was reported;
the other, taking a different road, to avoid falling in
with any of the marauders, proceeded to the place
where the ships were moored, fourteen miles from
the town. The latter party, slaying the guards, who
were unaware of their approach, made a rush for the
ships, and the terrified sailors were forced to get
them over to the other side of the stream. On land,

365

LIVY

palatos praedatores proelium fuerat refugientibusque

11 ad stationem Graecis Veneti obsistunt; ita in medio circumventi hostes caesique; pars capti classem indicant regemque Cleonymum tria milia abesse.

12 Inde captivis proximo vico in custodiam datis pars fluviatiles naves, ad superanda vada stagnorum apte planis alveis fabricatas, pars captiva navigia armatis complent profectique ad classem immobiles naves et loca ignota plus quam hostem timentes circumvadunt;

13 fugientesque in altum acrius quam repugnantes usque ad ostium amnis persecuti captis quibusdam incensisque navibus hostium, quas trepidatio in vada

14 intulerat, victores revertuntur. Cleonymus vix quinta parte navium incolumi, nulla regione maris Hadriatici prospere adita, discessit. Rostra navium spoliaque Laconum in aede Iunonis veteri fixa multi supersunt

15 qui viderunt Patavi.¹ Monumentum navalis pugnae eo die quo pugnatum est quotannis sollemne certamen navium in flumine oppidi medio exercetur.

III. Eodem anno Romae cum Vestinis petentibus amicitiam ictum est foedus. Multiplex deinde ex-

2 ortus terror. Etruriam rebellare ab Arretinorum

---

¹ For Patavium see Introduction, Vol. I. p. ix f.

too, the battle waged against the straggling
plunderers was equally successful, and when the
Greeks would have fled back to their station, the
Veneti stood in their way. Thus the enemy
were caught between two parties and were cut to
pieces. Some of them, being taken prisoners, told
how the fleet and King Cleonymus were three miles
off. Thereupon the captives were consigned to the
next village for safe-keeping, and armed men filling
the river boats—suitably constructed with flat
bottoms, to enable them to cross the shallow lagoons
—and others manning the craft they had captured
from the invaders, they descended upon the fleet
and surrounded the unwieldy ships; which, being
more fearful of the unknown waters than of the
enemy, and more bent on escaping to the deep sea
than on resisting, they pursued clear to the river's
mouth, and having captured some of them and
burnt them, after they had been run aground in the
confusion, returned victorious. Cleonymus sailed off
with barely a fifth part of his ships intact. In no
quarter of the Adriatic had his attempts succeeded.
There are many now living in Patavium [1] who have
seen the beaks of the ships and the spoils of the
Laconians which were fastened up in the old temple
of Juno. In commemoration of the naval battle a
contest of ships is held regularly, on the anniversary
of the engagement, in the river that flows through
the town.

III. A treaty was entered into at Rome this year
with the Vestini, who solicited friendship. Thereafter there were alarms in several quarters. It was
reported that Etruria was up in arms, in consequence
of an outbreak that had its origin in dissensions at

LIVY

seditionibus motu orto nuntiabatur, ubi Cilnium genus
praepotens divitiarum invidia pelli armis coeptum;
simul Marsos agrum vi tueri, in quem colonia Carseoli
deducta erat quattuor milibus hominum scriptis.

3 Itaque propter eos tumultus dictus M. Valerius
Maximus dictator magistrum equitum sibi legit M.

4 Aemilium Paulum.—Id magis credo quam Q. Fabium
ea aetate atque eis honoribus Valerio subiectum;
ceterum ex Maximi cognomine ortum errorem haud

5 abnuerim.—Profectus dictator cum exercitu proelio
uno Marsos fundit; compulsis deinde in urbes munitas, Milioniam, Plestinam, Fresiliam intra dies paucos
cepit et parte agri multatis Marsis foedus restituit.

6 Tum in Etruscos versum bellum; et cum dictator
auspiciorum repetendorum causa profectus Romam
esset, magister equitum pabulatum egressus ex insidiis
circumvenitur signisque aliquot amissis foeda militum

7 caede ac fuga in castra est compulsus.—Qui terror
non eo tantum a Fabio abhorret quod, si qua alia
arte cognomen suum aequavit tum maxime bellicis

8 laudibus, sed etiam quod memor Papirianae saevitiae
nunquam ut dictatoris iniussu dimicaret adduci
potuisset.

IV. Nuntiata ea clades Romam maiorem quam res
2 erat terrorem excivit. Nam ut exercitu deleto ita

---

[1] Maecenas, the patron of Horace and Virgil, belonged to
this family.

[2] This appears to be a mistake, Carseoli was probably not
planted until four years later (chap. xiii. § 1).

[3] Cf. p. 156, note.

[4] *i.e.* that a confusion arose between M. Valerius Maximus
and Quintus Fabius Maximus Rullianus.

[5] See the story of Papirius and Fabius at VIII. xxx–xxxv.

Arretium, where a movement was begun to drive out B.C. 302
the Cilnii—a very powerful family [1]—because of the
envy occasioned by their wealth. At the same time
the Marsi forcibly resisted the confiscation of their
land, where the colony of Carseoli had been planted
with an enrolment of four thousand men.[2] In view,
therefore, of these tumults, Marcus Valerius Maximus
was appointed dictator[3] and named Marcus Aemilius
Paulus to be his master of the horse. This I choose
rather to believe than that Quintus Fabius, at his
time of life and after the offices he had held, was
made subordinate to Valerius; but I would not deny
that the error might have originated in the surname
of Maximus.[4]—Setting out with his army, the dictator
overthrew the Marsi in a single battle; then shutting
them up in their walled cities, he captured Milionia,
Plestina, and Fresilia, in the course of a few days, and
having fined the Marsi in a part of their territory,
renewed the treaty with them. The campaign was
then directed against the Etruscans; the dictator
having set out for Rome, to take the auspices over
again, the master of the horse went out to forage,
and being ambushed, lost a number of standards and
was driven back into his camp, with a shameful rout
and slaughter of his soldiers.—This discomfiture is
very unlikely to have befallen Fabius, not only
because if in any quality he came up to his surname,
he assuredly did so in the glory of a soldier, but also
because, remembering the severity of Papirius, he
could never have been brought to engage in battle
without the orders of the dictator.[5]

IV. The news of this reverse gave rise in Rome
to a greater alarm than the situation warranted.
For, as though the army had been destroyed, a

iustitium indictum, custodiae in portis, vigiliae vicatim
3 exactae, arma tela in muros congesta. Omnibus
iunioribus sacramento adactis dictator ad exercitum
missus omnia spe tranquilliora et composita magistri
4 equitum cura, castra in tutiorem locum redacta,
cohortes quae signa amiserant extra vallum sine tentoriis destitutas invenit, exercitum avidum pugnae,
5 quo maturius ignominia aboleretur. Itaque confestim castra inde in agrum Rusellanum promovit.
6 Eo et hostes secuti, quamquam ex bene gesta re
summam et in aperto certamine virium spem habebant, tamen insidiis quoque, quas feliciter experti
7 erant, hostem temptant. Tecta semiruta vici per
vastationem agrorum deusti haud procul castris
Romanorum aberant. Ibi abditis armatis pecus in
conspectu praesidii Romani, cui praeerat Cn. Fulvius
8 legatus, propulsum. Ad quam inlecebram cum
moveretur nemo ab Romana statione, pastorum unus
progressus sub ipsas munitiones inclamat alios,
cunctanter ab ruinis vici pecus propellentes, quid
cessarent cum per media castra Romana tuto agere
9 possent. Haec cum legato Caerites quidam interpretarentur et per omnes manipulos militum indignatio

---

[1] By way of punishment for their cowardice. *Cf.* the
punishment meted out to his soldiers in 209 B.C. by
Marcellus (XXVII. xiii. 9).

[2] In Western Etruria, on the river Umbro.

[3] The Caerites were citizens (without the suffrage), and as
such might serve in the Roman army.

cessation of legal business was proclaimed, guards
were called into service at the gates, and night-
watches in the several streets, arms and missiles
being heaped upon the walls. After summoning
all of military age to take the oath, the dictator was
dispatched to the army, and there found everything
more tranquil than he had expected and reduced to
order by the careful measures of the master of the
horse. The camp had been withdrawn to a safer
site, the cohorts that had lost their standards had
been left outside the rampart without tents,[1] and
the army was eager for battle, that it might the
sooner wipe out its disgrace. Accordingly he
advanced without delay into the district of Rusellae.[2]
To this place the enemy followed him ; and although
in consequence of their success they had every confidence in their ability to cope with the Romans
even in the open field, yet they also attempted an
ambuscade, which they had successfully essayed
before. Not far from the Roman camp stood the
half-ruined buildings of a village which had been
burned when the country was laid waste. Concealing armed men in these ruins, they drove out some
cattle in full sight of a Roman outpost, which was
under the command of the lieutenant Gnaeus
Fulvius. But when this tempting bait failed to
lure any of the Romans from their post, one of the
shepherds came up under the very works and called
out to the others, who were hesitating to drive out
their flock from amongst the tumble-down buildings,
asking why they were so slow, for they could safely
drive them through the midst of the Roman camp.
Some men from Caere [3] interpreted these words to
the lieutenant, and great was the indignation aroused

A.U.C.
452

ingens esset nec tamen iniussu movere auderent,
iubet peritos linguae attendere animum, pastorum
10 sermo agresti an urbano propior esset. Cum referrent sonum linguae et corporum habitum et nitorem
cultiora quam pastoralia esse, "Ite igitur, dicite,"
inquit, "detegant nequiquam conditas insidias:
omnia scire Romanum nec magis iam dolo capi quam
11 armis vinci posse." Haec ubi audita sunt et ad eos
qui consederant in insidiis perlata, consurrectum
repente ex latebris est et in patentem ad conspectum
12 undique campum prolata signa. Visa legato maior
acies quam quae ab suo praesidio sustineri posset
itaque propere ad dictatorem auxilia accitum mittit;
interea ipse impetus hostium sustinet.

V. Nuntio allato dictator signa ferri ac sequi iubet
armatos. Sed celeriora prope omnia imperio erant;
2 rapta extemplo signa armaque, et vix ab impetu et
cursu tenebantur. Cum ira ab accepta nuper clade
stimulabat, tum concitatior accidens clamor ab in-
3 crescente certamine. Urgent itaque alii alios hor-
tanturque signiferos ut ocius eant. Quo magis
festinantes videt dictator, eo impensius retentat

through all the maniples of soldiers; yet they dared
not stir without the orders of their leader, who commanded those familiar with the language to mark
whether the shepherds' speech were more like that
of rustics or of city-folk. On their reporting that in
accent, in carriage, and in complexion they were
too refined for shepherds, "Go then," said he,
"and bid them uncover the ambuscade they have
laid in vain; for the Romans know all, and can now
no more be entrapped than they can be conquered
by force of arms." These words were no sooner
heard and repeated to those who lay in ambush
than they suddenly all rose up from their hiding-
places and advanced in martial array into the plain
which was spread open to the view on every side
Their army seemed to the lieutenant to be greater
than his own detachment could withstand, and he
therefore sent in all haste to the dictator to summon
help, in the meantime resisting by himself the
enemy's charges.

V. On receiving his message the dictator bade
advance the standards, and commanded his men to
arm and follow them. But everything was almost
sooner done than ordered; standards and arms were
hurriedly caught up, and the soldiers could hardly
be restrained from pushing forward at a run. It
was not anger alone that spurred them on, as they
thought of the defeat they had recently sustained,
but the shouts, as well, that fell faster on their
hearing as the fight waxed more hot. So they
urged one another forward and exhorted the
standard-bearers to a faster pace. But the more
haste the dictator saw them make, the more earnest
was he to hold them in, and commanded them to

A.U.C.
452

4 agmen ac sensim incedere iubet. Etrusci contra,
principio exciti pugnae, omnibus copiis aderant ; et
super alios alii nuntiant dictatori omnes legiones
Etruscorum capessisse pugnam nec iam ab suis
resisti posse, et ipse cernit ex superiore loco in
5 quanto discrimine praesidium esset. Ceterum satis
fretus esse etiam nunc tolerando certamini legatum nec se procul abesse periculi vindicem, quam
maxime volt fatigari hostem, ut integris adoriatur
6 viribus fessos. Quamquam lente procedunt, iam
tamen ad impetum capiundum,[1] equiti utique, modi-
cum erat spatium. Prima incedebant signa legionum,
ne quid occultum aut repentinum hostis timeret ;
sed reliquerat intervalla inter ordines peditum, qua
7 satis laxo spatio equi permitti possent. Pariter
sustulit clamorem acies et emissus eques libero
cursu in hostem invehitur incompositisque adversus
equestrem procellam subitum pavorem offundit.
8 Itaque, ut prope serum auxilium iam paene circumventis, ita universa requies data est. Integri accepere
9 pugnam, nec ea ipsa[2] longa aut anceps fuit. Fusi
hostes castra repetunt inferentibusque iam signa
Romanis cedunt et in ultimam castrorum partem

[1] capiundum *M* : capiendum *TDLA* : capiunt dum *PFU* :
wanting in O.
[2] nec ea ipsa ς (IX. xi. 5) : nec a ipsa *M* : nec ipsa Ω : ex
ipsa *P* : nec h$^{\text{e}}_{\text{c}}$ ipsa *P*[2] *or P*[3] : nec hec ipsa *O* : nec hec
ex ipsa *U* : nec h$^{\text{e}}_{\text{c}}$ exposita *F.*

slow down their march. The Etruscans, on the B.C. 302
contrary, having been called out at the beginning
of the battle, had taken the field with all their
troops. One messenger after another informed the
dictator that all the Etruscan legions were engaged
and that his own men could hold out no longer;
and looking down from the higher ground, he could
see for himself the perilous situation of his people.
Still, feeling fairly confident that his lieutenant was
capable, even then, of maintaining the fight, and
that he was himself not too far off to rescue him
from danger, he desired the enemy to become com-
pletely exhausted, that he might fall upon them
with undiminished vigour when their strength was
spent. Yet although the Romans advanced but
slowly, they had now but a little space to charge in,
especially the horse. In the van were the standards
of the legions, lest the enemy should be apprehen-
sive of any concealed or rapid movement; but the
dictator had left intervals between the files of the
infantry, to allow ample room for the horses to go
through. The legionaries gave a cheer, and simultaneously the horsemen were let loose and with a
free course galloped straight upon the enemy, who
were not prepared to resist a shock of cavalry and
were overwhelmed with a sudden panic. And so,
though the help had nearly come too late for men
who were already well-nigh surrounded, yet they
were now all given a respite, and the battle was
taken over by fresh troops—a battle of no long
duration nor of doubtful issue. The routed enemy
fled back to their camp, and when the Roman
standard-bearers pressed in after them, they gave
way and huddled up together in the farthest part

LIVY

10 conglobantur. Haerent fugientes in angustiis portarum; pars magna aggerem vallumque conscendit,
si aut ex superiore loco tueri se aut superare aliqua et
11 evadere posset. Forte quodam loco male densatus
agger pondere superstantium in fossam procubuit;
atque ea, cum deos pandere viam fugae conclamas-
sent, plures inermes quam armati evadunt.

12   Hoc proelio fractae iterum Etruscorum vires, et
pacto annuo stipendio et duum mensum frumento
permissum ab dictatore ut de pace legatos mitterent
Romam. Pax negata, indutiae biennii datae.
13 Dictator triumphans in urbem rediit.—Habeo auctores sine ullo memorabili proelio pacatam ab
dictatore Etruriam esse seditionibus tantum Arretinorum compositis et Cilnio[1] genere cum plebe in
14 gratiam reducto.—Consul ex dictatura factus M.
Valerius. Non petentem atque adeo etiam absen-
tem creatum tradidere quidam et per interregem ea
comitia facta; id unum non ambigitur, consulatum
cum Apuleio Pansa gessisse.

    VI. M. Valerio et Q. Apuleio consulibus satis
2 pacatae foris res fuere: Etruscum adversae[2] belli

---

[1] Cilnio *Gruter*: licinio iacilnio *M*: licinio (*omitted by F*) Ω.
[2] adversae ς: aduersa Ω: aduersi *U*.

---

[1] The other occasion was in 309 B.C. (IX. XXXIX. 11).
[2] This was the fifth consulship of M. Valerius Corvus.
The first was 348 B.C. (VII. XXVI, 12). The year 301 B.C.
according to the *Fasti Consulares*, had no consuls but only a
dictator. Livy conceives the dictatorship as occupying a
part of the year when Livius and Aemilius were consuls
(302 B.C.).

of the enclosure. The narrow gates became choked
with fugitives and a great part of them climbed
upon the mound and palisade, in hopes that from
that elevation they might be able either to defend
themselves, or to climb over somewhere and escape.
It chanced that in a certain place the mound had
not been solidly rammed down, and this, over-
burdened with the weight of those who stood upon
it, slid over into the trench. By that opening—
crying out that the gods were providing them a
means of flight—they saved themselves, but more
got away without their arms than with them.

In this battle the might of the Etruscans was
broken for the second time.[1] By promising a year's
pay for the soldiers, with two months' corn, they
obtained permission from the dictator to send
envoys to Rome to negotiate a peace. Peace was
denied them, but they were granted a truce of
two years. The dictator returned to Rome and
triumphed.—I find historians who say that Etruria
was pacified by the dictator without any memorable
battle, only by settling the dissensions of the
Arretini and reconciling the Cilnian family with
the plebs.—Marcus Valerius resigned as dictator,
to enter immediately upon the consulship.[2] Some
authors have recorded that he was elected without
seeking the office, indeed without even being
present, and that the election was presided over
by an interrex; this only is not disputed, that he
held the consulship in company with Apuleius
Pansa.

VI. During their year of administration the
foreign relations of the state were fairly peaceful:
the Etruscans were kept quiet by their failure in

LIVY

res et indutiae quietum tenebant ; Samnitem multo-
rum annorum cladibus domitum hauddum foederis
novi paenitebat. Romae quoque plebem quietam
3 exonerata[1] in colonias multitudo praestabat. Tamen
ne undique tranquillae res essent, certamen iniectum
inter primores civitatis, patricios plebeiosque, ab
4 tribunis plebis Q. et Cn. Ogulniis,[2] qui undique
criminandorum patrum apud plebem occasionibus
quaesitis, postquam alia frustra temptata erant, eam
actionem susceperunt qua non infimam plebem
5 accenderent sed ipsa capita plebis, consulares
triumphalesque plebeios, quorum honoribus nihil
praeter sacerdotia, quae nondum promiscua erant,
6 deesset. Rogationem ergo promulgarunt ut, cum
quattuor augures, quattuor pontifices ea tempestate
essent placeretque augeri sacerdotum numerum,
quattuor pontifices, quinque augures, de plebe
7 omnes, adlegerentur.—Quemadmodum ad quattuor
augurum numerum nisi morte duorum id redigi
collegium potuerit, non invenio, cum inter augures
constet imparem numerum debere esse, ut tres
antiquae tribus, Ramnes Titienses Luceres, suum
8 quaeque augurem habeant aut, si pluribus sit opus,
pari inter se numero sacerdotes multiplicent, sicut
multiplicati sunt cum ad quattuor quinque adiecti
novem numerum, ut terni in singulas essent, expleve-

---

[1] exonerata *Madvig*: exhoneratam deducta *A*: et exon
(*or* -hon-)eratam deducta Ω: et exon(*or*-hon-)eratam deductam *MPFTL*.
[2] Ogulniis ϛ: Oguiniis Ω: oguinus *L*: ognimus *F*.

---

[1] Weissenborn thinks that Livy has in mind the colonies
of a later day whose principal aim was to lighten the City

war and by the truce; the Samnites, tamed by the
defeats of many years, had not wearied as yet of the
new covenant. At Rome also the relief afforded by
the emigration of large numbers to the colonies had
quieted the commons.[1] Nevertheless, that tranquillity might not be found everywhere, the plebeian
tribunes Quintus and Gnaeus Ogulnius stirred up
a quarrel among the first men of the state, both
patrician and plebeian. They had sought in every
quarter occasions for maligning the Fathers to the
plebs; and having tried everything else in vain,
they set on foot a project by which they might
inflame, not the lowest of the rabble, but the very
leaders of the plebs—the commoners, namely, who
had enjoyed consulships and triumphs, and who
lacked nothing but priesthoods, which were not yet
open to all, to complete their list of honours. The
Ogulnii accordingly proposed a law, that whereas
there were then four augurs and four pontiffs and it
was desired to augment the number of priests, four
pontiffs and five augurs should be added, and should
all be taken from the plebs.—How this college
could have been reduced to four augurs, unless by
the death of two, I cannot discover; since it is a
settled principle amongst the augurs that their
number should be uneven, to the end that the three
ancient tribes, the Ramnes, Titienses and Luceres,
should each have its augur, or else—if a larger
number should be needed—that they should increase
the priests in the same proportion; as in fact they
were increased when five were added to the four,
and, making up the number of nine, gave each tribe

of its over-population. The colonies actually alluded to
were intended primarily to protect the frontiers.

379

LIVY

9 **runt.** Ceterum, quia de plebe adlegebantur, iuxta eam rem aegre passi patres quam cum consulatum
10 volgari viderent. Simulabant ad deos id magis quam ad se pertinere : ipsos visuros ne sacra sua polluantur ; id se optare tantum, ne qua in rem publicam
11 clades veniat. Minus autem tetendere, adsueti iam tali [1] genere certaminum vinci ; et cernebant adversarios non, id quod olim vix speraverint, adfectantes magnos honores sed omnia iam in quorum spem dubiam erat certatum adeptos, multiplices consulatus censurasque et triumphos.

VII. Certatum tamen suadenda dissuadendaque lege inter Ap. Claudium maxime ferunt et inter P.
2 Decium Murem. Qui cum eadem ferme de iure patrum ac plebis quae pro lege Licinia quondam contraque eam dicta erant cum plebeiis consulatus
3 rogabatur disseruissent,[2] rettulisse dicitur Decius parentis sui speciem, qualem eum multi qui in contione erant viderant, incinctum Gabino cultu super telum stantem, quo se habitu pro populo ac
4 legionibus Romanis devovisset : tum P. Decium

[1] tali Ω : in tali *Harant* (*supported by PF which have* in certaminum *below*).
[2] disseruissent ς : disseruisset Ω : deseruisset *L.*

[1] Livy means that originally there had been three augurs and that each subsequent increase in their number had been by multiples of three. He can only account for the tradition that there were four at this time on the assumption that two had died, and their places had not yet been filled when the Ogulnii made their proposal.

three.[1]—But since they were to be added from the B.C. 300 plebs, the patricians were as distressed by the proposal as they had been when they saw the consulship thrown open. They pretended that the gods were more concerned than they themselves were : the gods would see to it that their rites should not be contaminated ; for their own part they only hoped that no disaster might come upon the state. They made, however, no great struggle, accustomed as they now were to being worsted in contests of this kind ; and they beheld their adversaries no longer reaching out after great honours which they had formerly scarce any hopes of attaining, but in full possession of all the things for which they had striven with dubious prospects of success—repeated consulships, censorships, and triumphs.

VII. There is said, however, to have been a vigorous discussion as to the passage or rejection of the bill, in which Appius Claudius and Publius Decius Mus were the principal speakers. After they had brought up nearly the same arguments concerning the rights of patricians and plebeians as had formerly been employed in behalf of and against the Licinian Law,[2] when the plebeians sought access to the consulship, it is related that Decius evoked the image of his father as he had been seen by many who were then present in the assembly, wearing his toga with the Gabine cincture,[3] and standing over his weapon, as he had done when offering himself a sacrifice for the Roman People and the legions. Publius Decius the consul had

---

[2] Enacted 367 B.C. (VI. XXXV. 5).
[3] Prescribed in the ceremony of devotion, as in certain others.

A.U.C.
454

consulem purum piumque deis immortalibus visum
aeque ac si T. Manlius collega eius devoveretur :
5 eundem P. Decium qui sacra publica populi Romani
faceret legi rite non potuisse ? Id esse periculum, ne
suas preces minus audirent di quam Ap. Claudi ?
Castius eum sacra privata facere et religiosius deos
6 colere quam se ? Quem paenitere votorum quae pro
re publica nuncupaverint tot consules plebeii, tot
dictatores, aut ad exercitus euntes aut inter ipsa
7 bella ? Numerarentur duces eorum annorum, quibus plebeiorum ductu et auspicio res geri coeptae
sint ; ¹ numerarentur triumphi : iam ne nobilitatis
8 quidem suae plebeios paenitere. Pro certo habere,
si quod repens bellum oriatur non plus spei fore
senatui populoque Romano in patriciis quam in
plebeiis ducibus.
9   " Quod cum ita se habeat, cui deorum hominumve
indignum videri potest " inquit, " eos viros, quos vos
sellis curulibus, toga praetexta, tunica palmata et
toga picta et corona triumphali laureaque honoraritis,
quorum domos spoliis hostium adfixis insignes inter
alias feceritis, pontificalia atque auguralia insignia

¹ coeptae sint *Duker*: coeptae sunt Ω: coepta sunt *F*:
c$_{c}^{e}$pte sunt *O*: cepte s *A*   coactae sunt *L*.

---

¹ The *toga praetexta* (white with purple border) was worn
by those who had been elected to curule magistracies ; the
tunica palmata (embroidered with palm-leaves) and the *toga
picta* (of purple embroidered with gold) were worn by the
triumphator, who was also adorned with a wreath of laurel,
while a public slave who stood beside him in the chariot held
a golden chaplet over his head.

on that occasion seemed to the immortal gods an B.C. 300
oblation no less pure and holy than if his colleague
Titus Manlius had been offered up; could not then
this same Publius Decius—he asked—have been
duly chosen to solemnize the public sacrifices of the
Roman People? Or was it to be feared that the
gods would hearken less readily to the speaker's
prayers than to those of Appius Claudius? Did
Appius perform with more devotion the rites of
domestic religion, and worship the gods more
scrupulously than he did himself? Who was there
that repented him of the vows that had been uttered
in the state's behalf by so many plebeian consuls
and so many dictators, either on going to their
armies or in the midst of their campaigns? Let
them enumerate the generals of those years that
had elapsed since campaigns were first conducted
under the leadership and auspices of plebeians; let
them enumerate the triumphs; even on the score
of their nobility, the plebeians had now nothing to
regret. He felt quite sure that if suddenly some
war should arise, the senate and the Roman People
would rest their hopes no more on patrician than on
plebeian generals.

"Since this is so," he proceeded, "what god or
man can deem it inappropriate that those heroes
whom you have honoured with curule chairs, with
the purple-bordered robe, with the tunic adorned
with palms, and with the embroidered toga, the
triumphal crown and the laurel wreath,[1] whose
houses you have made conspicuous amongst the rest
with the spoils of your enemies which you have
fastened to their walls,—who, I say, can object if
such men add thereto the insignia of the pontiffs

383

10 adicere? Qui Iovis optimi maximi ornatu decoratus
curru aurato per urbem vectus in Capitolium ascen-
derit, is non[1] conspiciatur cum capide ac lituo, cum[2]
capite velato victimam caedet auguriumve ex arce
11 capiet? Cuius in imaginis[3] titulo consulatus censuraque et triumphus aequo animo legetur, si auguratum
aut pontificatum adieceritis, non sustinebunt legen-
12 tium oculi? Equidem—pace dixerim deum—eos nos
iam populi Romani beneficio esse spero, qui sacerdotiis
non minus reddamus dignatione nostra honoris[4]
quam acceperimus et deorum magis quam nostra
causa expetamus ut quos privatim colimus publice
colamus.

VIII. Quid autem ego sic adhuc egi, tamquam
integra sit causa patriciorum de sacerdotiis et non
iam in possessione unius amplissimi simus sacerdotii?
2 Decemviros sacris faciundis, carminum Sibyllae ac
fatorum populi huius interpretes, antistites eosdem
Apollinaris sacri caerimoniarumque aliarum plebeios
3 videmus. Nec aut tum patriciis ulla iniuria facta
est, cum duumviris sacris faciundis adiectus est
propter plebeios numerus, et nunc tribunus, vir

---

[1] is non *Weissenborn* : is Ω.
[2] cum capide ac lituo, cum *Walters* : cum capide ac lituo
ς : cum li capide ac tuo *M* : cum lituo *PFOT*[2] (*or T*[1]) : cum
litua *U* : cum *TDLA*.
[3] in imaginis *Wesenberg* : imaginis (*sic*) *A* : imaginis Ω.
[4] honoris *D*[x] : honores Ω.

---

[1] The *capis*, according to Varro (*L.L.*, v. 121), got its name
from *capere*, because it was provided with a handle; it was
used in the ceremonial of the pontiffs. The *lituus* was used

and the augurs? May the man who, decked with B.C. 300
the robes of Jupiter Optimus Maximus, has been
borne through the City in a gilded chariot and has
mounted the Capitol—may that man not be seen
with chalice and crook,[1] when, covering his head,
he offers up the victim, or receives an augury from
the Citadel? If men shall read with equanimity,
in the inscription that accompanies his portrait, of
consulship, censorship, and triumph, will their eyes
be unable to endure the brightness, if you add to
these the augurate or pontificate? For my own
part—under Heaven's favour be it spoken—I trust
that we are now, thanks to the Roman People, in
a position to reflect upon the priesthoods—in consequence of our recognized fitness for office—no less
credit than we shall receive from them, and to
seek, more for the service of the gods than for ourselves, that those whom we worship privately we
may also worship in the name of the state.

VIII. "But why have I been reasoning hitherto
as if the patrician claim on the priesthoods were
intact, and we were not already in possession of the
one supremely honourable priesthood? We see that
plebeians are members of the Ten charged with the
sacred rites, interpreters of the Sibylline oracles and
the destinies of this people, the same being also
overseers of Apollo's ritual and of other ceremonies.
And yet the patricians were in no way wronged at
the time when the two commissioners in charge of
sacred rites were increased in number on account
of the plebeians; and our brave and vigorous
tribune, in proposing at the present time to

---

[1] by the augur; Livy says (I. xviii. 7) that it was a crooked
staff without a knot.

A.U.C.
454
fortis ac strenuus, quinque augurum loca, quattuor
4 pontificum adicit,[1] in quae plebeii nominentur, non
ut vos, Appi, vestro loco pellant sed ut adiuvent vos
homines plebeii divinis quoque rebus procurandis,
sicut in ceteris humanis pro parte virili adiuvant.
5 Noli erubescere, Appi, collegam in sacerdotio habere
quem in censura quem in consulatu collegam habere
potuisti, cuius tam dictatoris magister equitum quam
6 magistri equitum dictator esse potes.   Sabinum
advenam, principem nobilitatis[2] vestrae, seu Attium[3]
Clausum seu Ap. Claudium mavoltis, illi antiqui
patricii in suum numerum acceperunt: tu ne[4]
fastidieris nos in sacerdotum numerum accipere.
7 Multa nobiscum decora adferimus, immo omnia
8 eadem quae vos superbos fecerunt: L. Sextius
primus de plebe consul est factus, C. Licinius
Stolo primus magister equitum, C. Marcius Rutulus[5]
primus et dictator et censor, Q. Publilius Philo
9 primus praetor.   Semper ista audita sunt eadem,
penes vos auspicia esse, vos solos gentem habere, vos
solos iustum imperium et auspicium domi militiae-
10 que ; aeque adhuc prosperum plebeium et patricium
fuit porroque erit. En umquam fando audistis
patricios primo esse factos non de caelo demissos sed
qui patrem ciere possent, id est nihil ultra quam
11 ingenuos?   Consulem iam patrem ciere possum,

[1] adicit *Duker*: adiciet A^2 (*or* A^3): adiecit Ω.
[2] nobilitatis A^1 (*or* A^2) ς: nobilitati Ω.
[3] Attium *Alschefski* (II. xvi. 4): at(*or* ac-)ium *MPFUO*:
app̄ tum *TDLA*.
[4] tu ne *Siesbye*: ne Ω.
[5] Rutulus *Conway and Walters on* III. vii. 6: rutilius (*or*
-cil-) Ω.   *The same correction at chap.* ix. § 2.

add five augurs' places and four pontiffs', to which B.C. 300
plebeians may be named, has not desired to oust
you patricians, Appius, from your places, but that
men of the plebs may help you in the administration
also of divine affairs, even as they help you in other
and human matters, to the measure of their strength.
Blush not, Appius, to have a colleague in the priesthood whom you might have had in the censorship
or consulship. It is quite as possible that he should
be dictator and you his master of the horse as that
it should be the other way about. A Sabine immi-
grant, the first of your house to be ennobled—call
him Attius Clausus or Appius Claudius, as you will—
was admitted to their number by the patricians of
that olden time : be not too proud to admit us into
the number of the priests. We bring many distinctions with us, aye, every one of those same distinctions that have made you so high and mighty.
Lucius Sextius was the first plebeian consul, Gaius
Licinius Stolo the first master of the horse ; Gaius
Marcius Rutulus the first dictator and censor, Quintus
Publilius Philo the first praetor. From you we
have heard always the same song—that the auspices
belong to you, that you alone are of noble birth,
that you alone have the full *imperium* and right to
divination, both at home and in the field. But the
authority and divination of plebeian and patrician
have prospered in equal measure until now, and so
they shall do in the future. Pray, has it ever been
wafted to your ears that those who were first
appointed to be patricians were not beings descended
from celestial regions, but were such as could name
their fathers—were free-born men, that is, and
nothing more? I can already name a consul for

A.U.C.
454

avumque iam poterit filius meus.   Nihil est aliud in
re, Quirites, nisi ut omnia negata adipiscamur;
certamen tantum patricii petunt nec curant quem
12 eventum certaminum habeant.   Ego hanc legem,
quod bonum faustum felixque sit vobis ac rei
publicae, uti rogas, iubendam [1] censeo."

A.U.C.
455

IX. Vocare tribus extemplo populus iubebat,
apparebatque accipi legem; ille tamen dies inter-
2 cessione est sublatus.   Postero die deterritis tribunis
ingenti consensu accepta est.   Pontifices creantur
suasor legis P. Decius Mus P. Sempronius Sophus
C. Marcius Rutulus M. Livius Denter; quinque
augures item de plebe, C. Genucius P. Aelius Paetus
M. Minucius Faesus C. Marcius T. Publilius.   Ita
octo pontificum, novem augurum numerus factus.

3 Eodem anno M. Valerius consul de provocatione
legem tulit diligentius sanctam.   Tertio ea tum post
reges exactos lata est, semper a familia eadem.
4 Causam renovandae saepius haud aliam fuisse reor
quam quod plus paucorum opes quam libertas plebis
poterat.   Porcia tamen lex sola pro tergo civium
lata videtur, quod gravi poena, si quis verberasset
5 necassetve civem Romanum, sanxit; Valeria lex cum

---

[1] iubendam ϛ: subendam ς: subeundam Ω.

---

[1] For the earlier laws *de provocatione*, see II. viii. 2, and
III. lv. 4.
[2] This law was not passed until (probably) 198 B.C., at the
instance of the elder Cato, who was then praetor.

my father, and my son will presently be able to B.C. 300
name one for his grandfather. In truth the matter
is simply, Quirites, that we must always be first
denied, and yet have our way in the end. A struggle
is all that the patricians ask : they care not what
may be the outcome of the struggle. I hold that
this law—and may good come of it and favour and
prosperity, to yourselves and to the state !—should
be ordered, as proposed."

IX. The people straightway commanded the tribes B.C. 299
to be called, and it seemed that the measure would
be accepted ; nevertheless it was put off for that day
on account of a veto. On the following day the
tribunes were cowed and the law was passed with
acclamation. To be pontiffs were chosen the advocate
of the law, Publius Decius Mus, with Publius Sempronius Sophus, Gaius Marcius Rutulus, and Marcus
Livius Denter ; the five augurs were likewise of the
plebs, Gaius Genucius, Publius Aelius Paetus, Marcus
Minucius Faesus, Gaius Marcius, and Titus Publilius.
Thus the number of pontiffs became eight and of
augurs nine.

In the same year Marcus Valerius the consul proposed a law of appeal with stricter sanctions. This
was the third time since the expulsion of the kings
that such a law had been introduced, by the same
family in every instance.[1] The reason for renewing
it more than once was, I think, simply this, that the
wealth of a few carried more power than the liberty
of the plebs. Yet the Porcian law alone seems to
have been passed to protect the persons of the
citizens, imposing, as it did, a heavy penalty if
anyone should scourge or put to death a Roman
citizen.[2] The Valerian law, having forbidden that

A.U.C.
455
eum qui provocasset virgis caedi securique necari
vetuisset, si quis adversus ea fecisset, nihil ultra
6 quam "improbe factum" adiecit. Id, qui tum
pudor hominum erat, visum, credo, vinculum satis
validum legis : nunc vix serio [1] ita minetur quisquam.
7   Bellum ab eodem consule haudquaquam memorabile adversus rebellantes Aequos, cum praeter
animos feroces nihil ex antiqua fortuna haberent,
8 gestum est. Alter consul Apuleius in Vmbria
Nequinum oppidum circumsedit. Locus erat arduus
atque in parte una praeceps, ubi nunc Narnia sita
9 est, nec vi nec munimento capi poterat. Itaque
eam infectam rem M. Fulvius Paetus T. Manlius
Torquatus novi consules acceperunt.
10   In eum annum cum Q. Fabium consulem non
petentem omnes dicerent centuriae, ipsum auctorem
fuisse Macer Licinius ac Tubero tradunt differendi
11 sibi consulatus in bellicosiorem annum : eo anno
maiori se usui rei publicae fore urbano gesto magistratu. Ita nec dissimulantem quid mallet nec
petentem tamen, aedilem curulem cum L. Papirio
12 Cursore factum. Id ne pro certo ponerem vetustior
annalium auctor Piso effecit, qui eo anno aediles
curules fuisse tradit Cn. Domitium [2] Cn. filium Calvi-

---

[1] vix serio ς *Pithoeus, Perizonius*: uix seruo OTA^2 : uix
seru (*or other corruptions*) Ω.
[2] Cn. Domitium *Pighius* (*C.I.L.* i[2], *p.* 134): CĪ (*or* cl *or*
C̄.L. *or* C.L.) Domitium Ω : l.c. domitium *T*.

---

[1] The *Acta Triumphorum* (*C.I.L.*, i[2], p. 171) give him as
son of Gnaeus and grandson of Gnaeus ; he is therefore not
the same as the M. Fulvius who was consul in 305 B.C. (IX.
xliv. 15), whose father and grandfather were both named
Lucius.
[2] Fabius had already held this office, 331 B.C. (VIII.
xviii. 4).

he who had appealed should be scourged with rods
or beheaded, merely provided that if anyone should
disregard these injunctions it should be deemed a
wicked act. This seemed, I suppose, a sufficiently
strong sanction of the law, so modest were men in
those days; at the present time one would hardly
utter such a threat in earnest.

The same consul conducted an insignificant campaign against the rebellious Aequi, who retained
nothing of their ancient fortune but a warlike spirit.
Apuleius, the other consul, laid siege to the town
of Nequinum in Umbria. It was a steep place and
on one side precipitous—the site is now occupied by
Narnia—and could be captured neither by assault
nor by siege operations. The enterprise was therefore still unfinished when Marcus Fulvius Paetus[1]
and Titus Manlius Torquatus, the new consuls, took
it over.

Licinius Macer and Tubero declare that all the
centuries were for naming Quintus Fabius consul
for this year, though he was not a candidate,
but that Fabius himself urged them to defer his
consulship to a year when there was more fighting;
just then he would be of greater service to the state
if invested with an urban magistracy. And so,
neither dissembling what he had in mind nor yet
seeking it, he was elected curule aedile, with Lucius
Papirius Cursor.[2] I have been unable to put this
down for certain, because Piso, one of the older
annalists,[3] states that the curule aediles for that
year were Gnaeus Domitius Calvinus, the son of

[3] For Piso and the other annalists see Vol. I. pp. xxviii-
xxx.

A.U.C.
455
13 num et Sp. Carvilium Q. filium Maximum. Id credo
cognomen errorem in aedilibus fecisse secutamque
fabulam mixtam ex aediliciis et consularibus comitiis,
14 convenientem errori. Et lustrum eo anno conditum
a P. Sempronio Sopho[1] et P. Sulpicio Saverrione
censoribus, tribusque additae duae, Aniensis ac
Terentina.[2] Haec Romae gesta.

X. Ceterum ad Nequinum oppidum cum segni
obsidione tempus tereretur, duo ex oppidanis, quorum
erant aedificia iuncta muro, specu facto ad stationes
2 Romanas itinere occulto perveniunt; inde ad consulem deducti praesidium armatum se intra moenia
3 et muros accepturos confirmant. Nec aspernanda
res visa neque incaute credenda. Cum altero eorum
—nam alter obses retentus—duo exploratores per
4 cuniculum missi; per quos satis comperta re trecenti
armati transfuga duce in urbem ingressi nocte portam quae proxima erat cepere. Qua refracta consul
5 exercitusque Romanus sine certamine urbem invasere. Ita Nequinum in dicionem populi Romani
venit. Colonia eo adversus Umbros missa a Nare
flumine[3] Narnia appellata; exercitus cum magna
praeda Romam reductus.
6   Eodem anno ab Etruscis adversus indutias paratum bellum; sed eos talia[4] molientis Gallorum ingens

---

[1] P. Sempronio Sopho et *edd* (*from* § 2): P. Sulpicio Sopho
et *MTDLA*: *omitted by PFUO?*.
[2] Terentina Ω: tarentina *TDLA*: terentia *Periocha*:
Teretina *Mommsen* (*cf. Conway, Italic Dialects*, i, *p*. 340).
[3] Nare flumine ς: flumine Ω.
[4] talia *Glareanus:* alia Ω.

---

[1] The "closing of the lustrum" was accomplished by the
sacrifice of a swine, a sheep and an ox (the *suovetaurilia*),
and completed the ceremonies incidental to the census.

Gnaeus, and Spurius Carvilius Maximus, the son of B.C. 299
Quintus. I fancy that this surname occasioned an
error in regard to the aediles, and that a story afterwards grew up in harmony with the error, from a
confusion of the aedilician with the consular elections. This year witnessed also the closing of the
lustrum,[1] by the censors Publius Sempronius Sophus
and Publius Sulpicius Saverrio, and two tribes were
added—the Aniensis and the Terentina. So much
for affairs at Rome.

X. Meantime, at the town of Nequinum, while
the siege dragged slowly on, two of the townsmen,
whose dwellings abutted on the wall, dug a tunnel
and made their way in secret to the Roman outposts.
Thence they were conducted to the consul, whom
they assured of their readiness to admit a party of
soldiers within the fortifications and the walls. It
was not thought wise to spurn this offer, nor yet
rashly to confide in it. In company with one of
these men—the other being held as a hostage—two
scouts were sent through the tunnel; the result
of their investigation was satisfactory, and three
hundred armed men, with the renegade as guide,
effected an entrance by night into the city and
seized the nearest gate. Once this had been broken
down, the Roman consul and his army captured the
place without a struggle. Thus Nequinum came
under the sway of the Roman People. A colony
was sent there to make head against the Umbrians,
and was given the name of Narnia from the river
Nar. The army, enriched with spoil, marched back
to Rome.

The Etruscans planned to go to war that year in
violation of the truce; but while they were busy

exercitus finis ingressus paulisper a proposito avertit.

7 Pecunia deinde, qua multum poterant, freti, socios ex hostibus facere Gallos conantur ut eo adiuncto

8 exercitu cum Romanis bellarent. De societate haud abnuunt barbari: de mercede agitur. Qua pacta acceptaque cum parata cetera ad bellum essent sequique Etruscus iuberet, infitias eunt mercedem

9 se belli Romanis inferendi pactos: quidquid acceperint accepisse ne agrum Etruscum vastarent armis-

10 que lacesserent cultores; militaturos tamen se, si utique Etrusci velint, sed nulla alia mercede quam ut in partem agri accipiantur tandemque aliqua sede

11 certa consistant. Multa de eo concilia populorum Etruriae habita, nec perfici quicquam potuit, non tam quia imminui agrum quam quia accolas sibi quisque adiungere tam efferatae gentis homines

12 horrebat. Ita dimissi Galli pecuniam ingentem sine labore ac periculo partam[1] rettulerunt. Romae terrorem praebuit fama Gallici tumultus ad bellum Etruscum adiecti; eo minus cunctanter foedus ictum cum Picenti populo est.

XI. T. Manlio consuli provincia Etruria sorte evenit; qui vixdum ingressus hostium finis cum

---

[1] partam ς: paratam Ω.

[1] Now mentioned for the first time by Livy.

with this project an enormous army of Gauls in- B.C. 299
vaded their borders and diverted them for a little
while from their purpose. Afterwards, putting
their trust in money, of which they had great store,
they endeavoured to convert the Gauls from enemies
into friends, to the end that, uniting the Gallic
army with their own, they might fight the Romans.
The barbarians made no objection to an alliance :
it was only a question of price. When this had
been agreed upon and received, and the Etruscans,
having completed the rest of their preparations for
the war, bade their new allies follow them, the
Gauls demurred. They had made no bargain, they
said, for a war with Rome ; whatever they had
received had been in consideration of their not
devastating the Etruscan territory and molesting
its inhabitants ; nevertheless they would take the
field, if the Etruscans were bent on having them,
but on one condition only—that the Etruscans
admit them to a share in their land, where they
might settle at last in a permanent home. Many
councils of the peoples of Etruria were held to consider this offer, but nothing could be resolved upon,
not so much from a reluctance to see their territory
lessened as because everyone shrank from having
men of so savage a race for neighbours. So the
Gauls were dismissed, and departed with a vast sum
of money, acquired without any toil or risk. The
Romans were alarmed by the rumour of a Gallic
rising in addition to a war with the Etruscans, and
lost no time in concluding a treaty with the people
of Picenum.[1]

XI. The command in Etruria fell by lot to Titus B.C. 298
Manlius the consul. He had barely entered the

A.U.C.
456

exerceretur inter equites, ab rapido cursu circuma-
gendo equo effusus extemplo prope exspiravit; ter-
2 tius ab eo casu dies finis vitae consuli fuit. Quo
velut omine belli accepto deos pro se commisisse
3 bellum memorantes Etrusci sustulere animos. Romae
cum desiderio viri tum incommoditate temporis
tristis nuntius fuit; patres ab iubendo dictatore consulis subrogandi comitia ex sententia principum
4 habita deterruerunt.[1] M. Valerium consulem omnes
centuriae[2] dixere, quem senatus dictatorem dici
iussurus fuerat. Tum extemplo in Etruriam ad
5 legiones proficisci iussit. Adventus eius compressit
Etruscos adeo ut nemo extra munimenta egredi
auderet timorque ipsorum obsidioni similis esset.
6 Neque illos novus consul vastandis agris urendisque
tectis, cum passim non villae solum sed frequentes
quoque vici incendiis fumarent, elicere ad certamen
potuit.
7 Cum hoc segnius bellum opinione esset, alterius
belli, quod multis in vicem cladibus haud immerito
terribile erat, fama, Picentium novorum sociorum
indicio exorta est: Samnites arma et rebellionem
8 spectare seque ab iis sollicitatos esse. Picentibus
gratiae actae et magna pars curae patribus ab Etruria
in Samnites versa est.

[1] patres . . . deterruerunt *Gronovius*: ut patres . . . de-
lirruerint Ω.
[2] centuriae *Cobet*: sententiae centuriaeque Ω.

territory of the enemy, and was exercising with the B.C. 298
cavalry, when, in wheeling his horse about after a
swift gallop, he was thrown and ere long breathed
his last, for the third day following the accident saw
the end of the consul's life. Taking this as an omen
of the war, and declaring that the gods had begun
hostilities in their behalf, the Etruscans plucked up
courage. It was sad news to the Romans; not only
could they ill spare the man, but his death occurred
at an embarrassing moment. The Fathers would have
ordered the nomination of a dictator had not the election held to choose a substitute for the consul fallen
out in accordance with the wishes of the leaders.
Marcus Valerius was the choice of all the centuries
for consul. It was he whom the senate had intended
to have named as dictator, and they now commanded
him to proceed forthwith to the legions in Etruria.
His arrival so damped the ardour of the Etruscans
that none ventured outside their fortifications, and
their own fear was like a besieging host. Nor
could the new consul entice them into giving
battle by wasting their lands and firing their buildings, though the smoke was rising on every side
from the conflagration not only of farm-houses but
of many villages as well.

While this war was prolonged beyond anticipation,
another war—justly dreaded by reason of the many
losses which the parties to it had inflicted on each
other—was beginning to be talked of in consequence
of information given by the Picentes, Rome's new
allies. The Samnites, they said, were looking to
arms and a renewal of hostilities, and had solicited
their help. The Picentes were thanked, and the
senate's anxiety was diverted, in great measure,
from Etruria to the Samnites.

LIVY

9 Caritas etiam annonae sollicitam civitatem habuit ventumque ad inopiae ultimum foret, ut scripsere quibus aedilem fuisse eo anno Fabium Maximum placet, ni eius viri cura, qualis in bellicis rebus multis tempestatibus fuerat, talis domi tum in annonae dispensatione praeparando ac convehendo frumento fuisset.

10 Eo anno—nec traditur causa—interregnum initum. interreges fuere Ap. Claudius, dein P. Sulpicius. Is comitia consularia habuit; creavit L. Cornelium Scipionem, Cn. Fulvium consules.

11 Principio huius anni oratores Lucanorum ad novos consules venerunt questum, quia condicionibus perlicere se nequiverint ad societatem armorum, Samnites infesto exercitu ingressos fines suos vastare

12 belloque ad bellum cogere. Lucano populo satis superque erratum quondam nunc ita obstinatos animos esse: ut omnia ferre ac pati tolerabilius ducant, quam ut unquam postea nomen Romanum

13 violent. Orare patres ut et Lucanos in fidem accipiant et vim atque iniuriam ab se Samnitium arceant: se, quamquam bello cum Samnitibus suscepto necessaria iam facta adversus Romanos fides sit, tamen obsides dare paratos esse.

XII. Brevis consultatio senatus fuit; ad unum omnes iungendum foedus cum Lucanis resque

---

[1] This is said to be the first recorded instance of the aediles being charged with the oversight of the City's food-supply.

[2] The Lucanians had entered upon friendly relations with the Romans in 326 B.C. (VIII. xxv. 3), but had been seduced from their loyalty by the Samnites (VIII. xxvii. 10). A Roman army invaded them in 317 (IX. xx. 9).

The citizens were also concerned at the dearness of provisions, and would have experienced the direst need, as those writers have recorded who are pleased to represent Fabius Maximus as having been aedile in that year, if that heroic man, who had on many occasions managed military undertakings, had not at this juncture shown himself equally expert in the administration of the market and the purchase and importation of corn.[1]

In this year—for no cause assigned—there befell an interregnum. The interreges were Appius Claudius, and afterwards Publius Sulpicius. The latter held a consular election, and announced that the choice had fallen on Lucius Cornelius Scipio and Gnaeus Fulvius.

In the beginning of this year Lucanian envoys came to the new consuls to complain that the Samnites, since they had been unable by offering inducements to entice them into an armed alliance, had invaded their territories with a hostile army and by warring on them were obliging them to go to war. The people of Lucania, they said, had on a former occasion strayed all too far from the path of duty, but were now so resolute as to deem it better to endure and suffer anything than ever again to offend the Romans.[2] They besought the Fathers both to take the Lucanians under their protection and to defend them from the violence and oppression of the Samnites. Though their having gone to war with the Samnites was necessarily a pledge of loyalty to the Romans, yet they were none the less ready to give hostages.

XII. Discussion in the senate was soon over. Every opinion was for entering into a treaty with

A.U.C.
456

2 repetendas ab Samnitibus censent. Benigne responsum Lucanis ictumque foedus ; fetiales missi, qui
Samnitem decedere agro sociorum ac deducere exercitum finibus Lucanis iuberent ; quibus obviam missi
ab Samnitibus, qui denuntiarent, si quod adissent in
3 Samnio concilium, haud inviolatos abituros. Haec
postquam audita sunt Romae, bellum Samnitibus et
patres censuerunt et populus iussit.

Consules inter se provincias partiti sunt : Scipioni
Etruria, Fulvio Samnites obvenerunt, diversique ad
4 suum quisque bellum proficiscuntur. Scipioni segne
bellum et simile prioris anni militiae exspectanti
hostes ad Volaterras instructo agmine occurrerunt.
5 Pugnatum maiore parte diei magna utrimque caede ;
nox incertis qua data victoria esset intervenit. Lux
insequens victorem victumque ostendit ; nam Etrusci
6 silentio noctis castra reliquerant.[1] Romanus egressus
in aciem, ubi profectione hostium concessam victoriam videt, progressus ad castra vacuis cum plurima
praeda—nam et stativa et trepide deserta fuerant—
7 potitur. Inde in Faliscum agrum copiis reductis
cum impedimenta Faleriis cum modico praesidio

---

[1] reliquerant *Heusinger* : reliquerunt Ω.

---

[1] This was the so-called Third Samnite War.
[2] The phrase *instructo agmine* seems to be used of a column
formed for marching in such a way that the soldiers merely

Lucania and demanding satisfaction of the Samnites. B.C. 298 The Lucanians received a friendly answer, and the league was formed. Fetials were then sent to command the Samnites to leave the country belonging to Rome's allies, and withdraw their army from the territory of Lucania. They were met on the way by messengers, whom the Samnites had dispatched to warn them that if they went before any Samnite council they would not depart unscathed. When these things were known at Rome, the senate advised and the people voted a declaration of war against the Samnites.[1]

The consuls divided the commands between them, Scipio getting Etruria and Fulvius the Samnites, and set out for their respective wars. Scipio looked forward to a slow campaign like that of the previous year, but was met near Volaterrae by the enemy drawn up in column.[2] The fighting, which lasted for the best part of a day, was attended with heavy losses on both sides; and night came on while it was yet uncertain to which nation victory had been vouchsafed. The morning showed who was victor and who vanquished, for in the silence of the night the Etruscans had decamped. The Romans marched out into line of battle; and when they saw that the enemy by his retreat had conceded their superiority, they advanced and possessed themselves of the camp, which was unoccupied and contained much booty, for it had been a permanent post and had been hurriedly abandoned. Scipio then led his troops back into the Faliscan territory, and having left his baggage with a small guard in Falerii, set out with

by executing a *right* (or *left*) *face* would constitute a battle-line.

reliquisset, expedito agmine ad populandos [1] hostium
8 fines incedit. Omnia ferro ignique vastantur; praedae
undique actae. Nec solum modo vastum hosti relictum sed castellis etiam vicisque inlatus ignis : urbibus
oppugnandis temperatum, in quas timor Etruscos
compulerat.

9 Cn. Fulvi consulis clara pugna in Samnio ad
Bovianum haudquaquam ambiguae victoriae fuit.
Bovianum inde adgressus nec ita multo post Aufide-
nam vi cepit.

XIII. Eodem anno Carseolos colonia in agrum
2 Aequicolorum deducta. Fulvius consul de Samnitibus triumphavit. Cum comitia consularia instarent,
fama exorta Etruscos Samnitesque ingentes conscribere
3 exercitus : palam omnibus conciliis vexari principes
Etruscorum, quod non Gallos quacumque condicione
traxerint ad bellum ; increpari [2] magistratus Samnitium, quod exercitum adversus Lucanum hostem
4 comparatum obiecerint Romanis ; itaque suis sociorumque viribus consurgere hostes ad bellum, et
haudquaquam pari defungendum esse certamine.

5 Hic terror, cum illustres viri consulatum peterent,
omnes in Q. Fabium Maximum primo non petentem,
deinde, ut inclinata studia vidit, etiam recusantem
6 convertit : quid se iam senem ac perfunctum laboribus

---

[1] populandos *MPUOA*[2] : depopulandos *FTDLA*.
[2] increpari ς : increpare Ω.

---

[1] We had already been told of the colony at Carseoli in
chap. iii. § 2. Livy seems here to be following a different
authority, and perhaps a better one, as the town is here
correctly located among the Aequicoli (mentioned in 1
xxxii. 5 as an ancient tribe from whom Ancus Marcius copied
the ritual of the fetials) instead of among the Marsi.

his army in light marching order to ravage the
territory of the enemy. The whole country was
laid waste with fire and sword and booty was brought
in from all directions. Not only was the soil left
bare for the enemy, but even strongholds and villages
were burned. The consul stopped short of attacking the walled towns, into which the frightened
Etruscans had fled for refuge.

The other consul, Gnaeus Fulvius, fought a famous
battle in Samnium, near Bovianum, and gained a
victory that was by no means doubtful. He then
attacked and captured Bovianum, and not long
afterwards Aufidena.

XIII. A colony was founded in that same year at
Carseoli in the land of the Aequicoli.[1] The consul
Fulvius triumphed over the Samnites. As the
consular elections drew near, a rumour arose that
the Etruscans and the Samnites were levying huge
forces; it was said that in all their councils the
leaders of the Etruscans were openly censured for
not having brought the Gauls into the war, on
whatever terms; and the Samnite magistrates were
attacked for having confronted the Romans with an
army raised to oppose a Lucanian foe; thus their
enemies were girding themselves for war, in their
own might and the might of their allies, and they
would have to contend with them on far from even
terms.

This danger, though illustrious men were candidates for the consulship, made everyone turn to
Quintus Fabius Maximus, who was not a candidate,
in the first place, and who, when he saw the
direction of the people's wishes, actually refused
to stand. Why must they trouble him, he asked,

403

LIVY

laborumque praemiis sollicitarent? Nec corporis nec
animi vigorem remanere eundem, et fortunam ipsam
vereri, ne cui deorum nimia iam in se et constantior
7 quam velint humanae res videatur. Et se gloriae
seniorum succrevisse et ad suam gloriam consurgentes
alios laetum aspicere; nec honores magnos fortissimis
viris Romae nec honoribus deesse fortes viros.
8 Acuebat hac moderatione tam iusta studia; quae
verecundia legum restinguenda ratus, legem recitari
iussit qua intra decem annos eundem consulem refici
9 non liceret. Vix prae strepitu audita lex est tribunique plebis nihil id impedimenti futurum aiebant:
10 se ad populum laturos uti legibus solveretur. Et
ille quidem in recusando perstabat: quid ergo attineret
leges ferri,[1] quibus per eosdem qui tulissent fraus
11 fieret. Iam regi leges, non regere. Populus[2] nihilo
minus suffragia inibat, et ut quaeque intro vocata
erat centuria, consulem haud dubie Fabium dicebat.
12 Tum demum consensu civitatis victus, "Dei appro-
bent" inquit, "quod agitis acturique estis, Quirites.
Ceterum, quoniam in me quod vos voltis facturi
estis, in collega sit meae apud vos gratiae locus:

[1] ferri *Walters*: ferri ros(*or*-rof-)itans *M*: ferri cogitans
O: ferri rogitans (*in PFU* rogitans *comes after* quibus) Ω.
[2] populus *A*[2]: populos Ω (*uncertain which letter in O*).

---

[1] The statute dated from 342 B.C. and applied equally to
all magistracies, but was frequently disregarded. As Fabius
had not been consul since 308, his election now would not
have contravened the statute, and Luterbacher suggests that
the story may have originated in connexion with the election
of two years before (chap. ix. § 10).
[2] There was an enclosure (the *saepta*) in the Campus
Martius, into which the centuries were summoned, and
there, one by one, proclaimed their choice.

who was an old man now and had done with
toil and the rewards of toil? Neither his body
nor his mind retained their vigour undiminished,
and he feared Fortune herself, lest some god might
deem that she had already been too kind to him
and more constant than human beings were meant
to find her. He himself had risen to the glory
of his elders, and he rejoiced to see others growing
up to the measure of his own. There was no lack
of great offices in Rome for the bravest men, nor of
brave men for the offices.

Such moderation but intensified the well-merited
enthusiasm of his friends; and Fabius, thinking
that it would have to be restrained by respect for
the laws, bade read aloud the statute which
prohibited the re-election of the same man to the
consulship within ten years.[1] Whereupon there was
such a clamouring that the law could scarce be
heard, and the tribunes of the plebs declared that
it should be no impediment, for they would propose
to the people that he be granted a dispensation from
the laws. Fabius, for his part, stoutly persisted in
his refusal. What, in that case, he demanded, was
the good of making laws, when their very makers
broke them? The laws were no longer in control,
but were themselves controlled. Nevertheless the
people proceeded to the election, and every century,
as it was summoned within, in no uncertain terms
named Fabius consul.[2] Then at last, overborne by
the consent of all the citizens, "May Heaven," he
said, "approve, Quirites, of what you are doing
and propose to do. For the rest, since you are
bound to have your way with me, grant me a favour
in the matter of my colleague and make consul

LIVY

13 P. Decium, expertum mihi concordi collegio virum,
dignum vobis, dignum parente suo, quaeso mecum
consulem faciatis." Iusta suffragatio visa. Omnes
quae supererant centuriae Q. Fabium, P. Decium
consules dixere.

14 Eo anno plerisque dies dicta ab aedilibus, quia
plus quam quod lege finitum erat agri possiderent;
nec quisquam ferme est purgatus vinculumque ingens
immodicae cupiditati[1] iniectum est.

XIV. Consules novi, Q. Fabius Maximus quartum
et P. Decius Mus tertium, cum inter se agitarent
2 uti alter Samnites hostes, alter Etruscos deligeret,
quantaeque in hanc aut in illam provinciam copiae
satis et uter ad utrum bellum dux idoneus magis
3 esset, ab Sutrio et Nepete et Faleriis legati, auctores
concilia[2] Etruriae populorum de petenda pace
haberi,[3] totam belli molem in Samnium averterunt.
4 Profecti consules, quo expeditiores commeatus essent
et incertior hostis qua venturum bellum foret, Fabius
per Soranum, Decius per Sidicinum agrum, in
Samnium legiones ducunt.
5 Ubi in hostium fines ventum est, uterque popula-
bundus effuso agmine incedit. Explorant tamen
6 latius quam populantur; igitur non fefellere ad
Tifernum hostes in occulta valle instructi, quam
ingressos Romanos superiore ex loco adoriri para-

---

[1] cupiditati ς : cupiditatis Ω.
[2] concilia D³: concilii Ω : aoncilii M : concilium U.
[3] haberi Ω : habiti Conway (reading concilii above with the MSS.).

---

[1] The elder Decius had devoted himself in 340 B.C. The
son had been consul with Fabius in 308 B.C. (VIII. ix.
and xli).

with me Publius Decius, a man whose friendliness
I have experienced in the fellowship of office, a man
worthy of you and worthy of his sire." [1] The
recommendation seemed a reasonable one. All the
remaining centuries voted for Quintus Fabius and
Publius Decius.

In that year many men were prosecuted by the
aediles on the charge of possessing more land than
the law allowed. Hardly anybody was acquitted,
and exorbitant greed was sharply curbed.

XIV. While the new consuls, Quintus Fabius
Maximus (in his fourth term) and Publius Decius
Mus (in his third), were laying plans together how
one should take the field against the Samnites,
and the other against the Etruscans, and were
considering what forces would suffice for these respective provinces and which of them was the better
suited to the one command and which to the
other, there came deputies from Sutrium and Nepete
and Falerii, with the news that the nations of
Etruria were counselling together how they might
sue for peace, and thus diverted upon Samnium the
whole burden of war. When the consuls set out, in
order to lessen the difficulty of getting supplies and
to keep the enemy uncertain where the attack would
come, Fabius marched into Samnium by way of Sora,
Decius through the territory of the Sidicini.

Arrived at the borders of the enemy, each spread
his army over a wide front and pillaged. Yet they
scouted more widely than they pillaged, and the
enemy were therefore unable to surprise them near
Tifernum, where they had drawn their forces up
in a secluded valley, and were preparing to assail
the Romans from above, once they should have

A.U.C.
457

7 bant. Fabius impedimentis in locum tutum remotis praesidioque modico imposito praemonitis militibus adesse certamen, quadrato agmine ad praedictas
8 hostium latebras succedit. Samnites desperato improviso tumultu, quando in apertum semel discrimen evasura esset res, et ipsi acie iusta maluerunt concurrere. Itaque in aequum descendunt ac fortunae
9 se maiore animo quam spe committunt. Ceterum, sive quia ex omnium Samnitium populis, quodcumque roboris fuerat contraxerant, seu quia discrimen summae rerum augebat[1] animos, aliquantum aperta quoque[2] pugna praebuerunt terroris.
10 Fabius, ubi nulla ex parte hostem loco moveri vidit, Maximum filium et M. Valerium tribunos militum, cum quibus ad primam aciem procurrerat,
11 ire ad equites iubet et adhortari ut, si quando unquam equestri ope adiutam rem publicam meminerint, illo die adnitantur ut ordinis eius gloriam invictam
12 praestent: peditum certamine immobilem hostem restare; omnem reliquam spem in impetu esse equitum. Et ipsos nominatim iuvenes, pari comitate utrumque, nunc laudibus nunc promissis onerat.
13 Ceterum quando ne ea quoque temptata vis parum proficeret timeri poterat, consilio[3] grassandum, si

---

[1] augebat *ς*: agebat *TDL*: angebat *MO*: āgebat *A*.

[2] aliquantum aperta quoque *ς*: aliquantum quoque aperta *MOTDLA*.

[3] ceterum . . . consilio *Madvig*: ceterum quando ne (nec *OL*) ea quoque temptata vis proficeret consilio *Ω*.

entered it. Removing the baggage to a place of
safety and appointing a small force to guard it,
Fabius warned his troops that a struggle was at
hand, and forming them into a hollow square, led
them up towards the place where the enemy lay,
as I have said, concealed. Balked of their surprise
attack, the Samnites—since it must ultimately come
to an open trial of strength—likewise preferred to
fight a regular engagement. They accordingly
descended to level ground, and committed their
cause to Fortune, with courage greater than their
hopes. However, whether owing to their having
assembled the fighting strength of all the Samnite
nations, or because a contest on which everything
was staked heightened their valour, they occasioned
some perturbation amongst the Romans, even in an
open battle.

When Fabius saw that the enemy were nowhere
giving way, he ordered Maximus his son [1] and Marcus
Valerius—military tribunes with whom he had
hurried to the front—to go to the horsemen and
tell them that if they remembered ever an occasion
when the state had been helped by the horse, now
was the time for them to exert their strength to
preserve untarnished the glory of that body: in the
struggle of infantry the enemy were yielding not
an inch; no hope remained save in a charge of
cavalry. Addressing each of the young men by
name, he loaded them now with praise and now
with promises. But since it was conceivable that
even their prowess might prove to be inadequate,
he thought proper to resort to strategy, if strength

---

[1] Quintus Fabius Maximus Gurges, aedile two years later
(chap. xxxi. § 9) and consul 292 B.C. (chap. xlvii. § 5).

A.U.C.
457 14 nihil vires iuvarent ratus, Scipionem legatum hastatos
primae legionis subtrahere ex acie et ad montes
proximos quam posset occultissime circumducere
iubet; inde ascensu abdito a conspectu erigere in
montes agmen aversoque hosti ab tergo repente se
ostendere.

15 Equites ducibus tribunis haud multo plus hostibus
quam suis ex improviso ante signa evecti praebuerunt

16 tumultus. Adversus incitatas turmas stetit immota
Samnitium acies nec parte ulla pelli aut perrumpi
potuit; et postquam inritum inceptum erat, recepti

17 post signa proelio excesserunt. Crevit ex eo hostium
animus, nec sustinere frons prima tam longum
certamen increscentemque fiducia sui vim potuisset,
ni secunda acies iussu consulis in primum succes-

18 sisset. Ibi integrae vires sistunt invehentem se iam
Samnitem; et tempore in ipso visa [1] ex montibus
signa clamorque sublatus non vero tantum metu

19 terruere Samnitium animos; nam et Fabius Decium
collegam adpropinquare exclamavit, et pro se quisque miles adesse alterum consulem, adesse legiones

20 gaudio alacres fremunt; errorque [2] utilis Romanis
oblatus fugae formidinisque Samnites implevit,
maxime [3] territos ne ab altero exercitu integro

21 intactoque fessi opprimerentur. Et quia passim in

---

[1] et tempore in ipso visa *Drakenborch:* et tempore inpro-
visa *MOTDLA:* et tempore in se uisa *PF:* eo tempore uisa
U: et tempore ipso visa *I. Perizonius:* et tempore inferri uisa
Conway.

[2] errorque ς *Modius:* terrorque Ω.

[3] maxime ς: maximeq. Ω.

---

[1] These "spearmen" formed the first of the three lines of
battle, but would ordinarily after being engaged a little
while be reinforced or replaced (as here) by the *principes*
(second line troops).

should not achieve his purpose. So he ordered B.C. 297
Scipio, his lieutenant, to withdraw the *hastati*[1] of
the first legion from the battle and conduct them,
as secretly as possible, by a circuitous route to the
nearest mountains; they were then, concealing
their ascent from observation, to climb the heights
and suddenly show themselves on the enemy's rear.

The cavalry, led by the tribunes, occasioned
hardly more confusion in their enemies than in their
friends, as they rode out unexpectedly in front of
the standards. The Samnite line held firm against
their galloping squadrons, and could at no point
be forced back or broken, and the cavalry, finding
their attack abortive, retired behind the lines and
left the battle. This gave the enemy a fresh access
of spirits; and the front ranks would have been
incapable of sustaining so long a struggle and the
increasing violence with which the enemy's confidence inspired him, had not the second line, by
the consul's order, come up to relieve them. Their
fresh strength halted the Samnites, who were now
pressing forward; and catching sight just at this
juncture of our detachments descending from the
mountains, and hearing the cheer they gave, the
enemy was filled with terror of worse things than
actually threatened him; for Fabius shouted that
his colleague Decius was approaching, and the
soldiers themselves in their joy and eagerness cried
out that the other consul was at hand—that the
legions were at hand; and this mistake, occurring
in a good hour for the Romans, filled the Samnites
with fear and bewilderment, for they dreaded
nothing so much as that the other army, fresh and
entire, might overwhelm them in their exhausted

A.U.C.
457
fugam dissipati sunt, minor caedes quam pro tanta
victoria fuit : tria milia et quadringenti caesi, capti
octingenti ferme et triginta, signa militaria capta
tria et viginti.

A.U.C.
458
XV. Samnitibus Apuli se ante proelium coniun-
xissent, ni P. Decius consul iis ad Maleventum castra
obiecisset, extractos deinde ad certamen fudisset.
2 Ibi quoque plus fugae fuit quam caedis : duo milia
Apulorum caesa ; spretoque eo hoste Decius in Sam-
3 nium legiones duxit. Ibi duo consulares exercitus
diversis vagati partibus omnia spatio quinque men-
4 sum evastarunt. Quinque et quadraginta[1] loca in
Samnio fuere in quibus Deci castra fuerunt, alterius
5 consulis sex et octoginta ; nec valli tantum ac fossa-
rum vestigia relicta, sed multo alia illis[2] insigniora
monumenta vastitatis circa regionumque depopula-
6 tarum. Fabius etiam urbem Cimetram cepit. Ibi
capta armatorum duo milia nongenti, caesi pugnantes
ferme nongenti triginta.
7   Inde comitiorum causa Romam profectus maturavit eam rem agere. Cum primo vocatae[3] Q.
Fabium consulem dicerent omnes centuriae, Ap.
8 Claudius, consularis candidatus, vir acer et ambi-
tiosus, non sui magis honoris causa quam ut patricii
reciperarent duo consularia loca, cum suis tum totius
nobilitatis viribus incubuit ut se cum Q. Fabio con-

[1] quinque et quadraginta *Walters and Conway :* xl et v (*or
at length*) *MPFUO :* et xl et xv (*or at length*) *TDLA.*
[2] alia illis *Walters and Conway :* aliis Ω : illis ς.
[3] vocatae ς : uocatum Ω.

[1] Later Beneventum. See IX. xxvii. 14 and note.

state. The slaughter was less than is usual in so _{B.C. 297} great a victory, for the enemy scattered far and wide in their flight. Three thousand four hundred were slain; about eight hundred and thirty were made prisoners, and twenty-three standards were taken.

XV. The Apulians would have joined the Samnites _{B.C. 296} before the battle had not Publius Decius the consul encamped over against them at Maleventum,[1] and then drawn them into an engagement and defeated them. In this instance also the rout was greater than the slaughter: two thousand Apulians were killed, and Decius, scorning such an enemy, led his legions into Samnium. There the two consular armies, overrunning the land in different directions, had laid all waste within four months' time. There were forty-five places in Samnium where Decius had encamped; the other consul had encamped in eighty-six. Nor did they leave behind them only the traces of their ramparts and their trenches, but other much more conspicuous memorials, in the havoc and devastation of the country round about. Fabius also captured the city of Cimetra. In this siege two thousand nine hundred men-at-arms were taken and some nine hundred and thirty were slain fighting.

After this he set out for Rome for the election, which he made haste to call. The centuries that voted first were all naming Quintus Fabius for consul, when Appius Claudius, who was a candidate for that post and a pushing and ambitious man, but no more eager to gain the honour for himself than to have the patricians recover two consular places, exerted his own strength and that of the whole nobility to induce them to elect him as Fabius's

LIVY

9 sulem dicerent. Fabius de se[1] eadem fere quae
priore anno dicendo abnuere. Circumstare sellam
omnis nobilitas; orare ut ex caeno plebeio consulatum extraheret maiestatemque pristinam cum
10 honori tum patriciis gentibus redderet. Fabius
silentio facto media oratione studia hominum
sedavit; facturum enim se fuisse dixit ut duorum
patriciorum nomina reciperet, si alium quam se con-
11 sulem fieri videret; nunc se suam rationem comitiis,
cum contra leges futurum sit, pessimo exemplo non
12 habiturum. Ita L. Volumnius de plebe cum Ap.
Claudio consul est factus, priore item consulatu inter
se comparati. Nobilitas obiectare Fabio fugisse
eum Ap. Claudium collegam, eloquentia civilibusque
artibus haud dubie praestantem.

XVI. Comitiis perfectis veteres consules iussi
bellum in Samnio gerere prorogato in sex menses
2 imperio. Itaque insequenti quoque anno L. Volumnio
Ap. Claudio consulibus P. Decius, qui consul in
Samnio relictus a collega fuerat, proconsul idem
populari non destitit agros, donec Samnitium exercitum nusquam se proelio committentem postremo
3 expulit finibus.

Etruriam pulsi petierunt, et quod legationibus
nequiquam saepe temptaverant, id se tanto agmine

---

[1] de se *Walters* (*note*): primo de se Ω: de se primo *F*.

---

[1] 307 B.C. (IX. xlii. 2).

colleague. Fabius would not have it so, raising b.c. 296
virtually the same objections he had raised in the
previous year. The nobles all thronged about his
seat, and besought him to lift up the consulship
out of the plebeian mire and restore both to the
office and to the aristocratic families their old-time
dignity. Obtaining silence, Fabius soothed their
excited feelings with a temperate speech, in which
he said that he would have done as they desired
and have received the names of two patricians, if
he had seen another than himself being made
consul ; as it was, he would not entertain his own
name at an election, for to do so would violate
the laws and establish a most evil precedent. So
Lucius Volumnius, a plebeian, was returned, together
with Appius Claudius, with whom he had also been
paired in an earlier consulship.[1] The nobles taunted
Fabius with having avoided Appius Claudius for a
colleague, as a man clearly his superior in eloquence
and statecraft.

XVI. The election over, the old consuls were
bidden to carry on the war in Samnium, having
received an extension of their command for six
months. So in the following year likewise—the
consulship of Lucius Volumnius and Appius Claudius
—Publius Decius, who had been left behind in
Samnium, when consul, by his colleague, ceased not
as proconsul to lay waste the farms, until finally
he forced the army of the Samnites—which would
nowhere risk a battle—to withdraw from the
country.

They retreated into Etruria, and thinking that
what they had often tried in vain to bring about
by means of embassies they might with so great

armatorum mixtis terrore precibus acturos efficacius rati, postulaverunt principum Etruriae con-
4 cilium. Quo coacto per quot annos pro libertate
dimicent cum Romanis exponunt: omnia expertos
esse si suismet ipsorum viribus tolerare tantam
5 molem belli possent; temptasse etiam haud magni
momenti finitimarum gentium auxilia. Petisse
pacem a populo Romano, cum bellum tolerare non
possent; rebellasse, quod pax servientibus gravior
6 quam liberis bellum esset. Unam sibi spem reliquam
in Etruscis restare; scire gentem Italiae oppulen-
tissimam armis, viris, pecunia esse; habere accolas
Gallos, inter ferrum et arma ˙natos, feroces cum
suopte ingenio tum adversus Romanum populum,
quem captum a se auroque redemptum, haud vana
7 iactantes, memorent; nihil abesse, si sit animus
Etruscis qui Porsinnae quondam maioribusque eorum
fuerit, quin Romanos omni agro cis Tiberim pulsos
dimicare pro salute sua non de intolerando Italiae
8 regno cogant. Samnitem illis exercitum paratum,
instructum armis, stipendio venisse, et confestim secu-
turos, vel si ad ipsam Romanam urbem oppugnandam
ducant.

XVII. Haec eos in Etruria iactantes molientesque
bellum domi Romanum urebat.   Nam P. Decius, ubi

---

[1] See II. ix.–xv.

a body of armed men and the menace which would B.C. 296 be added to their entreaties accomplish more effectually, called for a council of the Etruscan leaders. On its assembling, they pointed out for how many years they had been fighting with the Romans for their liberty. They had made every effort, they said, if haply they might of their own strength bear up under so great a war; and had also—but to little purpose—made trial of the help of neighbouring nations. Unable to sustain the war, they had sought peace of the Roman People; but had renewed hostilities, because peace with servitude was harder to endure than war with liberty. Their sole remaining hope lay in the Etruscans, whom they knew for the richest nation of Italy, in arms, in men, and in money; a nation, too, that marched with the Gauls, men born amid the clash of arms and possessing not only an instinctive love of fighting but a feeling of enmity to the Roman People, whose defeat at their hands and ransom for gold they were wont to relate with no idle boast. If the Etruscans had the spirit that once had animated Porsinna [1] and their forefathers, there was no reason why they should not expel the Romans from all the country north of the Tiber, and compel them to fight, not for an intolerable sovereignty over Italy, but for their own existence. Here was a Samnite army, provided with arms and pay, and ready to follow on the instant, though they should lead it to the assault of Rome itself.

XVII. While they were thus boasting and intriguing in Etruria, the Roman invasion was distressing their countrymen at home. For Publius Decius, having

417

comperit per exploratores profectum Samnitium
2 exercitum, advocato consilio "Quid per agros" inquit
"vagamur vicatim circumferentes bellum? Quin urbes
et moenia adgredimur? Nullus iam exercitus Samnio
3 praesidet; cessere finibus ac sibimet ipsi exsilium
conscivere." Adprobantibus cunctis ad Murgantiam,
validam urbem, oppugnandam ducit, tantusque ardor
militum fuit et caritate ducis et spe maioris quam ex
agrestibus populationibus praedae ut uno die vi atque
4 armis urbem caperent. Ibi duo milia Samnitium
et centum pugnantes circumventi captique, et alia
praeda ingens capta est. Quae ne impedimentis
gravibus agmen oneraret, convocari milites Decius
5 iubet. "Hacine" inquit "victoria sola aut hac
praeda contenti estis futuri? Voltis vos pro virtute
spes gerere? Omnes Samnitium urbes fortunaeque
in urbibus relictae vestrae sunt, quando legiones
eorum tot proeliis fusas postremo finibus expulistis.
6 Vendite ista et inlicite lucro mercatorem ut sequatur
agmen; ego subinde suggeram quae vendatis. Ad
Romuleam urbem hinc eamus, ubi vos labor haud
maior, praeda maior manet."
7 Divendita praeda ultro adhortantes imperatorem
ad Romuleam pergunt. Ibi quoque sine opere, sine
tormentis, simul admota sunt signa, nulla vi deterriti

ascertained through scouts that the Samnite army had departed, summoned a council, and said, " Why do we range about the countryside, bringing war to this, that, and the other village ? Why do we not assail cities and walled towns ? There is no longer any army defending Samnium ; they have withdrawn beyond their borders, sentenced to banishment by their own decree." With their unanimous approval he led them to the assault of Murgantia, a strong city ; and such was the ardour of the troops, by reason both of affection for their general and the hopes that they entertained of greater booty than was to be got by ranging the country, that they took the place by force of arms in a single day. There two thousand one hundred Samnites were surrounded and made prisoners as they fought, and vast spoils of other kinds were seized. Lest these should encumber the marching army with heavy baggage, Decius called the soldiers together and thus addressed them : " Will this single victory or these spoils content you ? Will your expectations not be equal to your courage ? All the cities of the Samnites and the riches left behind in them are yours, since, after defeating their legions in so many battles, you have in the end expelled them from their country. Sell these prizes and with hope of gain lure the traders on to follow your column ; I will find you from time to time wares to dispose of. Let us go from here to the city Romulea, where no greater toil awaits you, but greater booty."

The booty was sold off, and the men themselves urging on their general, they marched to Romulea. There, too, they used no siege-works or artillery ; but once they had come up under the walls, no force

LIVY

a muris, qua cuique proximum fuit, scalis raptim
8 admotis in moenia evasere. Captum oppidum ac
direptum est; ad duo milia et trecenti occisi et sex
9 milia hominum capta, et miles ingenti praeda potitus,
quam vendere, sicut priorem, coactus; Ferentinum
inde, quamquam nihil quietis dabatur, tamen summa
10 alacritate ductus est.[1] Ceterum ibi plus laboris ac
periculi fuit: et defensa summa vi moenia sunt, et
locus erat munimento naturaque tutus; sed evicit
omnia adsuetus praedae miles. Ad tria milia hostium
circa muros caesa; praeda militis fuit.

11 Huius oppugnatarum urbium decoris pars maior in
quibusdam annalibus ad Maximum trahitur: Murgantiam ab Decio, a Fabio Ferentinum Romu-
12 leamque oppugnatas tradunt. Sunt qui novorum
consulum hanc gloriam faciant, quidam non am-
borum sed alterius, L.[2] Volumni: ei Samnium provinciam evenisse.

XVIII. Cum [3] ea in Samnio cuiuscumque ductu
auspicioque gererentur, Romanis in Etruria interim
bellum ingens multis ex gentibus concitur, cuius
2 auctor Gellius Egnatius ex Samnitibus erat. Tusci
fere omnes consciverant bellum; traxerat contagio
proximos Umbriae populos, et Gallica auxilia mercede
sollicitabantur; omnis ea multitudo ad castra Sam-
3 nitium conveniebat. Qui tumultus repens postquam

---

[1] ductus est *Madvig*: ductus Ω.
[2] L. Sigonius (*cf.* § 3 *and Chap.* xvi. § 2, *and C.I.L.* i², *p.*
132): p̄. Ω (*wanting in O*).
[3] cum *Gronovius*: dum Ω (*wanting in O*).

could constrain them to retire; quickly setting up B.C. 296 their ladders at the nearest places, they swarmed over the battlements. The town was captured and sacked; two thousand three hundred were slain and six thousand made prisoners, and the soldiers came into possession of huge spoils which they were obliged, as before, to sell. After that they marched with the utmost alacrity—though they had been allowed no time to rest—to Ferentinum. But there they encountered more difficulty and danger: the city was defended with the utmost energy, and fortification and nature had combined to make it safe; yet all obstacles were overcome by a soldiery grown used to plunder. Some three thousand of the enemy were slain about the walls; the spoils went to the men.

Of the glory accruing from these sieges the larger share is in certain annals assigned to Maximus; they allow that Murgantia was stormed by Decius, but give to Fabius Ferentinum and Romulea. There are those who claim the credit for the new consuls, and some give it not to both but to one of them, Lucius Volumnius, to whom, they say, fell the command in Samnium.

XVIII. Whilst these operations were being carried out in Samnium—whoever had the command and auspices—a mighty war was preparing against the Romans in Etruria, on the part of many nations, at the instigation of a Samnite named Gellius Egnatius. The Tuscans had almost all voted for war; the nearest Umbrian tribes had caught the contagion; and Gallic auxiliaries were being solicited for pay. All this multitude was assembling at the camp of the Samnites. When news of this sudden rising

A.U.C.
458

est Romam perlatus, cum iam L. Volumnius consul
cum legione secunda ac tertia sociorumque milibus
quindecim profectus in Samnium esset, Ap. Claudium
primo quoque tempore in Etruriam ire placuit.

4 Duae Romanae legiones secutae, prima et quarta, et
sociorum duodecim milia; castra haud procul ab
hoste posita.

5 Ceterum magis eo profectum est quod mature ventum erat ut quosdam spectantes iam arma Etruriae
populos metus Romani nominis comprimeret quam
quod ductu consulis quicquam ibi satis scite aut

6 fortunate gestum sit: multa proelia locis et temporibus iniquis commissa, spesque in dies graviorem
hostem faciebat, et iam prope erat ut nec duci

7 milites nec militibus dux satis fideret. Litteras ad
collegam accersendum ex Samnio missas in trinis
annalibus invenio; piget tamen in certo[1] ponere,
cum ea ipsa inter consules populi Romani, iam iterum
eodem honore fungentes, disceptatio[2] fuerit, Appio
abnuente missas, Volumnio adfirmante Appi se litteris
accitum.

8 Iam Volumnius in Samnio tria castella ceperat, in
quibus ad tria milia hostium caesa erant, dimidium
fere eius captum, et Lucanorum seditiones a plebeiis
et egentibus ducibus ortas summa optimatium voluntate per Q. Fabium, pro consule missum eo cum

9 vetere exercitu, compresserat. Decio populandos hos-

---

[1] in certo *Walters*: incertum Ω: id certum *Buettner*.
[2] disceptatio M^1 or M^2: discepatio M: discrepatio M^1 (or
M^2) *PFUOTDLA.*

---

[1] This is the first time that Livy has designated the legions
by number. A consular army regularly comprised two
legions (with their cavalry and auxiliaries), but in the present instance the consular armies of the previous year are
still in the field.

was brought to Rome, Lucius Volumnius the consul, B.C. 296
with the second and third legions and fifteen thousand of the allies, had already set out for Samnium,
and it was resolved to send Appius Claudius into
Etruria at the earliest possible moment. Two
Roman legions followed him, the first and fourth,
and twelve thousand of the allies. They encamped
not far from the enemy.[1]

But the consul's prompt arrival accomplished
more, by checking, through dread of the Roman
name, certain peoples of Etruria that were already
meditating war, than he gained by his generalship,
which was characterized neither by much ability nor
by good fortune. He repeatedly joined battle at
untoward times and places, and the enemy grew
every day more hopeful and more formidable, until
now the soldiers were near losing confidence in their
commander and he in them. I find it recorded by
three annalists that he dispatched a letter sending
for his colleague out of Samnium ; yet am I loath to
set it down for certain, since the consuls of the
Roman People, now holding that office for the second
time, disputed about that very point—Appius denying
that he had sent a letter, Volumnius affirming that
a letter from Appius had summoned him.

Volumnius had already captured three fortresses
in Samnium, in which some three thousand of the
enemy had been slain and about half as many taken
prisoners ; and dispatching Quintus Fabius as proconsul with a seasoned army into Lucania, he had
suppressed—with the hearty approval of the opti-
mates—certain insurrections which had broken out
there at the instigation of necessitous plebeian
agitators. Leaving to Decius the devastation of

423

A.U.C.
458

tium agros relinquit, ipse cum suis copiis in Etruriam
ad collegam pergit.   Quem advenientem laeti omnes
10 accepere.   Appium ex conscientia sua credo animum
habuisse—haud immerito iratum si nihil scripserat,
inliberali et ingrato animo, si eguerat ope, dissimu-
11 lantem,—vix enim salute mutua reddita cum obviam
egressus esset, "Satin salvae"[1] inquit, "L. Volumni?
Ut sese in Samnio res habent?   Quae te causa, ut
12 provincia tua excederes induxit?"   Volumnius in
Samnio res prosperas esse ait, litteris eius accitum
venisse; quae si falsae fuerint nec usus sui sit in
13 Etruriam, extemplo conversis signis abiturum.   "Tu
vero abeas" inquit, "neque te quisquam moratur;
etenim minime consentaneum est, cum bello tuo
forsitan vix sufficias, huc[2] te ad opem ferendam aliis
14 gloriari venisse."   Bene Hercules verteret, dicere
Volumnius: malle frustra operam insumptam, quam
quicquam incidisse cur non satis esset Etruriae unus
consularis exercitus.

XIX. Digredientes iam consules legati tribunique
ex Appiano exercitu circumsistunt.   Pars imperatorem suum orare, ne collegae auxilium, quod accien-
dum ultro fuerit, sua sponte oblatum sperneretur;
2 plures abeunti Volumnio obsistere; obtestari ne
pravo cum collega certamine rem publicam prodat:

---

[1] salvae ς : salue Ω (*wanting in O*).
[2] huc A^3 (*or* A^4) ς : hic Ω (*wanting in O*).

the fields, Volumnius himself with his own troops B.C. 296 marched to join his colleague in Etruria, where he was welcomed on his arrival with general rejoicings. But what Appius was feeling his conscience alone could tell!—indeed he was justly angered if he had sent no word, but illiberal and ungracious if he had needed help and now sought to dissemble —for coming forth to meet his colleague, before they had fairly greeted one another, he demanded, " Is all well, Lucius Volumnius? How stand affairs in Samnium? What has moved you to come out of your own province?" Volumnius replied that affairs were prospering in Samnium, and that he was come being sent for by Appius' own letter; but if this were a forgery and he were not needed in Etruria, he would immediately face about and march back. " By all means go!" cried Appius. " No one hinders you! For truly it is no way fitting that when, perhaps, you are hardly equal to your own war, you should boast of coming hither to help others." Volumnius prayed that Hercules might direct all for the best; he had rather, he said, his trouble should go for naught than that anything should have befallen to make one consular army insufficient for Etruria.

XIX. The consuls were parting, when the lieutenants and tribunes from the army of Appius gathered round them. Some of them besought their general not to spurn his colleague's help—which ought even to have been asked for—now that it was proffered voluntarily; the greater number threw themselves in the way of Volumnius, as he turned to go, and conjured him not to betray the welfare of the state by an unworthy quarrel with his colleague: if any

si qua clades incidisset, desertori magis quam deserto
3 noxae fore; eo rem adductam ut omne[1] rei bene
aut secus gestae in Etruria decus dedecusque ad L.
Volumnium sit delegatum; neminem quaesiturum
quae verba Appi sed quae fortuna exercitus fuerit;
4 dimitti ab Appio eum sed a re publica et ab exercitu
retineri; experiretur modo voluntatem militum.
5   Haec monendo obtestandoque prope restitantes
consules in contionem pertraxerunt. Ibi orationes
longiores habitae in eandem ferme sententiam in
6 quam inter paucos certatum verbis fuerat. Et cum
Volumnius, causa superior, ne infacundus quidem
adversus eximiam eloquentiam collegae visus esset,
7 cavillansque Appius sibi acceptum referre diceret
debere, quod ex muto atque elingui facundum etiam
consulem haberent; priore consulatu, primis utique
8 mensibus, hiscere eum nequisse, nunc iam populares
orationes serere, "Quam mallem" inquit Volumnius,
"tu a me strenue facere quam ego abs te scite loqui
didicissem." Postremo condicionem ferre quae de-
cretura sit non orator—neque enim id desiderare rem
9 publicam—sed imperator uter sit melior. Etruriam
et Samnium provincias esse; utram mallet eligeret;
suo exercitu se vel in Etruria vel in Samnio rem
gesturum.
10   Tum militum clamor ortus ut simul ambo bellum

---

[1] omne *ς Muretus* : omni Ω : omnis *TDLA*.

---

[1] In their former consulship (307 B.C.) Volumnius had con-
ducted a successful campaign against the Sallentini, while
Appius had been left in Rome without any military command.
See IX. xlii. 4–5.

disaster should occur, the blame would lie more B.C. 296
with the deserter than the deserted ; to such a pass
had matters come that the entire credit or disgrace
of success or failure in Etruria was referred to Lucius
Volumnius; no one would enquire what the words
of Appius had been, but what the fortune of the
army ; he was being dismissed by Appius, but
retained by the republic and the army ; let him but
test the wishes of the soldiers.

Thus admonishing and entreating them they
dragged the all but resisting consuls to the place
of assembly. There they spoke at greater length,
but substantially to the same effect as they had
argued before in the hearing of a few ; and when
Volumnius, besides having the better cause, likewise
showed himself to be no mean orator in opposing
the rare eloquence of his colleague, Appius jeeringly
remarked that they ought to give himself the credit,
for that instead of a mute and tongue-tied consul
they had got one who was actually fluent, since in
his former consulship, at all events in its early
months, he had been incapable of opening his
mouth, but was now delivering popular orations.—
" How I could wish," exclaimed Volumnius, " that
you might rather have learnt from me to act with
vigour than that I should have learnt to speak
cleverly from you ! " In conclusion he proposed a
compact which would determine, not which was the
better orator—for this was not what the republic
wanted—but the better general.[1] Etruria and
Samnium were the nations to be conquered; let
Appius choose which he liked ; with his own army
he would campaign either in Etruria or in Samnium.

Then the soldiers began to cry out that both

LIVY

A.U.C.
458

11 Etruscum susciperent. Quo animadverso consensu
Volumnius "Quoniam in collegae voluntate interpre-
tanda" inquit "erravi, non committam ut quid vos
velitis obscurum sit: manere an abire me velitis
12 clamore significate." Tum vero tantus est clamor
exortus ut hostes e castris exciret. Armis arreptis in
aciem[1] descendunt. Et Volumnius signa canere ac
vexilla efferri castris iussit; Appium addubitasse
13 ferunt, cernentem seu pugnante seu quieto se fore
collegae victoriam; deinde veritum ne suae quoque
legiones Volumnium sequerentur, et ipsum flagitan-
tibus suis signum dedisse.

14 Ab neutra parte satis commode instructi fuerunt;
nam et Samnitium dux Gellius Egnatius pabulatum
cum cohortibus paucis ierat suoque impetu magis
milites quam cuiusquam ductu aut imperio pugnam
capessebant et Romani exercitus nec pariter ambo
15 ducti nec satis temporis ad instruendum fuit. Prius
concurrit Volumnius quam Appius ad hostem per-
16 veniret; itaque fronte inaequali concursum est; et
velut sorte[2] quadam mutante adsuetos inter se
hostes Etrusci Volumnio, Samnites parumper cunctati,
17 quia dux aberat, Appio occurrere. Dicitur Appius
in medio pugnae discrimine, ita ut inter prima signa
manibus ad caelum sublatis conspiceretur, ita precatu:

---

[1] in aciem T^2A^2: in acie Ω (*wanting in O*).
[2] et velut sorte ς *Duker* (VI. xxi. 2): et velut fort⊢
MTDLA: et ut forte *PFO*: ut et forte *U*.

---

[1] *i.e.* from the higher ground on which their camp lay
into the plain below.
[2] The ancients prayed with the arms outstretched an⊢
palms turned upwards.

should undertake the Etruscan war together. Perceiving them to be of one mind in this, Volumnius
said, "Since I erred in interpreting my colleague's
wishes, I will not make the blunder of leaving yours
in doubt: do you signify by a shout whether you
would have me stay or go." Then in truth they
cheered so loud that the enemy were drawn out
from their camp, and snatching up their arms went
down[1] into line of battle. Volumnius, too, bade
sound the signal and advance the banners from the
camp. Appius, they say, was uncertain what to do,
perceiving that, whether he fought or refrained
from fighting, the victory would be his colleague's;
then, fearing that even his own legions would follow
Volumnius, he, too, gave his men the signal for
which they were clamouring.

On neither side had the forces been very advan-
tageously marshalled; for the Samnite commander
Gellius Egnatius had taken a few cohorts and gone
off to forage, and his soldiers were entering the
battle more as their own impulse guided them than
under anybody's leadership or orders, and the
Roman armies were not both led out together nor
had they sufficient time to form. Volumnius was
engaged before Appius came within reach of the
enemy, and the line of attack was accordingly uneven. Moreover, as though lots had been cast,
there was a shifting of the customary opponents,
the Etruscans confronting Volumnius, and the
Samnites—after a little hesitation, owing to the
absence of their general—meeting Appius. It is
said that when the conflict was at its hottest, Appius
was seen to lift up his hands[2] in the very forefront
of the standards and utter this petition: "Bellona,

A.U.C.
458 esse : " Bellona, si hodie nobis victoriam duis, ast
18 ego tibi templum voveo." Haec precatus, velut
instigante dea, et ipse collegae et exercitus virtutem
aequavit ducis. Iam et duces imperatoria[1] opera
exsequuntur, et milites ne ab altera parte prius
19 victoria incipiat adnituntur. Ergo fundunt fugantque
hostes, maiorem molem haud facile sustinentes quam
20 cum qua manus conserere adsueti fuerant. Urgendo
cedentes insequendoque effusos compulere ad castra.
Ibi interventu Gelli cohortiumque Sabellarum paulisper recruduit pugna. Iis quoque mox fusis iam a
21 victoribus castra oppugnabantur; et cum Volumnius
ipse portae signa inferret, Appius Bellonam victricem
identidem celebrans accenderet[2] militum animos,
22 per vallum, per fossas inruperunt. Castra capta
direptaque; praeda ingens parta et militi concessa
est. Septem milia octingenti[3] hostium occisi, duo
milia et centum viginti capti.

XX. Dum ambo consules omnisque Romana vis
in Etruscum bellum magis inclinat, in Samnio novi
exercitus exorti ad populandos imperii Romani fines
per Vescinos[4] in Campaniam Falernumque agrum
2 transcendunt ingentesque praedas faciunt. Volumnium magnis itineribus in Samnium redeuntem—
iam enim Fabio Decioque prorogati imperii finis

[1] Iam et duces imperatoria *Walters and Conway* (*note*) : et
duces imperatoria *Weissenborn* : imperatoria Ω.
[2] accenderet ς : accenderant *MPTDLA* : accenderat Ω.
[3] octingenti *edd.* : accc *PFUOTDLA* : acccc *MA²*.
[4] Vescinos *Sigonius* (*Conway*, *Ital. Dial.* i, p. 283):
uestinos Ω.

if to-day thou grant us the victory, then do I vow thee a temple." Having pronounced this prayer, as though the goddess were inspiring him, he kept pace with the courage of his colleague and the army kept pace with his. And now the generals were quitting themselves like true commanders, and the soldiers were striving that victory might not come first on the other wing. They therefore routed and put to flight the enemy, who found it no easy task to withstand a greater force than they had been wont to engage with. Pressing hard upon them when they faltered and pursuing where they fled, the Romans drove them to their camp. There, on the appearance of Gellius and the Sabellian cohorts, the battle was renewed for a little while; but presently, when these too had been dispersed, the conquering troops assailed the camp, and while Volumnius himself led a charge against the gate, and Appius, calling from time to time on Bellona, goddess of victory, inspirited his soldiers, they burst through the trenches and the rampart. The camp was taken and pillaged, and the vast booty found there was given over to the soldiers. Seven thousand eight hundred of the enemy were slain, two thousand one hundred and twenty taken prisoners.

XX. While both consuls and all the strength of Rome were being devoted mainly to the Etruscan war, new armies rose up in Samnium to waste the territories under Roman sway, and crossing over into Campania and the Falernian district, through the land of the Vescini, gathered in huge spoils. As Volumnius was returning by long marches into Samnium—for now the extension of authority granted to Fabius and Decius was drawing to a

431

aderat—fama de Samnitium exercitu populationi-
busque Campani agri ad tuendos socios convertit.
3 Ut in Calenum venit, et ipse cernit recentia cladis
vestigia et Caleni narrant tantum iam praedae hostes
4 trahere ut vix explicare agmen possint : itaque iam
propalam duces loqui extemplo eundum in Samnium
esse, ut relicta ibi praeda in expeditionem redeant
nec tam oneratum agmen dimicationibus committant.
5 Ea quamquam similia veris erant, certius tamen
exploranda ratus dimittit equites, qui vagos praedatores in agris palantes intercipiant ;[1] ex quibus
6 inquirendo cognoscit ad Volturnum flumen sedere
hostem, inde tertia vigilia moturum ; iter in Samnium
esse.
7 His satis exploratis profectus tanto intervallo ab
hostibus consedit ut nec adventus suus propinquitate
nimia nosci posset et egredientem e castris hostem
8 opprimeret. Aliquanto ante lucem ad castra accessit
gnarosque Oscae linguae exploratum quid agatur
mittit. Intermixti hostibus, quod facile erat in
nocturna trepidatione, cognoscunt infrequentia armatis signa egressa, praedam praedaeque custodes
exire, immobile agmen et sua quemque molientem

---

[1] intercipiant M^3 (or M^4)A^2 : incipiant M : excipiant Ω.

---

[1] Their command had been extended for six months
(chap. xvi. § 1).

close [1]—a rumour about the Samnite army and its depredations in the territory of Campania turned him aside to the defence of the allies. When he came to the Calenian country, he saw for himself the fresh traces of the enemy's ravages, and the Calenians informed him that the Samnites had already so great a train of booty as to march with difficulty, and their leaders were saying openly that they must retire at once into Samnium, and leaving their plunder there, return to the invasion, and not subject an army so heavily burdened to the risks of battle. These reports were plausible enough; nevertheless he thought it right to obtain more authentic information. He therefore sent out horsemen in various directions, to intercept straggling plunderers in the fields, from whom he learned, on questioning them, that their army was encamped at the Volturnus river, whence they would set forward in the third watch and march towards Samnium.

Being satisfied of the truth of these reports, he followed the enemy and encamped at such a distance from them that while they could not learn of his arrival from his being too close at hand, he yet might surprise them as they were leaving their camp. A little before dawn he approached the camp and sent ahead men who knew the Oscan language to find out what was being done. Mingling with their enemies, as they could easily do in the confusion of the dark, they learned that the standards had gone forward with a scanty following of men-at-arms, that the booty and its escort were just setting out, but that the column was incapable of progress, since every man was intent upon his

nullo inter ullos[1] consensu nec satis certo imperio.
9 Tempus adgrediendi aptissimum visum est, et iam
lux adpetebat; itaque signa canere iussit agmenque
10 hostium adgreditur. Samnites praeda impediti,
infrequentes armati, pars addere gradum ac prae se
agere praedam, pars stare incerti utrum progredi an
regredi in castra tutius foret: inter cunctationem
opprimuntur et Romani iam transcenderant vallum
11 caedesque ac tumultus erat in castris. Samnitium
agmen praeterquam hostili tumultu, captivorum
etiam repentina defectione turbatum erat, qui partim
12 ipsi soluti vinctos solvebant, partim arma in sarcinis
deligata rapiebant tumultumque proelio ipso terri-
biliorem intermixti agmini praebebant. Memo-
13 randum deinde edidere facinus; nam Staium Mi-
natium ducem adeuntem ordines hortantemque
invadunt; dissipatis inde equitibus qui cum eo
aderant ipsum circumsistunt insidentemque equo
14 captum ad consulem Romanum rapiunt. Revocata
eo tumultu prima signa Samnitium, proeliumque iam
profligatum integratum est; nec diutius sustineri
15 potuit. Caesa ad sex milia hominum, duo milia et
quingenti capti—in eis tribuni militum quattuor—
signa militaria triginta, et quod laetissimum

---

[1] inter ullos *Madvig*: inter alios Ω: *deleted as a gloss by
Walters and Conway.*

---

[1] The Samnites, not anticipating any fighting, had put up
their arms in the bundles, which were tied to a pole that
was carried on the shoulder.

own affairs, with no common understanding among B.C. 296
any of them nor any very definite leadership. The
time seemed highly suitable for delivering an attack,
and the day was breaking. Volumnius therefore
ordered them to sound the charge and assailed the
enemy's column. The Samnites were impeded by
their booty and few of them were armed; some
quickened their pace and drove the cattle before
them, some stood still, uncertain whether it were
safer to go on or to return to camp; while they
hesitated, the Romans were upon them, and now
they had scaled the rampart and the camp was
filled with carnage and commotion. The Samnite
column, besides being charged by the enemy, had
also been disordered by a sudden outbreak of the
prisoners, some of whom, being loose, were releasing
those who were bound, while others were catching
up the weapons tied up in the soldiers' packs,[1] and,
mixed up with the column as they were, caused a
hurly-burly that was more terrifying than the battle
itself. They presently performed a remarkable
exploit; for as Staius Minatius, the Samnite general,
was riding along the ranks and encouraging them,
they made a rush at him, and scattering the horsemen who were with him, surrounded him, and
hurried him off a prisoner, horse and all, to the
Roman consul. This tumult had the effect of
bringing back the vanguard of the Samnites, who
renewed the battle, which had been almost finished.
But prolonged resistance was impossible. The slain
amounted to six thousand men, and twenty-five
hundred were captured—among them four military
tribunes—as well as thirty standards. What caused
most joy among the victors was the recovery of

LIVY

victoribus fuit, captivorum recepta septem milia et
quadringenti, et praeda[1] ingens sociorum; accitique
edicto domini ad res suas noscendas recipiendasque
16 praestituta die. Quarum rerum non exstitit domi-
nus, militi concessae, coactique vendere praedam, ne
alibi quam in armis animum haberent.

XXI. Magnum ea populatio Campani agri tu-
2 multum Romae praebuerat; et per eos forte dies ex
Etruria allatum erat post deductum inde Volumnia-
num exercitum Etruriam concitam in arma, et
Gellium Egnatium, Samnitium ducem, et Umbros
ad defectionem vocari et Gallos pretio ingenti solli-
3 citari. His nuntiis senatus conterritus iustitium
indici, dilectum omnis generis hominum haberi iussit.
4 Nec ingenui modo aut iuniores sacramento adacti
sed seniorum etiam cohortes factae libertinique
centuriati; et defendendae urbis consilia agitabantur
summaeque rerum praetor P. Sempronius praeerat.
5 Ceterum parte curae exonerarunt senatum L. Volumni consulis litterae, quibus caesos fusosque
6 populatores Campaniae cognitum est. Itaque et
supplicationes ob rem bene gestam consulis nomine
decernunt et[2] iustitium remittitur quod fuerat dies
duodeviginti; supplicatioque perlaeta fuit.

---

[1] et praeda *Madvig*: praeda Ω.
[2] decernunt et ς *Madvig*: decernunt Ω (-tur *F*³).

seven thousand four hundred prisoners and a vast B.C. 296
quantity of spoils belonging to the allies. The
owners were summoned by proclamation to identify
and recover their property on an appointed day.
Those things for which no owner appeared were
made over to the soldiers, and they were compelled
to sell their booty, that they might have no concern
in anything but fighting.

XXI. This raid upon the Campanian country-
side had occasioned a great alarm in Rome; and
just at that time, as it happened, there came news
out of Etruria, that after the withdrawal of the
army of Volumnius the Etruscans had been induced to arm, that Gellius Egnatius, the Samnite
general, and the Umbrians were being invited to
join in the revolt, and that the Gauls were being
tempted with great sums of money. Terrified by
these reports, the senate ordered that a cessation
of the courts should be proclaimed, and that a levy
should be held of every sort of men. Not only was
the oath administered to free citizens of military
age, but cohorts were also formed out of older men,
and freedmen were mustered into centuries. Plans
were discussed for defending the City, and the
supreme command was given to the praetor, Publius
Sempronius. But the senators were relieved of a
part of their anxiety by a dispatch from Lucius
Volumnius, the consul, apprising them of the
slaughter and dispersion of the army that had
ravaged Campania. They accordingly voted a
thanksgiving for the victory, in the consul's name,
and reopened the courts, which had been closed
for eighteen days. The thanksgiving was a very
joyful one.

7 Tum de praesidio regionis depopulatae ab Samnitibus agitari coeptum; itaque placuit ut duae coloniae circa Vescinum[1] et Falernum agrum deducerentur,

8 una ad ostium Liris fluvii, quae Minturnae appellata, altera in saltu Vescino Falernum contingente agrum, ubi Sinope dicitur Graeca urbs fuisse, Sinuessa

9 deinde ab colonis Romanis appellata. Tribunis plebis negotium datum est, ut plebei scito iuberetur P. Sempronius praetor triumviros in ea loca colonis

10 deducendis creare. Nec qui nomina darent facile inveniebantur, quia in stationem se prope perpetuam infestae regionis, non in agros mitti rebantur.

11 Avertit ab eis curis senatum Etruriae ingravescens bellum et crebrae litterae Appi monentis ne regionis

12 eius motum neglegerent: quattuor gentes conferre arma, Etruscos Samnites Umbros Gallos; iam castra bifariam facta esse, quia unus locus capere tantam

13 multitudinem non possit. Ob haec et—iam[2] appetebat tempus—comitiorum causa L. Volumnius consul Romam revocatus; qui priusquam ad suffragium centurias vocaret, in contionem advocato populo

14 multa de magnitudine belli Etrusci disseruit: iam tum cum ipse ibi cum collega rem pariter gesserit, fuisse tantum bellum ut nec duce uno nec exercitu

---

[1] Vescinum (*and in* § 8, Vescino) *as at chap.* xx. § 1.
[2] et—iam *Walters and Conway* : et iam Ω : et nam *Madvig* . et iam enim *Weissenborn.*

---

[1] Perhaps situated between *Mons Massicus* and the sea or the heights of *Mondragone.*

They next considered how they might protect the region devastated by the Samnites, and resolved to plant two colonies in the Vescinian and Falernian country, one, which was named Minturnae, at the mouth of the river Liris, the other in the Vescinian forest,[1] hard by the Falernian district, where the Greek city of Sinope is said to have stood, thereafter called Sinuessa by the Roman settlers. The tribunes of the plebs were assigned the task of obtaining a plebiscite directing Publius Sempronius the praetor to appoint three commissioners to conduct the colonists to these places; yet it was not easy to find men who would enroll, since they regarded themselves as sent, not to settle on the land, but to serve almost as a perpetual outpost in a hostile territory.

The senate's attention was diverted from these cares by the growing seriousness of the war in Etruria, and by a succession of dispatches from Appius, in which he warned them not to make light of the disturbance in that region. Four races, he said, were uniting their arms, the Etruscans, Samnites, Umbrians, and Gauls; and they had already divided their camp into two, one place not being able to hold so great a multitude. For these reasons and because of the elections—the time for which was rapidly approaching—the consul Lucius Volumnius was recalled to Rome. Before summoning the centuries to vote, he brought the people together in an assembly, and discoursed at length of the magnitude of the war in Etruria: even earlier, when he himself and his colleague had campaigned there together, the war had been so great that one general and one army could not have conducted it;

439

geri potuerit; accessisse postea dici Umbros et
15 ingentem exercitum Gallorum; adversus quattuor
populos duces consules illo die deligi meminissent.
Se, nisi confideret eum consensu populi Romani
consulem declaratum iri qui haud dubie tum primus
omnium ductor habeatur, dictatorem fuisse extemplo
16 dicturum.

XXII. Nemini dubium erat quin Fabius quintum
omnium consensu destinaretur; eumque et praerogativae et primo vocatae omnes centuriae consulem
2 cum L. Volumnio dicebant. Fabi oratio fuit qualis
biennio ante; deinde, ut vincebatur consensu, versa
3 postremo ad collegam P. Decium poscendum: id
senectuti suae adminiculum fore. Censura duo-
busque consulatibus simul gestis expertum se nihil
concordi collegio firmius ad rem publicam tuendam
esse. Novo imperii socio vix iam adsuescere senilem
4 animum posse; cum moribus notis facilius se
communicaturum consilia. Subscripsit orationi eius
consul cum meritis P. Deci laudibus, tum quae ex
concordia consulum bona quaeque ex discordia mala
in administratione rerum militarium evenirent me-
5 morando, quamque[1] prope ultimum discrimen suis
et collegae certaminibus nuper ventum foret, admo-
6 nendo; Decium Fabiumque uno animo, una mente[2]

---

[1] quamque *Duker*: quam Ω.
[2] uno . . . vivere *Ussing*: ut uno . . . uiuerent Ω: qui
uno . . . viverent *Harant*.

---

[1] The *praerogativae* were the 18 centuries of knights; the
others here referred to were the 80 centuries of the first
class, *cf.* I. xliii. 11.

but it was said that the Umbrians had since then been added to the enemy's forces, as well as a huge army of Gauls; they should remember that on that day they were choosing consuls to oppose four peoples; for his own part, were he not confident that the Roman People would unanimously choose for consul the man who was then looked upon as unquestionably the first of all commanders, he would at once have named him dictator.

XXII. No one doubted that Fabius would by the common voice of all be for the fifth time elected; and in fact the prerogative centuries and all those which were summoned first [1] were naming him consul, together with Lucius Volumnius. Fabius then made a speech, to the same purport as he had done two years before; but, overborne by the general agreement, he ended by requesting that he might have for colleague Publius Decius, who would be a prop to his old age. In the censorship and the two consulships which he had shared with Decius, he had found that nothing more tended to the preservation of the commonwealth than the harmony of colleagues. To a new partner in authority he could now hardly hope to adapt an old man's mind: with one whose character he knew, it would be easier to share his counsels. His plea was seconded by the consul, who bestowed well-merited praise on Publius Decius, and recalling the advantages that accrued from harmony betwixt the consuls to the administration of military measures and the harm that resulted from their discord, reminded his hearers how dire had been the danger occasioned lately by the strife between himself and his colleague. Decius and Fabius, he said, were of one heart and

441

LIVY

vivere; esse praeterea viros natos militiae, factis magnos, ad verborum linguaeque certamina rudes.
7 Ea ingenia consularia esse : callidos sollertesque, iuris atque eloquentiae consultos, qualis Ap. Claudius esset, urbi ac foro[1] praesides habendos praetoresque
8 ad reddenda iura creandos esse. His agendis dies est consumptus. Postridie ad praescriptum consulis
9 et consularia et praetoria comitia habita. Consules creati Q. Fabius et P. Decius, Ap. Claudius praetor, omnes absentes; et L. Volumnio ex senatus consulto et scito plebis prorogatum in annum imperium est.

XXIII. Eo anno prodigia multa fuerunt, quorum averruncandorum causa supplicationes in biduum
2 senatus decrevit; publice vinum ac tus praebitum;[2]
3 supplicatum iere frequentes viri feminaeque. Insignem supplicationem fecit certamen in sacello Pudicitiae Patriciae, quae in foro Bovario est ad aedem
4 rotundam Herculis, inter matronas ortum. Verginiam, Auli filiam, patriciam plebeio nuptam, L. Volumnio consuli, matronae, quod e patribus enupsisset, sacris arcuerant. Brevis altercatio inde ex iracundia muliebri in contentionem animorum ex-

---

[1] foro $F^3D^3A^3$: fori (tori M) Ω : fortes A.
[2] praebitum A^2 : prae(or pre-)bituum MPA : p (or per-) biduum P^2FUT^2 : plebitum TD : plebi tuum L.

---

[1] Where the law-courts were held.
[2] Fabius and Decius can only have been absent from the voting place, but Appius was away from Rome.
[3] It is likely that the tradition of a shrine to Pudicitia in the Forum Boarium is due to a confusion of this goddess with Fortuna Virgo, who had a chapel there near the temple of Mater Matuta (a birth-goddess), and was, like her, a woman's goddess. Young brides dedicated to her their maiden's dress, on marrying, and the mistake was favoured

one mind, and were, besides, men born for war, B.C. 296 great in their deeds, but unskilled in the strife of words and of the tongue. Theirs were talents meet for the consul's office. But shrewd and clever men, masters of the law and of eloquence, like Appius Claudius, should be had to preside over the City and the Forum,[1] and should be elected praetors to administer justice. With these transactions the day was taken up. On the following day, by the direction of the consul, elections were held both of consuls and of praetors. Quintus Fabius and Publius Decius were chosen consuls and Appius Claudius praetor—all three being absent[2]—and the senate passed a decree, which the people ratified, prolonging for a year the command of Lucius Volumnius.

XXIII. In that year were many portents, to avert which the senate decreed supplications for two days. Wine and incense were provided by the state, and the people went in throngs to offer their prayers —both men and women. The supplication was rendered memorable by a quarrel that broke out among the matrons in the chapel of Patrician Modesty, which stands in the Cattle Market, by the round temple of Hercules.[3] Virginia, Aulus's daughter, a patrician wedded to a commoner, Lucius Volumnius the consul, had been excluded by the matrons from their ceremonies, on the ground that she had married out of the patriciate. This led to a short dispute, which the hot anger of the sex soon kindled to a blaze of passionate contention.

by the unusual circumstance that the image of Fortuna Virgo was veiled. The story preserved by Livy is an attempt to explain the epithet of Pudicitia Plebeia (§ 7). See Wissowa, *Religion und Kultus der Römer* (1912²), pp. 257, 333.

A.U.C.
459

5 arsit, cum se Verginia et patriciam et pudicam in
Patriciae Pudicitiae templum ingressam et uni nuptam ad quem virgo deducta sit, nec se viri honorumve
eius ac rerum gestarum paenitere, ex vero[1] gloriaretur.

6 Facto deinde egregio magnifica verba adauxit : in
vico Longo, ubi habitabat, ex parte aedium quod satis
esset loci modico sacello exclusit, aramque ibi posuit
et convocatis plebeiis matronis conquesta iniuriam

7 patriciarum " Hanc ego aram " inquit " Pudicitiae
Plebeiae dedico vosque hortor, ut quod certamen

8 virtutis viros in hac civitate tenet, hoc pudicitiae
inter matronas sit detisque operam ut haec ara
quam illa, si quid potest, sanctius et a castioribus

9 coli dicatur." Eodem ferme ritu et haec ara quo
illa antiquior culta est, ut nulla nisi spectatae pudicitiae matrona et quae uni viro nupta fuisset ius

10 sacrificandi haberet. Volgata dein religio a pollutis,[2]
nec matronis solum sed omnis ordinis feminis, postremo in oblivionem venit.

11 Eodem anno Cn. et Q. Ogulnii aediles curules aliquot
12 feneratoribus diem dixerunt ; quorum bonis multatis
ex eo quod in publicum redactum est aenea in
Capitolio limina et trium mensarum argentea vasa in
cella Iovis Iovemque in culmine cum quadrigis et ad
ficum Ruminalem simulacra infantium conditorum

---

[1] ex vero *Madvig* : uero Ω : uerum *A*[2] : vere *Douiatius*.
[2] a pollutis Ω : cum pollutis *H. J. Mueller* : pollutis
Duker.

---

[1] Popular etymology made *Ruminalis* come from *Romularis*
and that from *Romulus*. It was in the overflow of the Tiber
near this fig-tree that the twins were exposed (I. iv. 5).

Verginia boasted, and with reason, that she had
entered the temple of Patrician Modesty both a
patrician and a modest woman, as having been
wedded to the one man to whom she had been
given as a maiden, and was neither ashamed of her
husband nor of his honours and his victories. She
then added a noble deed to her proud words. In
the Vicus Longus, where she lived, she shut off a
part of her mansion, large enough for a shrine of
moderate size, and, erecting there an altar, called
together the plebeian matrons, and after complaining
of the injurious behaviour of the patrician ladies,
said, "I dedicate this altar to Plebeian Modesty;
and I urge you, that even as the men of our state
contend for the meed of valour, so the matrons may
vie for that of modesty, that this altar may be said
to be cherished—if it be possible—more reverently
than that, and by more modest women." This altar,
too, was served with almost the same ritual as that
more ancient one, so that no matron but one of
proven modesty, who had been wedded to one man
alone, should have the right to sacrifice. Afterwards
the cult was degraded by polluted worshippers, not
matrons only but women of every station, and
passed finally into oblivion.

In that same year Gnaeus and Quintus Ogulnius
the curule aediles brought a number of usurers to
trial, and, confiscating their possessions, employed
the share which came into the public treasury to
put brazen thresholds in the Capitol, and silver
vessels for the three tables in the shrine of Jupiter,
and a statue of the god in a four-horse chariot on
the roof, and at the fig-tree Ruminalis[1] a repre-
sentation of the infant Founders of the City being

LIVY

13 urbis sub uberibus lupae posuerunt semitamque saxo
quadrato a Capena porta ad Martis straverunt. Et
ab aedilibus plebeiis L. Aelio Paeto et C. Fulvio
Curvo ex multaticia item pecunia, quam exegerunt
pecuariis damnatis, ludi facti pateraeque aureae ad
Cereris positae.

XXIV. Q. inde Fabius quintum et P. Decius
2 quartum consulatum ineunt, tribus consulatibus
censuraque collegae nec gloria magis rerum, quae
ingens erat, quam concordia inter se clari. Quae
ne perpetua esset, ordinum magis quam ipsorum
inter se certamen intervenisse reor, patriciis tenden-
3 tibus ut Fabius Etruriam [1] extra ordinem provinciam
haberet, plebeis auctoribus Decio ut ad sortem rem
4 vocaret.[2] Fuit certe contentio in senatu et postquam ibi Fabius plus poterat, revocata res ad populum est. In contione,[3] ut inter militares viros et
factis potius quam dictis fretos, pauca verba habita.
5 Fabius, quam arborem consevisset,[4] sub ea legere
alium fructum indignum esse dicere ; [5] se aperuisse
Ciminiam silvam viamque per devios saltus Romano
6 bello fecisse. Quid se id aetatis sollicitassent, si
alio duce gesturi bellum essent ? Nimirum adver-

---

[1] Etruriam ς : in Etruriam *MPFTLA*[2] : in etruria *U*.

[2] rem vocaret *Conway* : rem revocaret *Listovius* : reuocaret
Ω.

[3] in contione ς : in contionem *MTA*[2] : in contentionem
PFUDLA.

[4] consevisset *P³F³A²(or A³)Glareanus* : conseruisset (-set
et *P*) Ω.

[5] dicere *A²* or *A³* : diceret Ω.

---

[1] Convicted probably of using for grazing purposes more
of the public domain than they were legally entitled to
control.

suckled by the wolf. They also made a paved walk B.C. 296
of squared stone from the Porta Capena to the
temple of Mars. And the plebeian aediles Lucius
Aelius Paetus and Gaius Fulvius Curvus, likewise
with the money from fines, which they exacted from
convicted graziers,[1] held games and provided golden
bowls for the temple of Ceres.

XXIV. After that Quintus Fabius (for the fifth B.C. 295
time) and Publius Decius (for the fourth) began
their consulship, having thrice been colleagues in
that office and once in the censorship, and being
not more distinguished for the renown, great though
that was, of their achievements than for their
harmonious co-operation. This, however, was not
destined to be permanent, though its interruption
was due, I think, more to rivalry between the orders
than to their own; for the patricians strove that
Fabius should have the command in Etruria without
drawing lots, and the plebeians insisted that Decius
should demand that method of determining the
question. At all events there was a contention
in the senate, and Fabius proving to be the stronger
there, the case was carried before the people. In
the assembly the speeches were short, as befitted
soldiers and men who trusted more to deeds than to
words.

Fabius argued that when one man had planted a
tree, it was unfair that another should gather the
fruit that dropped from it; it was he that had
opened up the Ciminian Forest and had made a
path for Roman arms through remote and desert
tracts. Why, pray, had they troubled him, old as
he was, if they had meant to wage the war with
another general? It was only too clear, he said—

447

sarium se, non socium imperii legisse sensim expro-
brat et invidisse Decium concordibus collegiis tribus.

7 Postremo se tendere nihil ultra quam ut, si dignum
provincia ducerent, in eam mitterent : in senatus
arbitrio se fuisse et in potestate populi futurum.

P. Decius senatus iniuriam querebatur : quoad
8 potuerint, patres adnisos ne plebeiis [1] aditus ad
magnos honores esset; postquam ipsa virtus pervi-
9 cerit ne in ullo genere hominum inhonorata esset,
quaeri quemadmodum inrita sint non suffragia modo
populi sed arbitria etiam fortunae et in paucorum
10 potestatem vertantur. Omnes ante se consules
sortitos provincias esse : nunc extra sortem Fabio
11 senatum provinciam dare,—si honoris eius causa, ita
eum de se deque re publica meritum esse ut faveat
Q. Fabi gloriae quae modo non sua contumelia
12 splendeat. Cui autem dubium esse, ubi unum bellum
sit asperum ac difficile, cum id alteri extra sortem
mandetur, quin alter consul pro supervacaneo atque
13 inutili habeatur ? Gloriari Fabium rebus in Etruria
gestis : velle et P. Decium gloriari. Et forsitan, quem
ille obrutum ignem reliquerit, ita ut totiens novum
14 ex improviso incendium daret, eum se exstincturum.
Postremo se collegae honores praemiaque conces-

---

[1] plebeiis (or plebeis) *Dx edd.* : plebis (plebi *A*[4]) Ω.

taking gradually a more reproachful tone—that he B.C. 295
had selected an adversary, not a partner in command, and that Decius had begrudged the friendly
spirit in which they had administered three offices
together. Finally, he asked no more than that if
they thought him worthy of the command they
should give it to him; he had submitted to the
decision of the senate and would obey the people.

Publius Decius complained of the senate's injustice: as long as they were able, the Fathers had
striven to deny the plebeians access to great honours;
and since native worth had of its own strength won
the right to be recognized in any class of men, they
were seeking to make of none effect not only the
suffrages of the people but also the awards of
Fortune, and to subject them to the control of a
few. All the consuls who had preceded him had
drawn lots for their commands, but the senate was
now conferring a command on Fabius without the
lot. If they were doing this to honour him, he
would say that the man had deserved so well both
of himself and of the state that he stood ready to
promote the glory of Fabius, provided only that its
lustre were not purchased with insult to himself.
But who could doubt, when there was one difficult,
dangerous war, and this was entrusted without lots
to one of the consuls, that the other was regarded
as superfluous and useless? Fabius gloried in his
Etruscan victories: Publius Decius would fain glory
too. And perhaps that fire which Fabius had left
covered up, but so that it was continually breaking
out into new flames, might be by him extinguished.
In short he was willing, for the reverence he bore
his colleague's years and dignity, to yield to him

449

LIVY

surum verecundia aetatis eius maiestatisque ; cum
periculum, cum dimicatio[1] proposita sit, neque cedere
15 sua sponte neque cessurum ; et si nihil aliud ex eo
certamine tulerit, illud certe laturum ut quod populi sit populus iubeat potius quam patres gratificen-
16 tur. Iovem optimum maximum deosque immortales
se precari ut ita sortem aequam sibi cum collega
dent si eandem virtutem felicitatemque in bello
17 administrando daturi sint. Certe et id natura aequum
et exemplo utile esse et ad famam populi Romani
pertinere, eos consules esse quorum utrolibet duce
bellum Etruscum geri recte possit.
18   Fabius nihil aliud precatus populum Romanum
quam ut, priusquam intro vocarentur ad suffragium
tribus, Ap. Claudi praetoris allatas ex Etruria litteras
audirent, comitio abiit.[2] Nec minore populi consensu quam senatus provincia Etruria extra sortem
Fabio decreta est.

XXV. Concursus inde ad consulem factus omnium
ferme iuniorum et pro se quisque nomina dabant ;
tanta cupido erat sub eo duce stipendia faciendi.
2 Qua circumfusus turba "Quattuor milia" inquit
"peditum et sescentos equites dumtaxat scribere in
animo est ; hodierno et crastino die qui nomina
3 dederitis mecum ducam. Maiori mihi curae est ut
omnes locupletes reducam quam ut multis rem
4 geram militibus." Profectus apto exercitu et eo

---

[1] cum dimicatio ς : tum dimicatio MA^2 : dimicatio Ω.
[2] comitio abiit A^2 or A^4 : comitio abit ς : comitia habuit
(*perhaps* abuit A) Ω.

honours and rewards; but when peril, when strife, was set before them—he yielded not, of his own consent—nor ever would. And if he got nothing else by this contest, one thing at any rate he would get—that what belonged to the people should be disposed of by the people, not bestowed by the Fathers as a favour. To Jupiter Optimus Maximus and the immortal gods he prayed that they would grant him an equal chance in the lot with his colleague only if they were ready to grant him the same courage and the same good fortune in the administration of the war. At least it was a thing in its nature reasonable, in its example salutary, and material to the reputation of the Roman People, that the consuls should be such that the Etruscan war could be managed aright under the leadership of either one of them.

Fabius only prayed the Roman people to listen, before the tribes were called to vote, to a dispatch of Appius Claudius the praetor that had been brought in from Etruria. He then left the comitium, and the people then, as unanimously as the senate had done, decreed that Fabius should have the command in Etruria without drawing lots.

XXV. Nearly all the younger men now flocked about the consul, and each gave in his name, so eager were they to serve under such a captain. Surrounded by this throng he said, "I have in mind to enrol no more than four thousand foot and six hundred horse; I will take with me those of you who give in your names to-day and to-morrow. I am more concerned to bring all my men back with their purses filled than to wage war with many soldiers." Marching out with a fit army, which was

plus fiduciae ac spei gerente quod non desiderata
multitudo erat, ad oppidum Aharnam, unde haud
procul hostes erant, ad castra Appi praetoris pergit.

5 Paucis citra milibus lignatores ei cum praesidio
occurrunt; qui ut lictores praegredi viderunt Fabiumque esse consulem accepere, laeti atque alacres
dis populoque Romano grates agunt quod eum sibi

6 imperatorem misissent. Circumfusi deinde cum
consulem salutarent, quaerit Fabius quo pergerent,
respondentibusque lignatum se ire, " Ain tandem ? "

7 inquit, " num castra vallata non habetis ? " Ad hoc
cum succlamatum esset duplici quidem vallo et fossa
et tamen in ingenti metu esse, " Habetis igitur "
inquit " adfatim lignorum ; redite et vellite vallum."

8 Redeunt in castra terroremque ibi vellentes vallum
et iis qui in castris remanserant militibus et ipsi

9 Appio fecerunt ; tum pro se quisque alii aliis dicere
consulis se Q. Fabi facere iussu. Postero inde die
castra mota et Appius praetor Romam dimissus.

10 Inde nusquam stativa Romanis fuere. Negabat
utile esse uno loco sedere exercitum ; itineribus ac
mutatione locorum mobiliorem ac salubriorem esse.
Fiebant autem itinera, quanta fieri sinebat hiemps
hauddum exacta.

11 Vere inde primo relicta secunda legione ad Clu-

---

1 Probably = Arna, across the Tiber from Perusia, and
about six miles due east of it.
2 sc. for use as firewood.

all the more confident and hopeful because he had B.C. 295
not desired a great host, he took his way towards
the town of Aharna,[1] from which the enemy were
not far distant, to the camp of Appius the praetor.
A few miles this side the camp he encountered some
men who had come out with an armed escort to
gather wood. These people, seeing the lictors in
the van and learning that Fabius was consul, with
lively manifestations of satisfaction gave thanks to
the gods and to the Roman People for having sent
him to be their general. Then, as they trooped
about him and hailed him consul, Fabius asked
whither they were bound, and they answered that
they were come out to get wood. "Is it possible,"
he cried, "that you have no rampart round your
camp?" and, on their shouting back that they had
a double rampart and a trench and yet were in
mortal fear, "Then you have quite wood enough,"
said he; "go back and pull up your stockade."[2]
Returning to camp they began pulling up the palings,
to the terror of their comrades who had stayed
behind, as well as of Appius himself, till the news
was spread, as each talked with his neighbours, that
they were acting under orders of the consul Quintus
Fabius. On the morrow the camp was removed and
the praetor Appius was sent away to Rome. Thenceforward the Romans had no permanent camp anywhere. It was of no use, Fabius maintained, for
the army to sit down in one place: by marching
and shifting its position it grew more mobile and
more healthy. The marches, of course, were such
as could be made at a season when winter was not
yet over.

In the early spring, leaving the second legion in

453

LIVY

sium, quod Camars olim appellabant, praepositoque
castris L. Scipione pro praetore Romam ipse ad con-
12 sultandum de bello rediit, sive ipse sponte sua, quia
bellum ei maius in conspectu erat quam quantum
esse famae crediderat sive senatus consulto accitus;
13 nam in utrumque auctores sunt. Ab Ap. Claudio
praetore retractum quidam videri volunt, cum in
senatu et apud populum, id quod per litteras adsidue
fecerat, terrorem belli Etrusci augeret: non suffectu-
rum ducem unum nec exercitum unum adversus
14 quattuor populos; periculum[1] esse, sive iuncti unum
premant sive diversi gerant bellum, ne ad omnia
15 simul obire unus non possit. Duas se ibi legiones
Romanas reliquisse et minus quinque milia peditum
equitumque cum Fabio venisse. Sibi placere P.
Decium consulem primo quoque tempore in Etruriam
ad collegam proficisci, L. Volumnio Samnium provinciam dari; si consul malit in suam provinciam
16 ire, Volumnium in Etruriam ad consulem cum exer-
17 citu iusto consulari proficisci. Cum magnam partem
moveret oratio praetoris, P. Decium censuisse ferunt
ut omnia integra ac libera Q. Fabio servarentur,
donec vel ipse, si per commodum rei publicae posset,
Romam venisset vel aliquem ex legatis misisset, a
18 quo disceret senatus quantum in Etruria belli esset.

---

[1] periculum ⸱ *Gronovius*: periculos *MP*: periculosum Ω.

---

[1] *i.e.* two Roman legions with the usual complement of
cavalry and allies.

the neighbourhood of Clusium—which they used of b.c. 295 old to call Camars—and putting Lucius Scipio, as propraetor, in charge of the camp, Fabius himself returned to Rome to consult about the war, either voluntarily, because he had a task in prospect that was greater than he had believed the reports to signify, or, it may be, summoned by the senate; for both accounts are vouched for. Some would have it appear that he was compelled to return by Appius Claudius the praetor, who continued to exaggerate the perils of the Etruscan war in the senate and before the people, as he had done persistently in his dispatches. It was not enough, he said, to have one commander and one army against four nations: the danger was—whether they united to overwhelm him or campaigned separately—that one man would be incapable of meeting simultaneously all emergencies. He himself had left on the ground two Roman legions, and less than five thousand infantry and cavalry had come with Fabius. It was his opinion that Publius Decius the consul should march at the very earliest moment to Etruria, to join his colleague, and that Lucius Volumnius should be given the command in Samnium; or, if the consul preferred to go out to his own province, that Volumnius should set out for Etruria with a regular consular army.[1] The majority were moved by the praetor's speech, but Publius Decius—so they say—advised that all be left to the free and unhampered judgment of Quintus Fabius, until Fabius should either come to Rome himself—if this were compatible with public policy—or send some one of his lieutenants, to inform the senate how great a war was on foot

quantisque administrandum copiis et quot per duces esset.

XXVI. Fabius, ut Romam rediit, et in senatu et productus ad populum mediam orationem habuit, ut nec augere nec minuere videretur belli famam magisque in altero adsumendo duce aliorum indulgere timori quam suo aut rei publicae periculo con-

2 sulere. Ceterum si sibi adiutorem belli sociumque imperii darent, quonam modo se oblivisci P. Deci

3 consulis per tot collegia experti posse? Neminem omnium secum coniungi malle; et copiarum satis sibi cum P. Decio et nunquam nimium hostium fore; sin collega quid aliud mallet,[1] at sibi L. Volumnium

4 darent adiutorem. Omnium rerum arbitrium et a populo et a senatu et ab ipso collega Fabio permissum est; et cum P. Decius se vel in Samnium vel [2] in Etruriam proficisci paratum esse ostendisset, tanta laetitia ac gratulatio fuit ut praeciperetur victoria animis triumphusque non bellum decretum consulibus videretur.

5 Invenio apud quosdam extemplo consulatu inito profectos in Etruriam Fabium Deciumque sine ulla mentione sortis provinciarum certaminumque inter

6 collegas quae exposui. Sunt quibus ne haec quidem

---

[1] mallet *Weissenborn*: mallit Ω: malit $P^2FUT^2D^xA^x$.
[2] vel in Samnium vel *H. J. Mueller*: in Samnium uel Ω.

456

in Etruria, and with what forces, commanded by B.C. 295
how many generals, it ought to be conducted.

XXVI. Fabius, when he returned to Rome, both
in the senate and afterwards in speaking to the
people, steered a middle course, that he might
appear neither to exaggerate the current reports
about the war nor minimize them, and in accepting
an additional commander to be rather consulting
the fears of others than guarding against a danger
to himself or the republic. For the rest, if they
chose to give him a helper in the war and a partner
in authority, how—he asked—could he possibly
forget Publius Decius the consul, whom he had
proved so often when they had been colleagues?
There was no one living with whom he would sooner
share his commission; he should have troops enough,
if Decius were with him, and his enemies would
never be too numerous. But if his colleague preferred some other arrangement, let them give him
Lucius Volumnius to be his coadjutor. The decision
in regard to everything was left by the people and
the senate, and by his colleague himself, entirely
to Fabius; and when Publius Decius had made
known his readiness to set out either for Samnium
or Etruria, there were such rejoicings and congratulations that men tasted the sweets of victory
in anticipation, and it seemed as though the consuls
had been voted a triumph and not a war.

I find in some historians that Fabius and Decius
set out for Etruria at the very beginning of their
consulship, and they make no mention of the casting
of lots for provinces or of the disputes betwixt the
colleagues which I have described. On the other
hand, even these disputes have not been enough

LIVY

certamina exponere satis fuit; adiecerunt[1] et Appi
criminationes de Fabio absente ad populum et pertinaciam adversus praesentem consulem praetoris
contentionemque aliam inter collegas, tendente Decio
7 ut suae quisque provinciae sortem tueretur. Constare res incipit ex eo tempore quo profecti ambo
consules ad bellum sunt.

Ceterum antequam consules in Etruriam perveni-
rent, Senones Galli multitudine ingenti ad Clusium
venerunt legionem Romanam castraque oppugnaturi.
8 Scipio, qui castris praeerat, loco adiuvandam paucitatem suorum militum ratus, in collem[2] qui inter
9 urbem et castra erat aciem erexit. Sed, ut in re
subita, parum explorato itinere ad iugum perrexit
quod hostes ceperant parte alia adgressi. Ita caesa
ab tergo legio atque in medio, cum hostis undique
10 urgeret, circumventa. Deletam quoque ibi legionem, ita ut nuntius non superesset, quidam auctores
11 sunt, nec ante ad consules, qui iam haud procul a
Clusio aberant, famam eius cladis perlatam quam
in conspectu fuere Gallorum equites, pectoribus
equorum suspensa gestantes capita et lanceis infixa
12 ovantesque moris sui carmine. Sunt qui Umbros
fuisse non Gallos tradant, nec tantum cladis acceptum et circumventis pabulatoribus cum L. Manlio
Torquato legato Scipionem propraetorem subsidium

---

[1] adiecerunt *Heinsius*: adiecerint Ω.
[2] in collem ς: in colle (cole *P*) Ω.

---

[1] Possibly a son of the consul who was thrown from his
horse and killed in 299 B.C. See chap. xi. § 1.

for some, but they have added invectives pronounced
by Appius before the people against the absent
Fabius, and stubborn opposition on the praetor's
part to the consul who was present, and another
quarrel between the colleagues, when Decius urged
that each should attend to his allotted province.
The authorities begin to be in agreement from the
moment that both consuls set out for the seat of war.

But before the consuls could reach Etruria, the
Senonian Gauls were come with a great multitude
to Clusium, to besiege the Roman legion in camp
there. Scipio, who was in command, thought it
necessary that he should gain the advantage of
position to eke out the smallness of his numbers,
and marched his troops up a hill situated between
the city and his camp; but, as happens in sudden
emergencies, he had sent no scouts ahead of him,
and led his men up to a ridge which was held by
the enemy, who had approached it from another
direction. Thus the legion was attacked in the
rear and found itself surrounded, with the enemy
assailing it from every quarter. Some writers say
that the legion was even annihilated there, so that
none survived to bear away the tidings, and that
the consuls, who were not far from Clusium, got no
report of the disaster till some Gallic horsemen
came in sight, with heads hanging at their horses'
breasts or fixed on their lances, and singing their
customary song of triumph. Others allege that
they were not Gauls but Umbrians, and that the
reverse experienced was not so great. Some
foragers, according to their account, under Lucius
Manlius Torquatus,[1] a lieutenant, had been cut off,
and Scipio the propraetor sallied forth from the

LIVY

e castris tulisse victoresque Umbros **redintegrato**
proelio victos esse captivosque eis ac praedam
13 ademptam. Similius vero est a Gallo hoste quam
Umbro eam cladem acceptam, quod cum saepe alias
tum eo anno Gallici tumultus praecipuus terror
14 civitatem tenuit. Itaque praeterquam quod ambo
consules profecti ad bellum erant cum quattuor
legionibus et magno equitatu Romano Campanisque
mille equitibus delectis, ad id bellum missis, et
sociorum nominisque Latini maiore exercitu quam
15 Romano, alii duo exercitus haud procul urbe Etruriae
oppositi, unus in Falisco alter in Vaticano agro.
Cn. Fulvius et L. Postumius Megellus[1] propraetores
ambo, stativa in eis locis habere iussi.

XXVII. Consules ad hostes transgressos Appenninum[2] in agrum Sentinatem pervenerunt. Ibi
quattuor milium ferme intervallo castra posita.
2 Inter hostes deinde consultationes habitae atque
ita convenit ne unis castris miscerentur omnes
3 neve in aciem descenderent simul; Samnitibus
Galli, Etruscis Umbri adiecti. Dies indicta pugnae;
Samniti Gallisque delegata pugna; inter ipsum
certamen Etrusci Umbrique iussi castra Romana
4 oppugnare. Haec consilia turbarunt transfugae
Clusini tres clam nocte ad Fabium consulem
transgressi, qui editis hostium consiliis dimissi cum

---

[1] Megellus *Sigonius* (*from chap.* xxxii. § 1): megillus
(megillius *A*) Ω.
[2] transgressos Appenninum *Gronovius:* transgresso Ap-
pennino Ω.

camp to their relief, and renewing the battle defeated the victorious Umbrians and took from them
their prisoners and their booty. It is more probable
that the discomfiture was incurred at the hands of
a Gallic than of an Umbrian enemy, since apprehensions of a Gallic rising, which had often at other
times troubled the Romans, were in that year
particularly alarming. And so, not only did both
consuls go out to war, having four legions and a
strong body of Roman cavalry, together with a
thousand picked horse from Campania—furnished
for this campaign—and an army of allies and Latins
that outnumbered the Romans; but two other
armies were posted over against Etruria, not far
from the City, one in the Faliscan district and the
other in the Vatican. Gnaeus Fulvius and
Lucius Postumius Megellus—propraetors both—were
ordered to maintain a standing camp there.

XXVII. The consuls came up with the enemy—
who had crossed the Apennines—in the territory
round Sentinum, and went into camp about four
miles off. Consultations were then held amongst
the enemy and they decided not to unite all their
forces in one camp nor to give battle all together ;
to the Samnites were joined the Gauls and to the
Etruscans the men of Umbria. A day was designated
for the battle, and the Samnites and Gauls were
appointed to make the attack ; in the midst of the
engagement the Etruscans and the Umbrians were
to assault the Roman camp. These plans were
upset by three Clusinian deserters who came over
secretly in the night to Fabius, and having informed
him of the enemy's designs were rewarded and sent
back again, so that from time to time, as each new

461

LIVY

donis, ut subinde ut quaeque res nova decreta esset
5 exploratam perferrent. Consules Fulvio ut ex
Falisco, Postumio ut ex Vaticano exercitum ad
Clusium admoveant summaque vi fines hostium
6 depopulentur scribunt. Huius populationis fama
Etruscos ex agro Sentinate ad suos fines tuendos
movit. Instare inde consules, ut absentibus iis
7 pugnaretur. Per biduum lacessiere proelio hostem;
biduo nihil dignum dictu actum : pauci utrimque
cecidere magisque inritati sunt ad iustum certamen
animi quam ad discrimen summa rerum adducta.[1]
Tertio die descensum in campum omnibus copiis
est.
8 Cum instructae acies starent, cerva fugiens lupum
e montibus exacta per campos inter duas acies decurrit; inde diversae ferae, cerva ad Gallos, lupus
ad Romanos cursum deflexit. Lupo data inter
9 ordines via; cervam Galli confixere. Tum ex ante-
signanis Romanus miles "Illac fuga" inquit "et
caedes vertit, ubi sacram Dianae feram iacentem
videtis; hinc victor Martius lupus, integer et
intactus, gentis nos Martiae et conditoris nostri
admonuit."
10 Dextro cornu Galli, sinistro Samnites constiterunt.
Adversus Samnites Q. Fabius primam ac tertiam
legionem pro dextro cornu, adversus Gallos pro
11 sinistro Decius quintam et sextam instruxit; secunda

[1] adducta A^2 (or A^4): adducti F^3: addicta (-dita U) Ω.

---

[1] See chap. xxiii. § 12 for the bronze group which had
recently been erected of the wolf suckling the twins (the
Sons of Mars) and cf. the reference at XXII. i. 12 to a statue
of Mars and images of wolves (a group?) on the Appian Way.
Virgil uses the epithet *Martius* of the wolf (*Aen.* IX. 566)
and Horace has *Martialis lupos*, at *Carm.* I. xvii. 9.

step should be decided on, they might find it out and report upon it. The consuls wrote to Fulvius and Postumius to march from their respective posts in the Faliscan and Vatican districts to Clusium, and lay waste the territories of the enemy with the utmost rigour. The reports of this devastation drew off the Etruscans from the region of Sentinum to the defence of their own frontiers. Thereupon the consuls strove to bring about an engagement in their absence. For the space of two days they harassed the enemy, but in these two days there was nothing done worth telling : a few were slain on either side and spirits were whetted for a downright battle, but the main issue was not brought to a decision. On the third day the opposing armies descended in full strength into the field.

As they stood arrayed for battle, a hind, pursued by a wolf that had chased it down from the mountains, fled across the plain and ran between the two lines. They then turned in opposite directions, the hind towards the Gauls, the wolf towards the Romans. For the wolf a passage was opened between the ranks, but the hind was killed by the Gauls. Then one of the front-rankers on the Roman side called out, "That way flight and slaughter have shaped their course, where you see the beast lie slain that is sacred to Diana; on this side the wolf of Mars, unhurt and sound, has reminded us of the Martian race and of our Founder." [1]

On the right wing stood the Gauls, on the left the Samnites. Facing the Samnites, Quintus Fabius drew up the first and third legions, to form the Roman right, while Decius marshalled the fifth and sixth on the Roman left, against the Gauls. The

463

et quarta cum L. Volumnio proconsule in Samnio gerebant[1] bellum. Primo concursu adeo aequis viribus gesta res est ut si adfuissent Etrusci et Umbri, aut in acie aut in castris, quocumque se inclinassent accipienda clades fuerit.

XXVIII. Ceterum quamquam communis adhuc Mars belli erat necdum discrimen Fortuna fecerat qua datura vires esset, haudquaquam similis pugna 2 in dextro laevoque cornu erat. Romani apud Fabium arcebant magis quam inferebant pugnam extrahebaturque in quam maxime serum diei cer- 3 tamen, quia ita persuasum erat duci, et Samnites et Gallos primo impetu feroces esse, quos sustinere satis sit; longiore certamine sensim residere Sam- 4 nitium animos, Gallorum quidem etiam corpora intolerantissima laboris atque aestus fluere primaque eorum proelia plus quam virorum, postrema minus 5 quam feminarum esse. In id tempus igitur quo vinci solebat hostis, quam integerrimas vires militi 6 servabat. Ferocior Decius et aetate et vigore animi quantumcumque virium habuit certamine primo effudit. Et quia lentior videbatur pedestris pugna, 7 equitatum in pugnam concitat et ipse fortissimae iuvenum turmae immixtus orat proceres iuventutis in hostem ut secum impetum faciant: duplicem

---

[1] gerebant ς : gerebat Ω.

second and the fourth were campaigning in Samnium
under Lucius Volumnius the proconsul. At the
first shock the strength put forth on both sides was
so equal that if the Etruscans and the Umbrians
had been present either in the battle or at the
camp, in whichever quarter they had thrown their
weight the Romans must have suffered a disaster.

XXVIII. But, though so far it was a doubtful
battle and Fortune had given no indication where
she intended to bestow her might, the fighting was
very different on the right wing from what it was
on the left. The Romans with Fabius were rather
defending themselves than attacking, and were
trying to prolong the struggle to as late an hour
in the day as possible. This was because their
general was persuaded that both Samnites and
Gauls fought fiercely at the outset of an engagement, but only needed to be withstood; when a
struggle was prolonged, little by little the spirits
of the Samnites flagged, while the physical prowess
of the Gauls, who could least of all men put up with
heat and labour, ebbed away, and, whereas in the
early stages of their battles they were more than
men, they ended with being less than women. So
until the time should come when the enemy were
wont to fail, he was keeping his men as fresh as he
could contrive to do. But Decius, with the greater
impetuosity of his youth and spirits, expended all
the strength he could muster in the first encounter.
And because the fighting of the infantry seemed to
languish, he called on the cavalry to attack, and
attaching himself to the bravest squadron of troopers
besought the youthful nobles to join him in a
charge. Theirs, he said, would be a double share

465

illorum gloriam fore si ab laevo cornu et ab equite

8 victoria incipiat. Bis avertere Gallicum equitatum;
iterum longius evectos et iam inter media peditum [1]
agmina proelium cientes novum pugnae conterruit

9 genus: essedis carrisque superstans armatus hostis
ingenti sonitu equorum rotarumque advenit et insolitos [2] eius tumultus Romanorum conterruit equos.

10 Ita victorem equitatum velut lymphaticus pavor
dissipat; sternit inde ruentes equos virosque im-

11 provida fuga. Turbata hinc etiam signa legionum
multique impetu equorum ac vehiculorum raptorum
per agmen obtriti antesignani; et insecuta, simul
territos hostes vidit, Gallica acies nullum spatium
respirandi recipiendique se dedit.

12 Vociferari Decius, quo fugerent quamve in fuga
spem haberent; obsistere cedentibus ac revocare
fusos; deinde, ut nulla vi perculsos sustinere poterat,

13 patrem P. Decium nomine compellans "Quid ultra
moror" inquit "familiare fatum? Datum hoc nostro
generi est ut luendis periculis publicis piacula simus.
Iam ego mecum hostium legiones mactandas Telluri
ac dis Manibus dabo."

14 Haec locutus M. Livium pontificem, quem de-
scendens in aciem digredi vetuerat ab se, praeire

---

[1] peditum *Madvig*: equitum (quitum *M*) Ω.
[2] insolitos ς: insolitus Ω.

of glory, if victory should come first to the left wing B.C. 295
and to the cavalry. Twice they drove the Gallic
cavalry back. The second time they were carried
on for a considerable distance and soon found themselves in the midst of the companies of infantry,
when they were subjected to a new and terrifying
kind of assault; for, standing erect in chariots and
waggons, armed enemies came rushing upon them
with a mighty clattering of hoofs and wheels,
frightening the horses of the Romans with the
unfamiliar din. Thus the victorious cavalry were
scattered, as if by a panic fit of madness, and,
suddenly fleeing, were overthrown, both horse and
rider. From them the disorder was communicated
to the standards of the legions, and many of the
first line were trodden underfoot, as horses and
chariots swept through their ranks. No sooner did
the Gallic infantry perceive the confusion of their
enemies than they charged, without leaving them
a moment to recover or regain their breath.

Decius cried out to them to tell him whither they
were fleeing, or what hope they had in flight; he
endeavoured to stop them as they broke and ran,
and to call them back; then, his exertions proving
powerless to stay their rout, he cried aloud on the
name of his father Publius Decius. "Why," he
asked, "do I seek any longer to postpone the doom
of our house? It is the privilege of our family that
we should be sacrificed to avert the nation's perils.
Now will I offer up the legions of the enemy, to be
slain with myself as victims to Earth and the Manes."

On going down into the field of battle he had
ordered Marcus Livius the pontifex not to leave his
side. He now commanded this man to recite before

467

A.U.C.
459

iussit verba quibus se legionesque hostium pro
15 exercitu populi Romani Quiritium devoveret. Devotus inde eadem precatione eodemque habitu quo
pater P. Decius ad Veserim bello Latino se iusserat
16 devoveri, cum secundum sollemnes precationes
adiecisset prae se agere sese formidinem ac fugam
17 caedemque ac cruorem, caelestium inferorum iras, contacturum[1] funebribus diris signa tela arma hostium,
locumque eundem suae pestis ac Gallorum ac Sam-
18 nitium fore,—haec exsecratus in se hostesque, qua
confertissimam cernebat Gallorum aciem concitat
equum inferensque se ipse infestis telis est interfectus.

XXIX. Vix humanae inde opis videri pugna potuit.
Romani duce amisso, quae res terrori alias esse solet,
sistere fugam ac novam de integro velle instaurare
2 pugnam : Galli, et maxime globus circumstans consulis corpus, velut alienata mente vana in cassum
iactare tela ; torpere quidam et nec pugnae memi-
3 nisse nec fugae. At ex parte altera pontifex Livius,
cui lictores Decius tradiderat iusseratque pro praetore[2] esse, vociferari vicisse Romanos defunctos
4 consulis fato ; Gallos Samnitesque Telluris matris ac
deorum Manium esse ; rapere ad se ac vocare Decium
devotam secum aciem furiarumque ac formidinis
5 plena omnia ad hostes esse. Superveniunt deinde

[1] contacturum ς: contracturum Ω.
[2] pro praetore ς: propr. T^2 (or T^1): pro pr. T^3: ꝑ p̄ A^1?: propraetorem (or other corruptions) Ω.

---

[1] For the details of this earlier devotion consult VIII.
ix. 12.

him the words with which he proposed to devote B.C. 295
himself and the enemy's legions in behalf of the army
of the Roman People, the Quirites. He was then
devoted with the same form of prayer and in the same
habit his father, Publius Decius, had commanded to
be used, when he was devoted at the Veseris, in the
Latin war [1]; and having added to the usual prayers
that he was driving before him fear and panic, blood
and carnage, and the wrath of gods celestial and gods
infernal, and should blight with a curse the standards,
weapons and armour of the enemy, and that one and
the same place should witness his own destruction
and that of the Gauls and Samnites,—having uttered,
I say, these imprecations upon himself and the enemy,
he spurred his charger against the Gallic lines, where
he saw that they were thickest, and hurling himself
against the weapons of the enemy met his death.

XXIX. From that moment the battle seemed
scarce to depend on human efforts. The Romans,
after losing their general—an occurrence that is wont
to inspire terror—fled no longer, but sought to
redeem the field; the Gauls, and especially the press
about the body of the consul, as though deprived of
reason, were darting their javelins at random and
without effect, while some were in a daze, and could
neither fight nor run away. But in the other army
the pontifex Livius, to whom Decius had handed over
his lictors, bidding him act as propraetor, cried aloud
that the Romans had won the victory, being quit of
all danger by the consul's doom. The Gauls, he said,
and the Samnites were made over to Mother Earth
and to the Manes; Decius was haling after him their
devoted host and calling it to join him, and with the
enemy all was madness and despair. While the

his restituentibus pugnam L. Cornelius Scipio et C. Marcius cum subsidiis ex novissima acie iussu Q. Fabi consulis ad praesidium collegae missi. Ibi auditur P. Deci eventus, ingens hortamen ad omnia
6 pro re publica audenda. Itaque cum Galli structis ante se scutis conferti starent nec facilis pede con- lato videretur pugna, iussu legatorum collecta humi pila quae strata inter duas acies iacebant atque in
7 testudinem hostium coniecta; quibus plerisque in scuta rarisque[1] in corpora ipsa fixis sternitur cuneus ita ut magna pars integris corporibus attoniti con- ciderent. Haec in sinistro cornu Romanorum for- tuna variaverat.
8 Fabius in dextro primo, ut ante dictum est, cunc- tando extraxerat diem; dein, postquam nec clamor hostium nec impetus nec tela missa eandem vim
9 habere visa, praefectis equitum iussis ad latus Samni- tium circumducere alas, ut signo dato in transversos quanto maximo possent impetu incurrerent, sensim suos signa inferre iussit et commovere hostem.
10 Postquam non resisti vidit et haud dubiam lassitudi- nem esse, tum collectis omnibus subsidiis, quae ad id tempus reservaverat, et legiones concitavit et signum
11 ad invadendos hostes equitibus dedit. Nec sustinue- runt Samnites impetum praeterque aciem ipsam

---

[1] rarisque (or raris) *Hertz*: uerarisque rutis *MTDLA*: uerutis *U*: uerrutis *PF*: uerutisque *ς*: plerisque uerutus *A*⁴*ς*: uerutisque raris *Walters and Conway* (rarisque verutis *Drakenborch*).

---

[1] *Testudo*, "tortoise," was the name given to a formation in which the shields were held so close together as to form a sort of pent-house or *shell* over the soldiers.

Romans were restoring the battle, up came Lucius B.C. 295
Cornelius Scipio and Gaius Marcius, whom Quintus
Fabius the consul had ordered to take reserves from
the rearmost line and go to his colleague's support.
There they learned of Decius's death, a great
incentive to dare everything for the republic.   And
so, though the Gauls stood crowded together with their
shields interlocked in front of them, and it looked no
easy battle at close quarters, the lieutenants bade
their men gather up the javelins that were scattered
about on the ground between the hostile lines and
cast them against the *testudo* [1] of their enemies; and
as many of these missiles stuck fast in the shields
and now and then one penetrated a soldier's body,
their phalanx was broken up—many falling, though
unwounded, as if they had been stunned.   Such
were the shifts of Fortune upon the Roman left.

On the right, Fabius had begun, as has been said
before, by holding back and delaying the decision;
later, when neither the shouts of the foe, nor their
assaults, nor the missiles they discharged, seemed to
have any longer the same force, he ordered the
praefects of the cavalry to lead their squadrons
round the wing of the Samnites, that, on the signal
being given, they might attack them in the flank
with all possible vigour, and commanded his own
men to push forward by degrees and dislodge
the enemy.   When he saw that they made no
resistance and there could be no question of their
weariness, he gathered up all the troops which he
had hitherto held in reserve, and, sending in his
legions, made a signal to the cavalry to charge.
The Samnites could not withstand their onset and
fled in confusion past the Gallic line itself, abandon-

Gallorum relictis in dimicatione sociis ad castra effuso
12 cursu ferebantur : Galli testudine facta conferti stabant. Tum Fabius audita morte collegae Campanorum alam, quingentos fere equites, excedere acie iubet
et circumvectos ab tergo Gallicam invadere aciem ;
13 tertiae deinde legionis subsequi principes, et qua
turbatum agmen hostium viderent impetu equitum,
14 instare ac territos caedere. Ipse aedem Iovi Victori
spoliaque hostium cum vovisset, ad castra Samnitium
perrexit, quo multitudo omnis consternata agebatur.
15 Sub ipso vallo, quia tantam multitudinem portae non
recepere, temptata ab exclusis turba suorum pugna
16 est ; ibi Gellius Egnatius, imperator Samnitium,
cecidit. Compulsi deinde intra vallum Samnites
parvoque certamine capta castra et Galli ab tergo
17 circumventi. Caesa eo die hostium viginti quinque
milia, octo capta. Nec incruenta victoria fuit ;
18 nam ex P. Deci exercitu caesa septem milia, ex Fabi
mille septingenti.[1] Fabius dimissis ad quaerendum
collegae corpus spolia hostium coniecta in acervum
19 Iovi Victori cremavit. Consulis corpus eo die, quia
obrutum superstratis Gallorum cumulis erat, inveniri
non potuit ; postero die inventum relatumque est

---

[1] septingenti A^6*Drakenborch* : acc *MPUTL* : ac. c. FT^2 :
·a· cc *DA* : ac ducenti ç.

ing their comrades in the midst of the fighting and
seeking refuge in their camp. The Gauls had
formed a *testudo* and stood there closely packed
together. Then Fabius, who had learned of his
colleague's death, commanded the squadron of Campanians, about five hundred lances, to withdraw
from the line, and fetching a compass, assail the
Gallic infantry in the rear; these the *principes*, or
middle line, of the third legion were to follow, and,
pushing in where they saw that the cavalry charge
had disordered the enemy's formation, make havoc
of them in their panic. He himself, after vowing a
temple and the enemy's spoils to Jupiter Victor,
kept on to the Samnite camp, whither the whole
affrighted throng was being driven. Under the
very rampart, since the gates could not receive so
great a multitude, those who were shut out by the
crowding of their fellows attempted some resistance;
there Gellius Egnatius, the commander-in-chief of
the Samnites, fell; in the upshot the Samnites were
driven within the rampart and after a short struggle
their camp was taken and the Gauls were cut off in
the rear. There were slain that day five-and-twenty
thousand of the enemy, and eight thousand were
captured; nor was it a bloodless victory; for of the
army of Publius Decius seven thousand were slain
and seventeen hundred of the army of Fabius.
Fabius sent out men to search for the body of his
colleague, and, piling up the spoils of the enemy,
burned them in sacrifice to Jupiter the Victor.
The consul's body could not be found that day,
having been buried under heaps of Gauls who had
been slain above him; on the day after, it was found
and brought in, amidst the lamentations of the

LIVY

20 cum multis militum lacrimis. Intermissa inde
omnium aliarum rerum cura Fabius collegae funus
omni honore laudibusque meritis celebrat.

XXX. Et in Etruria per eosdem dies ab Cn.
Fulvio propraetore res ex sententia gesta et praeter
ingentem inlatam populationibus agrorum hosti
2 cladem pugnatum etiam egregie est Perusinorumque
et Clusinorum caesa amplius milia tria et signa
3 militaria ad viginti capta. Samnitium agmen cum
per Paelignum agrum fugeret, circumventum a
Paelignis est; ex milibus quinque ad mille caesi.

4 Magna eius diei quo in Sentinati agro bellatum
5 fama est, etiam vero stanti; sed superiecere quidam
augendo fidem, qui in hostium exercitu peditum
sexiens centena milia,[1] equitum sex et quadraginta
milia, mille carpentorum scripsere fuisse, scilicet cum
6 Umbris Tuscisque, quos et ipsos pugnae adfuisse; et
ut Romanorum quoque augerent copias, L. Volumnium pro consule ducem consulibus exercitumque
7 eius legionibus consulum adiciunt. In pluribus
annalibus duorum ea consulum propria victoria est,
Volumnius in Samnio interim res gerit Samnitiumque exercitum in Tifernum montem compulsum, non
deterritus iniquitate loci, fundit fugatque.

8 Q. Fabius, Deciano exercitu relicto in Etruriae
praesidio, suis legionibus deductis ad urbem de
Gallis Etruscisque ac Samnitibus triumphavit.

---

[1] sexiens centena milia *Walters* (deciens centena milia
Niebuhr): x. cccxxx *M* : xi. cccxxx *PFU* : (*i.e.* xl) x̄l̄• (*or* xl)
cccxxx *DLA* : quadraginta milia trecentos triginta (tricentos
triginta milia *T*) *T²*.

soldiers. Postponing his concern for everything else, B.C. 295 Fabius celebrated the funeral of his colleague with every show of honour and well-merited eulogiums.

XXX. In Etruria too at the same time Gnaeus Fulvius the propraetor was succeeding according to his wishes, and, besides the enormous damage which his forays inflicted on the enemy, fought also a victorious battle with them. The Perusini and Clusini lost upwards of three thousand men, and some twenty military standards were captured from them. The Samnite army, as it fled through the Paelignian territory, was surrounded by the inhabitants, and of five thousand men about a thousand were slain.

Great is the glory of that day on which the battle was fought in the district of Sentinum, even if a man hold fast to truth ; but some writers have so exaggerated as to over-shoot the credible, and have written that in the army of the enemy—including, of course, the Umbrians and Tuscans, for these, too, were present in the battle—there were six hundred thousand infantry, forty-six thousand horse, and a thousand cars ; and, to enlarge in like manner the forces of the Romans, they add to the consuls as a general Lucius Volumnius the proconsul, and his army to their legions. In the majority of histories this victory is reserved to the two consuls, and Volumnius is waging war at the same time in Samnium, where, having driven the Samnite army up Mount Tifernus, he routs and scatters them, undeterred by the difficulties of the ground.

Quintus Fabius, leaving the Decian army on guard over Etruria, led down his own legions to Rome and triumphed over the Gauls, the Etruscans, and the

9 Milites triumphantem secuti sunt. Celebrata in-
conditis militaribus non magis victoria Q. Fabi quam
mors praeclara P. Deci est, excitataque memoria
parentis, aequata eventu publico privatoque, filii
10 laudibus. Data ex praeda militibus aeris octogeni
bini sagaque et tunicae, praemia illa tempestate
militiae haudquaquam spernenda.

XXXI. His ita rebus gestis nec in Samnitibus
adhuc nec in Etruria pax erat; nam et Perusinis
auctoribus post deductum ab consule exercitum
2 rebellatum fuerat et Samnites praedatum in agrum
Vescinum[1] Formianumque et parte alia in Aeserninum[2] quaeque Volturno adiacent flumini descendere.
3 Adversus eos Ap. Claudius praetor cum exercitu
Deciano missus. Fabius in Etruria rebellante denuo
quattuor milia et quingentos Perusinorum occidit,
cepit ad mille septingentos quadraginta, qui redempti
4 singuli aeris trecentis decem ; praeda alia omnis mili-
5 tibus concessa. Samnitium legiones, cum partem Ap.
Claudius praetor partem L. Volumnius pro consule
sequeretur, in agrum Stellatem convenerunt. Ibi ad
Caiatiam omnes[3] considunt et Appius Volumniusque
6 castra coniungunt. Pugnatum infestissimis animis,
hinc ira stimulante adversus rebellantes totiens,

---

[1] Vescinum *Sigonius* (*cf. chap.* xx. § 1) : uestinum Ω.
[2] Aeserninum *Gronovius* : aesernium *MA*³: aeserunium
PFUT : aes (*or* es-)etrunium *DLA*.
[3] ad Caiatiam omnes *Conway* : ad Samnitium omnes *PF* :
ad Samnium omnes *U* : et Samnitium omnes *MTDLA* : et
Samnitium legiones *A*⁶: et Samnitium legiones omnes *ς* : et
Samnitium omnes copiae *Madvig*.

Samnites. The soldiers followed his triumphal chariot and in their rude verses celebrated no less the glorious death of Publius Decius than the victory of Fabius, reviving by their praise of the son the memory of the father, whose death (and its service to the commonwealth) had now been matched. Every soldier received from the spoils a present of eighty-two *asses* of bronze, with a cloak and tunic, a reward for military service in those days far from contemptible.

XXXI. Despite these victories, there was not yet peace either with the Samnites or in Etruria; for war had broken out afresh at the instigation of the Perusini, after the consul had withdrawn his army, and the Samnites were raiding the lands of Vescini and of Formiae on the one hand, and on the other the territory of Aesernia and the region adjacent to the Volturnus river. Against these the praetor Appius Claudius was dispatched with the army that Decius had commanded. Fabius dealt with the new outbreak in Etruria, where he slew four thousand five hundred of the Perusini and took one thousand seven hundred and forty prisoners, who were ransomed at three hundred and ten *asses* each, the rest of the booty being made over to the soldiers. The Samnite levies, of whom a part were being pursued by Appius Claudius the praetor and a part by Lucius Volumnius the pro-consul, effected a junction in the Stellate district, where they all took up a position near Caiatia. Appius and Volumnius also combined their forces. The ensuing battle was very bitterly contested, the Romans being incited by resentment against a people who had so often rebelled, while those on the other side were staking their last hopes

LIVY

7 illinc ad ultimam iam dimicantibus spem. Caesa
ergo Samnitium sedecim milia trecenti, capta duo
milia septingenti ; ex Romano exercitu cecidere duo
milia septingenti.

8 Felix annus bellicis rebus, pestilentia gravis
prodigiisque sollicitus ; nam et terra [1] multifariam
pluvisse et in exercitu Ap. Claudi plerosque fulmini-
9 bus ictos nuntiatum est, librique ob haec aditi. Eo
anno Q. Fabius Gurges, consulis filius, aliquot matronas ad populum stupri damnatas pecunia multavit ;
ex quo multaticio aere Veneris aedem quae prope
circum est faciendam curavit.

10 Supersunt etiam nunc Samnitium bella, quae
continua per quartum iam volumen annumque
sextum et quadragensimum a M. Valerio A. Cornelio
consulibus,[2] qui primi Samnio arma intulerunt,
11 agimus. Et ne tot annorum clades utriusque gentis
laboresque actos nunc referam, quibus nequiverint
12 tamen dura illa pectora vinci, proximo anno Samnites
in Sentinati agro, in [3] Paelignis, ad Tifernum,
Stellatibus campis, suis ipsi legionibus mixti alienis,
ab quattuor exercitibus, quattuor ducibus Romanis
13 caesi fuerant ; imperatorem clarissimum gentis suae
amiserant ; socios belli, Etruscos Umbros Gallos, in
14 eadem fortuna videbant qua ipsi erant ; nec suis nec

---

[1] terra ς (cf. III. x. 6 and VII. xxviii. 7) : terram Ω.
[2] consulibus A^2(or A^4) : consule Ω.
[3] agro, in Luterbacher : agro Ω : agros PF.

---

[1] Fabius was presumably an aedile (cf. chap. xxiii. § 11 and
chap. xxxiii. § 9). We learn from Servius, the commentator
on Virgil, that the goddess was worshipped as Venus Obse-
quens (ad Aen. I. 720).
[2] i.e. the mountain of that name ; or perhaps Livy means
the town, Tifernum.

on the conflict. The Samnites accordingly lost six- _{B.C. 295}
teen thousand three hundred slain and two thousand
seven hundred captured; in the Roman army two
thousand seven hundred fell.

The year, though one of success in war, was
saddened by a pestilence and vexed with prodigies.
Showers of earth were reported to have fallen in
many places, and it was said that in the army of
Appius Claudius many had been struck by lightning.
On account of these signs the Sibylline books were
consulted. In this year Quintus Fabius Gurges, the
consul's son, assessed a fine of money against a
number of married women who were convicted
before the people of adultery, and with this money
erected the temple of Venus which is near the Circus.[1]

There are more Samnite wars still to come, though
we have dealt with them continuously throughout
four books, covering a period of forty-six years, from
the consulship of Marcus Valerius and Aulus Cornelius, who were the first that made war on Samnium;
and—not to go over now the disasters sustained in
so many years on either side and the toils endured,
by which nevertheless those sturdy hearts could not
be daunted—in the year just past the Samnites had
fought in the territory of Sentinum, in the Paelignian country, at Tifernus,[2] and in the Stellate plains,
now by themselves, with their own levies, now in
company with troops from other nations, and had
been cut to pieces by four armies under four Roman
generals; they had lost their nation's most distinguished commander; they beheld their comrades in
war, the Etruscans, Umbrians, and Gauls, in the
same plight as their own; nor could they longer
maintain themselves, either by their own resources

LIVY

externis viribus iam stare poterant ; tamen bello non
abstinebant. Adeo ne infeliciter quidem defensae
libertatis taedebat et vinci quam non temptare
15 victoriam malebant.   Quinam sit ille, quem pigeat
longinquitatis bellorum scribendo legendoque, quae
gerentes non fatigaverunt ?

XXXII. Q. Fabium P. Decium L. Postumius
Megellus [1] et M. Atilius Regulus consules secuti
2 sunt. Samnium ambobus decreta provincia est, quia
tres scriptos hostium exercitus, uno Etruriam, altero
populationes Campaniae repeti, tertium tuendis
3 parari finibus, fama erat. Postumium valetudo
adversa Romae tenuit ; Atilius extemplo profectus,
ut in Samnio hostes—ita enim placuerat patribus—
4 nondum egressos opprimeret. Velut ex composito
ibi obvium habuere hostem ubi et vastare ipsi
Samnitium agrum prohiberentur et egredi inde in
pacata sociorumque populi Romani fines Samnitem
5 prohiberent. Cum castra castris conlata essent,
quod vix Romanus totiens victor auderet ausi
Samnites sunt—tantum desperatio ultima temeritatis
facit—castra Romana oppugnare ; et quamquam non
venit ad finem tam audax inceptum, tamen haud
6 omnino vanum fuit. Nebula erat ad multum diei
densa adeo ut lucis usum eriperet non prospectu

---

[1] Megellus (megallus T) Ω : megillus *F*³ (*cf. chap.* xxvi.
§ 15).

---

[1] Livy seems to forget that the *fighters* were now and then
relieved.

or by those of outside nations; yet would they not abstain from war;—so far were they from wearying of a liberty which they had unsuccessfully defended, preferring rather to be conquered than not to try for victory. Who, pray, could grudge the time for writing or reading of these wars, when they could not exhaust the men who fought them?[1]

XXXII. Quintus Fabius and Publius Decius were succeeded in the consulship by Lucius Postumius Megellus and Marcus Atilius Regulus. Samnium was assigned them both for their province, in consequence of a report that the enemy had raised three armies, with one of which they meant to return into Etruria, with another to resume the devastation of Campania, while the third was making ready for the defence of their frontiers. Postumius was detained in Rome by ill health: Atilius marched out at once, that he might put down the enemy in Samnium— for such was the senate's plan—ere they could cross the border. As though it had been prearranged, they encountered the foe in a place where they themselves were prevented from laying waste the territory of their enemies, while they prevented the Samnites from coming out into the district which had been pacified and the territory of the allies of the Roman People. On the camps being established over against each other, what the Romans would hardly have dared to do, victorious as they had so often been, the Samnites ventured—such temerity does utter hopelessness beget,—that is, to assault the enemy's camp; and although their desperate enterprise did not fully succeed, still, it was not altogether futile. There was a fog which lasted well on into the day, so dense as to shut out the light and

LIVY

modo extra vallum adempto sed propinquo etiam
7 congredientium inter se conspectu. Hac velut
latebra insidiarum freti Samnites vixdum satis certa
luce et eam ipsam premente caligine ad stationem
Romanam in porta segniter agentem vigilias per-
8 veniunt. Improviso oppressis nec animi satis ad
resistendum nec virium fuit. Ab tergo castrorum
9 decumana porta impetus factus; itaque captum
quaestorium quaestorque ibi L. Opimius Pansa
occisus. Conclamatum inde ad arma.

XXXIII. Consul tumultu excitus cohortes duas
sociorum, Lucanam Suessanamque, quae proximae
forte erant, tueri praetorium iubet; manipulos
2 legionum principali via inducit. Vixdum satis
aptatis armis in ordines eunt et clamore magis quam
oculis hostem noscunt nec quantus numerus sit
3 aestimari potest. Cedunt primo incerti fortunae
suae et hostem introrsum in media castra accipiunt;
inde, cum consul vociferaretur, expulsine extra
4 vallum castra deinde sua oppugnaturi essent,[1]
clamore sublato conixi primo resistunt, deinde
inferunt pedem urgentque et impulsos semel terrore
eodem quo[2] coeperunt expellunt extra portam
5 vallumque. Inde pergere ac persequi, quia turbida
lux metum circa insidiarum faciebat, non ausi,

---

[1] essent ⸗ *Duker* (*Walters, Class. Quart,* 12 (1918) *p.* 113)
essent rogitans Ω.
[2] eodem quo *Madvig* : eodem agunt (*or* cogunt) quo Ω.

---

[1] Situated behind the *praetorium* (headquarters) and
between it and the decuman gate.
[2] A wide street parallel with the front and rear lines of the
camp, at either end of which was a gate—the *porta principalis
dextra* and *porta principalis sinistra* respectively.

render it impossible to see, not only beyond the
rampart, but even at a little way off, when people
approached each other. Relying on this, as on a
screen for their operations, the Samnites came up,
when day had scarcely dawned, and even so was
hidden behind the murk, to the Roman outpost that
was negligently standing guard before the gate.
Falling upon them unawares they encountered
neither courage nor strength sufficient to hold them
in check. They charged in by the decuman gate in
the rear of the camp, captured the quaestor's tent,[1]
and slew the quaestor, Lucius Opimius Pansa ;
whereupon a general alarm was cried.

XXXIII. The consul, aroused by the din, commanded the two allied cohorts which happened to
be nearest—those from Lucania and Suessa—to
guard headquarters, and put himself at the head of
the legionary maniples in the *via principalis*.[2] The
men fell in ere they had fairly fitted on their armour,
and, knowing the enemy more by their shouting
than by the sight of them, were unable to form any
estimate of their numbers. At first they gave
ground, uncertain how fortune stood with them, and
admitted the foe into the middle of the camp ; then,
on the consul's asking them whether they meant to
be driven without the wall and afterwards make an
assault on their own camp, they gave a cheer, and,
exerting themselves, first made a successful stand,
and afterwards pushed forward and forced their
enemies back, and, having once repulsed them, left
them no time to recover their first dismay, but thrust
them out of gate and rampart. Not venturing then
to go on and pursue them, since the dim light made
them fear an ambush, they retired—content to have

LIVY

A.U.C.
460 liberatis castris contenti receperunt se intra vallum
6 trecentis ferme hostium occisis. Romanorum statio-
nis primae [1] et eorum qui circa quaestorium oppressi
periere ad septingentos [2] triginta.

7   Animos inde Samnitibus non infelix audacia auxit
et non modo proferre inde castra Romanum sed ne
pabulari quidem per agros suos patiebantur; retro
in pacatum Soranum agrum pabulatores ibant.
8 Quarum rerum fama, tumultuosior etiam quam res
erant, perlata Romam coegit L. Postumium consulem
9 vixdum validum proficisci ex urbe. Prius tamen
quam exiret, militibus edicto Soram iussis convenire
ipse aedem Victoriae, quam aedilis curulis ex multa-
10 ticia pecunia faciendam curaverat, dedicavit. Ita ad
exercitum profectus, ab Sora in Samnium ad castra
collegae perrexit. Inde postquam Samnites diffisi
duobus exercitibus resisti posse recesserunt, diversi
consules ad vastandos agros urbesque oppugnandas
discedunt.

XXXIV. Postumius Milioniam oppugnare adortus
vi [3] primo atque impetu, dein, postquam ea parum
procedebant, opere ac vineis demum iniunctis muro
2 cepit. Ibi capta iam urbe ab hora quarta usque ad
octavam fere horam omnibus partibus urbis diu
incerto eventu pugnatum est; postremo potitur

---

[1] primae *Conway*: primae uigilumque (*or* uigiliumque *or*
uiciumque *or* uiiiumque) Ω.
[2] septingentos *edd.*: acc (*for* DCC) *or other corruptions* Ω.
[3] vi ς: ut *PFUT*: *omitted by MDLA.*

---

[1] Probably on the Palatine, since Livy mentions a shrine
of Victory as being there at XXIX. xiv. 13.
[2] An unidentified Samnite city.

cleared their camp—within the palisade, having B.C. 294
slain about three hundred of the enemy. The
Roman loss, at the outpost and amongst those who
were taken by surprise at the quaestor's tent, was
some seven hundred and thirty.

This bold and not unsuccessful venture of the
Samnites raised their spirits; and not only would
they not permit the Romans to go forward, but
they would not even permit them to forage in
their fields; the foragers fell back on the peaceful
territory about Sora. The rumour of these events—
more startling even than the events themselves—
being brought to Rome compelled the consul
Lucius Postumius, though barely recovered, to take
the field. But after issuing a proclamation calling
upon his soldiers to assemble at Sora, he himself,
before leaving the City, dedicated a shrine to
Victory, which he had built,[1] as curule aedile, with
money received from fines. Having then set out
to join the army, he led it from Sora to his colleague's camp in Samnium. The Samnites then
retreated, having no confidence in their ability to
resist two armies, and the consuls separated and
marched in different directions to waste their fields
and attack their cities.

XXXIV. Postumius essayed to capture Milionia.[2]
Unsuccessful in his first attempt to storm the place,
he proceeded against it by regular approaches, and,
having brought his pent-houses into contact with
the walls, effected an entrance. Thereupon, though
the city was already taken, there ensued in every
quarter without interruption, from the fourth hour
till about the eighth, a desperate struggle, the
result of which was long in doubt. At last the

485

3 oppido Romanus. Samnitium caesi tria milia ducenti, capti quattuor milia septingenti[1] praeter praedam aliam.

4 Inde Feritrum ductae legiones, unde oppidani omnibus rebus suis quae ferri agique potuerunt nocte 5 per aversam portam silentio excesserunt. Igitur, simul advenit consul, primo ita compositus instructusque moenibus successit, tamquam idem quod ad 6 Milioniam fuerat certaminis foret; deinde, ut silentium vastum in urbe nec arma nec viros in turribus ac muris vidit, avidum invadendi deserta moenia militem detinet, ne quam occultam in fraudem in- 7 cautus rueret; duas turmas sociorum Latini nominis circumequitare moenia atque explorare omnia iubet. Equites portam unam alteramque eadem regione in propinquo patentes conspiciunt itineribusque iis 8 vestigia nocturnae hostium fugae. Adequitant deinde sensim portis urbemque ex tuto rectis itineribus perviam conspiciunt et consuli[2] referunt excessum urbe; solitudine haud dubia id perspicuum esse et recentibus vestigiis fugae ac strage rerum in trepi- 9 datione nocturna relictarum passim. His auditis consul ad eam partem urbis quam adierant equites circumducit agmen. Constitutis haud procul porta

---

[1] septingenti *A*[6] *Drakenborch* : acc (*or other corruptions*) Ω.
[2] et consuli ⸱ : et coñs (*or other corruptions*) Ω.

---

[1] Otherwise unknown.

Romans made themselves masters of the place.
The Samnites lost three thousand two hundred
slain and four thousand seven hundred captured,
besides other booty.

From there the legions were led to Feritrum,[1]
which the townspeople, with all their possessions
which they could carry or drive away, evacuated
in the silence of the night, by the opposite gate.
So, then, the consul was no sooner come than he
advanced up to the walls with all the order and
circumspection of one who looked for the same
resistance that he had met with at Milionia; but
afterwards, finding the city as silent as a desert and
neither arms nor men upon the battlements and
towers, he restrained his soldiers, who were eager
to scale the abandoned walls, lest they should rush
improvidently into some hidden trap. He ordered
two squadrons of Latin allies to make a circuit of
the fortifications and effect a thorough reconnais-
sance. The troopers discovered a wide-open gate,
and near it in the same quarter another one, and
saw in the roads leading out of them the traces
of the enemy's nocturnal flight. Riding up then
slowly and cautiously to the gates, they saw that
the city could be safely traversed by streets that
led straight through it, and reported to the consul
that it had been abandoned. This was evident, they
said, from the unmistakable solitude and the fresh
signs of flight and the objects that lay scattered
about where they had been discarded in the confusion of the darkness. On receiving this account,
the consul led his army round to that side of the
city which the horsemen had approached. Halting
the troops not far from the gate, he commanded

A.U.C.
460

signis quinque equites iubet intrare urbem et modi-
cum spatium progressos tres manere eodem loco, si
10 tuta videantur, duos explorata ad se referre. Qui
ubi redierunt rettuleruntque eo se progressos unde
in omnes partes circumspectus esset longe lateque
11 silentium ac solitudinem vidisse, extemplo consul
cohortes expeditas in urbem induxit, ceteros interim
12 castra communire iussit. Ingressi milites refractis
foribus paucos graves aetate aut invalidos inveniunt
13 relictaque quae migratu difficilia essent. Ea direpta ;
et cognitum ex captivis est communi consilio aliquot
circa urbes conscisse fugam ; suos prima vigilia profectos ; credere eandem in aliis urbibus solitudinem
14 inventuros. Dictis captivorum fides exstitit, desertis
oppidis consul potitur.

XXXV. Alteri consuli M. Atilio nequaquam tam
facile bellum fuit. Cum ad Luceriam duceret
legiones, quam oppugnari ab Samnitibus audierat,
ad finem Lucerinum ei hostis obvius fuit. Ibi ira
2 vires aequavit; proelium varium et anceps fuit,
tristius tamen eventu Romanis, et quia insueti erant
vinci et quia digredientes magis quam in ipso certamine senserunt quantum in sua parte plus volnerum

five horsemen to enter and advance for a short
distance; then, if all seemed safe, three of these
were to remain there together, and the other two
were to report to him what they had found. When
they came back and reported that they had advanced
to a place from which a view could be had in all
directions, and that silence and solitude reigned far
and wide, the consul at once led some light-armed
cohorts into the city and ordered the rest to con-
struct a camp in the meanwhile. Having entered
the place and broken in the house-doors, the soldiers
discovered some few decrepit or bed-ridden people
and certain things abandoned as too difficult to
remove. These things were seized. It was learned
from the prisoners that a number of communities
in the vicinity had agreed together in planning
flight; their own people had left in the first watch;
they believed that the Romans would find the same
solitude in the other cities. The statements of the
prisoners turned out to be true, and the consul
took possession of the deserted towns.

XXXV. The other consul, Marcus Atilius, had
by no means so easy a war. He was marching, at
the head of his legions, towards Luceria, which he
had heard was being besieged by the Samnites,
when the enemy met him at the Lucerine frontier.
On this occasion rage made their strength as great
as his, and the battle was one of shifting fortunes
and doubtful issue. Yet its outcome was more
discouraging to the Romans, both as having been
unaccustomed to defeat, and because, as they were
retiring from the field, they could see, even better
than during the actual engagement, how much their
side had got the worst of it in killed and wounded.

LIVY

3 ac caedis fuisset. Itaque is terror in castris ortus, qui si pugnantes cepisset, insignis accepta clades foret; tum quoque sollicita nox fuit iam invasurum castra Samnitem credentibus aut prima luce cum victoribus conserendas manus.

4 Minus cladis ceterum non plus animorum ad hostes erat. Ubi primum inluxit, abire sine certamine cupiunt; sed via una et ea ipsa praeter hostes erat, qua ingressi praebuere speciem recta tendentium ad 5 castra oppugnanda. Consul arma capere milites iubet et sequi se extra vallum; legatis tribunis praefectis sociorum imperat quod apud quemque facto opus est. 6 Omnes adfirmant se quidem omnia facturos, sed militum iacere animos; tota nocte inter volnera et 7 gemitus morientium vigilatum esse; si ante lucem ad castra ventum foret, tantum pavoris fuisse ut relicturi signa fuerint; nunc pudore a fuga contineri, alioqui pro victis esse.

8 Quae ubi consul accepit, sibimet ipsi circumeundos adloquendosque milites ratus, ut ad quosque venerat, 9 cunctantes arma capere increpabat: quid cessarent tergiversarenturque? Hostem in castra venturum nisi illi extra castra exissent, et pro tentoriis suis pugnaturos si pro vallo nollent. Armatis ac dimi-

The consequence of this was such a panic in the B.C. 294
camp as, had it come over them whilst they were
fighting, must have led to a signal overthrow. Even
so the night was an anxious one, for they thought
that the Samnites would soon be attacking the
camp, or else that they would have to fight their
victorious enemy at break of day.

The enemy had suffered less, but was not less
faint-hearted. As soon as it grew light they wished
to retire without giving battle. But there was only
one road, and this led past their enemies, and when
they had started to go that way, they looked as if
marching straight to attack the camp. The consul
ordered the soldiers to arm and follow him outside
the rampart. To the lieutenants, tribunes, and
prefects of the allies he explained what part it was
needful for their several commands to play. They
all assured him that, as for themselves, they were
ready for anything, but that the soldiers were
dispirited; all night long they had been kept awake
by the groans of the wounded and the dying; had
the enemy attacked the camp before daylight, their
fear would have been so great as to cause them to
desert their ranks; as it was, they were withheld
by shame from running away, but were otherwise
as good as beaten.

On hearing this, the consul thought he had best
go about himself among the men and talk to them.
Wherever he went he scolded those who were
hesitating to arm themselves: Why did they linger
and hold back? The enemy would come into the
camp, unless they went out; and they would be fighting before their tents, if they were not willing to
fight before the palisade. If men armed themselves

10 cantibus dubiam victoriam esse; qui nudus atque
inermis hostem maneat, ei aut mortem aut servitutem
11 patiendam. Haec iurganti increpantique responde-
bant confectos se pugna hesterna esse, nec virium
quicquam nec sanguinis superesse; maiorem multitudinem hostium apparere quam pridie fuerit.

12 Inter haec appropinquabat agmen; et iam breviore
intervallo certiora intuentes, vallum secum portare
Samnitem adfirmant nec dubium esse quin castra
13 circumvallaturi sint. Tunc enimvero consul indignum
facinus esse vociferari tantam contumeliam igno-
14 miniamque ab ignavissimo accipi hoste. "Etiamne
circumsedebimur" inquit "in castris, ut fame potius
per ignominiam quam ferro, si necesse est, per
virtutem moriamur?" Di bene verterent; facerent
15 quod[1] se dignum quisque ducerent: consulem M.
Atilium vel solum, si nemo alius sequatur, iturum
adversus hostes casurumque inter signa Samnitium
potius quam circumvallari castra Romana videat.
16 Dicta consulis legati tribunique et omnes turmae
equitum et centuriones primorum ordinum appro-
bavere.
17 Tum pudore victus miles segniter arma capit,
segniter e castris egreditur longo agmine nec continenti; maesti ac prope victi procedunt adversus
18 hostem nec spe nec animo certiorem. Itaque simul
conspecta sunt Romana signa, extemplo a primo

---

[1] Di bene verterent; facerent quod *Duker*: di (*or* dii) bene
uerterent facerentque quod Ω.

---

[1] The true explanation being that the Samnites were
quitting their camp and were carrying the stakes to use in
constructing the next one.

492

and fought, it was a question whose the victory _{B.C. 294} would be; but a man who waited for the enemy, unarmed and helpless, must put up with either death or slavery. To these objurgations and reproaches they replied that they were exhausted with the battle of the previous day and had no strength left nor blood to shed; while the enemy appeared to be in greater numbers than on the day before.

Meanwhile the column was approaching; and presently, as the soldiers obtained a closer view of them, they declared that the Samnites were carrying stakes and were doubtless going to fence in the camp.[1] At this the consul lost all patience, and shouted out that it was a shameful thing to suffer such disgrace and humiliation at the hands of the most cowardly of foes. "Shall we even be pent up within our camp," he cried, "to die shamefully of hunger, rather than, if need be, by the sword, like gallant men?" Heaven prosper them! They must act as each thought worthy of himself; but the consul, Marcus Atilius—alone if there were none to follow him—would charge the enemy, and sooner fall amongst the standards of the Samnites than see a Roman camp beleaguered. The consul's words were approved by the lieutenants and the tribunes and by all the squadrons of horse and the centurions of highest rank.

Then the soldiers began, for very shame, to arm, and slowly emerged from the stockade; in a long and straggling column, discouraged and almost beaten, they advanced towards the enemy, who were no better off for hopefulness or courage. Accordingly, no sooner had they beheld the Roman standards than a murmur ran through the column

Samnitium agmine ad novissimum fremitus perfertur,
exire, id quod timuerint, ad impediendum iter
19 Romanos; nullam inde ne fugae quidem patere
viam; illo loco aut cadendum esse aut stratis hostibus
per corpora eorum evadendum.

XXXVI. In medium[1] sarcinas coniciunt; armati
2 suis quisque ordinibus instruunt aciem. Iam exiguum
inter duas acies erat spatium, et stabant exspectantes
dum ab hostibus prius impetus prius clamor inci-
3 peret. Neutris animus est ad pugnandum, diversique
integri atque intacti abissent, ni cedenti instaturum
alterum timuissent. Sua sponte inter invitos ter-
giversantesque segnis pugna clamore incerto atque
impari coepit; nec vestigio quisquam movebatur.
4 Tum consul Romanus, ut rem excitaret, equitum
paucas turmas extra ordinem immisit; quorum cum
plerique delapsi ex equis essent et alii turbati, et a
Samnitium acie ad opprimendos eos qui ceciderant
5 et ad suos tuendos ab Romanis procursum est. Inde
paulum inritata pugna est; sed aliquanto et impigre
magis et plures procurrerant Samnites et turbatus
eques sua ipse subsidia territis equis proculcavit.
6 Hinc fuga coepta totam avertit aciem Romanam;
iamque in terga fugientium Samnites pugnabant,
cum consul equo praevectus ad portam castrorum ac

---

[1] in medium *Iac. Gronovius*: in medio Ω.

of the Samnites, from the foremost to the hindmost, that the Romans—just as they had feared—were coming out to dispute their passing; there was no way open even for flight; they must fall where they stood, or else cut down their foes and escape over their bodies.

XXXVI. They heaped up their baggage together, and, being armed, went every man to his own place in the ranks, and the battle-line was formed. And now there was but a little space between the armies, and they halted, each waiting for the other to be first to attack and first to raise a cheer. Neither side had any stomach for fighting, and they would have gone off in opposite directions, scatheless and unhurt, had they not been afraid that, if they retired, their enemies would advance. No signal was given, but though unwilling and reluctant, they began to fight, in a half-hearted manner, with an uncertain and unequal shout; nor would any man stir from his place.

Then the Roman consul, to put some life into the work, detached a few troops of cavalry and sent them in. Of these the most part were unhorsed, and, the rest being thrown into confusion, there was a rush on the part of the Samnites to dispatch the fallen and on that of the Romans to save their comrades. This infused a little spirit into the fighting; but the Samnites had charged somewhat more briskly and in greater numbers, and the disordered cavalry, their horses becoming terrified, rode down their own supports, who began a flight that spread to the whole Roman army. And now the Samnites were on the backs of the fugitives, when the consul, galloping on before to the gate of the camp, posted

7 statione equitum ibi opposita edictoque ut quicumque
ad vallum tenderet, sive ille Romanus sive Samnis
esset, pro hoste haberetur,[1] haec ipse minitans obstitit
8 profuse tendentibus suis in castra. "Quo pergis"
inquit, "miles? Et hic arma et viros invenies nec
vivo consule tuo nisi victor castra intrabis; proinde
elige, cum cive an hoste pugnare malis."

9 Haec dicente consule equites infestis cuspidibus
circumfunduntur ac peditem in pugnam redire iubent.
Non virtus solum consulis sed fors etiam adiuvit, quod
non institerunt Samnites spatiumque circumagendi
signa vertendique aciem a castris in hostem fuit.
10 Tum alii alios hortari ut repeterent pugnam; centuriones ab signiferis rapta signa inferre et ostendere
suis paucos et ordinibus inconpositis effuse venire
11 hostes. Inter haec consul manus ad caelum attollens
voce clara, ita ut exaudiretur, templum Iovi Statori
vovet, si constitisset a fuga Romana acies redinte-
gratoque proelio cecidisset vicissetque legiones Sam-
12 nitium. Omnes undique adnisi ad restituendam
pugnam, duces milites, peditum equitumque vis.
Numen etiam deorum respexisse nomen Romanum
visum; adeo facile inclinata res repulsique a castris
hostes, mox etiam redacti ad eum locum in quo

___

[1] haberetur (*followed by erasure*) *A* ς: haberent Ω: haberet
*MA*² (*or A*⁴).

there a guard of horse and commanded them, whosoever should make for the rampart, be he Roman or Samnite, to treat him as a foe. He likewise threatened the men himself, and stopped them as they made in disorder for the camp. "Where are you going, men?" he shouted: "Here too you will find arms and soldiers, and while your consul lives you shall not enter the camp, except as victors. Choose, therefore, whether you would sooner fight with fellow-citizens or enemies!"

As the consul spoke these words, the cavalry gathered round the infantry and levelling their spears bade them return into the battle. Not only the consul's bravery but Fortune also helped; for the Samnites did not press their advantage, and he had time to reverse his standards and change his front from the camp to the enemy. They then began to encourage each other to resume the fight; the centurions snatched the standards from the standard-bearers and carried them forward, pointing out to their men that the enemy were few in number and were coming on in irregular and ill-formed ranks. At this juncture the consul lifted up his hands to heaven, and in a clear voice, so as to be overheard, vowed a temple to Jupiter the Stayer, if the Roman army should stay its flight, and renewing the struggle cut to pieces and overcome the legions of the Samnites. Everybody, all along the line— officers, soldiers, infantry and horse—made an effort to restore the day. It even seemed that the divine power of the gods was concerned for the renown of Rome, so easily was the struggle turned and the enemy repulsed from the camp, and in a short time driven back to the place where the fighting had

LIVY

A.U.C. 13 commissa pugna erat. Ibi obiacente sarcinarum
460 cumulo, quas coniecerant in medium, haesere impediti; deinde, ne diriperentur res, orbem armatorum

14 sarcinis circumdant. Tum vero eos a fronte urgere
pedites, ab tergo circumvecti equites; ita in medio
caesi captique. Captivorum numerus fuit septem
milium octingentorum,[1] qui omnes nudi sub iugum
missi; caesos rettulere ad quattuor milia octingentos.

15 Ne Romanis quidem laeta victoria fuit; recensente
consule biduo acceptam cladem amissorum militum
numerus relatus septem milium octingentorum.

16 Dum haec in Apulia gerebantur, altero exercitu
Samnites Interamnam, coloniam Romanam, quae via
Latina est, occupare conati urbem non tenuerunt;

17 agros depopulati, cum praedam aliam inde mixtam
hominum atque pecudum colonosque captos agerent,
in victorem incidunt consulem ab Luceria redeuntem;
nec praedam solum amittunt sed ipsi longo atque

18 impedito agmine incompositi caeduntur. Consul
Interamnam edicto dominis ad res suas noscendas
recipiendasque revocatis et exercitu ibi relicto

19 comitiorum causa Romam est profectus. Cui de
triumpho agenti negatus honos et ob amissa tot
milia militum et quod captivos sine pactione sub
iugum misisset.

XXXVII. Consul alter Postumius, quia in Samnitibus materia belli deerat, in Etruriam[2] transducto

---

[1] octingentorum (dccc) A⁶ *Drakenborch*: accc (*or other
corruptions*) Ω.

[2] in Etruriam ς: etruriam Ω.

---

[1] The consul was blamed not for humiliating the enemy, but
for letting them off with the humiliation—as though they had
surrendered upon that understanding—instead of selling them
as slaves, which he had it in his power to do.

498

begun. There they were held up by the heap of B.C. 294
bundles which they had piled together, and, to
keep their effects from being rifled, they formed
around them a circle of armed men. Then the
foot-soldiers fell hotly upon them in the front, and
the cavalry rode round and assailed them in the
rear ; and so between the two they were slaughtered
or made prisoners. The number of the captives was
seven thousand eight hundred, who were all stripped
and sent under the yoke : the slain were reported
at four thousand eight hundred. Even the Romans
had no joy of their victory, for the consul found, on
reckoning up the two days' casualties, that he had
lost seven thousand eight hundred men.

Whilst these affairs were taking place in Apulia,
the Samnites with a second army attempted to seize
Interamna, a Roman colony on the Latin Way, but
could not take it ; having pillaged the farms, they
were driving off a miscellaneous booty of men and
beasts, together with the captured settlers, when
they encountered the victorious consul returning
from Luceria, and not only lost their spoils, but,
marching without order in a long and encumbered
column, were massacred themselves. The consul
made proclamation summoning the owners back to
Interamna to identify and receive again their
property, and, leaving there his army, went to Rome
for the purpose of conducting the elections. When
he sought to obtain a triumph, the honour was denied
him, on the ground that he had lost so many
thousand men, and because he had sent the prisoners
under the yoke, though they had made no terms.[1]

XXXVII. The other consul, Postumius, in default
of enemies in Samnium, transferred his army to

exercitu primum pervastaverat Volsiniensem agrum;
2 dein cum egressis ad tuendos fines haud procul
moenibus ipsorum depugnat; duo milia octingenti[1]
Etruscorum caesi; ceteros propinquitas urbis tutata
3 est. In Rusellanum[2] agrum exercitus traductus;
ibi non agri tantum vastati sed oppidum etiam ex-
pugnatum; capta amplius duo milia hominum, minus
4 duo milia circa muros caesa. Pax tamen clarior
maiorque quam bellum in Etruria eo anno fuerat
parta est. Tres validissimae urbes, Etruriae capita,
5 Volsinii Perusia Arretium, pacem petiere; et vestimentis militum frumentoque pacti cum consule, ut
mitti Romam oratores liceret, indutias in quadraginta
annos impetraverunt. Multa praesens quingentum
milium aeris in singulas[3] civitates imposita.
6 Ob hasce res gestas consul cum triumphum ab
senatu moris magis causa quam spe impetrandi
7 petisset videretque alios quod tardius ab urbe exis-
set, alios quod iniussu senatus ex Samnio in Etruriam
transisset, partim suos inimicos, partim collegae
amicos ad solacium aequatae repulsae sibi quoque
8 negare triumphum, "Non ita" inquit, "patres conscripti, vestrae maiestatis meminero, ut me consulem
esse obliviscar. Eodem iure imperii quo bella gessi,

---

[1] octingenti (dccc) A^5 *Drakenborch*: accc (*or other corruptions*) Ω.

[2] Rusellanum *Gronovius* (*chap.* iv. § 5): rosellanum (*or other corruptions*) Ω.

[3] aeris in singulas *Andreas* (*ed. Rom.* 1469): aerisingulas MPT: aeris singulas M^3: aeris singulis $P^2UT^2A^6$: aeris R: aeris in R^2: *omitted by DLA*.

Etruria. There he first devastated the lands of the B.C. 294
Volsinienses, and then, when they came out to defend
their territory, defeated them at no great distance
from their own walls. Two thousand eight hundred
Etruscans were slain; the rest were saved by their
nearness to the city. The army was then led into
the territory of Rusellae. There not only were the
fields laid waste, but the town was captured too.
More than two thousand were made prisoners and
somewhat fewer were killed in the fighting about the
walls. Yet a peace was made that year in Etruria
that was more glorious and of more importance than
the fighting had been. Three very powerful cities,
the chief places in that country, namely Volsinii,
Perusia, and Arretium, made overtures of peace, and
arranged with the consul, in return for clothing and
corn for his troops, to be permitted to send
ambassadors to Rome, who obtained a truce for forty
years. A fine of five hundred thousand *asses,* to be
paid at once, was assessed upon each state.

In view of these achievements, the consul asked
the senate for a triumph, more as a matter of custom
than with any hope of obtaining his request. When
he perceived that some were for denying him on the
ground of his tardiness in leaving the City, and others
because he had gone over without the authorization
of the senate from Samnium into Etruria—a part of
these critics being his personal enemies, and the rest
friends of his colleague, who were minded to console
the latter for his rebuff by denying a triumph to
Postumius also—seeing, I say, how matters stood, he
spoke as follows: " I shall not be so mindful,
Conscript Fathers, of your dignity as to forget that
I am consul. In virtue of the same authority with

LIVY

bellis feliciter gestis, Samnio atque Etruria subactis,
9 victoria et pace parta triumphabo." Ita senatum
reliquit. Inde inter tribunos plebis contentio orta;
pars intercessuros, ne novo exemplo triumpharet
aiebat, pars auxilio se adversus collegas triumphanti
10 futuros. Iactata res ad populum est vocatusque eo
consul cum M. Horatium L.[1] Valerium consules,
C. Marcium Rutulum[2] nuper, patrem eius qui tunc
censor esset, non ex auctoritate senatus sed iussu
11 populi triumphasse diceret, adiciebat se quoque
laturum fuisse ad populum, ni sciret mancipia nobilium, tribunos plebis, legem impedituros; voluntatem sibi ac favorem consentientis populi pro
12 omnibus iussis esse ac futura. Posteroque die
auxilio tribunorum plebis trium adversus interces-
sionem septem tribunorum et consensum senatus
celebrante populo diem triumphavit.

13 Et huius anni parum constans memoria est. Postumium auctor est Claudius in Samnio captis aliquot
urbibus in Apulia fusum fugatumque saucium ipsum
cum paucis Luceriam compulsum: ab Atilio in
14 Etruria res gestas eumque triumphasse. Fabius
ambo consules in Samnio et ad Luceriam res gessisse

---

[1] M. Horatium L. *Glareanus and Sigonius*: L. Horatium
M. Ω (*cf. C.I.L.* i[2], *p.* 44, A.U.C. 305).
[2] Rutulum (*see* III. vii. 6 *and* VII. xxxviii. 8) rutilium Ω.

---

[1] *i.e.* the law granting the triumph.
[2] Compare chap. xxvi. §§ 5–7, and chap. xxx. §§ 4–7.
[3] Q. Claudius Quadrigarius composed his annals about
80 B.C., covering the period from the Gallic invasion to his
own times.
[4] Q. Fabius Pictor was a contemporary of Hannibal and
wrote an annalistic history of Rome in Greek.

which I conducted my wars, I intend, now that those B.C. 294
wars are happily concluded with the subjugation of
Samnium and Etruria and the winning of victory and
peace, to celebrate a triumph." So saying he left the
senate. A dispute then arose amongst the tribunes
of the plebs; some declared that they would
interpose their veto to prevent this unprecedented
kind of triumph, others that they would support his
claims against the opposition of their colleagues.
The question was discussed in an assembly and the
consul was asked to speak. He reminded them that
Marcus Horatius and Lucius Valerius, the consuls,
and lately Gaius Marcius Rutulus, father of him who
was then censor, had triumphed not by authorization
of the senate but by command of the people; and he
added that he, too, would have referred the question
to the people, had he not known that there were
tribunes who were owned by the nobles and would
obstruct the law [1]; but the wishes and approbation
of the people when they were of one accord had all
the binding force with him—and ever would have—
of any orders whatsoever. And so, on the following
day, with the support of three tribunes of the plebs,
against the opposition of seven who forbade the
proceedings and a unanimous senate, Postumius
triumphed, with the people thronging in attendance.

Of this year, too, the tradition is uncertain.[2]
Postumius, if we follow Claudius,[3] after capturing
several cities in Samnium, was defeated in Apulia and
put to flight, and, being wounded himself, was forced
to take refuge with a few followers in Luceria; while
Atilius campaigned in Etruria and obtained a
triumph. Fabius [4] writes that both consuls fought
in Samnium and at Luceria; that the army was led

LIVY

scribit traductumque in Etruriam exercitum—sed ab
utro consule non adicit[1]—et ad Luceriam utrimque
15 multos occisos inque ea pugna Iovis Statoris aedem
votam, ut Romulus ante voverat ; sed fanum tantum,
16 id est locus templo effatus, fuerat. Ceterum hoc
demum anno ut aedem etiam fieri senatus iuberet
bis eiusdem voti damnata re publica[2] in religionem
venit.

XXXVIII. Sequitur hunc annum et consul insignis, L. Papirius Cursor, qua paterna gloria qua
sua, et bellum ingens victoriaque quantam de Samnitibus nemo ad eam diem praeter L. Papirium
2 patrem consulis[3] pepererat. Et forte eodem conatu
apparatuque omni opulentia insignium armorum
bellum adornaverant, et deorum etiam adhibuerant
opes, ritu quodam sacramenti vetusto velut initiatis
militibus, dilectu per omne Samnium habito nova
3 lege, ut qui iuniorum non convenisset ad imperatorum edictum quique iniussu abisset eius caput[4]
4 Iovi sacraretur.[5] Tum exercitus omnis Aquiloniam
est indictus. Ad quadraginta[6] milia militum, quod
roboris in Samnio erat, convenerunt.

5 Ibi mediis fere castris locus est consaeptus crati-
bus pluteisque et linteis contectis, patens ducentos
6 maxime pedes in omnes pariter partis. Ibi ex libro

[1] adicit (adii-) *Madvig* : adiecit Ω.
[2] re publica A^{x2} *Gronovius* : respublica Ω.
[3] consulis ς : cōs *P* : consulem *MTDLA* : eius consulem *U*.
[4] eius caput *M. Mueller* (II. viii. 2) : caput (capud *A*) Ω.
[5] sacraretur *Madvig* : sacratum erat Ω.
[6] quadraginta (XL) *MULA²* (*or A⁶*) : sexaginta (LX)
PTDA.

---

[1] The same, that is, as in the year 309 B.C., when they had

over into Etruria—by which consul he does not state B.C. 294
—and that at Luceria both sides suffered heavy
losses; in the course of the battle a temple was
vowed to Jupiter Stator, as Romulus had vowed one
before; but only the *fanum*, or place set apart for the
temple, had been consecrated; this year, however,
their scruples demanded that the senate should order
the erection of the building, since the state had now
been obligated for the second time by the same vow.

XXXVIII. The following year brought with it a B.C. 293
consul, Lucius Papirius Cursor, remarkable both for
his father's glory and for his own, and a mighty war,
with a victory such as no one, save Lucius Papirius,
the consul's father, had until that day obtained over
the Samnites. And it happened that the enemy had
made their preparations for the war with the same[1]
earnestness and pomp and all the magnificence of
splendid arms, and had likewise invoked the assistance of the gods, initiating, as it were, their soldiers,
in accordance with a certain antique form of oath.
But first they held a levy throughout Samnium under
this new ordinance, that whosoever of military age
did not report in response to the proclamation of the
generals, or departed without their orders, should
forfeit his life to Jupiter. Which done, they
appointed all the army to meet at Aquilonia, where
some forty thousand soldiers, the strength of
Samnium, came together.

There, at about the middle of the camp, they had
enclosed an area, extending approximately two
hundred feet in all directions, with wicker hurdles,
and roofed it over with linen. In this place they

[1] ought against the Romans, who were commanded by the
elder Papirius (ix. xl. 2 ff.).

LIVY

vetere linteo lecto[1] sacrificatum sacerdote Ovio
Paccio quodam, homine magno natu, qui se id sacrum
petere adfirmabat ex vetusta Samnitium religione,
qua quondam usi maiores eorum fuissent, cum adi-
mendae Etruscis Capuae clandestinum cepissent
7 consilium. Sacrificio perfecto per viatorem imperator acciri iubebat nobilissimum quemque genere
8 factisque; singuli introducebantur. Erat cum alius
apparatus sacri qui perfundere religione animum
posset, tum in loco circa omni contecto arae in
medio victimaeque circa caesae et circumstantes cen-
9 turiones strictis gladiis. Admovebatur altaribus
magis ut victima quam ut sacri particeps adigebaturque[2] iure iurando quae visa auditaque in eo loco
10 essent,[3] non enuntiaturum. Dein iurare cogebant
diro quodam carmine, in exsecrationem capitis familiaeque et stirpis composito, nisi isset in proelium
quo[4] imperatores duxissent et si aut ipse ex acie
fugisset aut si quem fugientem vidisset non ex-
11 templo occidisset. Id primo quidam abnuentes
iuraturos se obtruncati circa altaria sunt; iacentes
deinde inter stragem victimarum documento ceteris
12 fuere ne abnuerent. Primoribus Samnitium ea
detestatione obstrictis, decem nominatis ab imperatore, eis dictum ut vir virum legerent donec sedecim

---

[1] lecto Ω: tecto *Madvig.*
[2] adigebaturque D^3_5: adicebaturque *MPTDA*: adicieba-
turque *UL.*
[3] essent M^2 (*or* M^1) P^2 (*or* P^3) *u* T^2 (*or* T^1) D^3A^6: co essent
MP: coissent *TDLA.*
[4] quo P^2uT^2 (*or* T^1) A^6: quod *MPTDLA.*

---

[1] At IV. xxxvii. 1 f. we were told how the Etruscan city of
Volturnum was captured by the Samnites and renamed
Capua.

offered sacrifice in accordance with directions read B.C. 293
from an old linen roll. The celebrant was one
Ovius Paccius, an aged man, who claimed to derive
this ceremony from an ancient ritual of the Samnites
which the forefathers of those present had formerly
employed when they had gone secretly about to get
Capua away from the Etruscans.[1] On the conclusion
of the sacrifice, the general by his apparitor commanded to be summoned all those of the highest
degree in birth and deeds of arms ; and one by one
they were introduced. Besides other ceremonial
preparations, such as might avail to strike the mind
with religious awe, there was a place all enclosed,
with altars in the midst and slaughtered victims
lying about, and round them a guard of centurions [2]
with drawn swords. The man was brought up to the
altar, more like a victim than a partaker in the rite,
and was sworn not to divulge what he should there
see or hear. They then compelled him to take an
oath in accordance with a certain dreadful form of
words, whereby he invoked a curse upon his head,
his household, and his family, if he went not into
battle where his generals led the way, or if he either
fled from the line himself or saw any other fleeing
and did not instantly cut him down. Some there
were at first who refused to take this oath ; these
were beheaded before the altars, where they lay
amongst the slaughtered victims—a warning to the
rest not to refuse. When the leading Samnites had
been bound by this imprecation, the general named
ten of them and bade them choose every man
another, and so to proceed until they had brought

[2] These are called "armed priests" at chap. xli. § 3.

milium numerum confecissent. Ea legio linteata ab
integumento consaepti, in quo[1] sacrata nobilitas
erat, appellata est; his arma insignia data et cri-
13 statae galeae, ut inter ceteros eminerent. Paulo
plus viginti milium alius exercitus fuit nec corporum
specie nec gloria belli nec apparatu linteatae legioni
dispar.[2] Hic hominum numerus, quod roboris erat,
ad Aquiloniam[3] consedit.

XXXIX. Consules profecti ab urbe, prior Sp. Carvilius, cui veteres legiones quas M. Atilius superioris
anni consul in agro Interamnati reliquerat decretae
2 erant. Cum eis in Samnium profectus, dum hostes
operati superstitionibus concilia secreta agunt, Ami-
3 ternum oppidum de Samnitibus vi cepit. Caesa ibi
milia hominum duo ferme atque octingenti, capta
4 quattuor milia ducenti septuaginta. Papirius novo
exercitu—ita enim decretum erat—scripto Duroniam
urbem expugnavit; minus quam collega cepit hominum, plus aliquanto occidit; praeda opulenta utro-
5 bique est parta. Inde pervagati Samnium consules,
maxime depopulato Atinate agro, Carvilius ad Cominium, Papirius ad Aquiloniam, ubi summa rei Samni-
6 tium erat, pervenit. Ibi aliquamdiu nec cessatum
ab armis est neque naviter pugnatum; lacessendo
quietos, resistentibus cedendo comminandoque magis

---

[1] in quo *Freudenberg*: a quo ς: quo Ω.
[2] dispar Ω (*Walters*): par u (*Conway*).
[3] ad Aquiloniam ς: Aquiloniam Ω.

---

[1] See IX. xxxix. 5, where this mode of selection is described as having been employed by the Etruscans.
[2] To be consistent with the total given in § 4, this number
should be 24,000.

their number up to sixteen thousand.[1]   These were B.C. 293
named the "Linen Legion," from the roof of the
enclosure wherein the nobles had been sworn, and
were given splendid arms and crested helmets, to
distinguish them from the rest.   A little over twenty
thousand[2] men composed another corps, which
neither in physical appearance nor in martial renown
nor in equipment was inferior to the Linen Legion.
This was the size of the army, comprising their
effective forces, which encamped at Aquilonia.

XXXIX. The consuls set out from the City,
Spurius Carvilius, to whom had been assigned the
veteran legions which Marcus Atilius the consul of
the previous year had left in the territory of
Interamna, being the first to take the field.   Proceeding with these forces into Samnium, while the
enemy, busy with their superstitious rites, were
holding secret councils, he carried the Samnite town
of Amiternum by assault.   There about two thousand
eight hundred men were slain and four thousand two
hundred and seventy made prisoners.   Papirius,
having levied a new army—for so it had been
decreed—took by storm the city of Duronia, making
fewer prisoners than his colleague but killing many
more.   In each place a rich booty was obtained.
Afterwards, the consuls having ranged over Samnium
and laid waste especially the district of Atina,
Carvilius appeared before Cominium and Papirius
before Aquilonia, where the main power of the
Samnites lay encamped.   There for some days there
was neither cessation from hostilities nor downright
fighting, but the time was spent in provoking the
enemy when they were quiet and retreating when
they offered resistance—in a word, in feinting rather

7 quam inferendo pugnam dies absumebatur. Quodcumque[1] inciperetur remittereturque, omnium rerum
etiam parvarum eventus perferebatur inde in[2] altera
Romana castra, quae viginti milium spatio aberant,
et absentis collegae consilia omnibus gerendis inte-
rerant rebus, intentiorque Carvilius, quo in maiore[3]
discrimine res vertebatur, in Aquiloniam quam ad
8 Cominium, quod obsidebat, erat.

L. Papirius, iam per omnia ad dimicandum satis
paratus, nuntium ad collegam mittit sibi in animo
9 esse postero die, si per auspicia liceret, confligere
cum hoste; opus esse et illum quanta maxima vi
posset Cominium oppugnare, ne quid laxamenti sit
10 Samnitibus ad subsidia Aquiloniam mittenda. Diem
ad proficiscendum nuntius habuit; nocte rediit,
11 approbare collegam consulta referens. Papirius
nuntio misso extemplo contionem habuit; multa
de universo genere belli, multa de praesenti hostium
apparatu, vana magis specie quam efficaci ad even-
12 tum, disseruit: non enim cristas volnera facere,
et per picta atque aurata scuta transire Romanum
pilum, et candore tunicarum fulgentem aciem, ubi
13 res ferro geratur, cruentari. Auream olim atque
argenteam Samnitium aciem a parente suo occidione occisam spoliaque ea honestiora victori hosti
14 quam ipsis arma fuisse. Datum hoc forsan nomini
familiaeque suae, ut adversus maximos conatus
Samnitium opponerentur duces spoliaque ea referrent quae insignia publicis etiam locis decorandis

---

[1] Quodcumque *Madvig*: quodcum Ω: quaecum $A^6\varsigma$.
[2] inde in *Madvig*: in dies Ω.
[3] quo in maiore *Madvig*: quom aiore *T*: quo maiore Ω.

---

[1] In 310 B.C. See IX. xl. 1–17.

than attacking. Whatever was undertaken or given B.C. 293
over, the result of every skirmish, no matter how
trivial it might be, was reported at the other camp,
which was twenty miles away. The other colleague,
Carvilius, though absent, shared in every plan of
operations, and was more intent upon Aquilonia,
as the crisis became more imminent, than upon
Cominium, to which he was laying siege.

Lucius Papirius, being now prepared at all points
for the battle, sent word to his colleague that he
purposed, if the auspices permitted, to engage the
enemy on the following day; it was needful, he
said, that Carvilius should also direct an assault, as
violent as possible, on Cominium, that no relaxation
of the pressure there might allow of the Samnites'
sending relief to Aquilonia. The messenger had a
day for the journey. Returning in the night, he
reported that Carvilius approved the measures taken
by his colleague. Papirius had no sooner sent off the
courier than he addressed his troops, and said many
things of war in general and much regarding the
present equipment of the enemy, more vain and
showy than effective. For crests, said he, dealt no
wounds, and painted and gilded shields would let
the Roman javelin through, and their battle-array,
resplendent in white tunics, would be stained with
blood when sword met sword. Long ago a gilt and
silvern Samnite army had been utterly destroyed by
his father, and the spoils had done their conquerors
more credit than the arms had brought to their
bearers.[1] It had perhaps been granted to his name
and family to be sent forth as generals against the
mightiest efforts of the Samnites, and to win such
trophies as should strikingly adorn even public

511

LIVY

15 essent. Deos immortales adesse propter totiens
16 petita foedera, totiens rupta; si[1] qua coniectura
mentis divinae sit, nulli unquam exercitui fuisse
infestiores quam qui nefando sacro mixta hominum pecudumque caede respersus, ancipiti deum
irae devotus, hinc foederum cum Romanis ictorum
17 testes deos, hinc iuris iurandi adversus foedera
suscepti exsecrationes horrens, invitus iuraverit,
oderit sacramentum, uno tempore deos cives hostes
metuat.

XL. Haec comperta perfugarum indiciis cum apud
infensos iam sua sponte milites disseruisset, simul
divinae humanaeque spei pleni clamore consentienti
pugnam poscunt; paenitet in posterum diem dilatum
2 certamen; moram diei noctisque oderunt. Tertia
vigilia noctis, iam relatis litteris a collega, Papirius
silentio surgit et pullarium in auspicium mittit.
3 Nullum erat genus hominum in castris intactum
cupiditate pugnae, summi infimique aeque intenti
erant; dux militum, miles ducis ardorem spectabat.
4 Is ardor omnium etiam ad eos qui auspicio inter-
erant pervenit; nam cum pulli non pascerentur,
pullarius auspicium mentiri ausus tripudium soli-
5 stimum consuli nuntiavit. Consul laetus auspicium

---

¹ si *Luterbacher* : tum si Ω.

---

[1] For the use of sacred chickens in augury see VI. xli. 8
and note (Vol. III., p. 344).

places.   The immortal gods, he said, were ready to b.c. 293
intervene in behalf of treaties so often sought and so
often broken.   If it were possible in any way to
surmise the feelings of the gods, they had never been
more enraged with any army than with this one,
which with horrid rites and stained with the com-
mingled blood of men and beasts, doubly devoted
to the wrath of Heaven, as it trembled now at
the gods that attested the treaties it had made with
the Romans, and now at the curses called down when
it undertook to break those treaties, had sworn
unwillingly, hated its oath, and dreaded at one and
the same moment its gods, its fellow-citizens, and
its enemies.

   XL. These fears had been made known to Papirius
by deserters; and when he had described them to
his soldiers, incensed as they already were of themselves, their hopes both of gods and men ran high,
and they called out in unison demanding battle;
they were vexed at the postponement of the
struggle until the morrow, and to wait for a day
and night disgusted them.   In the third watch of
the night, having now received his colleague's
answer, Papirius rose silently and sent the keeper
of the chickens ¹ to take the auspices.   There was
no class of men in camp who were not affected by
the lust of battle; both high and low felt the same
eagerness; the general could see the ardour of the
men, the men that of their general.   This universal
zeal spread even to those who took the auspices,
for when the chickens refused to feed, their keeper
dared to falsify the presage and reported that the
corn danced on the ground as it fell from their
greedy beaks.   The consul joyfully announced that

LIVY

6 egregium esse et deis auctoribus rem gesturos pro-
nuntiat signumque pugnae proponit. Exeunti iam
forte in aciem nuntiat perfuga viginti cohortes
Samnitium—quadringenariae ferme erant—Cominium profectas. Quod ne ignoraret collega, extemplo nuntium mittit; ipse signa ocius proferri
7 iubet; subsidia[1] suis quaeque locis et praefectos
subsidiis attribuerat; dextro cornu L. Volumnium,
sinistro L. Scipionem, equitibus legatos alios, C.
8 Caedicium et T. Trebonium,[2] praefecit; Sp. Nautium
mulos detractis clitellis cum tribus cohortibus[3] alariis
in tumulum conspectum propere circumducere iubet
atque inde inter ipsam dimicationem quanto maxime
posset moto pulvere se[4] ostendere.

9 Dum his intentus imperator erat, altercatio inter
pullarios orta de auspicio eius diei exauditaque ab
equitibus Romanis, qui rem haud spernendam rati
Sp. Papirio, fratis filio consulis, ambigi de auspicio
10 renuntiaverunt. Iuvenis ante doctrinam deos sper-
nentem natus inquisitam, ne quid incompertum
11 deferret, ad consulem detulit. Cui ille: "Tu quidem
macte virtute diligentiaque esto! Ceterum qui
auspicio adest si quid falsi nuntiat, in semet ipsum

---

[1] subsidia *Madvig*: subsidiaque Ω.
[2] T. Trebonium *Weissenborn*: Trebonium Ω.
[3] tribus cohortibus *Hertz*: cohortibus (cohortir *P*: cohortis *F*) Ω.
[4] moto pulvere se *Madvig*: moto puluere Ω.

---

[1] For a similar use of pack-animals to simulate cavalry, compare VII. xiv. 7-10.
[2] Compare the caustic remark at III. xx. 5: But there had not yet come about that contempt for the gods which possesses the present generation; nor did everybody seek to construe oaths and laws to suit himself, but rather shaped his own practices by them.

the omens were most favourable, and that the gods
would be with them as they fought. So saying, he
displayed the signal for a battle. It chanced, as he
was already moving out to the field, that a deserter
came up with the information that twenty cohorts
of the Samnites—of about four hundred each—had
set out for Cominium. That his colleague might
not be ignorant of this, he instantly dispatched a
messenger to him, and ordered his own troops to
advance in double time. He had assigned supports
to take their posts at favourable points and officers
to command them; the right wing he had given to
Lucius Volumnius, the left to Lucius Scipio; to lead
the cavalry he appointed the other lieutenants,
Gaius Caedicius and Titus Trebonius. Spurius
Nautius he directed to remove the pack-saddles
from the mules, and with three cohorts of auxiliaries
to make a hasty detour to a hill which lay in full
view, and thence to show himself, in the heat of the
engagement, raising as much dust as possible.[1]

While the general was thus employed, a dispute
which broke out amongst the keepers of the chickens
about the auspices for that day was overheard by
some Roman cavalrymen, who, deeming it no
negligible matter, reported to Spurius Papirius, the
consul's nephew, that the auspices were being called
in question. The young man had been born before
the learning that makes light of the gods,[2] and
having inquired into the affair, that he might not
be the bearer of an uncertain rumour, acquainted
the consul with it. The consul replied: "For yourself, I commend your conduct and your diligence;
but he who takes the auspices, if he reports aught
that is false, draws down the wrath of Heaven upon

A.U.C.
461

religionem recipit: mihi quidem tripudium nuntiatum; populo Romano exercituique egregium auspicium est.'' Centurionibus deinde imperavit uti pullarios inter prima signa constituerent. Promovent et Samnites signa; insequitur acies ornata armataque, ut hostium [1] quoque magnificum spectaculum esset. Priusquam clamor tolleretur concurrereturque, emisso temere pilo ictus pullarius ante signa cecidit. Quod ubi consuli nuntiatum est, " Di in proelio sunt'' inquit; "habet poenam noxium caput!'' Ante consulem haec dicentem corvus voce clara occinuit; quo laetus augurio consul, adfirmans nunquam humanis rebus magis praesentes interfuisse deos, signa canere et clamorem tolli iussit.

XLI. Proelium commissum atrox, ceterum longe disparibus animis: Romanos ira spes ardor certaminis avidos hostium sanguinis in proelium rapit; Samnitium magnam partem necessitas ac religio invitos magis resistere quam inferre pugnam cogit. Nec sustinuissent primum clamorem atque impetum Romanorum, per aliquot iam annos vinci adsueti, ni potentior alius metus insidens pectoribus a fuga retineret. Quippe in oculis erat omnis ille occulti paratus sacri et armati sacerdotes et promiscua hominum pecudumque strages et respersae fando nefandoque sanguine arae et dira exsecratio ac

---

[1] hostium Ω : hostibus (or hosti) edd.

himself; as for me, I was told that the corn had B.C. 293 danced; it is an excellent omen for the Roman People and the army." He then ordered the centurions to station the keepers of the chickens in the front rank. The Samnites, too, advanced their standards, which were followed by the battle-line in gorgeous armour—a splendid spectacle, though composed of enemies. Before the first shout and the clash of arms, a random javelin struck the chicken-keeper and he fell before the standards. The consul, on being told of this, exclaimed, "The gods are present in the battle; the guilty wretch has paid the penalty!" In front of the consul a raven, just as he spoke, uttered a clear cry, and Papirius, rejoiced with the augury, and declaring that never had the gods been more instant to intervene in human affairs, bade sound the trumpets and give a cheer.

XLI. The battle was fought fiercely, but with far from equal spirit. The Romans were filled with rage and hope and ardour for the combat, and, thirsting for their enemies' blood, rushed into the engagement. As for the Samnites, in most cases it was necessity and the fear of Heaven that compelled them, however reluctant, rather to resist than to attack. Nor would they have held out against the first battle-cry and onset of the Romans, accustomed, as they had now been for some years, to being beaten, had not another yet more powerful fear benumbed their hearts and prevented them from fleeing. For their eyes beheld all that array of the secret rite, and the armed priests, and the mingled slaughter of men and beasts, and the altars spattered with the blood of victims—and with that other blood—and they could hear the baleful execrations

LIVY

furiale carmen, detestandae familiae stirpique com-
positum ; iis vinculis fugae obstricti stabant, civem
4 magis quam hostem timentes. Instare Romanus a
cornu utroque, a media acie, et caedere deorum
hominumque attonitos metu ; repugnatur segniter,
ut ab iis [1] quos timor moraretur a fuga.

5 Iam prope ad signa caedes pervenerat, cum ex
transverso pulvis velut ingentis agminis incessu
motus apparuit ; Sp. Nautius—Octavium Maecium
quidam eum tradunt—cum auxiliaribus [2] cohortibus
6 erat ; pulverem maiorem quam pro numero excita-
bant ; incidentes mulis calones frondosos ramos per
terram trahebant. Arma signaque per turbidam
lucem in primo apparebant ; post altior densiorque
pulvis equitum speciem cogentium agmen dabat
fefellitque non Samnites modo sed etiam Romanos ;
7 et consul adfirmavit errorem clamitans inter prima
signa, ita ut vox etiam ad hostis accideret, captum
Cominium, victorem collegam adesse : adniterentur
vincere, priusquam gloria alterius exercitus fieret.
8 Haec insidens equo ; inde tribunis centurionibusque
imperat, ut viam equitibus patefaciant ; ipse Trebonio
Caedicioque praedixerat, ubi se cuspidem erectam
quatientem vidissent, quanta maxima vi possent con-
9 citarent equites in hostem. Ad nutum omnia, ut

---

[1] iis ⌐ : his Ω : hiis *A*.
[2] cum auxiliaribus *Madvig* : dux alaribus (laribus *A*) Ω :
dux cum alaribus *Koch*.

and that dire oath, framed to invoke perdition on their families and on their stock. These were the chains that stayed them from flight, and they feared their countrymen more than they feared their foes. On came the Romans from either wing and from the centre, and cut them down as they stood there dazed by the dread of gods and men. They resisted, but sluggishly, like men whom cowardice restrained from running.

The carnage had now reached almost to the standards, when a cloud of dust appeared on their flank, as though raised by the oncoming of a mighty host. It was Spurius Nautius—some say Octavius Maecius—with the auxiliary cohorts; they made more dust than their numbers warranted, for the grooms who rode the mules were dragging leafy branches along the ground. Arms and standards were made out in the van through the murky air, and behind them another denser cloud of dust seemed to show that cavalry were closing the rear, and deceived not only the Samnites, but the Romans as well. This mistake the consul confirmed by calling out in the front ranks, so loud that his voice carried even to the enemy, that Cominium was taken, and that his victorious colleague was at hand; let them therefore strive to conquer before the other army won the glory. He was on horseback as he shouted these words. He then commanded the tribunes and centurions to open a path for the cavalry, having previously admonished Trebonius and Caedicius that when they saw him holding his lance aloft and shaking it, they should make their horsemen run full tilt against the enemy. Everything fell out according to his wishes,

519

ex ante praeparato, fiunt; panduntur inter ordines
viae; provolat eques atque infestis cuspidibus in
medium agmen hostium ruit perrumpitque ordines
quacumque impetum dedit. Instant Volumnius et
Scipio et perculsos sternunt.

10   Tum iam deorum hominumque victa vi, funduntur
linteatae cohortes; pariter iurati iniuratique fugiunt
11 nec quemquam praeter hostes metuunt. Peditum [1]
quod superfuit pugnae in castra aut Aquiloniam
compulsum est; nobilitas equitesque Bovianum perfugerunt. Equites eques sequitur, peditem pedes;
diversa cornua dextrum ad castra Samnitium, laevum
12 ad urbem tendit. Prior aliquanto Volumnius castra
cepit; ad urbem Scipioni maiore resistitur vi, non
quia plus animi victis est sed melius muri quam
vallum armatos arcent; inde lapidibus propulsant
13 hostem. Scipio, nisi in primo pavore priusquam
colligerentur animi transacta res esset, lentiorem
fore munitae urbis oppugnationem ratus, interrogat
milites satin aequo animo paterentur ab altero cornu
castra capta esse, se victores pelli a portis urbis.
14 Reclamantibus universis primus ipse scuto super
caput elato pergit ad portam; secuti alii testudine
facta in urbem perrumpunt deturbatisque Samnitibus
quae circa portam erant muri occupavere; penetrare

---

[1] peditum *Gronovius* : peditum agmen Ω.

as happens when plans are laid beforehand. Lanes B.C. 293 were opened up between the files; the cavalry dashed out, and with levelled spears assailed the midst of the enemy's array, and broke his ranks wherever they charged. Hard after them came Volumnius and Scipio, and made havoc of the disordered Samnites.

Then at last, overwhelmed by gods and men, the Linen Cohorts were put to rout; the sworn and the unsworn fled alike, and knew no fear but fear of the enemy. Such portion of the foot as survived the battle was driven to the camp or to Aquilonia; the nobles and cavalry escaped to Bovianum. Horse were pursued by horse, infantry by infantry. The Roman wings advanced on different objectives, the right on the Samnite camp, the left on their city. Volumnius succeeded somewhat sooner in capturing the camp. From the city Scipio met with a more violent resistance—not that vanquished men are more courageous, but walls avail better to keep out armed enemies than does a rampart; and from thence they drove their assailants off with stones. Scipio, fearing that it would be a tedious task to reduce a fortified city, unless the affair were concluded during the first panic of his enemies and before they should collect their spirits, asked his soldiers whether they could be content that the other wing should have taken the camp, while they, though victors, were repulsed from the city gates. When they all together cried out "No!" he himself led the way to the gate, shield over head, and the others, following him, formed a *testudo*, burst into the city, and hurling down the defenders seized the walls adjoining the gate; they durst not

in interiora urbis, quia pauci admodum erant, non audent.

XLII. Haec primo ignorare consul et intentus recipiendo exercitui esse; iam enim praeceps in occasum sol erat et appetens nox periculosa et 2 suspecta omnia etiam victoribus faciebat. Progressus longius ab dextra capta castra videt, ab laeva clamorem in urbe mixtum pugnantium ac paventium fremitu esse; et tum forte certamen ad portam erat. 3 Advectus deinde equo propius, ut suos in muris videt nec iam integri quicquam esse, quoniam temeritate paucorum magnae rei parta occasio esset, acciri quas receperat copias signaque in urbem inferri 4 iussit. Ingressi proxima ex parte [1] quia nox appropinquabat, quievere. Nocte oppidum ab hostibus desertum est.

5 Caesa illo die ad Aquiloniam Samnitium milia viginti trecenti quadraginta, capta tria milia octingenti et septuaginta, signa militaria nonaginta septem. 6 Ceterum illud memoriae traditur, non ferme alium ducem laetiorem in acie visum seu suopte ingenio 7 seu fiducia bene gerundae rei. Ab eodem robore animi neque controverso auspicio revocari a proelio potuit et in ipso discrimine quo templa deis immor-

---

[1] ex parte Ω : ea parte *Iac. Gronovius.*

venture into the middle of the city, because their B.C. 293 numbers were so small.

XLII. Of these events the consul was at first unaware, and was intent upon the withdrawal of his army; for the sun was now rapidly sinking in the west, and night coming on apace made all things dangerous and suspect, even to the victors. As he rode farther forward, he saw on his right hand that the camp was taken, while from the city, on his left, a confused uproar was rising in which the shouts of the combatants were mingled with screams of terror; and it so happened that at that very moment the struggle at the gate was in progress. Then, riding nearer and perceiving that his men were on the walls and that his course was already marked out for him, since the adventurousness of a few men had provided him with a great opportunity, he gave orders that the troops withdrawn should be called back and advance against the city. They entered it on the nearest side, and, as night was approaching, bivouacked; in the night the town was abandoned by the enemy.

There were slain that day of the Samnites at Aquilonia twenty thousand three hundred and forty, and three thousand eight hundred and seventy were captured, with ninety-seven military standards. Tradition also avers that hardly had there ever been a general more joyous in combat, whether owing to his native temper or to his confidence that he should gain the victory. It resulted from the same stoutness of heart that he was not to be recalled from giving battle by the dispute about the omen, and that in the hour of crisis, when it was customary to vow temples to the immortal gods, he made a

LIVY

talibus voveri mos erat voverat Iovi Victori, si
legiones hostium fudisset, pocillum mulsi priusquam
temetum biberet, sese facturum.   Id votum dis cordi
fuit et auspicia in bonum verterunt.

XLIII. Eadem fortuna ab altero consule ad
Cominium[1] gesta res.   Prima luce ad moenia omnibus copiis admotis corona cinxit urbem subsidiaque
2 firma, ne qua eruptio fieret, portis opposuit. Iam
signum dantem eum nuntius a collega trepidus de
viginti cohortium adventu et ab impetu moratus est
et partem copiarum revocare instructam intentamque
3 ad oppugnandum coegit.   D. Brutum Scaevam legatum cum legione prima et decem cohortibus alariis
equitatuque ire adversus subsidium hostium iussit :
4 quocumque in loco fuisset obvius, obsisteret ac
moraretur manumque, si forte ita res posceret, con-
ferret, modo ne ad Cominium eae copiae admoveri
5 possent.   Ipse scalas ferri ad muros ab omni parte
urbis iussit ac testudine ad portas successit ; simul
et refringebantur portae et vis undique in muros
fiebat.   Samnites sicut antequam in muris viderent
armatos satis animi habuerunt ad prohibendum urbis
6 aditu hostes, ita, postquam iam non ex intervallo nec
missilibus sed comminus gerebatur res et qui aegre

---

¹ Cominium *A*ˣ: cō(*or* com-)minium Ω : cōmonium *P*:
cōmineum (?) *F*.

---

¹ The consul's vow was by no means prompted by a spirit
of mockery, but was merely an hilarious expression of confidence and good understanding—not without a playful
assumption of superiority as a toper, implied in the contrast
between *pocillum mulsi* and *temetum*.   That Jupiter should
have savoured the jest shows him to have been blessed with
a livelier sense of humour than the elder Pliny, who cites
the anecdote (*N. H.*, xiv. 91) as evidence how sparingly wine
was used in the old days.

vow to Jupiter the Victor that if he routed the B.C. 293
legions of the enemy he would present him with
a thimbleful of mead before he drank strong wine
himself. This vow was pleasing to the gods and
they gave a good turn to the auspices.[1]

XLIII. The same good fortune attended the
other consul at Cominium. With the dawn he led
up all his forces under the walls and invested the
city, posting strong supports to prevent any sally
from the gates. He was in the act of giving the
signal when the courier from his colleague came up
with the alarming news about the twenty cohorts,[2]
thus delaying the assault and obliging him to recall
a part of his troops who were already drawn up and
eager to attack. He commanded Decimus Brutus
Scaeva, his lieutenant, to proceed with the first
legion, ten auxiliary cohorts, and the cavalry, to
confront the new forces of the enemy: wherever
he fell in with them, he was to block their path
and delay them, giving battle if the situation happened to require it; but on no account must these
troops be suffered to approach Cominium. He himself gave orders to bring up scaling-ladders from
every side against the walls of the city, and under
a mantlet of shields approached the gates. Thus
at the same instant the gates were burst open and
the walls assaulted. The Samnites, although, until
they beheld armed men upon their walls, they had
pluck enough to keep their enemies from coming
near the city, yet when the combat was no longer
carried on with missiles at long range, but was
fought hand-to-hand, and when those who had

[2] See chap. xl. § 6.

successerant ex plano in muros, loco quem magis
timuerant victo, facile in hostem imparem ex aequo

7 pugnabant, relictis turribus murisque in forum omnes
compulsi paulisper inde temptaverunt extremam

8 pugnae fortunam ; deinde abiectis armis ad undecim
milia hominum et quadringenti in fidem consulis
venerunt ; caesa ad quattuor milia octingenti[1]
octoginta.

9 Sic ad Cominium, sic ad Aquiloniam gesta res ; in
medio inter duas urbes spatio, ubi tertia exspectata
erat pugna, hostes non inventi. Septem milia
passuum cum abessent a Cominio, revocati ab suis

10 neutri proelio occurrerunt. Primis ferme tenebris,
cum in conspectu iam castra, iam Aquiloniam
habuissent, clamor eos utrimque par accidens susti-

11 nuit ; deinde regione[2] castrorum, quae incensa ab
Romanis erant, flamma late fusa[3] certioris cladis

12 indicio progredi longius prohibuit ; eo ipso loco
temere sub armis strati passim inquietum omne
tempus noctis exspectando timendoque lucem egere.

13 Prima luce incerti quam in partem intenderent iter
repente in fugam consternantur[4] conspecti ab equitibus, qui egressos nocte ab oppido Samnites persecuti
viderant multitudinem non vallo, non stationibus

---

[1] octingenti *Gronovius*: accc (*or other corruptions*) Ω.
[2] regione *uA*ˣς: regionem (*or* -ē)Ω: e regione ς.
[3] flamma late fusa *u*ς: flammae late fusae Ω.
[4] consternantur D²ς: consternuntur Ω.

mounted with difficulty from the plain on to the
walls—overcoming the inequality of position, which
was what they had chiefly dreaded—were making
easy work of it on the level ground with an enemy
that was no match for them, they forsook their
towers and battlements, and, huddled all together
in the market-place, made there one last brief
attempt to redeem the day. Then, throwing down
their arms, some eleven thousand four hundred men
cast themselves on the mercy of the consul; about
four thousand eight hundred had been slain.

Such were the operations at Cominium and at
Aquilonia. In the place between, where a third
battle had been looked for, the enemy were not
encountered. Recalled by their leaders when seven
miles from Cominium, they had not been present
at either engagement. As the evening shadows began to fall, when they had already come within sight
of the camp and of Aquilonia, they had been halted
by the shouts, which were equally loud from both
directions. But afterwards, from the direction of
the camp, which had been fired by the Romans,
the flames broke out so extensively, with their
warning of an unmistakable disaster, as to keep
them from advancing further, and throwing themselves on the ground at random, just where they
were, without stopping to remove their arms, they
passed the whole weary night in waiting for the
dawn, which at the same time they dreaded. As
the day broke, they were hesitating which way to
march, when the Roman cavalry, who had pursued
the Samnites when they left their town in the
night, caught sight of the army, lying there without
breastworks or outpost, and instantly routed them.

14 firmatam. Conspecta et ex muris Aquiloniae ea
multitudo erat iamque etiam legionariae cohortes
sequebantur; ceterum nec pedes fugientes persequi
potuit et ab equite novissimi agminis ducenti ferme
et octoginta interfecti; arma multa pavidi ac signa
15 militaria duodeviginti reliquere; alio agmine incolumi, ut ex tanta trepidatione, Bovianum perventum est.

XLIV. Laetitiam utriusque exercitus Romani
auxit et ab altera parte feliciter gesta res. Uterque
ex alterius sententia consul captum oppidum diri-
2 piendum militi dedit, exhaustis deinde tectis ignem
iniecit; eodemque die Aquilonia et Cominium defla-
gravere et consules cum gratulatione mutua legionum
3 suaque castra coniunxere. In conspectu duorum
exercituum et Carvilius suos pro cuiusque merito
laudavit donavitque; et Papirius, apud quem multiplex
in acie, circa castra, circa urbem fuerat certamen,
Sp. Nautium,[1] Sp. Papirium, fratris filium, et quattuor centuriones manipulumque hastatorum armillis
4 aureisque coronis donavit: Nautium propter expeditionem qua magni agminis modo terruerat hostes,
iuvenem Papirium propter navatam cum equitatu et
in proelio operam et nocte qua fugam[2] infestam
5 Samnitibus ab Aquilonia[3] clam egressis fecit, centuriones militesque quia primi portam murumque
Aquiloniae ceperant; equites omnes ob insignem

[1] Sp. Nautium ς (*chap.* xl. § 8): p. nautium Ω.
[2] qua fugam *Aldus* : quia fugam Ω.
[3] ab Aquilonia ς: ab Aquiloniam (*or* -ā) *PF* : ad aquiloniā
(*or* -am) Ω.

---

[1] Front-line troops.
[2] This interference was not mentioned at chap. xlii.
§ 4.

Their mass had been seen, too, from the walls of Aquilonia, and presently the legionary cohorts were likewise in pursuit of them. But the infantry could not overtake the fugitives, though the cavalry killed some two hundred and eighty of the rear-guard, who in their fright abandoned a quantity of arms and eighteen military standards. The rest of the column made good its escape, as safely as could be in so great a confusion, to Bovianum.

XLIV. The rejoicing in each of the Roman armies was enhanced by the good fortune the other had enjoyed. Each consul, with the approval of his fellow, made over the town he had captured to be sacked by the soldiers, and when the houses had been emptied, gave it to the flames. So on the same day Aquilonia and Cominium were destroyed by fire, and the consuls, amid the mutual exultations and good wishes of their legions and themselves, united their camps. In the full sight of both armies Carvilius commended his men as each had merited, and presented them with decorations; and Papirius, who had fought an engagement of many sorts—in line of battle, round the camp, and about the city— awarded armlets and wreaths of gold to Spurius Nautius and to his nephew Spurius Papirius, and to four centurions and a maniple of *hastati* [1]—to Nautius for the charge by which, as though with a huge force, he had dismayed the enemy; to the young Papirius for his valiant service with the cavalry, both in the battle and in the night when he harassed [2] the flight of the Samnites after their secret departure from Aquilonia; to the centurions and soldiers because they had been the first to capture the gate and wall of Aquilonia. All the horsemen, in recog-

multis locis operam corniculis armillisque argenteis
donat.

6 Consilium inde habitum iamne [1] tempus esset de-
ducendi de Samnio [2] exercitus aut utriusque aut
7 certe alterius, optimum visum, quo magis fractae res
Samnitium essent, eo pertinacius et infestius agere
cetera et persequi ut perdomitum Samnium insequentibus consulibus tradi posset.

8 Quando iam nullus esset hostium exercitus, qui
signis conlatis dimicaturus videretur, unum superesse
belli genus, urbium oppugnationes, quarum per
excidia militem locupletare praeda et hostem pro
9 aris ac focis dimicantem conficere possent. Itaque
litteris missis ad senatum populumque Romanum de
rebus ab se gestis diversi Papirius ad Saepinum,
Carvilius ad Veliam [3] oppugnandam legiones ducunt.

XLV. Litterae consulum ingenti laetitia et in
curia et in contione auditae, et quadridui supplica-
tione publicum gaudium privatis studiis celebratum
2 est. Nec populo Romano magna solum sed per-
opportuna etiam ea victoria fuit, quia per idem forte
3 tempus rebellasse Etruscos allatum est. Subibat
cogitatio animum quonam modo tolerabilis futura
Etruria fuisset si quid in Samnio adversi evenisset,
quae coniuratione Samnitium erecta, quoniam ambo

---

[1] iamne *Conway* : cum iam nec *TDLA* ϛ : cum iam *MPFu*.
[2] de Samnio *Weissenborn* : ab (*or* a) Samnio Ω.
[3] Veliam *A²* and *A⁵* (*marg.*) : uellam Ω.

nition of their distinguished conduct in many places,
he decorated with little silver horns and silver
armlets.

A council of war was then held, and the question
was debated whether the time were now come for
withdrawing both armies, or at any rate one of the
two, from Samnium. But they decided that the
greater the damage they had inflicted on the Samnites, the more sharply and pertinaciously ought
they to carry out such measures as remained, and
to persist until they could hand over to the consuls
who succeeded them a Samnium utterly subdued.

Since there was no longer any hostile army that
seemed likely to engage in a pitched battle with
them, one form of war alone remained, the storming
of cities; by destroying which they would be able
to enrich their troops with booty and crush their
enemies, who would fight for their altars and their
hearths. Accordingly, after dispatching letters to
the senate and the Roman People recounting their
achievements, the consuls parted company, Papirius
marching to attack Saepinum, and Carvilius Velia.

XLV. The consuls' letters were listened to with
vast exultation both in Senate-house and in assembly,
and the general rejoicing found expression in the
eagerness with which a thanksgiving of four days'
duration was observed by individual citizens. For
the Roman People, moreover, it was not only a great
but also a very seasonable victory, since it happened
that they got news at about the same time that the
Etruscans had commenced hostilities again. Men
wondered how they could have withstood Etruria if
anything had gone wrong in Samnium; for the
Samnite coalition and the diversion of both consuls

LIVY

consules omnisque Romana vis aversa in Samnium
esset, occupationem populi Romani pro occasione
rebellandi habuisset.

4 Legationes sociorum, a M. Atilio praetore in
senatum introductae, querebantur uri ac vastari
agros a finitimis Etruscis quod desciscere a populo

5 Romano nollent, obtestabanturque patres conscriptos
ut se a vi atque iniuria communium hostium tutarentur. Responsum legatis curae senatui futurum
ne socios fidei suae paeniteret: Etruscorum prope-
diem eandem fortunam quam Samnitium fore.

6 Segnius tamen, quod ad Etruriam attinebat, acta
res esset, ni Faliscos quoque, qui per multos annos
in amicitia fuerant, allatum foret arma Etruscis

7 iunxisse. Huius propinquitas populi acuit curam
patribus, ut fetiales mittendos ad res repetendas
censerent; quibus non redditis ex auctoritate pa-

8 trum iussu populi bellum Faliscis indictum est
iussique consules sortiri uter ex Samnio[1] in Etruriam
cum exercitu transiret.

9 Iam Carvilius Veliam[2] et Palumbinum et Herculaneum ex Samnitibus ceperat, Veliam[3] intra paucos

10 dies, Palumbinum eodem quo ad muros accessit. Ad
Herculaneum etiam signis conlatis ancipiti proelio
et cum maiore sua quam hostium iactura dimicavit;
castris deinde positis moenibus hostem inclusit;

11 oppugnatum oppidum captumque. In his tribus

[1] Samnio $M^x P^2 F^3 u D^3 A^2$: samnito $MTDA$: samnitio L :
samntio PF ?
[2] Veliam A^2_5 : ueletiam Ω : uellam etiam u.
[3] Veliam M^1 (or M^2) TA^3 : ueletiam DLA : uetiam M.

---

[1] The situation of none of these three towns is known.

and all Rome's military strength to Samnium had B.C. 293 encouraged these other enemies to revolt while the Roman People had their hands full.

Deputations from the allies, introduced into the senate by Marcus Atilius the praetor, complained that their lands were being burnt and devastated by the neighbouring Etruscans, because they were not willing to forsake the Roman People, and besought the Conscript Fathers to defend them against the violence and injuries of their common foes. Answer was made to the deputations that the senate would see to it that the allies should not regret their loyalty: the Etruscans would shortly meet with the same fortune as the Samnites. Nevertheless, the Etruscan business would have dragged but for intelligence that the Faliscans likewise, who had for many years been friendly, were now united in arms with the Etruscans. The proximity of this people sharpened the anxiety of the Fathers, and they decreed that fetials should be dispatched to demand redress. On the refusal of this demand, war was declared against the Faliscans, by command of the people, on the authorization of the senate, and the consuls were bidden to cast lots to determine which should cross over with his army from Samnium into Etruria.

Carvilius had already taken Velia and Palumbinum and Herculaneum[1] from the Samnites—Velia in a few days' time, and Palumbinum the same day that he approached its walls. At Herculaneum he even fought a regular engagement, of which the issue was for some time in doubt and his losses heavier than the enemy's; he then pitched his camp and shut the enemy up within his walls, and finally stormed the town and captured it. In these three

urbibus capta aut caesa ad decem milia hominum,
ita ut parvo admodum plures caperentur. Sorti-
entibus provincias consulibus Etruria Carvilio evenit
secundum vota militum, qui vim frigoris iam in
12 Samnio non patiebantur. Papirio ad Saepinum
maior vis hostium restitit. Saepe in acie, saepe
in agmine, saepe circa ipsam urbem adversus
eruptiones hostium pugnatum. Nec obsidio sed
bellum ex aequo erat; non enim muris magis se
Samnites quam armis ac viris moenia tutabantur.
13 Tandem pugnando in obsidionem iustam coegit
hostes obsidendoque vi atque operibus urbem ex-
14 pugnavit. Itaque ab ira plus caedis editum capta
urbe; septem milia quadringenti caesi, capta minus
tria milia hominum. Praeda, quae plurima fuit congestis Samnitium rebus in urbes paucas, militi concessa est.

XLVI. Nives iam omnia oppleverant nec durari
extra tecta poterat; itaque consul exercitum de
2 Samnio deduxit. Venienti Romam triumphus omnium consensu est delatus. Triumphavit in magistratu, insigni, ut illorum temporum habitus erat,
3 triumpho. Pedites equitesque insignes donis tran-
siere ac transvecti sunt;[1] multae civicae coronae
4 vallaresque ac murales conspectae; inspectata spolia

---

[1] transvecti sunt ς : transuectis M?uς : transuecti Ω.

---

[1] The Samnites lived for the most part in small, unfortified
villages; cf. chap. xvii. § 2.
[2] The civic crown was conferred on a soldier who saved
the life of a fellow-citizen; the others on the first man to
mount the enemy's rampart and city wall, respectively.

places ten thousand or so of the enemy were taken
or put to death, with the prisoners very slightly
outnumbering the slain. When the consuls cast lots
for their commands, Etruria fell to Carvilius, thus
answering the prayers of his soldiers, who could
endure no longer the rigorous cold in Samnium.
Papirius, before Saepinum, had a larger body of the
enemy still to reckon with. His troops were many
times engaged in regular battle, many times when
marching, and many times about the city itself, in
resisting the sorties of the enemy. It was not a
siege, but war upon even terms; for the Samnites
protected their walls with arms and men full as
much as the walls protected them. At length,
fighting hard, he forced the enemy to submit to a
regular blockade, and by assault and siege-works
captured the place. The exasperation of the Romans
made the massacre more bloody when the city fell.
Seven thousand four hundred were slain and fewer
than three thousand were made prisoners. The
booty, which was very great, since the Samnites had
gathered their wealth together in a few cities,[1] was
handed over to the soldiers.

XLVI. The ground was now covered with snow
and men could no longer live out of doors. The
consul therefore withdrew his army from Samnium.
On his coming to Rome he was unanimously voted a
triumph. This he celebrated, while still holding
office, in a style which, for the circumstances of those
days, was magnificent. Foot-soldiers and horsemen
marched or rode past the crowds adorned with their
decorations; many civic crowns were seen, and many
that had been won at the escalade of a rampart or a
city wall.[2] Men inspected the spoils that he had

A.U.C.
461

Samnitium et decore[1] ac pulchritudine paternis spoliis, quae nota frequenti publicorum ornatu locorum erant, comparabantur; nobiles aliquot captivi,[2] 5 clari suis patrumque factis, ducti. Aeris gravis travecta viciens centum milia et quingenta[3] triginta tria milia; id aes redactum ex captivis dicebatur; argenti quod captum ex urbibus erat pondo mille[4] octingenta[5] triginta. Omne aes argentumque in aerarium conditum, militibus nihil datum ex praeda 6 est; auctaque ea invidia est ad plebem quod tributum etiam in stipendium militum conlatum est, cum, si spreta gloria fuisset captivae pecuniae in aerarium inlatae, et militi tum donum[6] dari ex praeda et 7 stipendium militare praestari[7] potuisset. Aedem Quirini dedicavit—quam in ipsa dimicatione votam apud neminem veterem auctorem invenio neque hercule tam exiguo tempore perficere potuisset—ab dictatore patre votam filius consul dedicavit exor- 8 navitque hostium spoliis; quorum tanta multitudo fuit ut non templum tantum forumque iis ornaretur sed sociis etiam coloniisque[8] finitimis ad templorum 9 locorumque publicorum ornatum dividerentur. Ab triumpho exercitum in agrum Vescinum,[9] quia regio ea infesta ab Samnitibus erat, hibernatum duxit.

---

[1] decore $M^x u D^3 A^2$: decorem MPT : decoram F : decor DLA.

[2] captivi $I^2 u T^2 D^3 A^x$: actiui F : captivis Ω.

[3] quingenta *Gelenius* : a Ω : ad $T^2 u$: *omitted by* L.

[4] pondo mille *Alschefski* : p̄ co (*or other corruptions*) Ω.

[5] octingenta *Alschefski* : accc (*or similar corruptions*) Ω.

[6] militi tum donum *Walters and Conway* : militi tum (*or* militum) Ω.

[7] praestari $F^3 u D^3$ (*or* D^5) A^2 (*or* A^1) : praestare Ω.

[8] coloniisque $u A^3 Madvig$: colonisque Ω.

taken from the Samnites, and compared them for B.C. 293
splendour and beauty with those his father had won,
which were familiar to them from being often used
in the decoration of public places. A number of
noble captives, famous for their own and their fathers'
deeds, were led in the procession. Of heavy bronze
there were carried past two million five hundred and
thirty-three thousand pounds. This bronze had been
collected, it was said, from the sale of captives. Of
silver which had been taken from the cities there
were eighteen hundred and thirty pounds. All the
bronze and silver was placed in the Treasury, none
of the booty being given to the soldiers. The ill-
feeling which this gave rise to in the plebs was
increased by the gathering of a war-tax to pay the
troops, since, if the consul had forgone the glory of
depositing the captured money in the Treasury, the
booty would then have afforded the soldiers a
donative, as well as providing for their pay. Papirius
dedicated the temple of Quirinus. I find no ancient
authority who states that it was vowed in the hour of
conflict, nor indeed could it possibly have been
completed in so short a time ; his father had vowed
it when dictator, and the son as consul dedicated it,
adorning it with the spoils of the enemy. Of these
there was such a great quantity that not only were
the temple and the Forum bedecked with them, but
they were distributed also amongst the allies and the
neighbouring colonies for the decoration of their
temples and public squares. After triumphing, Papirius led his army into the country of the Vescini—a
district infested by the Samnites—to pass the winter.

---

⁹ Vescinum *Sigonius* (*cf. chap.* **xx.** § 1): uestinum
MPFuDLA.

10   Inter haec Carvilius consul in Etruria Troilum primum oppugnare adortus quadringentos septuaginta ditissimos, pecunia grandi pactos ut abire inde

11 liceret, dimisit; ceteram multitudinem oppidumque ipsum vi cepit. Inde quinque castella locis sita

12 munitis expugnavit. Caesa ibi hostium duo milia quadringenti, minus duo milia capta. Et Faliscis pacem petentibus annuas indutias dedit, pactus centum milia gravis aeris et stipendium eius anni militi-

13 bus. His rebus actis ad triumphum decessit, ut minus clarum de Samnitibus quam collegae triumphus fuerat

14 ita cumulo Etrusci belli aequatum. Aeris gravis tulit in aerarium trecenta octoginta milia; reliquo aere aedem Fortis Fortunae de manubiis faciendam locavit prope aedem eius deae ab rege Ser. Tullio[1]

15 dedicatam, et militibus ex praeda centenos binos asses et alterum tantum centurionibus atque equitibus, malignitate collegae gratius accipientibus

16 munus, divisit. Favor consulis tutatus ad populum est L. Postumium legatum eius, qui dicta die a M. Scantio tribuno plebis fugerat legatione,[2] ut fama ferebat, populi iudicium; iactarique magis quam peragi accusatio eius poterat.

---

[1] Tullio *uç* : tullo Ω.
[2] legatione *Perizonius* : in legatione *F* : in legationem Ω.

---

[1] Site unknown.

[2] The temple was not mentioned by Livy in his account of that king's reign (I. xxxix.–xlviii.).

[3] The course of events somewhat obscurely indicated here would seem to have been as follows :—When Scantius lodged the indictment, Carvilius procured Postumius immunity for a year by making him a *legatus*. On the expiration of the year some successor of Scantius revived the prosecution, but was induced by the friends of Carvilius to let the proceedings drop.

In Etruria meanwhile the consul Carvilius, having made his preparations to begin with an attack on Troilum,[1] agreed with four hundred and seventy of the wealthiest inhabitants for a large sum of money to let them go ; the rest of the population and the town itself he took by assault. He then stormed five fortresses situated in positions of great strength. There he slew two thousand four hundred of the enemy, making fewer than two thousand prisoners. He also granted a year's truce to the Faliscans—who came to him seeking peace—having stipulated for a hundred thousand of heavy bronze and the year's pay for his soldiers. After these exploits he departed to enjoy his triumph, which, though less distinguished than his colleague's had been for success against the Samnites, was a match for it when the Etruscan war was counted in. Of heavy bronze he lodged in the Treasury three hundred and eighty thousand pounds ; with what remained he contracted for a temple to Fors Fortuna to be erected from the general's spoils, near the temple of that goddess dedicated by King Servius Tullius,[2] while to the soldiers he apportioned from the rest of the booty one hundred and two *asses* each, and as much again to the centurions and horsemen. These allowances were all the more welcome because of the parsimony of his colleague. The consul's popularity served to shield his lieutenant Lucius Postumius from the people. He had been indicted by Marcus Scantius, a plebeian tribune, but had escaped trial before the people—so the story ran —through his appointment to the lieutenancy ; so that it was easier to threaten him than to carry home the accusation.[3]

XLVII. Exacto iam anno novi tribuni plebis magistratum inierant; hisque ipsis, quia vitio creati

2 erant, quinque post dies alii[1] suffecti. Lustrum conditum eo anno est a P. Cornelio Arvina C. Marcio Rutulo[2] censoribus; censa capitum milia ducenta sexaginta duo trecenta viginti unum. Censores vicesimi sexti a primis censoribus, lustrum unde-

3 vicesimum fuit. Eodem anno coronati primum ob res bello bene gestas ludos Romanos spectarunt palmaeque tum primum translato e Graeco more victoribus datae. Eodem anno ab aedilibus curulibus qui

4 eos ludos fecerunt damnatis aliquot pecuariis, via a Martis silice ad Bovillas perstrata est.

5 Comitia consularia L. Papirius habuit; creavit consules Q. Fabium Maximi filium Gurgitem et D. Iunium Brutum Scaevam. Ipse Papirius praetor factus.

6 Multis rebus laetus annus vix ad solacium unius mali, pestilentiae urentis simul urbem atque agros, suffecit;[3] portentoque iam similis clades erat, et libri aditi quinam finis aut quod remedium eius mali

---

[1] alii $M^x u D^x A^x$: aliis Ω.
[2] Rutulo *Conway*: rutilo MP: rutilio Ω.
[3] suffecit uA^3; sufficit (*or* sub- Ω.

---

[1] This was a sacrifice of purification performed as the final ceremony of the census-taking. "To close the lustrum" is therefore to complete the census.

XLVII. The year having now run its course, new
tribunes of the plebs came in, but owing to a flaw in
their election they were themselves supplanted by
others, five days later. The lustrum[1] was closed
that year by the censors Publius Cornelius Arvina
and Gaius Marcius Rutulus ; there were enrolled two
hundred and sixty-two thousand three hundred and
twenty-one. The censors were the twenty-sixth
pair from the first censors ; the lustrum was the
nineteenth. This year for the first time those who
had been presented with crowns because of gallant
behaviour in the war wore them at the Roman games,
and palms were then for the first time conferred
upon the victors, in accordance with a custom
borrowed from the Greeks. The same year the
curule aediles who gave those games procured the
conviction of a number of graziers,[2] and with their
fines paved the road from the temple of Mars as far
as Bovillae.[3]

The consular comitia were held by Lucius Papirius,
who declared the election of Quintus Fabius Gurges,
the son of Maximus, and Decimus Junius Brutus
Scaeva. Papirius himself was chosen praetor.

The year had been one of many blessings, which
yet were hardly a consolation for one misfortune—
a pestilence which ravaged both city and country-
side. Its devastation was now grown portentous,
and the Books were consulted to discover what end

---

[2] The men were probably fined for appropriating more than
the legal maximum of public land. Compare chap. xxiii.
§ 13.

[3] This refers to the Via Appia itself (which had apparently
not been fully paved—*perstrata*—before) rather than to the
footway referred to at chap. xxiii. § 12.

A.U.C.
462 7 ab dis[1] daretur. Inventum in libris Aesculapium
ab Epidauro Romam arcessendum; neque eo anno,
quia bello occupati consules erant, quicquam de ea
re actum, praeterquam quod unum diem Aesculapio
supplicatio habita est.

[1] ab dis *Madvig* : ab (*or* a) diis Ω.

---

[1] It was two or three years later and the pestilence was
still raging when a deputation under Q. Ogulnius was dis-

or what remedy the gods proposed for this misfortune. B.C. 292
It was discovered in the Books that Aesculapius
must be summoned to Rome from Epidaurus; but
nothing could be done about it that year, because
the consuls were occupied with the war, except that
for one day a supplication to that god was held.[1]

patched to Epidaurus and brought away a serpent to Rome
which passed for the god himself. A temple of Aesculapius
was then erected on the island in the Tiber. See *Summary
of Book XI.*

---

[1] M. Valerius, according to Livy, chap. xi. §2.

BOOK X. xlvii. 6–7

LIBRI X PERIOCHA

Coloniae deductae sunt Sora et Alba et Carsioli. Marsi in deditionem accepti sunt. Collegium augurum ampliatum est, ut essent novem, cum antea quaterni fuissent. Lex de provocatione ad populum a Murena cos. tertio lata est. Duae tribus adiectae sunt, Aniensis et Terentina. Samnitibus bellum indictum est et adversus eos saepe prospere pugnatum est. Cum adversus Etruscos Umbros Samnites Gallos P. Decio et Q. Fabio ducibus pugnaretur et Romanus exercitus in magno discrimine esset, P. Decius, secutus patris exemplum, devovit se pro exercitu et morte sua victoriam eius pugnae populo R. dedit. Papirius Cursor Samnitium exercitum, qui de iureiurando obstrictus, quo maiore constantia virtutis pugnaret, in aciem descenderat, fudit. Census actus est, lustrum conditum. Censa sunt civium capita ccclxxii et cccxx.

---

[1] M. Valerius, according to Livy, chap. ix. § 3.

SUMMARY OF BOOK X

COLONIES were planted at Sora, at Alba, and at Carseoli. The surrender of the Marsi was received. The augural college was enlarged so that there were nine where before there had been four. A law about appeals was then for the third time laid before the people by the consul Murena.[1] Two tribes were added, the Aniensis and the Terentina. War was declared upon the Samnites and victories were often gained over them. When the Etruscans, Umbrians, Samnites, and Gauls were being fought under the leadership of Publius Decius and Quintus Fabius and the Roman army was in sore peril, Publius Decius, following the example of his father, devoted himself on behalf of the army and by his death gave the victory in that battle to the Roman People. Papirius Cursor routed the army of the Samnites, which had taken the field after binding itself with an oath, that it might fight with a more constant courage. The census was taken and the lustrum closed. There were enumerated 272,320 citizens.

LIVY

LIBRI XI PERIOCHA

Cum Fabius Gurges cos. male adversus Samnites pugnasset et senatus de removendo eo ab exercitu ageret,
Fabius Maximus pater deprecatus hanc fili ignominiam
eo maxime senatum movit quod iturum se filio legatum
pollicitus est, idque praestitit. Eius consiliis et opera
filius consul adiutus caesis Samnitibus triumphavit; C.
Pontium, imperatorem Samnitium, ductum in triumpho,
securi percussit. Cum pestilentia civitas laboraret, missi
legati ut Aesculapi signum Romam ab Epidauro transfer-
rent, anguem, qui se in navem eorum contulerat, in quo
ipsum numen esse constabat, deportaverunt; eoque in
insulam Tiberis egresso eodem loco aedis Aesculapio
constituta est. L. Postumius consularis, quoniam, cum
exercitui praeesset, opera militum in agro suo usus erat,
damnatus est. Pacem petentibus Samnitibus[1] foedus quarto
renovatum est. Curius Dentatus cos. Samnitibus caesis et
Sabinis, qui rebellaverant, victis et in deditionem acceptis
bis in eodem magistratu triumphavit. Coloniae deductae
sunt Castrum Sena Hadria. Triumviri capitales tunc
primum creati sunt. Censu acto lustrum conditum est.
Censa sunt civium capita CCLXXII. Plebs propter aes
alienum post[2] graves et longas seditiones ad ultimum
secessit in Ianiculum, unde a Q. Hortensio dictatore
deducta est; isque in ipso magistratu decessit. Res
praeterea contra Vulsinienses gestas continet, item adversus Lucanos, contra quos auxilium Thurinis[3] ferre
placuerat.

---

[1] petentibus Samnitibus *a late MS.*: petentibus *MSS.*
[2] post *Sigonius ex. vet. lib.*: propter *MSS.*
[3] Thurinis *Pighius* (*Plin. N. H.* XXXIV. 32, *Vat. Max.* I.
viii. 6, *Dion. Hal.* XIX. xiii): tyrrhenis *or* tyrrinis *MSS.*

SUMMARY OF BOOK XI

When Fabius Gurges the consul had fought an unsuccessful battle with the Samnites and the senate was debating his removal from the command, Fabius Maximus his father begged them to spare his son this ignominy. What particularly moved the senate was his promise to go out as his son's lieutenant, which he did. Aided by his advice and services, his son the consul defeated the Samnites and triumphed. Gaius Pontius, the general of the Samnites, was led in the triumph and beheaded. When the state was troubled with a pestilence, the envoys dispatched to bring over the image of Aesculapius from Epidaurus to Rome fetched away a serpent, which had crawled into their ship and in which it was generally believed that the god himself was present. On the serpent's going ashore on the island of the Tiber, a temple was erected there to Aesculapius. The consular Lucius Postumius was convicted of having used the labour of soldiers on his own land when in command of the army. The Samnites sought peace and the treaty with them was renewed for the fourth time. Curius Dentatus the consul having slaughtered the Samnites and conquered the Sabines, who had revolted, and received their submission, triumphed twice in the same year of office. Colonies were established at Castrum, Sena, and Hadria. A board of three to deal with capital offences was then chosen for the first time. The number of citizens was returned as 272,000. Because of their debts, the plebs, after serious and protracted quarrels, seceded to Janiculum, whence they were brought back by Quintus Hortensius the dictator, who died before the expiration of his term. The book contains also campaigns with the Vulsinienses and likewise with the Lucanians, against whom the Romans had voted to assist the people of Thurii.

547

LIBRI XII PERIOCHA

Cum legati Romanorum a Gallis Senonibus interfecti essent, bello ob id Gallis indicto, L. Caecilius praetor ab his cum legionibus caesus est. Cum a Tarentinis classis Romana direpta esset, iiviro qui praeerat classi occiso, legati ad eos a senatu, ut de his iniuriis quererentur, missi pulsati sunt. Ob id bellum his indictum est. Samnites defecerunt. Adversus eos et Lucanos et Brittios et Etruscos aliquot proeliis a conpluribus ducibus bene pugnatum est. Pyrrhus, Epirotarum rex, ut auxilium Tarentinis ferret, in Italiam venit. Cum in praesidium Reginorum legio Campana cum praefecto Decio Vibellio missa esset, occisis Reginis Regium [1] occupavit.

LIBRI XIII PERIOCHA

Valerius Laevinus cos. parum prospere adversus Pyrrhum pugnavit, elephantorum maxime inusitata facie territis militibus. Post id proelium cum corpora Romanorum qui in acie ceciderant Pyrrhus inspiceret, omnia versa in hostem invenit [2] populabundusque ad urbem Romanam processit. C. Fabricius missus ad eum a senatu, ut de redimendis captivis ageret, frustra ut patriam desereret a rege temptatus est. Captivi sine pretio remissi sunt. Cineas legatus a Pyrrho ad senatum missus petit ut conponendae pacis causa rex in urbem reciperetur. De qua re cum ad frequentiorem senatum referri placuisset, Appius Claudius, qui propter valetudinem oculorum iam diu consiliis publicis se abstinuerat,

---

[1] Regium *vulg.*: regnum *MSS.*
[2] invenit *vulg.*: venit *MSS.*

---

[1] *sc.* Bruttii.　　　　[2] *sc.* Rhegium.

SUMMARY OF BOOK XII

ROMAN envoys having been put to death by the
Senonian Gauls, war was for that reason declared against
the Gauls, and Lucius Caecilius the praetor and his
legions were cut to pieces by them. The Tarentines
plundered a Roman fleet, slew the duumvir who commanded it, and maltreated the envoys whom the senate
had dispatched to them to complain of these wrongs.
On this account war was declared against them. The
Samnites revolted. Several successful battles were fought
with them and with the Lucanians and the Brittii [1] and
the Etruscans, under a number of generals. Pyrrhus,
king of the Epirots, came to Italy to help the Tarentines.
A Campanian legion, commanded by Decius Vibellius,
being sent to protect the people of Regium, [2] put the
inhabitants to death and seized the city.

SUMMARY OF BOOK XIII

THE consul Valerius Laevinus fought a losing engagement with Pyrrhus, the soldiers being greatly terrified
by the strange sight of the elephants. After this battle,
when Pyrrhus was looking at the bodies of the Romans
who had fallen, he found that they all faced their
enemies, and laying waste the country, advanced towards
the city of Rome. Gaius Fabricius, being sent to him
by the senate to treat for the ransom of the prisoners,
was in vain solicited by the King to forsake his country.
The prisoners were released without a price. Cineas,
having been dispatched by Pyrrhus as an envoy to the
senate, asked that the King might be received into the
City for the purpose of arranging terms of peace. On
its having been resolved to refer this proposal to a fuller
meeting of the senate, Appius Claudius, who by reason of
a weakness of the eyes had long abstained from public

venit in curiam et sententia sua tenuit ut id Pyrrho
negaretur. Cn. Domitius censor primus ex plebe lustrum
condidit. Censa sunt civium capita ccxxxxvii ccxxii.
Iterum adversus Pyrrhum dubio eventu pugnatum est.
Cum Carthaginiensibus quarto foedus renovatum est.
Cum C. Fabricio consuli is qui ad eum a Pyrrho trans-
fugerat polliceretur venenum se regi daturum, cum
indicio ad regem remissus est. Res praeterea contra
Lucanos et Bruttios, Samnites et Etruscos[1] prospere
gestas continet.

LIBRI XIIII PERIOCHA

Pyrrhus in Siciliam traiecit. Cum inter alia prodigia
fulmine deiectum esset in Capitolio Iovis signum, caput
eius per haruspices inventum est. Curius Dentatus cos.
cum[2] dilectum haberet, eius qui citatus non responderat
bona primus vendidit; iterum Pyrrhum ex Sicilia in
Italiam reversum vicit et Italia expulit. Fabricius censor
P. Cornelium Rufinum consularem senatu movit, quod is x
pondo argenti facti haberet. Lustro a censoribus condito
censa sunt civium capita cclxxi ccxxiiii. Cum Ptolemaeo,
Aegypti rege, societas iuncta est. Sextilia, virgo Vestalis,
damnata incesti viva defossa est. Coloniae deductae sunt
Posidonia et Cosa. Carthaginiensium classis auxilio
Tarentinis venit, quo facto ab his foedus violatum est.
Res praeterea contra Lucanos et Bruttios et Samnites
feliciter gestas et Pyrrhi regis mortem continet.

---

[1] et Etruscos *vulg.* : etruscos *MSS.*
[2] cos. cum *Rossbach* : ˙is˙ cum *MSS.*

business, entered the Curia and by his speech prevailed on the senators to deny Pyrrhus his request. Gnaeus Domitius was the first plebeian censor to close the lustrum. The number of the citizens was returned as 287,222. There was a second battle with Pyrrhus, of an indecisive nature. The treaty with the Carthaginians was renewed for the fourth time. When a deserter from Pyrrhus promised Gaius Fabricius the consul that he would poison the King, Fabricius sent him back to the King with the story of his guilt. The book contains also successful campaigns against the Lucanians and the Bruttians, the Samnites and the Etruscans.

SUMMARY OF BOOK XIV

PYRRHUS crossed into Sicily. When, amongst other prodigies, the statue of Jupiter in the Capitol had been thrown down by a thunderbolt, its head was discovered by haruspices. The consul Curius Dentatus, on holding a levy, was the first to sell the goods of any man who did not answer the summons; he likewise defeated Pyrrhus, who had returned from Sicily into Italy, and drove him out of Italy. The censor Fabricius removed Publius Cornelius Rufinus, an ex-consul, from the senate, because he had in his possession ten pounds of wrought silver. When the censors had closed the lustrum, there were found to be 271,224 citizens. An alliance was made with Ptolemy, king of Egypt. Sextilia, a Vestal Virgin, was found guilty of unchastity and was buried alive. The colonies of Posidonia and Cosa were established. A fleet of the Carthaginians came to the assistance of the Tarentines, an act which constituted a violation of the treaty. The book also contains successful wars with the Lucanians, the Bruttians, and the Samnites, and the death of King Pyrrhus.

LIVY

LIBRI XV PERIOCHA

Victis Tarentinis pax et libertas data est.[1] Legio
Campana quae Regium occupaverat obsessa deditione
facta securi percussa est. Cum legatos Apolloniatium ad
senatum missos quidam iuvenes pulsassent, dediti sunt
Apolloniatibus. Picentibus victis pax data est. Coloniae
deductae Ariminum in Piceno, Beneventum in Samnio.[2]
Tunc primum populus R.[3] argento uti coepit. Umbri et
Sallentini[4] victi in deditionem accepti sunt. Quaestorum
numerus ampliatus est, ut essent octo.[5]

LIBRI XVI PERIOCHA

Origo Carthaginiensium et primordia urbis eorum refe-
runtur. Contra quos et Hieronem, regem Syracusanorum,
auxilium Mamertinis ferendum senatus censuit, cum de ea
re inter suadentes ut id fieret dissuadentesque contentio
fuisset; transgressisque tunc primum mare equitibus[6]
Romanis adversus Hieronem saepius bene pugnatum.
Petenti pax data est. Lustrum a censoribus conditum est.
Censa sunt civium capita ccclxxxii ccxxxiiii. Decimus
Iunius Brutus munus gladiatorium in honorem defuncti
patris primus edidit. Colonia Aesernia deducta est. Res
praeterea contra Poenos et Vulsinios[7] prospere gestas
continet.

---

[1] data est *vulg.* : nata est *MSS.*
[2] Beneventum in Samnio *editio princeps* : Beneventum *MSS.*
[3] populus R. *vulg.* : populus *MSS.*
[4] Sallentini *vulg.* : salleni (*or* saleni *or* salerni) *MSS.*
[5] ut essent octo *Sigonius* : ut essent *MSS.*
[6] equitibus *MSS* : exercitibus *Weissenborn.*

SUMMARIES

SUMMARY OF BOOK XV

The Tarentines, having been vanquished, were granted peace and liberty. The Campanian legion which had seized Regium [1] was besieged and forced to surrender and its members were beheaded. Envoys from Apollonium to the senate were beaten by certain youths, who were given up to the people of Apollonium. The Picentes were defeated and granted peace. Colonies were sent out to Ariminum in the Picentian district and to Beneventum in Samnium. Then for the first time the Roman People began to use silver.[2] The Umbrians and the Sallentines were conquered and their submission was received. The number of quaestors was enlarged, so that there were eight.

SUMMARY OF BOOK XVI

The origin of the Carthaginians and the beginnings of their city are described. Against them and against Hiero, king of the Syracusans, the senate determined to assist the Mamertines, after a bitter debate about the proposal between its advocates and its opponents. Then for the first time Roman cavalry [3] crossed the sea, and fought a number of victorious engagements against Hiero. On his suing for peace, it was granted him. The lustrum was closed by the censors. There were enumerated 382,234 citizens. Decimus Junius Brutus was the first to give a gladiatorial exhibition, in honour of his dead father. The colony of Aesernia was planted. The book contains also successful operations carried on against the Carthaginians and Vulsinii.

---

[1] sc. Rhegium.   [2] i.e. silver coinage.
[3] Or "armies," if we accept Weissenborn's emendation.

Vulsinios *vulg.* : uulsinos *MSS.*

LIBRI XVII PERIOCHA

Cn. Cornelius consul a classe Punica circumventus et
per fraudem, veluti in conloquium evocatus, captus est.
C. Duillius consul adversus classem Poenorum prospere
pugnavit, primusque omnium Romanorum ducum navalis
victoriae duxit triumphum.   Ob quam causam ei perpetuus
quoque honos habitus est, ut revertenti a cena tibicine
canente funale praeferretur.   L. Cornelius consul in
Sardinia et Corsica contra Sardos et Corsos et Hannonem,
Poenorum ducem, feliciter pugnavit.   Atilius Calatinus [1]
cos. cum in locum a Poenis circumsessum temere exercitum
duxisset, M. Calpurni, tribuni militum, virtute et opera
evasit, qui cum ccc militibus eruptione facta hostes in se
converterat.   Hannibal, dux Poenorum, victa classe cui
praefuerat, a militibus suis in crucem sublatus est. Atilius
Regulus cos. victis navali proelio Poenis in Africam
traiecit.

LIBRI XVIII PERIOCHA

Atilius Regulus in Africa serpentem portentosae magni-
tudinis cum magna clade militum occidit, et cum aliquot
proeliis bene adversus Carthaginienses pugnasset, succes-
sorque ei a senatu prospere bellum gerenti non mitteretur,
id ipsum per litteras ad senatum scriptas questus est, in
quibus inter causas petendi successoris erat [2] quod agellus
eius a mercennariis desertus esset.   Quaerente deinde
Fortuna ut magnum utriusque casus exemplum in Regulo

---

[1] Calatinus *vulg.* : calasinus *MSS.*
[2] successoris erat *vulg.* : successoris *MSS.*

---

[1] *cf.* Cic. *Cato Maior,* § 44.

SUMMARIES

SUMMARY OF BOOK XVII

The consul Gnaeus Cornelius was surrounded by a Carthaginian fleet and was made prisoner by fraud, having been lured out as to a colloquy. The consul Gaius Duillius fought a successful engagement with the fleet of the Carthaginians and was first of all Roman leaders to triumph for a naval victory. For this reason he was granted a perpetual honour—that a waxen torch should be borne before him and a flautist should make music when he returned from dining out.[1] The consul Lucius Cornelius fought successfully in Sardinia and Corsica against the Sardinians and Corsicans and against Hanno, the Carthaginian general. The consul Atilius Calatinus having rashly led his army into a place surrounded by the Carthaginians, escaped through the valiant services of Marcus Calpurnius, a tribune of the soldiers, who with three hundred men broke through the enemy and drew their attack upon himself. Hannibal, a Carthaginian general, on the defeat of the fleet which he commanded, was crucified by his own soldiers. Atilius Regulus the consul, having beaten the Carthaginians in a naval battle, crossed into Africa.

SUMMARY OF BOOK XVIII

Atilius Regulus in Africa slew a serpent of portentous size with the loss of many of his soldiers. Having fought several successful battles with the Carthaginians, and finding that owing to his good fortune in the prosecution of the war the senate was not disposed to send anyone to succeed him, he wrote to the senate and complained of this very thing, alleging, amongst other reasons for desiring a successor, that his little farm had been deserted by the labourers hired to work it. Afterwards, on Fortune's seeking to exhibit in the case of Regulus an

proderetur, arcessito a Carthaginiensibus Xanthippo,
Lacedaemoniorum duce, victus proelio et captus est. Res
deinde a ducibus Romanis omnibus terra marique prospere
gestas deformaverunt naufragia classium. Tib. Coruncanius primus ex plebe pontifex maximus creatus est. M'.
Valerius Maximus P. Sempronius Sophus [1] censores cum
senatum legerent, XVI senatu moverunt. Lustrum con-
diderunt, quo censa sunt civium capita CCXCVII DCCXCVII.
Regulus missus a Carthaginiensibus ad senatum ut de
pace, et si eam non posset impetrare, de commutandis
captivis ageret, et iureiurando adstrictus rediturum se
Carthaginem, si commutari captivos non placuisset, utrumque negandi auctor senatui [2] fuit, et cum fide custodita
reversus esset, supplicio a Carthaginiensibus de eo sumpto
perit.

LIBRI XVIIII PERIOCHA

Caecilius Metellus rebus adversus Poenos prospere
gestis speciosum egit triumphum, XIII ducibus hostium et
CXX elephantis in eo ductis. Claudius Pulcher cos. contra
auspicia profectus—iussit mergi pullos, qui cibari nolebant
—infeliciter adversus Carthaginienses classe pugnavit, et
revocatus a senatu iussusque dictatorem dicere Claudium
Gliciam dixit, sortis ultimae hominem, qui coactus abdicare
se magistratu postea ludos praetextatus spectavit. A.
Atilius Calatinus [3] primus dictator extra Italiam exercitum

[1] *The censors' names, variously corrupted in the MSS., are
corrected from the Fasti Capitolini, C.I.L.* i², *p.* 24.

[2] senatui *vulg.* : senatus *MSS.*

[3] calatinus *vulg*: calanus *MSS.*

---

[1] The Regulus story inspired Horace to write his finest
ode (*Carm.* III. 5).

example of both extremes, the Carthaginians sent for
Xanthippus, a general of the Lacedaemonians, who
defeated Regulus in battle and made him prisoner. After
that all the Roman generals gained victories on land and
sea; but these were marred by the wreck of fleets.
Tiberius Coruncanius was the first to be chosen pontifex
maximus from the plebs. Manius Valerius Maximus and
Publius Sempronius Sophus, when as censors they were
passing on the senate, removed sixteen from that order.
They closed the lustrum and the number of citizens
returned was 297,797. Regulus being sent by the Carthaginians to the senate to treat for peace, or, failing that,
for an exchange of prisoners, and being bound by an
oath to return to Carthage, if the Romans would not
exchange, advised the senate to grant neither request,
and having loyally returned, was tortured to death by
the Carthaginians.[1]

SUMMARY OF BOOK XIX

CAECILIUS METELLUS, after a prosperous campaign
against the Carthaginians, triumphed brilliantly, having
thirteen of the enemy's generals and a hundred and
twenty elephants in his procession. The consul Claudius
Pulcher having set out in opposition to the auspices—he
ordered the chickens to be drowned, when they would
not feed[2]—fought an unsuccessful naval engagement with
the Carthaginians, and on being recalled by the senate
and directed to name a dictator, named Claudius Glicia,
a man of the basest sort, who afterwards, when he had
been forced to abdicate the office, witnessed the games
in his purple-bordered toga. Aulus Atilius Calatinus
was the first dictator to lead an army out of Italy. An

[2] According to Cicero, *De Natura Deorum*, II. 7, Claudius
had the fowls thrown into water, "that they might drink,
since they would not eat."

duxit. Commutatio captivorum cum Poenis facta est.
Coloniae deductae sunt Fregenae, in agro Sallentino
Brundisium. Lustrum a censoribus conditum est. Censa
sunt civium capita ccxli ccxii. Claudia, soror P. Claudi,
qui contemptis auspiciis male pugnaverat, a ludis revertens
cum turba premeretur, dixit : Utinam frater meus viveret ;
iterum classem duceret. Ob eam causam multa ei dicta
est. Duo praetores tunc primum creati sunt. Caecilius
Metellus, pontifex maximus, A. Postumium[1] consulem,
quoniam idem et flamen Martialis erat, cum is ad bellum
gerendum proficisci vellet, in urbe tenuit nec passus est a
sacris recedere. Rebus adversus Poenos a pluribus ducibus prospere gestis, summam victoriae[2] C. Lutatius cos.
victa ad Aegates insulas classe Poenorum imposuit.
Petentibus Carthaginiensibus pax data est. Cum templum
Vestae arderet, Caecilius Metellus, pontifex maximus, ex
incendio sacra rapuit. Duae tribus adiectae sunt, Velina
et Quirina.

LIBRI XX PERIOCHA

Falisci cum rebellassent, sexto die perdomiti in deditionem venerunt. Spoletium colonia deducta est. Adversus
Liguras tunc primum exercitus promotus est. Sardi et
Corsi cum rebellassent, subacti sunt. Tuccia,[3] virgo
Vestalis, incesti damnata est. Bellum Illyriis propter
unum ex legatis qui ad eos missi erant occisum indictum
est, subactique in deditionem venerunt. Praetorum
numerus ampliatus est, ut essent iiii. Galli transalpini
qui in Italiam inruperant caesi sunt. Eo bello populum

---

[1] A. Postumium *vulg.* : aurelium postumium *MSS.*
[2] victoriae *vulg.*: victoriam *MSS.*
[3] Tuccia *Sigonius ex vet. lib.* : lucia (or Luccia) *MSS.*
Tucia *ed. prin.*

exchange of prisoners with the Carthaginians was effected. Colonies were founded at Fregenae [1] and in the Sallentine country at Brundisium. The lustrum was closed by the censors. 241,212 citizens were registered. Claudia, the sister of Publius Claudius, who had been defeated after making light of the auspices, being jostled by the crowd while returning from the games, exclaimed, " O that my brother were alive to command another fleet ! " For this she was fined. Then for the first time two praetors were elected. Caecilius Metellus, the pontifex maximus, kept Aulus Postumius, the consul, in the City, since he was also the flamen of Mars, when he desired to go forth to war, nor would he suffer him to forsake his sacred functions. After a number of generals had gained successes against the Carthaginians, Gaius Lutatius crowned the victory by defeating the Carthaginian fleet off the Aegatian Islands. The Carthaginians sued for peace and it was granted them. When the temple of Vesta was burning, Caecilius Metellus, the pontifex maximus, rescued the sacred objects from the flames. Two tribes were added, the Velina and the Quirina.

SUMMARY OF BOOK XX

THE Faliscans, having revolted, were on the sixth day subdued and permitted to surrender. A colony was planted at Spoletium. Then for the first time an army marched against the Ligurians. The Sardinians and Corsicans having revolted were reduced to subjection. Tuccia, a Vestal Virgin, was convicted of unchastity. War was declared against the Illyrians on account of the murder of one of the envoys who had been dispatched to them, and they were subdued and received in surrender. The number of praetors was enlarged to four. Transalpine Gauls who had made an incursion into Italy were cut to pieces. The author states that in that war the

[1] Near the coast about due W. of Rome.

R. sui Latinique nominis ᴅᴄᴄᴄ armatorum [1] habuisse dicit
Exercitibus Romanis tunc primum trans Padum ductis
Galli Insubres aliquot proeliis fusi in deditionem venerunt.
M. Claudius Marcellus cos. occiso Gallorum Insubrium
duce, Vertomaro,[2] opima spolia rettulit. Histri subacti
sunt. Iterum Illyrî cum rebellassent, domiti in deditionem venerunt. Lustrum a censoribus ter[3] conditum est.
Primo lustro censa sunt civium capita ᴄᴄʟxx ᴄᴄxɪɪ**.
Libertini in quattuor tribus redacti sunt, cum antea
dispersi per omnes fuissent, Esquilinam Palatinam Subura-
nam Collinam. C. Flaminius censor viam Flaminiam
muniit[4] et circum Flaminium exstruxit. Coloniae deductae sunt in agro de Gallis[5] capto Placentia et Cremona.

---

[1] ᴅᴄᴄᴄ armatorum *Mommsen*: ᴀᴄᴄᴄ *MSS.*

[2] Vertomaro *MSS.*: Virtomane *Propertius* IV. x. 41 (*codex
N*): Viridomaro *ed. prin.* (*cf. Serv. Verg. Aen.* VI. 855).

[3] ter *Madvig*: per *MSS.*

[4] C. Flaminius censor viam Flaminiam muniit *Sigonius*
muniit *MSS.*

[5] de gallis *Frobenius*: gallis *MSS.*

Roman People had under arms 800,000 men, of their own and of the Latin name. Then for the first time Roman armies crossed the Po, and defeating the Insubrian Gauls in several battles, received their submission. The consul Marcus Claudius Marcellus having slain the chief of the Insubrian Gauls, Vertomarus, brought back the spoils of honour.[1] The Histrians were subjugated. The Illyrians having gone to war a second time were defeated and their submission was received. The census was thrice taken by the censors. In the first census there were registered 270,212 citizens. . . . The freedmen were assigned to four tribes, whereas before they had been dispersed through them all—the four being the Esquilina, the Palatina, the Suburana, the Collina. The censor Gaius Flaminius built the Flaminian Way and the Flaminian Circus. Colonies were established in the territory taken from the Gauls, at Placentia and Cremona.

[1] The " spoils of honour " were those taken by the general in personal combat with the general of the enemy. See I. x. 6.

INDEX OF NAMES

(The References are to Pages.)

563

INDEX OF NAMES

INDEX OF NAMES

INDEX OF NAMES

567

INDEX OF NAMES

INDEX OF NAMES

(*ter*), 514, 516 (*bis*), 518, 520 (*bis*),
522, 524, 526, 528, 532 (*bis*), 534
(*bis*), 536 (*bis*), 538, 544 (*ter*),
546 (*quinquies*), 548, 550 (*bis*);
Pentri Samnites, 280; Samnis ager,
8; civis, 202; hostis, 8, 100;
populus, 6, 200; Samnites milites,
86
Sangus, *see* Semo.
Sardinia, 554; Sardi, 554, 558
Saticula, 244 (*bis*), 246, 248 (*bis*);
Saticulani, 244
Satricum, 2 (*bis*), 220; Satricanus
(*collective*), 222; Satricani, 206 (*bis*),
220, 222
Scantius, M., 538
Scaptia tribus, 68
Sceleratus campus, 62
Semo Sangus, 86 (*bis*)
Sempronius, Sophus, P., 288, 344 (*bis*),
388, 392, 436, 438, 556
Sena, 546
Setini, 2; Setinus ager, 74; homo, 18
Sextilia (virgo Vestalis), 550
Sextius, L., 386
Sibylla, 384
Sicilia, 550 (*bis*)
Sidicini, 4 (*bis*), 6 (*ter*); 121, 4, 16, 60
(*bis*), 62, 64, 66 (*bis*); Sidicinus
ager, 68, 406; hostis, 8
Signia, 10; Signini, 84
Sinope (= Sinuessa), 438
Sinuessa, 46, 438
Sipontum Apulorum, 94
Solonius ager, 48
Sora, 248 (*bis*), 252, 256 (*bis*), 258 (*bis*),
332, 344, 360 (*bis*), 484 (*bis*), 544;
Soranus ager, 406, 484; transfuga,
254; Sorana arx, 282
Sotimus, 96
Spoletium, 558
Stagna Inferna, 92
Stellatis ager, 476; campus, 340;
Stellates campi, 478
Suburana tribus, 560
Sucasina, *see* Interamna
Suessa Aurunca, 60, 272 (*bis*), 354;
Suessana cohors, 482
Suessula, 88; Suessulani, 60
Sulpicius Longus, C. (*cos.* 337, 323,
and 314; *dictator* 312 B.C.), 60, 62,
142 (*ter*), 226, 252, 268 (*bis*),
274; Sulpicius Saverrio, P. (*cos.*
304, *censor* 299 B.C.), 344, 392,
398

Sutrium, 284, 288 (*bis*), 298, 304,
406; Sutrini, 284
Syracusani, 552

TARENTUM, 100, 106; Tarentini, 92, 94,
100, 104, 110, 212 (*quater*), 548 (*bis*),
550, 552; Tarentini legati, 212 (*bis*)
Tarquiniensis (*collective*), 324
Tarquinius, L., 18; Tarquinii (*the
Tarquin kings*), 292
Teanenses, 242
Teates Apuli, *see* Apuli
Tellus, 36, 466; Tellus mater, 468
Terentina tribus, 392, 544
Terina Bruttiorum, 94
Terra mater, 20
Thebae, 232
Thesprotius sinus, 92
Thessali, 236
Thuriae (in Sallentinis), 362 (*bis*)
Thurii, 236; Thurini, 546
Tiberis, 58 (*bis*), 80, 416, 546
Tibur, 278 (*bis*); Tiburtes, 52, 54, 58;
Tiburtini, 278; Tiburs populus, 50
Tifernum (in Samnium), 340, 406;
Tifernus mons, 474, 478
Titienses, 378
Titinius, M., 362
Torquatus, *see* Manlius
Trebonius, T., 514, 518
Trebulani, 360
Trifanum, 46
Troilum, 538
Tubero, *see* Aelius
Tuccia (virgo Vestalis), 558
Tullius, Ser. (rex), 538
Tullus, *see* Hostilius
Tusci (*see also* Etrusci), 286, 308, 328,
420, 474
Tusculani, 58, 144 (*ter*); Tusculanus
populus, 144; Tusculani equites, 22

UFENTINA tribus, 242
Umbria, 236 (*bis*), 304, 326 (*bis*), 360,
390, 420; Umbri, 308, 326 (*quater*),
330, 354, 392, 436, 438, 440, 458,
460 *ter*), 464, 474, 478, 544, 552;
Camertes Umbri, 302 (*bis*); Umber
hostis, 460

VACCI Prata, 74
Vaccus, *see* Vitruvius
Valerius, L. (*cos.* 449 B.C.), 502
Valerius, M. (= Corvus?), 10, 36;
Valerius Corvus, M. (*cos.* 348, 346,

570

INDEX OF NAMES

PRINTED IN GREAT BRITAIN BY
RICHARD CLAY AND COMPANY, LTD.,
BUNGAY, SUFFOLK